ROBERT L.
HEILBRONER

—

LESTER C.
THUROW

Under-standing Macro-economics

fifth edition

Englewood Cliffs, New Jersey

PRENTICE-HALL INC.

Library of Congress Cataloging in Publication Data

HEILBRONER, ROBERT L
   Understanding macroeconomics.

   Includes index.
   1. Macroeconomics.   I. Thurow, Lester C., joint
   author. II. Title.
HB171.5.H392 1975   339   74-23395
ISBN   0-13-936401-3 pbk.

UNDERSTANDING MACROECONOMICS, *fifth edition*
by Robert L. Heilbroner and Lester C. Thurow

© 1975 by Prentice-Hall, Inc., Englewood Cliffs, New Jersey
© 1972, 1970, 1968, 1965 by Robert L. Heilbroner

10   9   8   7   6   5   4   3

Prentice-Hall International, Inc., *London*
Prentice-Hall of Australia, Pty. Ltd., *Sydney*
Prentice-Hall of Canada, Ltd., *Toronto*
Prentice-Hall of India Private Limited, *New Delhi*
Prentice-Hall of Japan, Inc., *Tokyo*

Contents

The Problem of Unemployment,   247

Problems of Economic Growth,   263

An Introduction to Statistics and Econometrics,   279

Wealth and Output

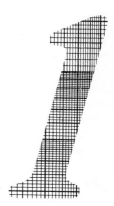

WHAT IS "MACROECONOMICS?" The word derives from the Greek *macro* meaning "big," and the implication is therefore that it is concerned with bigger problems than in microeconomics (*micro* = small). Yet microeconomics wrestles with problems that are quite as large as those of macroeconomics. The difference is really not one of scale. It is one of approach, of original angle of incidence. *Macroeconomics begins from a viewpoint that initially draws our attention to aggregate economic phenomena and processes,* such as the growth of total output. Microeconomics begins from a vantage point that first directs our analysis to the workings of the marketplace. Both views are needed to comprehend the economy as a whole, just as it takes two different lenses to make a stereophoto jump into the round. But we can learn only one view at a time, and now we turn to the spectacle of the entire national economy as it unfolds to the macroscopic gaze.

What does the economy look like from this perspective? The view is not unlike that from a plane. What we see first is the fundamental tableau of nature—the fields and forests, lakes and seas, with their inherent riches; then the diverse artifacts of man—the cities and towns, the road and rail networks, the factories and machines, the stocks of half-completed or unsold goods; and finally the human actors themselves with all their skills and talents, their energies, their social organization.

Thus our perspective shows us a vast panorama from which we single out for our special attention those elements and activities having to do with our overall economic performance. In fact, we concentrate on those processes that give rise to the *wealth* of our nation.

National Wealth

What is the wealth of a nation? In Table 1·1 we show the most recent inventory of our national wealth. Note that it consists of the value of those physical objects we noted from our aerial overview—land, buildings, equipment, and the like. Yet, a closer examination of the table reveals some odd facts.

To begin with, it does not include *all* our material goods. Such immense economic treasures as the contents of the Library of

TABLE 1 · 1

U.S. National Physical Wealth 1968 Value

	Billions of dollars, rounded
Structures	
Residential	$ 683
Business	394
Government	460
Equipment	
Producers (machines, factories, etc.)	377
Consumers durables (autos, appliances)	234
Inventories, business	216
Monetary gold and foreign exchange	14
Land	
Farm	152
Residential & business	419
Public	144
Net foreign assets	66
Total	**3,159**

Congress or the Patent Office cannot be accurately valued. Nor can works of art, nor military equipment—not any of them included in the total. Much of our public land is valued at only nominal amounts. Hence at best this is the roughest of estimates of the economic endowment at our disposal.

What is more important, the table omits the most important constituent of our wealth: the value of skills and knowledge in our population. If we estimate the value of those skills for 1968, they come to $5.15 trillion—more than the value of the material equipment with which they work! For reasons that we explain in the following box, "Human Wealth," we do not usually include human wealth along with physical wealth, although we shall return again and again to this all-important element of our economic system. But here we shall familiarize our-

selves with the material side of our national balance sheet, leaving the human side for later.

CAPITAL

One portion of the endowment of a nation's physical wealth has a special significance. This is its national *capital*—the portion of its productive wealth that is *man-made* and therefore *reproducible*. If we look back at the table, we can see that our own national capital in 1968 consisted of the sum total of all our structures, our producers' equipment and our consumer durables, our inventories, our monetary gold and foreign assets—$2,744 billion in all.

We can think of this national capital as consisting of whatever has been preserved out of the sum total of everything that has ever been produced from the very beginning of the economic history of the United States up to a certain date—here December 31, 1968. Some of that capital—inventories for example—might be used up the very next day. On the other hand, inventories might also be increased. In fact, our national capital changes from date to date, as we do add to our inventories or to our stocks of equipment or structures, etc., or more rarely, as we consume them and do not replace them. But at any date, our capital still represents *all that the nation has produced*—yesterday or a century ago—*and that it has not used up or destroyed.*

The reason that we identify our national capital within the larger frame of our wealth is that it is constantly changing and usually growing. Not that a nation's inheritance of natural resources is unimportant; indeed, the ability of a people to build capital depends to no small degree on the bounties or obstacles offered by its geography and geology—think of the economic limitations imposed by desert and ice on the Bushman and the Eskimo. But the point in singling out our

HUMAN WEALTH

Why do we not include the value of human skills in our inventory of wealth? The reason is that all our inventory consists of *property* that can be sold; that is, marketable goods. When our economy included slaves, they were part of our wealth; but in today's market system, men are not property. They can sell their labor but not themselves.

Ideally, our inventory of wealth should therefore include the "asset value" of that labor, or the human capital that gives rise to the various tasks, skilled and unskilled, that men perform.

How could we estimate that value? The method is much the same as that used to estimate the value of a machine. If a lathe produces a flow of output worth, say, $1,000 a year, we can "capitalize" the value of that flow of output to arrive at the current value of the machine itself.

In the same way we can capitalize the flow of output of humans. The value of human output is measured by the *incomes* that the factor of production labor earns. In 1968 that stream of income was worth $515 billion. If we capitalize it at 10 percent—a rough and ready figure that is comparable to the rate at which we might capitalize many assets—the value of our human capital was therefore $5.15 trillion.

capital is that it represents the portion of our total national endowment over which we have the most immediate control. As we shall later see, much of a nation's current economic fortune is intimately related to the rate at which it is adding to its capital wealth.

WEALTH AND CLAIMS

There remains to be noted one more thing before we leave the subject of wealth. Our table of national wealth omits two items that would be the very first to be counted in an inventory of personal wealth: bank accounts and financial assets such as stocks or bonds or deeds or mortgages. Why are these all-important items of personal wealth excluded from our summary of national wealth?

The answer to this seeming paradox is that we have already counted the *things*—houses, factories, machines, etc.,—that constitute the real assets behind stocks, bonds, deeds, and the like. Indeed these certificates tell us only who *owns* the various items of our national capital. Stocks and bonds and mortgages and deeds are *claims* on assets, but they are not those assets in themselves. The reality

of General Motors is its physical plant and its going organization, not the shares of stock that organization has issued. If by some curious mischance all its shares disintegrated, General Motors would still be there; but if the plants and the organization disintegrated instead, the shares would not magically constitute for us another enterprise.

So, too, with our bank accounts. The dollars we spend or hold in our accounts are part of our personal wealth only insofar as they command goods or services. The value of coin or currency as "objects" is much less than their official and legal value as money. But most of the goods over which our money exerts its claims (although not, it must be admitted, the services it also buys) are already on our balance sheet. To count our money as part of national wealth would thus be to count a claim as if it were an asset, much as in the case of stocks and bonds.

Why, then, do we have an item for monetary gold in our table of national wealth? The answer is that foreigners will accept gold in exchange for their own real assets (whereas they are not bound to accept our dollar bills) and that, therefore, monetary gold gives us a claim against *foreign* wealth.* In much the same way, the item of *net foreign assets* represents the value of all real assets, such as factories, located abroad and owned by U.S. citizens, less the value of any real wealth located in the United States and owned by foreigners.

REAL WEALTH VS. FINANCIAL WEALTH

Thus we reach a very important final conclusion. *National wealth is not quite the same thing as the sum of personal wealth.* When we add up our individual wealth, we include first of all our holdings of money or stocks or bonds—all items that are excluded from our national register of wealth. The difference is that as individuals we properly consider our own wealth to be the *claims* we have against one another, whereas as a society we consider our wealth to be the stock of material *assets* we possess, and the only claims we consider are those that we may have against other societies.

National wealth is thus a *real* phenomenon, the tangible consequence of past activity. Financial wealth, on the other hand —the form in which individuals hold their wealth—is only the way the claims of ownership are established vis-à-vis the underlying real assets of the community. The contrast between the underlying, slow-changing reality of national wealth and the overlying, sometimes fast-changing financial representation of that wealth is one of the differences between economic life viewed from the vantage point of the economist and that same life seen through the eyes of a participant in the process. We shall encounter many more such contrasts as our study proceeds.

---

*Gold has, of course, a value in itself—we can use it for jewelry and for dentistry. However, in the balance sheet of our national wealth, we value the gold at its formal international exchange price, rather than merely as a commodity.

The Flow of Production

WEALTH AND OUTPUT

But why is national wealth so important? Exactly what is the connection between the wealth of nations and the well-being of their citizens?

The question is not an idle one, for the connection between wealth and well-being is not a matter of direct physical cause and effect. For example, India has the largest inventory of livestock in the world, but its contribution to Indian living standards is far less than that of our livestock wealth. Or again, our national capital of goods (or skills) in 1933 was not significantly different from that in 1929, but one year was marked by widespread misery and the other by booming prosperity. Clearly then, the existence of great physical wealth by itself does not guarantee—it only holds out the possibility of—a high standard of living. It is only insofar as physical wealth interacts with the working population that it exerts its enormous economic leverage, and this interaction is not a mechanical phenomenon that we can take for granted, but a complex *social* process, whose motivations we must explore.

As the example of Indian livestock indicates, local customs and beliefs can effectively sterilize the potential physical benefits of wealth. Perhaps we should generalize that conclusion by observing that the political and social system will have a primary role in causing an effective or ineffective use of existing wealth. Compare the traditional hoarding of gold or gems in many backward societies with the possibility of their disposal to produce foreign exchange for the purchase of machinery.

In a modern industrial society, we take for granted some kind of effective social and political structure. Then why do we at times make vigorous use of our existing material assets and at other times seem to put them to little or no use? Why do we have "good times" and "bad times"? The question directs our attention back to the panorama of society to discover something further about its economic operation.

INPUTS AND OUTPUTS

This time, our attention fastens on a different aspect of the tableau. Rather than noticing our stock of wealth, we observe the result of our use of that wealth, a result we can see emerging in the form of a *flow of production.*

How does this flow of production arise? We can see that it comes into being as man combines his energies and his skills with his natural and man-made environment. We have already briefly described the long and painful history of his social and technical attempts to combine those energies and the environment successfully.

Hence we take for granted the fact that men organize their struggle with nature according to the rules of a market process whose operation was the main subject matter of Part Three. Now we want to know what happens to the flow of output emerging under our eyes from thousands of enterprises as their entrepreneurs hire the factors of production and combine their services as inputs to yield a saleable output.

It may help us picture the flow as a whole if we imagine that each and every good and service that is produced—each loaf of bread, each nut and bolt, each doctor's call, each theatrical performance, each car, ship, lathe, or bolt of cloth—can be identified in the way that a radioactive isotope allows us to follow the circulation of certain kinds of cells through the body. Then, if we look down on the economic panorama, we can see the continuous combination of land, labor, and capital giving off a continuous flow of "lights" as goods and services emerge in their saleable form.

INTERMEDIATE GOODS

Where do these lights go? Many, as we can see, are soon extinguished. The goods or services they represent are *intermediate goods* that have been incorporated into other products to form more fully finished items of output. Thus from our aerial perspective we can follow a product such as cotton from the fields to the spinning mill, where its light is extinguished, for there the cotton disappears into a new product: yarn. In turn, the light of the yarn traces a path as it leaves the spinning mill by way of sale to the textile mill, there to be doused as the yarn disappears into a new good: cloth. And again, the cloth leaving the textile mill lights a way to the factory where it will become part of an article of clothing.

FINAL GOODS: CONSUMPTION

And what of the clothing? Here at last we have what the economist calls a *final* good. Why "final"? Because once in the possession of its ultimate owner, the clothing passes out of the active economic flow. As a good in the hands of a consumer, it is no longer an object on the marketplace. Its light is now extinguished permanently—or if we wish to complete our image, we can imagine it fading gradually as the clothing "disappears" into the utility of the consumer. In the case of consumer goods like food or of consumer services like recreation, the light goes out faster, for these items are "consumed" when they reach their final destination.*

We shall have a good deal to learn in later chapters about the macroeconomic behavior of consumers. What we should notice in this first view is the supreme importance of this flow of production into consumers'

---

*In fact, of course, they are not *really* consumed but remain behind as garbage, junk, wastes, and so on. Economics used to ignore these residuals, but it does so no longer.

hands. By this vital process, the population replenishes or increases its energies and ministers to its wants and needs; it is a process that, if halted for very long, would cause a society to perish. That is why we speak of consumption as the ultimate end and aim of all economic activity.

A SECOND FINAL GOOD: INVESTMENT

Nevertheless, for all the importance of consumption, if we look down on the illuminated flow of output we see a surprising thing. Whereas the greater portion of the final goods and services of the economy is bought by the human agents of production for their consumption, we also find that a lesser but still considerable flow of final products is not. What happens to it?

If we follow an appropriate good, we may find out. Let us watch the destination of the steel that leaves a Pittsburgh mill. Some of it, like our cotton cloth, will become incorporated into consumers' goods, ending up as cans, automobiles, or household articles of various kinds. But some steel will not find its way to a consumer at all; instead, it will end up as part of a machine or an office building or a railroad track.

Now in a way, these goods are not "final," for they are used to produce still further goods or services—the machine producing output of some kind, the building producing office space, the rail track producing transportation. Yet there is a difference between such goods, used for production, and consumer goods, like clothing. The difference is that the machine, the office building, and the track are goods that are used by business enterprises as part of their productive equipment. In terms of our image, these goods slowly lose their light-giving powers as their services pass into flows of production, but usually they are replaced with new goods before their light is totally extinguished. That is why we call them *cap-*

ital goods or *investment goods* in distinction to consumers' goods. *As part of our capital, they will be preserved, maintained, and renewed, perhaps indefinitely. Hence the stock of capital, like consumers, constitutes a final destination for output.* *

GROSS AND NET INVESTMENT

We call the great stream of output that goes to capital *gross investment*. The very word *gross* suggests that it conceals a finer breakdown; and looking more closely, we can see that the flow of output going to capital does indeed serve two distinct purposes. Part of it is used to replace the capital—the machines, the buildings, the track, or whatever—that has been used up in the process of production. Just as the human agents of production have to be replenished by a flow of consumption goods, so the material agents of production need to be maintained and renewed if their contribution to output is to remain undiminished. We call the part of gross investment, whose purpose is to keep society's stock of capital intact, *replacement investment,* or simply *replacement*.

Sometimes the total flow of output going to capital is not large enough to maintain the existing stock; for instance, if we allow inventories (a form of capital) to become depleted, or if we simply fail to replace worn-out equipment or plant. This running-down of capital, we call *disinvestment,* meaning the very opposite of investment: instead of maintaining or building up capital, we are literally consuming it.

Not all gross investment is used for replacement purposes, however. Some of the flow may *increase* the stock of capital by

---

*We might note that some products, like automobiles, possess characteristics of both consumption goods and capital goods. We call such goods *consumer durables;* and unlike ordinary goods (such as food) held by consumers, we include them in our inventory of national wealth (see Table 1·1).

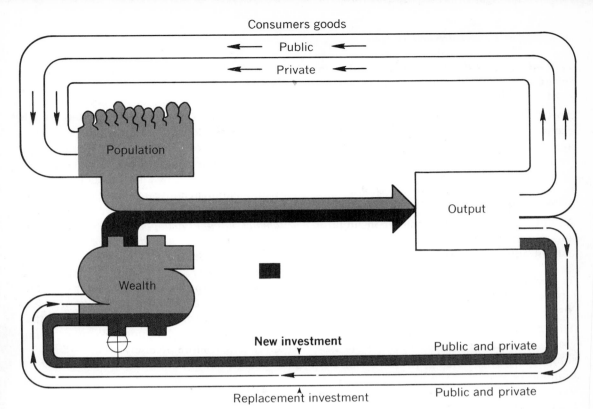

Consumers goods
Public
Private

Population

Output

Wealth

New investment

Public and private

Replacement investment

Public and private

FIGURE 1 · 1
The circular flow, view I

adding buildings, machines, track, inventory, and so on.* If the total output consigned to capital is sufficiently great not only to make up for wear and tear, but to increase the capital stock, we say there has been *new* or *net investment,* or *net capital formation.*

Sometimes it helps to have a homely picture in mind to keep things straight. The difference between replacement and net investment is made clear by using as an example the paving of streets. Each year some streets wear out, and we have to repave them to keep them passable. This is clearly *investment,* but it does not add to our ability to enjoy surface transportation. Hence it is solely *replacement* investment. Only when we

build *additional* streets do we undertake new or net investment. Also, sometimes we build a new street but allow an old one to deteriorate beyond usability. Here we have to offset the new investment with the *disinvestment* in our now unpassable road. Whether or not we have any net investment in street building as a whole depends on whether we have added or subtracted from street capacity when we consider gross investment and the disinvestment together.

CONSUMPTION AND INVESTMENT

A simple diagram may help us picture the flows of output we have been discussing. Figure 1·1 calls to our attention these important attributes of the economic system:

*Note carefully that *increased* inventory is a form of investment. Later this will take on a special importance.

7

1. It emphasizes the essential circularity, the self-renewing, self-feeding nature of the production flow.

This circularity is a feature of the macro-economic process to which we will return again and again.

2. It illumines a basic choice that all economic societies must make: a choice between consumption and investment.

At any given level of output, consumption and investment are, so to speak, rivals for the current output of society.

3. It makes clear that society can invest (that is, add to its capital) only the output that it refrains from consuming.

The economic meaning of *saving*, as our diagram shows, is to release resources from consumption so that they can be used for the building of capital. Whether they *will* be so used is a matter that will occupy us through many subsequent chapters.

4. It shows that both the consumption flow and the investment flow can be split between public uses and private uses in any manner that the nation sees fit.

But the only way to increase public consumption and investment is to refrain from private consumption and investment.

5. Finally, it reveals that output is the nation's "budget constraint."

It indicates the total quantity of goods and services available for all public and private consumption and investment uses. More goods and services might be desired, but they do not exist.

Gross National Product

There remains but one preliminary matter before we proceed to a closer examination of the actual determinants of the flow of pro-duction. We have seen that the annual output of the nation is a revealing measure of its well-being, for it reflects the degree of inter-action between the population and its wealth. Later we shall also find output to be a major determinant of employment. Hence it be-hooves us to examine the nature and general character of this flow and to become familiar with its nomenclature and composition.

We call the dollar value of the total annual output of final goods and services in the nation its gross national product. The gross national product (or GNP as it is usually abbreviated) is thus nothing but the dollar value of the total output of all consumption goods and of all investment goods produced in a year. We are already familiar with this general meaning, but now we must define GNP a little more precisely.

FINAL GOODS

We are interested, through the concept of GNP, in measuring the value of the *ultimate* production of the economic system—that is, the total value of all goods and services *enjoyed by its consumers or accumulated as new or replacement capital.* Hence we do not count the intermediate goods we have already noted in our economic panorama. To go back to an earlier example, we do not add up the value of the cotton *and* the yarn *and* the cloth *and* the final clothing when we compute the value of GNP. That kind of multiple counting might be very useful if we wanted certain information about our total economic activity, but it would not tell us accurately about the final value of output. For when we buy a shirt, the price we pay includes the cost of the cloth to the shirtmaker; and in turn, the amount the shirtmaker paid for his cloth included the cost of the yarn; and in turn, again, the seller of yarn included in his price the amount he paid for raw cotton. Em-bodied in the price of the shirt, therefore, is the value of all the intermediate products that went into it. Thus in figuring the value for GNP, we add only the values of all final goods, both for consumption and for investment purposes. Note as well that GNP includes only a given year's production of goods and services. Therefore sales of used car dealers, antique dealers, etc., are not included, because the value of these goods was picked up in GNP the year they were produced.

TYPES OF FINAL GOODS

In our first view of macroeconomic activity we divided the flow of output into two great streams: consumption and gross investment. Now, for purposes of a closer analysis, we impose a few refinements on this basic scheme.

First we must pay heed to a small flow of production that has previously escaped our notice. This is the net flow of goods or services that leaves this country; that is, the total flow going abroad minus the flow that enters. This international branch of our economy will play a relatively minor role in our analysis for quite a while; we will largely ignore it until Chapter 9. But we must give it its proper name: *net exports.* Because these net exports are a kind of investment (they are goods we produce but do not consume), we must now rename the great bulk of investment that remains in this country. We will henceforth call it *gross private domestic investment.*

By convention, gross private domestic investment refers only to investments in physical assets such as factories, inventories, homes. Personal expenditures on acquiring human skills, as well as expenditures for regular use, are considered *personal consumption expenditures*—the technical accounting term for *consumption.* As these accounting terms indicate, *public* consumption and investment are included in neither personal consumption expenditures nor gross private domestic investment. Here is our last flow of final output: all public buying of final goods and services is kept in a separate category called *government purchases of goods and services.*

C + I + G + X

We now have four streams of "final" output, each going to a final purchaser of economic output. Therefore we can speak of gross national product as being the sum of personal consumption expenditure (C), gross private domestic investment (I), government purchases (G), and net exports (X), or (to abbreviate a long sentence) we can write that

$$GNP \equiv C + I + G + X$$

This is a descriptive identity that should be remembered.

It helps, at this juncture, to look at GNP over the past decades. In Fig. 1·2 we show the long irregular upward flow of GNP from 1929 to the present, with the four component streams of expenditures visible. Later we will be talking at length about the behavior of each stream, but first we need to be introduced to the overall flow itself.

STOCKS AND FLOWS

One final point should be made about our basic identity. All through our discussion of GNP we have talked about *flows* of output. We do so to distinguish GNP, a "flow concept," from wealth or capital (or any asset) that is a *stock,* or a sum of wealth that exists at any given time.

A moment's reflection may make the distinction clear. When we speak of a stock of business capital or of land or structures, we mean a sum of wealth that we could actually

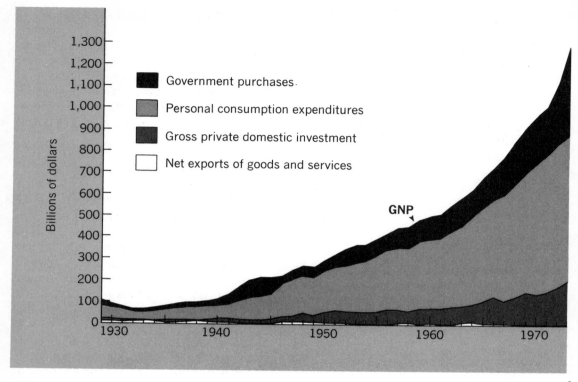

FIGURE 1 · 2
GNP and components, 1929–1973

inspect on a given date. GNP, however, does not "exist" in quite the same way. If our gross national product for a year is, say $1.5 trillion, this does not mean that on any day of that year we could actually discover this much value of goods and services. *Rather, GNP tells us the average annual rate, for that year, at which production was carried out; so that if the year's flow of output had been collected in a huge reservoir without being consumed, at the end of the year the volume in the reservoir would indeed have totaled $1.5 trillion.* GNP is, however, constantly being consumed as well as produced, and its rate of flow is constantly changing. Hence the $1.5 trillion figure refers to the value of the *sum of production over the year* and should not be pictured as constituting a given flow of output existing at any moment in time.

Cautions about GNP

GNP is an indispensable concept in dealing with the performance of our economy, but it is well to understand the weaknesses as well as the strengths of this most important single economic indicator.

1. GNP deals in dollar values, not in physical units.

That is, it does not tell us how many goods and services were produced, but only what their sales value was. Trouble then arises when we compare the GNP of one year with that of another, to determine whether or not the nation is better off. For if prices in the second year are higher, GNP will appear higher, even though the actual volume of output is unchanged or even lower!

We can correct for this price change very easily when all prices have moved in the same degree or proportion. Then it is easy to speak of "real" GNP—that is, the current money value of GNP adjusted for price changes—as reflecting the actual rise or fall of output. The price problem becomes more difficult, however, when prices change in different degrees or even in different directions, as they often do. Then a comparison of "real" GNP from one year to the next, and especially over a long span of years, is unavoidably arbitrary to some extent.

Figure 1·3 shows us the previous totals for GNP corrected as best we can for price changes. In this chart, 1963 is used as the "base," and the GNP's of other years use 1963 prices, so that price changes are eliminated to the greatest possible extent. One can, of course, choose any year for a base. Choosing a different year would alter the basic dollar measuring rod, but it would only slightly change the profile of "real" year-to-year changes.

2. *Changes in the quality of output may not be accurately reflected in GNP.*

The second weakness of GNP also involves its inaccuracy as an indicator of "real" trends over time. The difficulty revolves

FIGURE 1 · 3
GNP in constant and current prices, 1929–1973

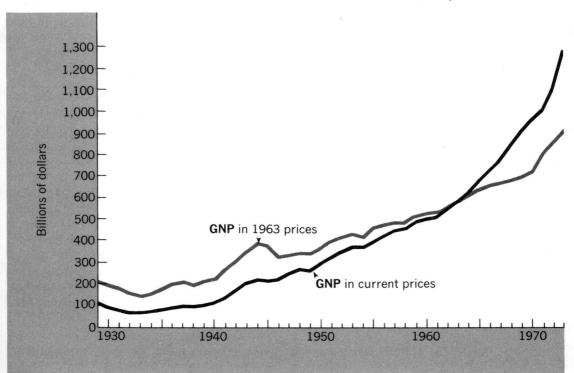

GNP in 1963 prices

GNP in current prices

REAL AND CURRENT GNP

How do we arrive at a figure for "real" GNP? *The answer is that we "correct" the value of GNP (or any other magnitude measured in dollars) for the price changes that affect the value of our dollars but not the real quantitites of goods and services our dollars buy.*

We make this correction by applying a *price index*. Such an index is a series of numbers showing the variation in prices, year to year, from a starting or *base year* whose price level is set at 100. Thus if prices go up 5 percent a year, a price index starting in year one will read 105 for year two, 110+ for year three (105 × 1.05), 115.5 for year four, and so on.

In correcting GNP we use a very complex price index called a GNP *price deflator*. This index, constructed by the Department of Commerce, allows for the fact that different parts of GNP, such as consumers goods and investment goods may change in price at different rates. The present price deflator uses GNP price levels in 1958 as a "base." In 1973, the value of the deflator was 153.9.

Now let us work out an actual example. *To arrive at a corrected GNP, we divide the current GNP by the deflator and then multiply by 100.* For example, GNP in current figures was $977 billion for 1970; $1,055 billion for 1971; and $1,155 billion for 1972. The deflator for those years was 135, 142, and 146 respectively. Here are the results:

around the changes in the utility of goods and services. In a technologically advancing society, goods are usually improved from one decade to the next, or even more rapidly, and new goods are constantly being introduced. In an urbanizing, increasingly high-density society, the utility of other goods may be lessened over time. An airplane trip today, for example, is certainly highly preferable to one taken twenty or thirty years ago; a subway ride is not. Television sets did not even exist 40 years ago.

Government statisticians attempt to correct for changes in the quality of goods and services. Committees composed of government statisticians and industry representatives meet to decide on the extent to which price increases represent quality improvements. It is very difficult to determine whether these committees over- or under-adjust for quality improvements. In the 1950s these committees counted the cost of putting "fins" on cars as a quality improvement rather than as a price increase. The fins did not affect the performance of the car, but they were thought to improve its beauty.

Completely new goods, such as the picture phones that have been demonstrated in some parts of the country, present an even more difficult problem. Clearly, a picture phone is not an ordinary telephone. Yet, how much of a quality improvement is it? Since there is no satisfactory answer to this question, picture phones will be valued at the price they are sold in any given year. If picture phones fall in price as they are introduced into the mass market, an evaluation of GNP in 1975 prices will give a much higher "weight" to picture phones than an evaluation of GNP in 1990 prices. This is a prime reason why base years and deflating formulas are periodically reconsidered.

3. GNP does not reflect the purpose of production.

A third difficulty with GNP lies in its blindness to the ultimate use of production. If in one year GNP rises by a billion dollars, owing to an increase in expenditure on education, and in another year it rises by the same amount because of a rise in cigarette production, the figures in each case show the same

$$\frac{\$977}{135} = \$7.23 \times 100 = \$723 \text{ billion}$$

$$\frac{\$1055}{142} = \$7.44 \times 100 = \$744 \text{ billion}$$

$$\frac{\$1155}{146} = \$7.93 \times 100 = \$793 \text{ billion}$$

Thus the "real value" of GNP in 1972 was $793 billion, *in terms of 1958 prices*, rather than the $1,115 billion of its current value. Two things should be noted in this process of correction. First, the "real value" of any series will differ, depending on the base year that is chosen. For instance, if we started a series in 1972, the "real value" of GNP for that year would be $1,115, the same as its money value.

Second, the process of constructing a GNP deflator is enormously difficult. In fact there is no single "accurate" way of constructing an index that will reflect all the variations of prices of the goods *within* GNP. To put it differently, we can construct different kinds of indexes, with different "weights" for different sectors, and these will give us differing results. The point then is to be cautious in using corrected figures. Be sure you know what the base year is. And remember that complex indexes, such as the GNP deflator, are only approximations of a change that defies wholly accurate measurement.*

*For a fuller discussion of price indexes and related problems, you might look into Chapter 18.

amount of "growth" of GNP. Even output that turns out to be wide of the mark or totally wasteful—such as the famous Edsel car that no one wanted or military weapons that are obsolete from the moment they appear—all are counted as part of GNP.

The problem of environmental deterioration adds another difficulty. Environmentalists concerned about the adverse impact of growth on our quality of life sometimes advocate Zero Economic Growth as a solution to our ecological ills. Unfortunately, the environmental problem is much more complicated than a "go" or "no go" decision on GNP. Some types of GNP growth directly contribute to pollution—cars, paper or steel production, for example. Other types of GNP growth are necessary to stop pollution—sewage disposal plants or the production of a clean internal combustion engine. Still other types of GNP have little impact on the environment; most personal services fall into this category.

The real problem therefore involves selecting the types of economic growth that are compatible with environmental safety. The sheer measure of GNP tells us nothing with respect to such a purpose. For example, our conventional measure of GNP makes no allowances for the harmful goods and services that are often generated by production. All forms of pollution and congestion are essentially *negative outputs*. They diminish individual pleasure or utility; they should be *subtracted* from GNP. Yet under our accounting procedures, they are included in GNP! So too, we fail to factor out of GNP those expenditures taken to repair the damage caused by other elements in the total. For instance, the cleaning bills we pay to undo damage caused by smoke from the neighborhood factory become part of GNP, although cleaning our clothes does not increase our well-being; it only brings it back to what it was in the first place.

These costs of cleaning up the harmful effects of economic growth are just one of a large number of *defensive expenditures* in GNP. Defensive expenditures are designed to prevent bad things from happening or to offset the impacts of adverse circumstances, rather than to cause good things to happen.

IMPUTED INCOMES

Imputed rents are calculated by determining the rent that an individual would have to pay for his own home if he did not own it. This hypothetical rent is added into the GNP to maintain consistency in the treatment of the nation's housing stock. The produce grown in personal vegetable gardens is handled in a similar fashion.

Given the precedent of imputed rents, why haven't government statisticians imputed the value of the housewifes services into the GNP? Statisticians can find market wages for cleaning women, babysitters, maids, cooks, and other servants. But is a wife or mother simply a combined cook, maid, and babysitter—a servant? While imputed values could be placed on these services, most wives and mothers would object strenuously (so would most husbands and children). As a result, government statisticians, and the politicians who hire them, do not want to get involved in placing a value on someone else's mother or wife. Only research economists are willing to be so presumptuous.

Imputing the value of housewives services also opens a Pandora's Box of problems with respect to other self-produced consumption goods. Men provide services in their homes as carpenters, bartenders, and do-it-yourselfers. Should imputed values also be placed on these services? Theoretically the answer is yes, but as with the housewife, the practical problems of assigning an actual value serves as a deterrent.

In addition to environmental expenditures, other major examples include military and police expenditures, flood control, repair bills, many medical outlays. These outlays are not desired in their own right; they are simply forced on us by man-made circumstances.

4. GNP does not include most goods and services that are not for sale.

Presumably GNP tells us how large our final output is. Yet it does not include one of the most important kinds of work and sources of consumer pleasure—the labor of wives in maintaining their households. Yet, curiously, if this labor were paid for—that is, if we engaged cooks and maids and baby sitters instead of depending on our wives for these services, GNP *would* include their services as final output, since they would be purchased on the market. But the labor of wives being unpaid, it is excluded from GNP.

The difficulty here is that we are constantly moving toward purchasing "outside" services in place of home services—laundries, bakeries, restaurants, etc., all perform work that used to be performed at home. Thus the process of *monetizing* activity gives an upward trend to GNP statistics that is not fully mirrored in actual output.

A related problem is that some parts of GNP are paid for by some members of the population and not by others. Rent, for example, measures the services of landlords for homeowners and is therefore included in GNP, but what of the man who owns his own home and pays no rent? Similarly, what of the family that grows some part of its food at home and therefore does not pay for it? In order to include such items of "free" consumption into GNP, the statisticians of the Commerce Department add an "imputed" value figure to include goods and services like these not tallied on a cash register.

5. GNP does not consider the value of leisure.

Leisure time is not only enjoyable in its own right, but it is also *necessary* in order to consume material goods and services. A boat without the time to use it is of little consumption value. Over the years, individual enjoyment and national well-being go up because each individual has more leisure time to spend as he pleases, *but leisure time does not show up in GNP*.

Leisure time has not been integrated into

measured GNP, since economists have not managed to find either a good technique for measuring its extent or for placing a value upon it. What should be subtracted from the 24-hour day to indicate hours of leisure? Presumably, leisure hours are those hours that give pleasure or utility. All hours that create pain or disutility should be subtracted.

Then what about work? Does it create utility or disutility? Does it create pleasure or pain? In economic theory, work is considered to be pain and should be subtracted. Yet this is clearly often incorrect. Many people enjoy their work. Even those who basically dislike their jobs often enjoy *parts* of work. Are those parts leisure or work?

And then, what about the maintenance activities—eating, sleeping, washing, etc.— that are necessary to keep the human body alive? Are they pleasure or pain? They are necessary to both consumption and work, yet they are neither pure leisure nor painful work. If you were asked to divide your own day into the hours that give pleasure (utility) and the hours that give you pain (disutility), how would you divide your day? Most of us would find many ambiguous hours that we could not really categorize one way or another. What you cannot do for yourself, economists cannot do for you.

As a result, people tend to focus on hours of paid labor on the assumption that leisure must be going up if hours of paid work are going down. While this assumption is probably correct, subtracting hours of paid work from the total quantity of available hours is obviously a very crude measure of the quality of leisure. For example, if people move to the suburbs and spend two hours a day commuting, their leisure has decreased, although their paid hours of labor have not.

6. The GNP does not indicate anything about the distribution of goods and services among the population.

Societies can and do differ in how they allocate their production of purchasable goods and services among their populations. A pure egalitarian society might allocate everyone the same quantity of goods and services. Many societies establish minimum consumption standards for individuals and families. Few deliberately decide to let someone starve if they have the economic resources to prevent such a possibility. Yet to know a nation's GNP, or even to know its average (per capita) GNP, is to know nothing about how broadly or how narrowly this output is shared. A wealthy country can be composed mainly of poor families. A poor country can have many wealthy families.*

GNP AND ECONOMIC WELFARE

These problems lead economists to treat GNP in a skeptical and gingerly manner, particularly insofar as its "welfare" considerations are concerned. Kenneth Boulding has suggested that we relabel the monster *Gross National Cost* to disabuse ourselves once and for all of the notion that a bigger GNP is necessarily a better one. Paul Samuelson suggests a new measure—Net Economic Welfare or NEW—to supplement GNP, the difference being mostly the maintenance or defensive or negative outputs we have mentioned. Economists Tobin and Nordhaus propose MEW—Measure of Economic Welfare—for much the same purposes, subtracting the outputs that contribute nothing to the sum of individuals' utilities and adding back other sums, mainly housewives' services, that are conventionally omitted. (We might note in passing that MEW, as calculated by Tobin and Nordhaus, grows much less rapidly per capita than does GNP. From 1929 to 1965, real per capita GNP mounted at 1.7 percent per year; MEW, at 1.1 percent.)

All these doubts and reservations should instill in us a permanent caution against using

---

*See the section on averages and bimodal distributions, Chapter 18, for more on this important statistical problem.

GNP as if it were a clearcut measure of social contentment or happiness. Economist Edward Denison once remarked that perhaps nothing affects national economic welfare so much as the weather, which does not get into the GNP accounts. Hence, because the U.S. has a GNP per capita that is higher than that of say, the Netherlands, life is not consequently better here; it may be worse. In fact, by the indices of longevity, health, quality of environment, or ease of retirement, it probably *is* worse.

Yet, with all its shortcomings, *GNP is still the simplest way we possess of summarizing the overall level of market activity of the economy.* If we want to summarize its welfare, we had better turn to specific social indicators of how long we live, how healthy we are, how cheaply we provide good medical care, how varied and abundant is our diet, etc.—none of which we can tell from GNP figures alone. But we are not always interested in welfare, partly because it is too complex to be summed up in a single measure. For better or worse, therefore, GNP has become the yardstick used by most nations in the world; and although other yardsticks are sure to become more important, GNP will be a central term in the economic lexicon for a long time to come.

KEY WORDS

Macroeconomics

Wealth

Capital
Claims

Production
Consumption

Replacement
investment

Net and gross
investment

Gross national
product
  Consumption
  Gross domestic
  private investment
  Government
  purchases
  Net exports

CENTRAL CONCEPTS

1. **Macroeconomics is an *approach* to economic problems through the study of certain aggregate processes.**
2. **We begin the study of macroeconomic processes by observing how a *flow of output* comes from human resources interacting with physical resources.**
3. **We note that capital consists of *real things*, and *not of the financial claims* against those things.**
4. **The flow of output shows us *the circular nature of the process of production*. From the interaction of population and wealth emerges a stream of goods going back to replenish consumers (consumption goods) and a stream to replenish and add to our capital wealth (gross investment).**
5. **A study of the flow of output and its division into consumption and investment emphasizes the essential choice that must be made between these *two basic uses of output*.**
6. **The investment flow can be subdivided into two: one flow *replaces or renews capital* that has been worn out or used up. This is *replacement investment*. The other flow *adds to the stock of capital wealth*, and is called *new or net capital* or *investment*. The two flows together are called *gross investment*.**
7. **The name for the total flow of output is *gross national product*. It is divided into four categories:**
   - **Consumption *(C)*, or the goods and services going to consumers.**
   - **Gross private domestic investment *(I)*, or that portion of output going to private businesses as replacements for, and additions to, their real domestic capital. It also includes housing.**
   - **Government purchases *(G)*, or those goods and services (both consumers' and capital) bought by all public agencies.**
   - **Net exports *(X)*, the net outflow of goods and services to other countries.**
   - **The formula GNP $\equiv$ C + I + G + X conveniently summarizes these four subdivisions.**

$GNP \equiv C + I$
$+ G + X$

8. Note that GNP counts only the dollar value of *final goods and services* in each of these categories. Intermediate goods or services are not counted, since their value is included in the value of final goods.

9. GNP is an indispensable concept in macroeconomics. It is a measure of the purchasable goods and services that the economy is producing. *It is not a measure of economic welfare.* To make judgments about economic welfare remember that:

Pitfalls of GNP
  Final goods
  Prices
  Quality
  Use
  Defensive output
  Output not for sale
  Leisure
  Distribution

  ● GNP deals in dollar values and not physical units. This leads to problems in adjusting for price changes, so that "real" GNP accurately reflects changes in output.

  ● GNP may not accurately reflect quality changes.

  ● GNP does not reveal the purpose or usefulness of production.

  ● GNP accounts include defensive expenditures that are made not to create utility but to prevent disutility, and "negative" outputs are not subtracted from it.

  ● GNP figures do not include output that is not for sale.

  ● GNP does not place a value upon leisure time.

  ● GNP does not reveal the distribution of output.

QUESTIONS

1. Why is capital so important a part of national wealth? Why is money not considered capital?

2. What is meant by the "circularity" of the economic process? Does it have something to do with the output of the system being returned to it as fresh inputs?

3. What is meant by net investment? by gross investment? What is the difference?

4. Write the basic identity for GNP and state carefully the exact names of each of the four constituents of GNP.

5. Suppose we had an island economy with an output of 100 tons of grain, each ton selling for $90. If grain is the only product sold, what is the value of GNP? Now suppose that production stays the same but that prices rise to $110. What is the value of GNP now? How could we "correct" for the price rise? If we didn't, would GNP be an accurate measure of output from one year to the next?

6. Now suppose that production rose to 110 tons but that prices fell to $81. The value of GNP, in terms of current prices, has fallen from $9,000 to $8,910. Yet, actual output, measured in tons of grain, has increased. Can you devise a price index that will show the change in real GNP?

7. Presumably, the quality of most products improves over time. If their price is unchanged, does that mean that GNP understates or overstates the real value of output?

8. When more and more consumers buy "do-it-yourself" kits, does the value of GNP (which includes the sale price of these kits) understate or overstate the true final output of the nation?

9. What is a public consumption good? A public investment expenditure? How would you classify the following: Blue Cross Insurance; airport flight controllers; museum fees? Are these public or private? Consumption or investment? It's not always easy to draw the line, is it?

10. What is an intermediate good, and why are such goods not included in the value of GNP? Is coal sold to a utility company an intermediate good? Coal sold to a consumer? Coal sold to the army? What determines whether a good will or will not be counted in the total of GNP?

11. A bachelor pays a cook $100 a week. Is this part of GNP? He then marries her and gives her an allowance of $100 a week. Allowances do not count in GNP. Hence the *measure* of GNP falls. Does welfare fall?

12. Do you think that we should develop measures other than GNP to indicate changes in our basic well-being? What sorts of measures?

The Tools of Economic Analysis

OUR INTRODUCTION TO THE PROBLEM OF gross national product gives us a general idea of the direction in which our macroeconomic inquiry will proceed. But before we come to grips with matters that await us—unemployment, inflation, growth—we should take a chapter to learn a few basic concepts on which economics, as an analytical discipline, is founded.

In this chapter we will take up a series of concepts that will be helpful to you as you go on. Some of them seem very simple but are more subtle than they appear at first look; others may seem demanding at first but are actually simple. There are seven of these intellectual tools. Try to master them all, for we will use them frequently.*

1. Ceteris paribus

The first concept is one that sounds simple but is actually very complex. It is the assump-

*Because this chapter is basic to all economics, it appears, in substantially the same form, in *Understanding Microeconomics.*

tion that when we examine the relationship between any two economic activities, we can disregard the effects of everything but the particular elements under examination.

This assumption of holding "other things equal" is called by its Latin name ceteris paribus. It is extremely easy to apply in theory—and extremely difficult to apply in practice. For example, in our examination of the demand curve, we assume that the *income* and *tastes* of the person (or of the collection of persons) are unchanged, while we examine the influence of price on the quantities of shoes they are willing and able to buy. The reason is obvious. If we allowed their incomes or tastes to change, both their willingness *and* their ability would also change. If prices doubled, but a fad for shoes developed; or if price tripled, but income quadrupled, we would not find that "demand" decreased as prices rose.

Ceteris paribus is applied every time we speak of supply and demand, and on many other occasions as well. Since we know that in reality prices, tastes, incomes, population size, technology, "moods," and many other elements of society are continually changing, we can see why this is a heroic assumption and one that is almost impossible to trace in actual life or to correct for fully by special statistical techniques.

Yet we can also see that unless we apply ceteris paribus, at least in our minds, we cannot isolate the particular interactions and causal sequences that we want to investigate. The economic world then becomes a vast Chinese puzzle. Every piece interlocks with every other, and no one can tell what the effect of any one thing is on any other. But if economics is to be useful, it must be able to tell us something about the effect of changing *just* price or *just* income or *just* taste or any *one* of a number of other things. We can do so only by assuming that other things are "equal" and by holding them unchanged in our minds while we perform the intellectual experiment in whose outcome we are interested.

2. Functional relationships

Economics, it is already very clear, is about relationships—relationships of man and nature, and relationships of man and man. The laws of diminishing marginal utility or diminishing returns or supply and demand are all statements of those relationships, which we can use to explain or predict economic matters.

We call these relationships, the effect of one thing on another, functional relationships. For example, functional relationships may relate the effect of price on the quantities offered or bought, or the effect of successive inputs of the same factor on outputs of a given product, or the effect of population growth on economic growth, or whatever.

One important point. Functional relationships are not "logical" relationships of the kind we find in geometry or arithmetic, such as that the square of the hypotenuse of a triangle is equal to the sum of the squares of the other two sides, or that the number six is the product of two times three or three times two. Functional relationships cannot be discovered by deductive reasoning. They are descriptions of real events that we can discover only by empirical investigation. We then search for ways of expressing these relationships in graphs or mathematical terms. In economics, the technique used for discovering these relationships is called *econometrics.* You can get a first taste of this subject, if you wish, in Chapter 18, pp. 295ff.

3. Identities

Before going on, we must clarify an important distinction between functional relationships and another kind of relationship called an *identity*. We need this distinction because both relationships use the word *equals,* although the word has different meanings in the two cases.

A few pages ahead we will meet the expression

$$Q_d = f(P)$$

which we read "Quantity demanded (Q_d) *equals f(P)*" or "*is* a function of price [$f(P)$]." This refers to the kind of relationship we have been talking about. But we will also find another kind of "equals," typified by the statement that $P \equiv S$ or purchases equals sales. $P \equiv S$ is *not* a functional relationship, because purchases do not "depend" on sales. They are *the same thing* as sales, viewed from the vantage point of the buyer instead of the seller. We have already met an identity in the definition of GNP on p. 9.

Identities are true by definition. They cannot be "proved" true or false, because there is nothing to be proved. On the other hand, when we say that the quantity purchased will depend on price, there is a great deal to be proved. Empirical investigation may disclose that the suggested relationship is not true. Or

THE IMPORTANCE OF TIME

Of all the sources of difficulty that creep into economic analysis, none is more vexing than *time*. The reason is that time changes all manner of things and makes it virtually impossible to apply *ceteris paribus*. That is why, for example, we always specify "within a fixed period of time" when we speak of something like diminishing marginal utility. There is no reason for the marginal utility of a meal tomorrow to be less than one today, but good reason to think that a second lunch on top of the first will bring a sharp decline in utilities.

So, too, supply and demand curves presumably describe activities that take place within a short period of time, ideally within an instant. The longer the time period covered, the less is *ceteris* apt to be *paribus*.

This poses many difficult problems for economic analysis, because it means that we must use a "static" (or timeless) set of theoretical ideas to solve "dynamic" (or time-consuming) questions. The method we will use to cope with this problem is called comparative statics. We compare an economic situation at one period with an economic situation at a later period, without investigating in much detail the path we travel from the first situation to the second. To inquire into the path requires calculus and advanced economic analysis. We'll leave that for another course.

---

it may show that a relationship exists but that the nature of the relationship is not always the same. Identities are changeless as well as true. They are logical statements that require no investigations of human action.

Sometimes identities and behavioral equations are written in the same manner with an equal sign (=). Technically, identities should be written with an identity sign (≡) Unfortunately for generations of students, that is also read "equals." Since it is important to know the difference between definitions, which do not need proof, and hypotheses, which *always* need demonstration or proof, we shall carefully differentiate between the equal sign (=) and the identity sign (≡). *Whenever you see an equal sign, you know that a behavioral relationship is being hypothesized. When you see the identity sign, you will know that a definition is being offered, not a statement about behavior.*

The fact that identities are always true does not make them unimportant. Definitions are very important. They are the way we establish a precise working language. Learning this language, with its special vocabulary, is essential to being able to speak economics accurately.

4. Tautologies

Tautologies are statements that resemble identities but are not quite the same thing. *They are statements that cannot be proven false because there is no empirical or operational way to examine them.*

Tautologies play an important part in economic thought. Take, for example, the conception of economic man, who is said to strive to maximize his utilities. Now this is a very elusive statement. If we had said that his aim was to maximize his *money* income, we might put the statement to the test of observation. We might discover that it was untrue. A businessman, for example, may refuse to cheat, although cheating might make his money income larger.

Thus, when economists say that individuals seek to maximize their *utilities*, they confront us with a concept that defies empirical testing. Whatever a person does—cheating or not cheating, working hard or not, seeking a fortune or leading a life of ease —we can always claim that he is maximizing his utilities, and there is no way of disproving the contention. We should know about tautologies, even though they play a larger role in micro theory than in macro theory.

We must realize that their untestability does not mean that tautologies are useless. If we say that maximizing refers to an acquisitive propensity, to an effort aimed at "bettering our condition," that has a ring of experiential truth. The problem is that there is no way of *measuring* this "betterment," which includes not alone money but our whole conduct of life. Thus the information conveyed by a tautology may be real and useful, but it cannot be objectively accepted or rejected in the way that functional relationships can be. Nor can tautologies be accepted as definitions, the way identities can. They occupy a special position, giving us statements about reality that reflect our beliefs or feelings, but not statements that can be subjected to empirical scrutiny.

5. Schedules

We are familiar with the next item in our kit of intellectual tools. It is one of the techniques used to establish functional relationships: the technique of drawing up *schedules* or lists of the different values of elements.

We have already met such schedules in our lists of the quantities of shoes supplied or demanded at various prices. *Schedules are thus the empirical or hypothetical data whose*

functional interconnection we wish to investigate. In our next chapter we will look into some of the problems of drawing up such schedules in real life. But we must understand that we use them in economic analysis as "examples" of the raw material of behavior scrutinized by economic theory.

6. Graphs

The depiction of functional relationships through schedules is simple enough, but economists usually prefer to represent these relationships by graphs or equations. This is so because schedules only show the relationship between *specific* quantities and prices, or specific data of any kind. Graphs and equations show the *generalized* relationship, the relationship that covers all quantities and prices or all values of any two things we are interested in.

The simplest and most intuitively obvious method of showing a functional relationship in its general form is through a graph. Everyone is familiar with graphs of one kind or another, but not all graphs show functional relationships. A graph of stock prices over time, as in Fig. 2·1, shows us the level of prices in different periods but

FIGURE 2·1
Stock market prices

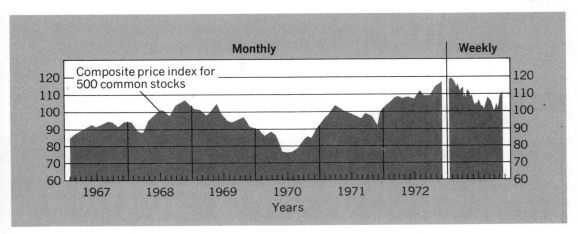

While most demand curves slope downward, in three interesting cases they don't. The first concerns certain *luxury goods* in which the price itself becomes part of the "utility" of the good. The perfume Joy is extensively advertized as "the world's most expensive perfume." Do you think its sales would increase if the price were lowered and the advertisement changed to read "the world's second-most expensive perfume"?

The other case affects just the opposite kind of good: certain basic staples. Here the classic case is potatoes. In 19th-century Ireland, potatoes formed the main diet for very poor farmers. As potato prices rose, Irish peasants were forced to cut back on their purchases of other foods, to devote more of their incomes to buying this necessity of life. More potatoes were purchased, even

does not show a behavioral connection between a date and a price. Such a graph merely describes and summarizes history. No one would maintain that such and such a date *caused* stock market prices to take such and such a level.

On the other hand, a graph that related the price of a stock and the quantities that we are willing and able to buy *at that price, ceteris paribus,* is indeed a graphic depiction of a functional relation. If we look at the hypothetical graph below, we can note the dots that show us the particular price/quantity relationships. Now we can tell the quantity that would be demanded at any price, simply by going up the "price" axis, over to the demand curve, and down to the "quantity" axis. In the graph, Fig. 2·2 (left) for example, at a price of $50, the quantity demanded is 5,000 shares per day.*

7. Equations

A third way of representing functional relationships is often used for its simplicity and brevity. *Equations are very convenient means of expressing functional relationships, since they allow us to consider the impact of more than one factor at a time.* A typical equation for demand might look like this:

$$Q_d = f(P)$$

Most of us are familiar with equations but may have forgotten their vocabulary. There are three terms in the equation above: Q_d, f, and P; and each has a name. Two of these names are simple. We are interested in seeing

FIGURE 2·2

Price/quantity relationship of a hypothetical stock

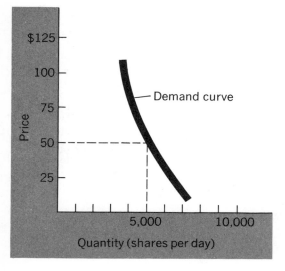

*Technically we would need a schedule of survey results showing the quantities demanded for every conceivable price, in order to draw a graph. In fact, we obtain results for a variety of prices and assume that the relationship between the measured points is like that of the measured points. The process of sketching in unmeasured points is called *interpolation*.

though their prices were rising, because potatoes were the cheapest thing to eat.

Such goods, with upward sloping demand curves, are called *inferior goods*. Up to a point, the higher the price, the more you (are forced to) buy. Of course, when potatoes reach price levels that compete with, say wheat, any further price rises will result in a fall in the quantity demanded, since buyers will shift into wheat.

Finally, there is a very important upward sloping curve that relates quantities demanded and *incomes:* the higher our incomes, the more we buy. We will use this special demand relationship a great deal in macroeconomics. However, in microeconomics, the functional relation is mainly between *price* and quantities demanded, not income and quantities demanded. Still, it is useful to remember that the functional relationships involving demand do not all slope in the same direction.

how our quantity demanded (Q_d) is affected by changes in prices (P). In other words, our "demand" is dependent on changes in price. Therefore the term Q_d is called the *dependent variable:* "variable" because it changes; "dependent" because it is the result of changes in P. As we would imagine, the name for P is the *independent variable*.

Now for the term f. The definition of f is simply "function" or "function of," so that we read $Q_d = f(P)$ as "quantity demanded is a function of price." If we knew that the quantity demanded was a function of both price *and* income (Y) we would write $Q_d = f(P, Y)$. Such equations tell us what independent variables affect what dependent variables, but they do not tell us *how* Q_d changes with changes in P or Y.

The "how" depends on our actual analysis of actual market behavior. Let us take a very simple case for illustrative purposes. Suppose that a survey of consumer purchasing intentions tells us that when the price of a particular product goes up by $1, the quantity demanded goes down by 2 units. In this case, the functional relationship would be represented by this equation:

$$Q_d = -2(P)$$

The function, f, has been found to be -2. Suppose we also find out that consumers would take 100 units of this product if its price were zero—that is, if it were given away free—and that they would buy one-half unit less each time the price went up by $1. The demand equation would then be:

$$Q_d = 100 - .5(P)$$

Thus, if price were $10, buyers would take $100 - .5 \times 10$, or 95 units.

We should stop to note one important property of ordinary price/quantity demand or supply functions. It is that they have opposite "signs." A normal demand function is negative, showing that quantities demanded *fall* as prices rise. A supply function is usually positive, showing that quantities supplied *rise* as prices rise. A survey of producers, for example, might tell us that the quantity supplied would go up by 2 units for every $1 increase in price, or

$$Q_s = 2(P)$$

Note that the sign of the function 2 is positive, whereas the sign of the demand function was negative, $-.5$.

ECONOMIC TECHNIQUES REVIEWED

The seven items in our kit of intellectual tools do not tell us more about the basic assumptions that economics makes with respect to the facts of economic society. We

EQUILIBRIUM IN EQUATIONS

It is very easy to see the equilibrium point when we have a supply curve and a demand curve that cross. But since equations are only another way of representing the information that curves show, we must be able to demonstrate equilibrium in equations. Here is a simple example:

Suppose the demand function, as before, is:
$Q_d = 100 - .5(P)$, and that the supply function is:
$Q_s = 2(P)$

The question is, then, what value for P will make Q_d equal to Q_s? The answer follows:

If $Q_d = Q_s$, then
$100 - .5(P) = 2(P)$.
Putting all the P's on one side
$2(P) + .5(P) = 100$, or $2.5P = 100$. Solving, $P = 40$.

Substituting a price of 40 into the demand equation we get a quantity of 80. In the supply equation we also get 80. Thus 40 must be the equilibrium price.

have seen that these facts can be summed up in two sets of general propositions or laws—laws about behavior and laws about production. What we have been learning in this chapter are the *techniques* of economic analysis, rather than its basic premises.

These techniques, as we have seen, revolve around the central idea of functional relationships. Because behavior or production is sufficiently "regular," functions enable us to explain or predict economic activity. Their relationships are presented in the form of graphs or equations derived from the underlying schedules of data.

As we have seen, the ability to establish functional relationships depends critically on the *ceteris paribus* assumption. Unless we hold other things equal, either by econometric means or simply "in our heads," we cannot isolate the effect of one variable on another.

Finally, economic analysis also relies on identities and tautologies. Identities are definitional—they are merely two names for one thing. Tautologies are descriptions that cannot be subjected to empirical investigation. Both identities and tautologies can be useful in clarifying our thought, but they must not be confused with functional relationships.

ECONOMIC FALLACIES

No chapter on the mode of economic thought would be complete without reference to economic fallacies. Actually there is no special class of fallacies that are called economic. The mistakes we find in economic thought are only examples of a larger class of mistaken ways of thinking that we call fallacies. But they are important enough to warrant a warning in general and some attention to one fallacy in particular.

The general warning can do no more than ask us to be on guard against the sloppy thinking that can make fools of us in any area. It is easy to fall into errors of false syllogisms,* of trying to "prove" an argument "post hoc, ergo propter hoc" ("after

*See the questions at the end of this chapter for examples.

the fact, therefore the cause of the fact"); for example, "proving" that government spending must be inflationary by pointing out that the government spent large sums during periods when inflation was present, ignoring other factors that may have been at work.

The gallery of such mistaken conclusions is all too large in all fields. But there is one fallacy that has a special relevance to the kinds of problems that economics considers. It is called the *fallacy of composition*. Suppose we had an island community in which all farmers sold their produce to one another. Suppose further that one farmer was able to get rich by cheating—selling his produce at the same price as everyone else, but putting fewer vegetables into his bushel baskets. Does it not follow that all farmers could get rich if all cheated?

We can see that there is a fallacy here. Where does it arise? In the first example, when our cheating farmer got rich, we ignored a small side effect of his action. The side effect was that a loss in real income was inflicted on the community. To ignore that side effect was proper so long as our focus of attention was what happened to the one farmer. But when we now broaden our inquiry to the entire community, the loss of income becomes important. Everyone loses as much by being shortchanged as he gains by shortchanging. The side effects have become central effects; what was true for one turns out not to be true for all. Later on, in macroeconomics, we will find a very important example of exactly such a fallacy when we encounter what is called the Paradox of Thrift.

KEY WORDS

Techniques vs. theory

Ceteris paribus

Functional relationships

Identities

Tautologies

Schedules

Graphs

Equations

CENTRAL CONCEPTS

1. **This is a chapter about the techniques of economic analysis, not about the basic assumptions underlying economic theory. We should become familiar with a few useful ideas, or tools.**

2. **Ceteris paribus is the assumption that everything other than the two variables whose relationship is being investigated is "kept equal." *Without* ceteris paribus we cannot discern functional relationships.**

3. **Functional relationships—relationships that show that x "depends" on y—lie at the very center of economic analysis. They are not logical or deductive relationships, but relationships that we discover by *empirical investigation*.**

4. **Identities are purely definitional and therefore *not subject to proof or to empirical investigation*. Such definitions can, however, be very important.**

5. **Tautologies are statements that may convey feelings or beliefs but are *not capable of empirical measurement* and therefore cannot be proved or disproved.**

6. **Functional relationships use three techniques:**

   schedules, or lists of data
   graphs, or visual presentations
   equations

● *Independent and
   dependent
   variables*
● *Function*

We should learn the meaning of three equational terms: the *independent variable*, the ''causative'' element that interests us; the *dependent variable*, the element whose behavior is affected by the independent variable; and the *function*, a mathematical statement of the relation between the two. We should learn to read the sentence $x = f(y)$ as ''x is a function of y.'' Here, x is the dependent variable; y is the independent variable.

*Fallacy of
composition*

7. We must be on guard against *economic fallacies*, especially against the *fallacy of composition*.

QUESTIONS

1. Suppose we discover that the quantity of food you buy per week increases by 10 percent every time the price of food goes down. If we have no more information than that, can we derive a functional relationship?

2. What other information would you need to know? Would changes in your income have to be taken into account? Changes in your tastes? Changes in the prices of other goods? Explain.

3. Can you write a hypothetical function that might relate your demand for food and the price of food, assuming *ceteris paribus*?

4. ''The quantity of food bought equals the quantity sold.'' Is this statement a functional relationship? If not, why not? Is it a tautology? An identity?

5. Which of the following are tautologies:

Everything always turns out for the best in the long run.

Men always act in their own self-interest.

Men always behave to maximize their incomes.

The effort to maximize incomes always results in economic success.

HINT: to which of these statements could you apply some kind of empirical test?

6. Here is a schedule of supply and demand:

Price	Units supplied	Units demanded
$1	0	50
2	5	40
3	10	30
4	20	25
5	30	20
6	50	10

Does the schedule show an equilibrium price? Can you draw a graph and approximate the equilibrium price? What is it?

7. How do we read aloud the following?

$C = f(Y)$ where C = consumption and Y = income.

Which is the independent variable? The dependent?

8. Which of the following statements is a fallacy?

> All *X* is *Y*
> *Z* is *Y*
> Therefore *Z* is *X*
>
> All *X* is *Y*
> *Z* is *X*
> Therefore *Z* is *Y*

Try substituting classes of objects for the *X*'s and *Y*, and individual objects for the *Z*'s. Example: All planets (*X*'s) are heavenly bodies (*Y*). The sun (*Z*) is a heavenly body (*Y*). Therefore the sun (*Z*) is a planet (*X*). Clearly, a false syllogism. But: the sun is a heavenly body (*Z* is *Y*) is correct.

Other fallacies:

If I can move to the head of the line, all individuals can move to the head of the line.

If I can save more by spending less, all individuals should be able to save more by spending less. (Hint: if all spend less, what will happen to our incomes?)

The fact that Lenin called inflation a major weapon that could destroy the bourgeoisie indicates that inflations are part of the Communist strategy for the overthrow of capitalism.

The Growth
of Output

Macroeconomics, it should by now be clear, is essentially about growth. At the center of its focus is the question of how an economy expands its output of goods and services (or if it fails to expand them, why growth does not take place). In out last chapter, we began to analyze this process by familiarizing ourselves with the way our stock of wealth interacts with our labor force to yield a flow of output that we call gross national product. In this chapter we are going to push forward by learning about the underlying trends and causes of growth in the American economy. That will set the stage for the work that still lies ahead, when we will narrow our focus down to the present and inquire into the reasons for the problems of our macrosystem—unemployment and inflation, booms and busts.

THE PRODUCTION POSSIBILITY CURVE

How much output can an economy produce, utilizing all its factors? If the economy produced only a single good, such as wheat, the answer would be some number of bushels

that we would discover by utilizing to the hilt every available acre, every tractor, every farmer's labor.

But obviously, economies produce many kinds of goods. Thus we cannot answer the question in terms of a single figure, but in terms of a range of possibilities, depending on which goods we produce. It would be difficult to represent this range of possibilities in a simple graph, so we abstract the range of possible outputs to two goods, say grain and milk, and we then show what *combinations* of outputs are possible, using all factors. We call such a schedule of alternative possibilities a *production possibility curve,* and we draw such a curve in Fig. 3·1.

THE EFFICIENCY FRONTIER

The production-possibility curve shows us a number of things. First it makes vivid the material meaning of the word *scarcity.* Any point outside the frontier of the curve is unattainable for our community, given its present resources. This is obviously true of point X. But look at point Y. This is an output that

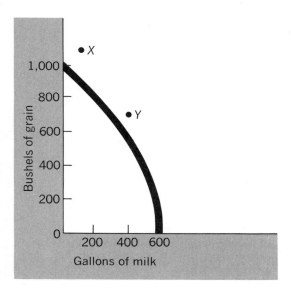

FIGURE 3 · 1
Production possibility curve

filled spinnaker sail. Any place on the sail represents some combination of consumption, investment, and government spending that is within the reach of the community. Any place "behind" the *efficiency frontier* represents a failure of the economy to employ all its resources. It is a graphic depiction of unemployment of men or materials.

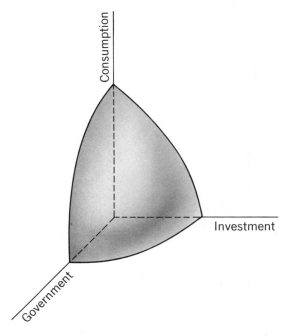

FIGURE 3 · 2
A production possibility surface

represents roughly 700 bushels of grain and 400 gallons of milk. Either one of these goals, taken separately, lies well within the production possibilities of the economy. What the curve shows us is that *we cannot have both at the same time.* If we want 700 bushels of grain, we must be content with less than 400 gallons of milk: and if we want 400 gallons of milk, we will have to settle for about 600 bushels of grain.

Such a two-commodity diagram may seem unreal. But remember that "milk" and "grain" can stand for consumption and investment (or any other choices available to an economy). In fact, with a little imagination we can construct a three-dimensional production-possibility *surface* that will show us the limits imposed by scarcity on a society that divides its output among three uses: such as consumption, investment, and government. Figure 3·2 shows what such a diagram looks like.

Note how the production-possibility surface swells out from the origin like a wind-

THE LAW OF INCREASING COST

One last point deserves clarification before we move on. The alert student may have noticed that all the production-possibility curves have bowed shapes. The reason for this lies in the *changing efficiency* of our resources as we shift them from one use to another.

We call this changing efficiency, represented by the bowed curve, the *law of increasing costs*. Note that it is a law imposed by nature, rather than behavior. For what would it mean if the curve connecting the two points of all-out grain or milk production were a straight line as in Fig. 3·3? It would mean that as we shifted resources from one use to the other, we would always get exactly the same results: the last man and

the last acre put into milk would give us exactly as much milk at the loss of exactly as much grain, as the first man and the first acre.

Such a straight-line production possibility curve is said to exhibit *constant returns to specialization*. Except perhaps in a very simple economy, where a population might choose between hunting or fishing, constant returns to specialization is an unrealistic assumption, for it implies that there is no difference from one man, or acre, to another, or that it made no difference as to the *proportions* in which factors, even if they were homogenous, were combined. That is a very unrealistic assumption. Men and land (and any other resource) *are* different and different products *do* utilize them in different proportions. Hence, as we shift them from one use to another, assuming that we always choose the resources best suited for the job, society's efficiency changes. At first we enjoy a very low cost in terms of what we must give up for what we get; thereafter, we pay an increasing cost. Although the shapes of production-possibility curves may have considerably different contours, the unevenness of nature's gifts make most of them bowed, or concave from below.

FIGURE 3 · 3
Constant returns to specialization

FIGURE 3 · 4
Shifts in the production frontier

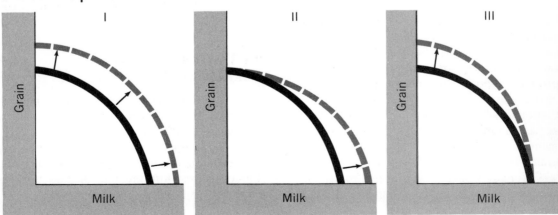

BEYOND THE FRONTIER

Our acquaintance with production possibility curves and their efficiency frontiers brings home the importance of economic growth. Consider point *A* in the diagram (right). It shows us an economy that is allowing attainable output to go to waste because it is not properly using the productive powers it possesses. Such an economy may expand output, but this is not really "growth" in the proper sense.

But now consider the shaded area outside the frontier. This represents combinations of goods that we cannot enjoy because we do not have the requisite productive capacity. We can enter this area only if we grow, thereby pushing our frontier outward.

This is by no means an exercise in mere imagination. For instance in 1960, a rather conservative Commission on National Goals established by President Eisenhower laid down a set of "goals," ranging from enhanced private consumption to a variety of improved public programs, to be achieved in some 15 areas of economic activity by 1975. A few years ago the National Planning Association "costed out" these goals to show how many of them were within reach. Its conclusion was that if output continued

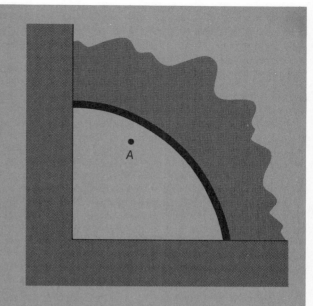

to grow at 4 percent a year (14 percent *faster* than the long-run 3.5 percent rate), our GNP in 1975 would fall short by $150 billion of achieving the aspirations of the Eisenhower Commission. Our production possibility curve was simply not moving out fast enough to place the Commission's targets within our efficiency frontier.

TECHNICAL PROGRESS

One last point about the shapes of production possibility curves. They are not static. As we know, technical progress or changes in skills change the amount of output we can derive from a given quantity of input. These changes move the production possibility curves outward, as in Fig. 3·4. Notice that in Panel 1 we enjoy a general increase in productivity that enables us to have more of both grain and milk (or any other two goods); but in Panels 2 and 3, productivity has increased in only one area of production, so that the maximum output available to us for one good stays the same, whereas the maximum for the other good increases.

Structural Requirements for Growth

An acquaintance with production possibility curves has given us a sense of the importance of growth. But it does not explain how an economy actually grows, how the production possibility frontiers move out. That is the question to which we will devote the remainder of this chapter.

We already know part of the answer from our study of GNP. An economy grows because it allocates a portion of its output to investment (public as well as private), rather than consuming the entire output it produces. But how does a society actually find the resources to devote to capital-building? In a rich, industrialized economy such as ours, the answer seems simple. We use our industrial equipment to make more industrial equipment. To put it differently, we use the people working in the steel and other capital-goods industries to make more steel and more capital goods.

Building Capital

But the matter-of-factness of our answer hides the real structural problem of growth. For when we look abroad or backward in time and ask how a poor society grows, the question is not so easy to answer. Such societies do not have steel mills waiting for orders, nor labor forces that are already deployed in capital-goods industries. How do they, then, create capital?

The process is by no means an obvious one. Suppose we have a very poor society (like an extremely underdeveloped nation) in which 80 percent of the population tills the soil, equipped with so little by way of capital —mere spades and hoes—that it produces only enough to maintain itself and the remaining 20 percent of society.

Who are the other 20 percent? In reality, of course, they might be government officials, landlords, and others, but we will simplify our model by assuming that the whole 20 percent is occupied in making the simple spades and hoes (the capital goods) used by the consumption-goods sector. Like the farmers, the toolmakers labor from dawn to dusk; and again like the farmers, they are so unproductive that they can produce only enough capital to replace the spades and hoes that wear out each year.

TWIN TASKS OF
THE CAPITAL SECTOR

Now how could such a society grow? If we look again at the capital-goods sector, we find a clue. For unlike the consumption-goods sector, we find here not one but two distinguishable kinds of economic activity going on. On the agricultural side, everyone is farming; but on the capital-goods side, not everyone is making the spades and hoes with which the agricultural laborers work. No matter how we simplify our model, we can see that *the capital-goods sector must carry out two different tasks.* It must turn out spades and hoes, to be sure. But part of the capital-goods labor force must also turn out a different kind of capital good—a very special kind that will produce not only spades and hoes, but also more of itself!

Is there such a kind of equipment? There is indeed, in a versatile group of implements known as *machine tools*. In our model economy, these may be only chisels and hammers that can be used to make spades, hoes, and more chisels and hammers. In a complex industrial system, machine tools consist of presses and borers and lathes that, when used ensemble, not only make all kinds of complicated machines but can also recreate themselves.

THE CAPITAL SECTOR

Thus we encounter the unexpected fact that there is a strategic branch of capital creation at the core of the whole sequence of economic growth.*

How does growth now ensue? Our model enables us to see that it is not simply a matter of bringing in peasants from the fields to make more spades and thereby to

---

*This raises the perplexing question of how the machine-tool industry *began,* since it needs it own output to grow. The answer is that it evolved as a special branch of industrial production during the industrial revolution when, for the first time, machinery itself began to be made by machinery instead of by hand. A key figure in the evolution of the machine-tool industry was Maudslay, whose invention of the screw-cutting lathe was "one of the decisive pieces of standardization that made the modern machine possible." (Lewis Mumford, *Technics and Civilization.* New York: Harcourt, 1963, p. 209.)

increase their productivity, for they will not be able to make spades until there is an increased output of spade-making tools. Before spades can be made, chisels and hammers must be made. Before textile or shoemaking or food-processing or transportation equipment can be made, machine tools must be made.

Thus at the core of the growth process—whether in a very backward nation or a highly industrialized one—we can see *two* great structural shifts that must take place:

1. Within the capital sector to increase its own productive capacity

2. From the consumption sector to the capital sector, to man the growing volume of equipment emerging from the enlarged capital sector.*

Can we actually trace this process in real life? The shifts *within* the capital sector are not always easy to see, because there is usually some excess capacity in the machine tool branch. By running overtime, for instance, it can produce *both* more machine tools *and* more hoes and spades. Yet if we examine a society in the process of rapid industrialization, such as the U.S.S.R. (or for that matter, the United States in its periods of rapid wartime industrial buildup), we can clearly see the importance of this critical branch in setting a *ceiling* on the overall pace of industrial expansion.

When we turn to the second shift, from the consumption sector into the capital sector, the movement in real life is very apparent. Table 3·1, for instance, shows us the proportion of the population engaged in agriculture for a number of industrialized nations at an early and a late stage of their transformations.

---

*How will these new factory workers be fed? Obviously, food must be diverted from the country to the city. This is discussed at length in Heilbroner and Thurow, *The Economic Problem*, 4th ed., Chap. 39.

TABLE 3·1
Labor Force in Agriculture

PERCENT OF LABOR FORCE IN AGRICULTURE		
	Early 19th century	*1971*
France	63% (1827)	13
Great Britain	31 (1811)	3
Sweden	63 (1840)	8
United States	72 (1820)	4

Sources: Colin Clark, *The Conditions of Economic Progress* (London: Macmillan, 1960), pp. 512, 514, 518; B. R. Mitchell, *Abstract of British Historical Statistics* (Cambridge: Cambridge University Press, 1962), pp. 60–61, and *Basic Statistics of the Community.*

Here we see in reality the internal emigration that takes place in the industrializing process (note that by 1811 Britain was already well on the road). Over the course of the nineteenth and twentieth centuries, these countries have lost two-thirds to four-fifths of their erstwhile farmers—not all to capital-building alone, of course, but to the whole industrial and commercial structure that capital-building makes possible. In this way, the process of economic growth can be seen in part as a great flow of human and material resources from simple consumption goods output to a hierarchy of industrial tasks — a flow that is even more dramatic in real life than we might have divined from our imaginary model.

THE HISTORICAL RECORD

Thus, behind the phenomenon of growth—of production possibility frontiers moving outward—we encounter a hidden structural shift of the greatest importance. Once the shift has taken place, however—once a large capital-building sector has been established—the process of adding to the stock of capital is greatly simplified. Indeed, we now get that long process of gradually increasing output that provides us with our ordinary starting point in the study of growth. In Fig. 3·5 we see the American experience from the middle of the nineteenth century, in terms of real per capita GNP in 1929 prices.

How regular has been our average rate of growth? The answer: astonishingly constant, whether we take an average over the past thirty-odd years since the Great Depression, or whether we go back to the earliest reliable statistics and calculate our growth rate since the 1870s (or even 1830s). As the chart shows, the swings are almost all contained within a range of 10 percent above or below the trend. The trend itself comes to about 3.5 percent a year in real terms, or a little over 1.5 percent a year per capita.

The Sources of Growth

How do we account for this long steady ascent? The answer takes us to a deeper consideration of the *sources of growth* in terms of the contribution of labor and capital (including land). Clearly, our growth reflects the fact that labor and capital have cooperated to bring about a rising stream of final goods and services. But this rising output could be the result of either or both of two quite separate trends:

1. *The quantity of labor and capital that we use may be growing; that is, the expansion of our production frontier may simply reflect a growth in the sheer volume of "inputs."*

FIGURE 3 · 5
Trend in real GNP per head, 1839–1973

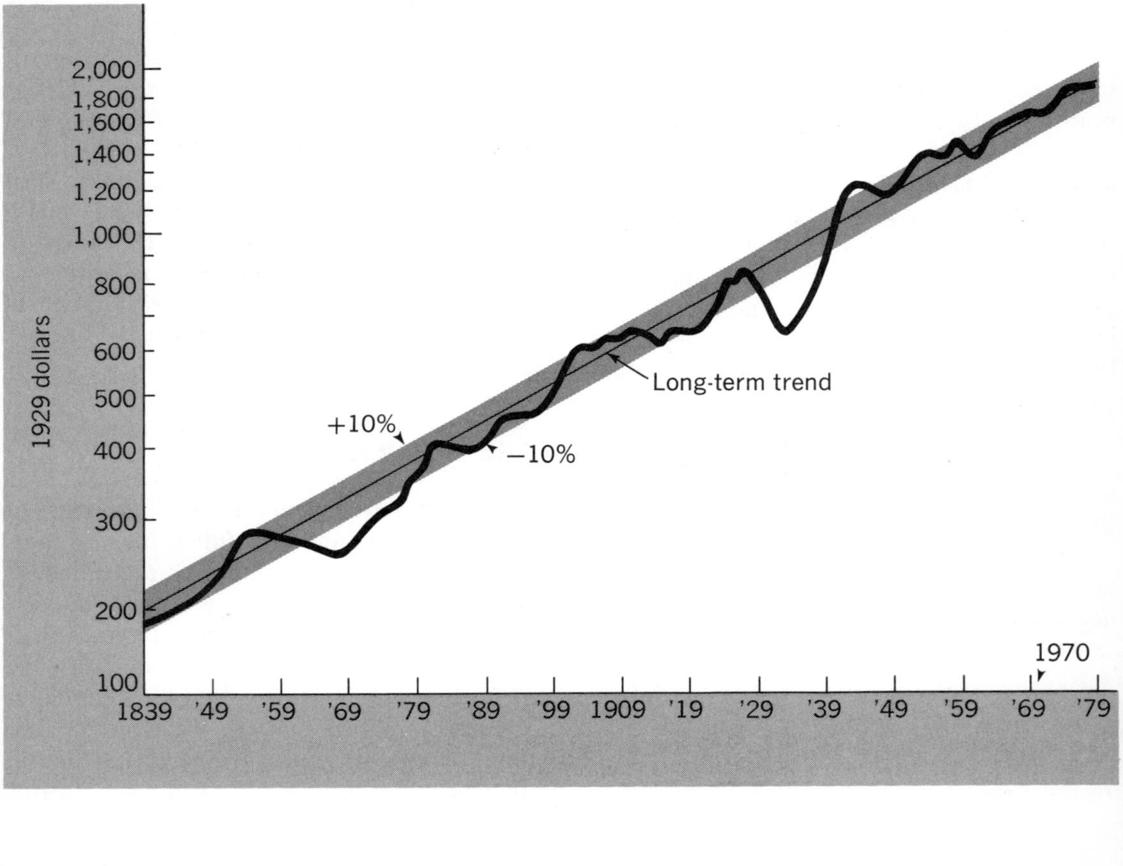

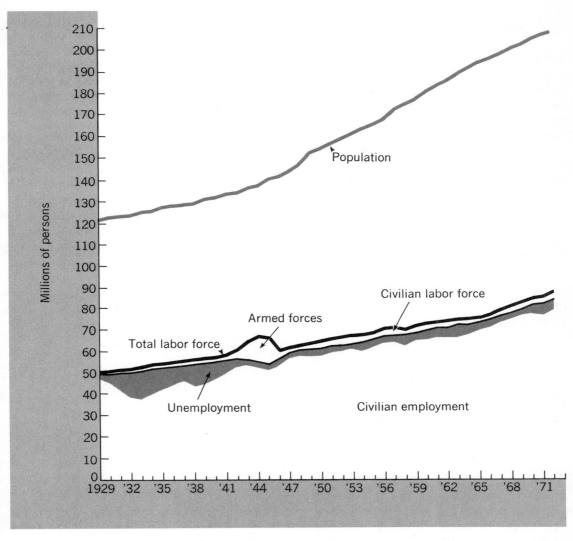

FIGURE 3·6
United States labor force, 1929–1973

2. Labor and capital may be increasing in productivity. If each working individual or each "unit" of land or capital can produce more goods and services over time, output will rise, even if the total number of working individuals or the value of the stock of capital remains unchanged.

Hence the next question on the agenda is to learn about the long-term trends in the quantity of labor and capital and their respective productivities.

EMPLOYMENT AND PRODUCTION

Output depends on work, and work depends on people working. Thus, the first source of growth that we study is the rise in the sheer numbers of people in the *labor force*. As we will see, this is a more complicated matter than might at first appear.

Figure 3·6 gives us a picture of the population and the labor force over the past almost half-century. As we would expect, the

35

size of the force has been rising because our population has been rising. Yet this trend is more puzzling than might at first appear. For one might expect that as our society grew richer and more affluent, fewer people would seek employment. But that is not the case. Looking back to 1890 or 1900, we find that only 52 out of every 100 persons over 14 sought paid work. Today about 60 out of every 100 persons of working age seek employment. Looking forward is more uncertain; but if we can extrapolate (extend) the trend of the past several decades to the year 2000, we can expect perhaps as many as 65 persons out of 100 to be in the labor market by that date.

PARTICIPATION IN THE LABOR FORCE

How can we explain this curious upward drift of the labor force itself? The answer is to be found in the *different labor participation trends* of different ages and different sexes. Figure 3·7 shows this very clearly.

Note that the overall trend toward a larger participation rate for the entire population masks a number of significant trends.

FIGURE 3 · 7
Participation rates

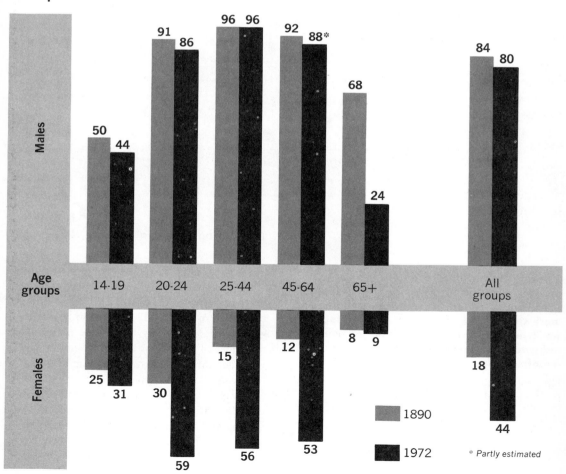

1. *Young males entering the labor force are older than those who entered in the past.*

A larger number of young men remain in high school now or go on to college. Only a third of elementary school pupils now go on to college, but the ratio is steadily growing.

2. *Older males show a dramatic withdrawal from the labor force.*

The reason is the advent of Social Security and private pension plans. It is probable that the proportion of older males in the labor force will continue to fall as the retirement age is slowly reduced.

3. *Counterbalancing this fall in male participation is a spectacular rise in total female participation. Indeed, the overall trend toward an increasing search for work within the population at large is entirely the result of the mass entrance of women into the labor force.*

This surge of women into the labor market reflects several changing factors in the American scene (many of these changes can be found abroad, as well). One factor is the growth of nonmanual, as contrasted with manual, jobs. Another is the widening cultural approval of working women and working wives—it is the amazing fact that the average American girl who marries today in her early twenties and goes on to raise a family will nevertheless spend *twenty-five years* of her life in paid employment after her children are grown. Yet another reason for the influx of women is that technology has released them from household work. And finally there is the pressure to raise living standards by having two incomes within the household.

4. *Actually, we must view the growing number of females in the labor force as part of a very old economic phenomenon whose roots we traced back to the Middle Ages—the monetization of work.*

The upward trend of female participation does not imply an increasing amount of labor performed within society. Rather, it measures a larger amount of *paid* labor. In the 1890s, many persons worked long and hard hours on a family farm or in a family enterprise, and above all within a household, *without getting paid* and, therefore, were not counted as members of the "labor force." To a very considerable extent, the rising numbers of female participants in the labor force mirror the transfer of these unpaid jobs onto the marketplace where the same labor is now performed in an economically visible way. There is every likelihood this process will continue.

These are not, of course, the only factors that bear on the fundamental question of how many persons will seek work out of a given population. The drift from country to city, the decline in the number of hours of labor per day expected of a jobholder, the general lengthening of life, the growth of general well-being—all these changes bear on the decision to work or not. *Overall, what the complex trends seem to show is that we are moving in the direction of a society where employment absorbs a larger fraction of the life (but not of the day) of an average woman, and a diminishing fraction of the life and of the day of an average man.*

HOURS OF WORK

In addition to deciding whether to participate in the labor force, individuals decide how much labor they wish to contribute as members of the labor force. That is, they must decide how many hours of work they wish to offer during a week or how many weeks they wish to work in a year.

Had we asked this question in the days of Adam Smith, it would have been relatively simple to answer. Wages were so close to subsistence that someone in the labor force

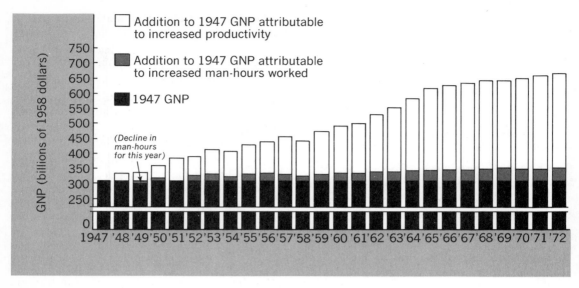

FIGURE 3·8
Source of GNP increases, 1947–1972

was obliged to work extremely long hours to keep body and soul together. Paid vacations were unknown to the employees of the cotton mills; unpaid vacations would have been tantamount to starvation.

But with the slow rise in productivity, working men and women gradually found their income rising above "subsistence," and a new possibility came into being: the possibility of deliberately working less than the physical maximum, *using part of their increased productivity to buy leisure for themselves instead of wages.* Thus, beginning in the early nineteenth century we find that labor organizations (still very small and weak) sought to shorten the workweek. In England, in 1847 a signal victory was won with the introduction of the Ten (!) Hour Day as the legal maximum for women and children. In America, in the prosperity of the 1920s, the 48-hour week finally became standard. More recently, the two-day weekend has become the general practice; and

now we hear talk of the coming of the three-day weekend.*

Thus the total supply of labor-time has not risen as fast as the labor force, because a decline in average hours has offset the rise in participation rates and population. On balance, the total supply of labor-hours has increased, but the supply of labor-hours *per employee,* male and female, has fallen.

LABOR PRODUCTIVITY

As we have seen, we can trace part of our long-term growth to increases in the total supply of man-hours of production. But this is by no means the most important source of growth. Far outpacing the growth in the sheer volume of labor-time has been the increase in the amounts of goods and services that each hour of labor-time gives rise to.

*The trend to shorter hours may now be at an end: we do not yet know.

MEASURING PRODUCTIVITY

As the accompanying table shows, the average increase in productivity of 3.5 percent masks wide swings from year to year. Compare 1950, when productivity per man grew at 9.2 percent, with 1956, when it actually declined by 0.1!

But there is a caution here. These sharp ups and downs do not so much reflect real variations in output per manhour as they do the way in which we measure productivity. *Productivity is measured by dividing total output by total man-hours.* When recessions occur and output falls, businesses reduce their labor forces as much as possible, but they find that there are considerable numbers of overhead laborers who cannot profitably be let go simply because output is down. If General Motors' production falls by 25 percent, it does not reduce the working time of its president by 25 percent.

Hence, in recession years, a smaller output is divided by a number of man-hours that has been "kept high." The underlying normal growth in productivity of the labor force may still be occurring, but it is masked by the overhead labor that is not reduced as much as output. In booming years, just the opposite occurs. Output increases faster than employment, since the company does not need to add overhead as rapidly as output. Result: *year-to-year productivity figures must be interpreted with great care.*

	Productivity index (G.N.P./man-hour)	Per cent change in productivity per man-hour in the private economy
1947	100	
1948	103.4	3.4%
1949	105.9	2.4
1950	115.7	9.2
1951	121.0	4.6
1952	124.5	2.9
1953	130.2	4.6
1954	133.7	2.7
1955	139.5	4.3
1956	139.5	−0.1
1957	143.3	2.7
1958	146.6	2.3
1959	152.5	4.0
1960	154.2	1.1
1961	158.4	2.7
1962	166.8	5.3
1963	172.3	3.3
1964	178.7	3.7
1965	184.6	3.3
1966	193.1	4.6
1967	197.0	2.0
1968	204.9	4.0
1969	207.1	1.1
1970	206.8	1.0
1971	214.6	4.1
1972	222.2	3.8
1973	227.9	2.9

Technology Review, March, 1971.

Economists measure the productivity of the labor force by dividing the total output of goods by the total number of man-hours. Figure 3·8 shows us the wide margin by which changes in labor productivity outweigh changes in labor-time as a source of increased output.

Over the postwar period, the *average* increase in productivity per man-hour has been growing at about 3½ percent a year. At that rate, productivity per man-hour doubles in just under 20 years. Of course, this increase varies from one sector to another; over the last two decades it increased by 80 percent in manufacturing and *tripled* in agriculture.

Sources of Labor Productivity

What is the explanation for this tremendous and persistent increase in the ability of labor to turn out goods? Here are the most important answers.

1. Growth of human capital

By human capital, as we know, we mean the skills and knowledge possessed by the labor force. The measurement of "human capital" is fraught with difficulties, but the difficulty of measuring it does not permit us to ignore this vital contributory element in labor productivity. Ferenc Jánossy, a Hungarian economist, has suggested a vivid imaginary experiment to highlight the importance of skills and knowledge.

Suppose, he says, that the populations of two nations of the same size could be swapped overnight, so that 50 million Englishmen would awake to find themselves in, say, Nepal, and 50 million Nepalese would find themselves in England. The newly transferred Englishmen would have to contend with all the poverty and difficulties of the Nepalese economy; the newly transferred Nepalese would confront the riches of England. Yet the Englishmen would bring with them an immense reservoir of literacy, skills, discipline, and training, whereas the Nepalese would bring with them the very low levels of "human capital" that are characteristic of underdeveloped countries. Is there any doubt, asks Jánossy, that growth rates in Nepal with its new skilled population would in all likelihood rise dramatically, and that those of England would probably fall catastrophically?

One way of indicating in very general terms the rising "amount" of human capital is to trace the additions to the stock of education that the population embodies. Table 3·2 shows the change in the total number of years of schooling of the U.S. population over the past three quarters of a century, as well as the rise in formal education per capita. While these measures of human capital are far from exact or all-inclusive, they give some dimensions to the importance of skills and knowledge in increasing productivity.

2. Shifts in the occupations of the labor force

A second source of added productivity results from shifts in employment from low productivity areas to high productivity areas. If workers move from occupations in which their productivity is low relative to other occupations in which output per manhour is high, the production possibility curve of the economy will move out, even if there are no increases in productivity *within* the different sectors.

A glance at Table 3·3 shows that very profound and pervasive shifts in the location of labor have taken place. What have been the effects of this shift on our long-term ability to produce goods?

The answer is complex. In the early years of the twentieth century, the shift of

TABLE 3·2
Stock of Education, U.S.

	1900	1971
Total man-years of schooling embodied in population (million)	228	991
Percent of labor force with high-school education or more	6.4%	66.9%
Percent of high-school graduates entering college	17%	40%

	1900	1972
Agriculture, forests, and fisheries	38.1	4.2
Manufacturing, mining, transportation, construction, utilities	37.7	36.3
Trade, government, finance, professional and personal services*	24.2	59.5

TABLE 3 · 3
Percent Distribution of all Employed Workers

Source: Calculated from *Historical Statistics*, p. 74; also from *Statistical Abstract.*

*It is customary to include transportation and utilities among the third, or service, area of activities. In this analysis, however, we group them with goods-producing or goods-handling activities, to highlight the drift into "purely" service occupations. Since domestic servants, proprietors, and the self-employed are omitted (owing to inadequate statistics), the table under-represents the labor force in the service and trade sector.

labor out of agriculture into manufacturing and services probably increased the overall productivity of the economy, since manufacturing was then the most technologically advanced sector. In more recent years, however, we would have to arrive at a different conclusion. Agriculture is now a highly productive but very small sector, in terms of employment. Moreover, the proportion of the labor force employed in manufacturing is roughly constant, up or down only a few percentage points, year to year, from its long-term level of 35 to 40 percent of all workers.

Today, growth in employment takes place mainly in the congeries of occupations we call the service sector: government, retail and wholesale trade, professions such as lawyers, accountants, and the like. The growth of output per capita is least evident in these occupations.* *Thus the drift of labor into the service sector means that average GNP per worker is growing more slowly today than if labor were moving into manufacturing or agriculture.*

Why is this growth-lowering shift taking

*It is only proper to note that we cannot measure productivity of output in the service sector nearly so unambiguously as in the goods sector, and there is no doubt that the *quality* of many services has increased substantially. Compare, for example, the "productivity" of a surgeon operating for appendicitis in 1900, 1930, and 1960. On the other hand, insofar as we are interested in increases of measurable output per capita, there seems little doubt of the considerable superiority of the goods-producing branches of the economy.

place? The reason has to do with the changing pattern of demand in an affluent society. There seems to be a natural sequence of wants as a society grows richer: first for food and basic clothing, then for the output of a wide range of industrial goods, then for recreation, professional advice, public administration, and enjoyments of other services. We will meet these trends again and study their implications when we examine the problems of automation and inflation.

3. Economies of large-scale production

A third source of increasing labor productivity is the magnifying effect of mass production on output. As we have seen, when the organization of production reaches a certain critical size, especially in manufacturing, economies of scale become possible. Many of these are based on the possibility of dividing complex operations into a series of simpler ones, each performed at high speed by a worker aided by specially designed equipment. It is difficult to estimate the degree of growth attributable to these economies of size. Certainly during the era of railroad-building and of the introduction of mass production, they contributed heavily to growth rate. In a careful study of the contemporary sources of U.S. growth, Edward F. Denison estimates that economies of large-scale production today are responsible for about one-tenth of our annual rate of productivity increase.

MASS PRODUCTION IN ACTION

Allan Nevins has described what mass production techniques looked like in the early Ford assembly lines.

Just how were the main assembly lines and lines of component production and supply kept in harmony? For the chassis alone, from 1,000 to 4,000 pieces of each component had to be furnished each day at just the right point and right minute; a single failure, and the whole mechanism would come to a jarring standstill.... Superintendents had to know every hour just how many components were being produced and how many were in stock. Whenever danger of shortage appeared, the shortage chaser—a familiar figure in all automobile factories—flung himself into the breach. Counters and checkers reported to him. Verifying in person any ominous news, he mobilized the foreman concerned to repair deficiencies. Three times a day he made typed reports in manifold to the factory clearing-house, at the same time chalking on blackboards in the clearing-house office a statement of results in each factory-production department and each assembling department. [1]

Such systematizing in itself resulted in astonishing increases in productivity. With each operation analyzed and subdivided into its simplest components, with a steady stream of work passing before stationary men, with a relentless but manageable pace of work, the total time required to assemble a car dropped astonishingly. Within a single year, the time required to assemble a motor fell from 600 minutes to 226 minutes; to build a chassis, from 12 hours and 28 minutes to 1 hour and 33 minutes. A stopwatch man was told to observe a 3-minute assembly in which men assembled rods and pistons, a simple operation. The job was divided into three jobs, and half the men turned out the same output as before.

[1] *Ford, the Times, the Man, the Company* (New York: Scribner's, 1954), I, 507.

---

4. Increases in the quantity and quality of capital

A fourth basic reason for the rising productivity of labor again harks back to Adam Smith's growth model. It is the fact that each additional member of the labor force has been equipped with at least as much capital as previous members; and that all members of the labor force have worked with a steadily more productive stock of capital.

We call the first kind of capital growth a *widening* of capital. It consists of matching additional workers with the same amounts and kinds of equipment that their predecessors had. The streams of additional part-time women workers coming into offices and stores, for example, would not be able to match the productivity of those who preceded them if they did not also get typewriters, cash registers, or similar equipment.

But we must also notice a *deepening* of capital as a source of increased labor productivity. This means that each worker receives *more* capital equipment over time. The ditch digger becomes the operator of a power shovel; the pencil-and-paper accountant uses a computer.

Over the long course of economic growth, increased productivity has required the slow accumulation of very large capital stocks per working individual. Thus investment that increases capital per worker is, and will probably continue to be, one of the most effective levers for steadily raising output per worker. But unlike the steady widening of capital, the deepening of capital is not a regular process. Between 1929 and 1947 there was no additional capital added per worker! This was, of course, a time of severe depression and thereafter of enforced wartime stringencies. Since 1947, the value of our stock of capital per worker has been growing at about 2.7 percent a year. As we shall see immediately following, however, the *size* of this additional stock of capital is of less crucial importance than the *productivity* of that capital—that is, its technological character.

5. Technology

We have just mentioned the fifth and last main source of increases in productivity—technology. During the past half-century, GNP has consistently grown faster than can be accounted for by increases in the work force or the size of the capital stock. (Even during the 1929–1947 era, for instance, when capital stock per worker remained fixed, the output of GNP per worker grew by 1.5 percent a year.) Part of this "unexplained" increase can be attributed to some of the sources of growth we have itemized above— mainly education and training and economies of scale. But contemporary economic investigation increasingly attributes the bulk of the "bonus" rate of growth to the impact of new technology.

The term is, admittedly, somewhat vague. By "new technology" we mean new inventions, innovations of a productivity-enhancing kind, the growth of knowledge in the form of research and development, changes in business organization or in techniques of management, and many other activities. What is increasingly apparent, however, is that the search for new products and processes is the main force behind much productivity-enhancing investment. Thus while investment has become less important for growth simply as a means of adding sheer quantities of capital to the labor force (although that is still a very important function, particularly in construction), it remains the strategic variable as the carrier of technological change.

CHANGING SOURCES OF GROWTH

It is time to sum up what we have covered. We have seen that long-term growth proceeds from two sources: *more* input and more *productive* input, and we have been concerned with studying some of the main facets of both kinds of growth. Perhaps we can summarize our findings in Fig. 3·9, comparing the sources of growth in two eras of our past.

Note the declining importance played by increases in numbers of workers or sheer dollar value of capital, and the increasing importance of the "intangibles" of education and technology. To a number of observers, this shift implies that we have been slowly moving into a new phase of industrial organization in which productivity will more and more reflect the application of scientific knowledge, rather than the brute leverage of mechanical strength and power. Whether this "postindustrial" society will grow at a faster or slower rate than in the past is a question that we will not be able to answer for many years.

WHAT WE DO NOT KNOW ABOUT LONG-RUN GROWTH

Last, we must take cognizance of an important fact. We have learned a good deal about the sources of growth in the United States, but we have not really unlocked the secret of the historical trajectory of that growth. In fact, we can now see that this trajectory was the result of crosscurrents of many kinds. The potential stimulus to growth of a rising participation rate was dampened by a decline in the numbers of hours worked per year. Increases in productivity of labor in manufacturing and agriculture were offset by a

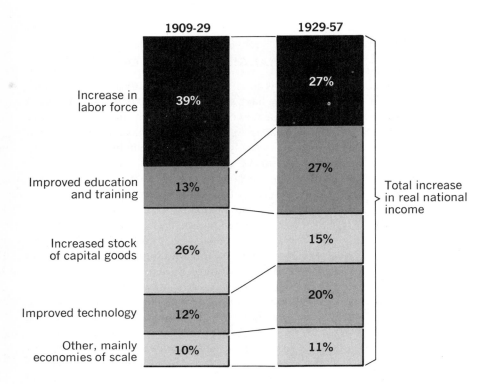

FIGURE 3·9
Sources of U.S. economic growth

shift of labor into the "low productivity" service sector.

The overall effect of these complex trends is the "steady" rate of 3.5 percent growth evidenced in the United States for many years. But we can now see that this steady rate was really the outcome of many contrary trends. Is there any underlying reason why the growth of GNP maintained such an even pace, or why that pace was 3.5 percent per year?

Not so far as we know. Other nations have different long-run growth rates; and those growth rates are not always as steady as those of the United States, by any means. Furthermore, within the United States, the steadiness of the average rate conceals a great deal of variation in shortrun rates as we shall see in our next chapter. The fact is, then, that we can describe but cannot really explain why our growth has followed the pattern shown in Fig. 3·9. This remains a profound problem for economists and economic historians.

DIFFERENT KINDS OF KNOWLEDGE

In thinking about technology and growth, it helps to differentiate among scientific knowledge, engineering knowledge, and economic knowledge. The relationship can best be understood if we look at the accompanying figure. Here we assume that knowledge can be arranged along a continuum from the least productive technologies to the most productive. On the extreme left are those techniques we have discarded; for example, water mills or treadmills for the production of energy. Next we come to the range of techniques

From an economist's point of view, the level of productivity in an economy depends not only on the location of all these techniques and frontiers, but on the distribution of plants *within* the bell curve. A high-productivity economy will have its curve of plants to the right of a low-productivity economy. Moreover, within that curve, its working equipment will be "bunched" toward the right-hand edge of *best-practice* plants; a low-productivity economy will have the opposite distribution. Incidentally, this is one reason why productivity is very high in industrial nations that have been severely damaged by war but have re-

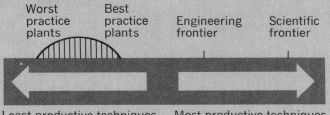

Worst practice plants | Best practice plants | Engineering frontier | Scientific frontier

Least productive techniques | Most productive techniques

in use. Here is a "bell curve" of plants, beginning with those that are still in use but almost obsolete—say, old-fashioned utilities—to the newest plant and equipment, perhaps nuclear power plants. Here we reach the *economic frontier*, the limit of knowledge that can be profitably used.

Still further to the right is another frontier—the limit of *engineering knowledge*. For instance, breeder reactors, still in "pilot plant stage" might be located near this point. Then to the far right is the boundary of *scientific knowledge*—for instance, fusion power—where our theoretical knowledge has not yet passed into the stage of engineering feasibility.

built their capital stock. Their factories will tend to incorporate the very newest and best in techniques, whereas an economy that was spared the damages of war will retain in use many older plants that still manage to show a small profit.

This consequence may help explain why the change in R&D expenditures has not significantly boosted American postwar productivity. *These expenditures have mainly moved out our engineering and scientific frontiers, without altering the distribution of actual techniques in use.* Most R&D in recent decades has been aimed at military and space technology, which has so far had only minor application to civilian use.

KEY WORDS

CENTRAL CONCEPTS

Production possibility curves

1. Total output possibilities for an economy cannot be represented simply by a given physical maximum. They involve choices that we represent by *production possibility curves* or surfaces.

2. The bowed shape of production-possibility curves reflects the *law of increasing costs*. This basic economic relationship describes the fact that our efficiency changes as we shift resources from one use to another, and that typically we experience a decreasing efficiency (with the consequence of increasing costs) as we move more and more resources into the production of any given item.

Law of increasing cost

3. Production possibility curves also make vivid the idea of an *efficiency frontier*. An economy that has not reached its frontier has unemployed or underutilized factors. *An economy cannot reach any point beyond a frontier unless it grows, thereby moving its frontier outwards.*

4. Growth in output derives from *investment that adds to our stock of capital wealth*. In an industrialized society, this investment is achieved by utilizing an existing capital-goods sector. But in a poor society, the process is much more difficult.

Efficiency frontier

5. In such a poor society, we can see that the *capital-goods sector consists of two subsectors:* one producing capital goods that, in turn, make the equipment used in the consumption-goods sector; and the other making machine tools, capital goods that can create more capital goods.

6. *Thus growth requires two shifts:* (1) the machine-tool capacity of the capital-goods sector must be enlarged and (2) resources must be shifted from the consumption sector to the capital goods sector.

Capital-goods sector

7. United States' growth has been shown a *persistently steady rate of 3.5 percent—1.5 percent per capita—*for well over a century. From year to year, however, the *rate of growth is very uneven.*

8. Growth results from two sources: *more inputs* and *more productive inputs* of both labor and capital.

9. *Participation* in the working force has slowly increased over the long run. This is the net result of three forces: the *large-scale entry of women* into the labor force after childbearing, partly offset by the *later entry and earlier retirement of males.*

Growth rates

10. *Higher participation rates have also been accompanied and offset by declines in the hours of work per year, per week, per day.*

11. *Increases in labor productivity have been much more important than increases in labor hours* in accounting for growth. The main sources of increased productivity have been:

Inputs and productivity

● Growth of human capital.

● Shifts in labor occupation (recently these shifts into services have slowed growth).

● Economies of large-scale production.

● Increases in the quantity and quality of capital. This involves both the *widening* and *deepening* of capital.

Participation rates

● Technology.

Technology and human capital have become increasingly important as sources of growth.

Sources of higher productivity

12. These factors present crosscurrents, some enhancing growth, some dampening it. We have no explanation of why the 3.5 average growth rate has been so steady.

QUESTIONS

1. Set up a production possibility curve for an economy producing food and steel. Show how there exists combinations of goods that cannot be produced, *although the quantity of either good alone is within the reach of economy.*

2. Describe carefully the difference between the law of diminishing returns and the law of increasing cost.

3. What kind of economy might display constant returns to specialization? Would a very simple, low-technology economy show such a straight-line efficiency frontier if its choice was, for example, to hunt or fish? Would this depend on the abundance of game or fish?

4. Explain why an economy would not want to operate to the left of its efficiency frontier.

5. What should an economy do if it does not *want* as many goods as it can have by being on its efficiency frontier? (Hint: remember that the efficiency frontier assumes that all factors of production are fully employed.)

6. Describe carefully the shifts in labor needed to begin the process of growth in a very simple economy. Are such shifts visible in an advanced economy?

7. What is the special property of machine tools? Is there a very simple article of output that is also capable of the dual uses of machine tools? How about the seed corn held back by a farmer?

8. How do you account for the fact that there are more people per hundred who want to work today than there were 70 years ago, when the nation was so much poorer? How much does the monetization of labor have to do with this? How much is it a change in life styles, especially for women? What do you expect for the very long run—say 100 years from now?

9. What is extensive investment? What is intensive investment? Which is more conducive to growth?

10. Why is productivity so important in achieving growth? What are its main sources? What would you recommend as a long-term program to raise American productivity? Asian productivity?

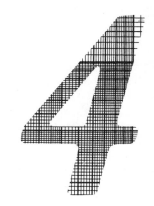

From Growth
to Fluctuations

WITH SOME UNDERSTANDING of how long-term growth emerges—and with a chastening sense of the limits of our understanding—it is time to change the focus of our lens. When we do, a second problem of macroeconomics emerges, as important as those we have been studying. It is concerned not with the course of long-term growth, but of *short-term fluctuations*—of boom and bust, business cycles, recessions and unemployment, inflation.

Take the years 1895 to 1905, very smooth-looking in Fig. 3·5, in our preced-

TABLE 4 · 1
U.S. Rates of Growth 1895–1905

1895–1896	− 2.5%	1900–1901	+11.5%
1896–1897	+9.4	1901–1902	+ 1.0
1897–1898	+2.3	1902–1903	+ 4.9
1898–1899	+9.1	1903–1904	− 1.2
1899–1900	+2.7	1904–1905	+ 7.4

Source: *Long Term Economic Growth* (U.S. Dept. of Commerce, 1966), p. 107.

ing chapter. As Table 4·1 reveals, those years were, in fact, anything but steady.

Or examine a more recent period, not year by year, but in groups of years. As we can see in Fig. 4·1 the rate of growth has varied greatly over the last fifty years.

BUSINESS CYCLES

This extraordinary sequence of ups and downs, rushes of growth followed by doldrums, introduces us to a fascinating aspect of the subject of growth—*business cycles.* For if we inspect the profile of the long ascent carefully, we can see that its entire length is marked with irregular tremors or peaks and valleys. Indeed, the more closely we examine year-to-year figures, the more of these tremors and deviations we discover, until the problem becomes one of selection: which vibrations to consider significant and which to discard as uninteresting.

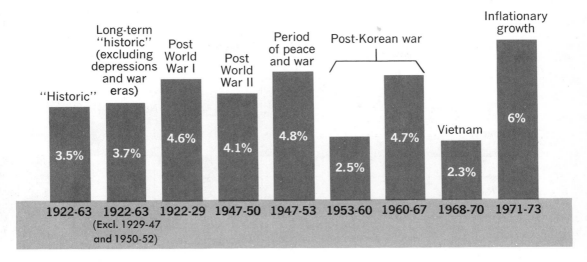

FIGURE 4 · 1
Short-term variations in the rate of growth

The problem of sorting out the important fluctuations in output (or in statistics of prices or employment) is a difficult one. Economists have actually detected dozens of cycles of different lengths and amplitudes, from very short rhythms of expansion and contraction that can be found, for example, in patterns of inventory accumulation and decumulation, to large background pulsations of seventeen or eighteen years in the housing industry, and possibly (the evidence is unclear) swings of forty to fifty years in the path of capitalist development as a whole.

Generally, however, when we speak of "the" business cycle we refer to a wavelike movement that lasts, on the average, about eight to ten years. In Fig. 4·2 this major oscillation of the American economy stands forth very clearly, for the chartist has eliminated the underlying tilt of growth, so that the profile of economic performance looks like a cross section at sea level rather than a cut through a long incline.

REFERENCE CYCLES

In a general way we are all familiar with the meaning of business cycles, for the alternation of "boom and bust" or prosperity and recession (a polite name for a mild depression) is part of everyday parlance. It will help us study cycles, however, if we learn to speak of them with a standard terminology. We can do this by taking the cycles from actual history, "superimposing" them, and drawing the general profile of the so-called *reference* cycle that emerges. It looks like Fig. 4·3. This model of a typical cycle enables us to speak of the "length" of a business cycle as the period from one peak to the next or from trough to trough. If we fail to measure from *similar* points on two or more cycles, we can easily get a distorted picture of short-term growth—for instance, one that begins at the upper turning point of one cycle and measures to the trough of the next. Much of the political charge and countercharge about

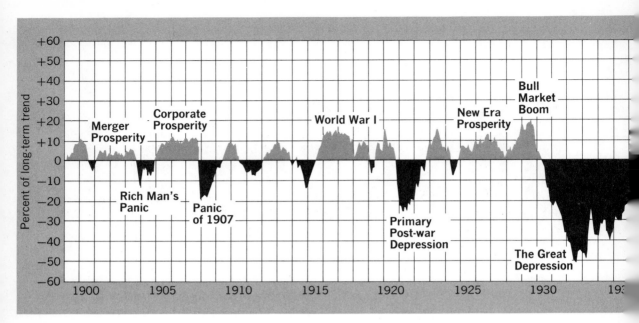

FIGURE 4 · 2
The business cycle

FIGURE 4 · 3
The reference cycle

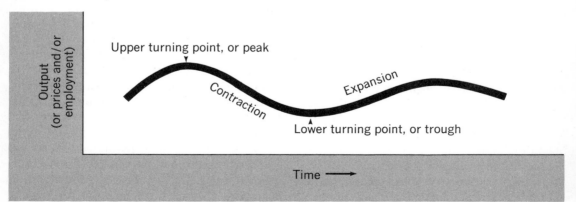

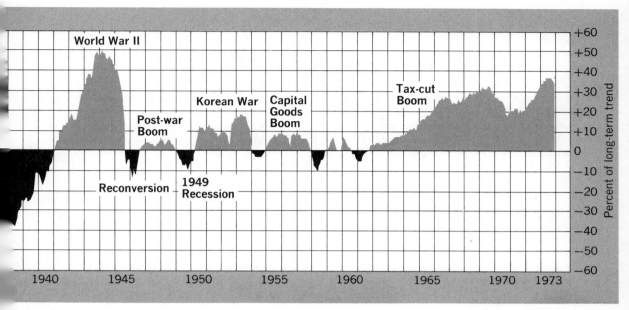

growth rates can be clarified if we examine the starting and terminating dates used by each side.

CAUSES OF CYCLES

What lies behind this more or less regular alternation of good and bad times?

Innumerable theories, none of them entirely satisfactory, have been advanced to explain the business cycle. A common business explanation is that waves of optimism in the world of affairs alternate with waves of pessimism—a statement that may be true enough, but that seems to describe the sequence of events rather than to explain it. Hence economists have tried to find the underlying cyclical mechanism in firmer stuff than an alternation of moods. One famous late-nineteenth-century economist, W. S. Jevons, for example, explained business cy-

cles as the consequence of sunspots—perhaps not as occult a theory as it might seem, since Jevons believed that the sunspots caused weather cycles that caused crop cycles that caused business cycles. The trouble was that subsequent investigation shows that the periodicity of sunspots was sufficiently different from that of rainfall cycles to make the connection impossible.

Other economists have turned to causes closer to home: to variations in the rate of gold mining (with its effects on the money supply); to fluctuations in the rate of invention; to the regular recurrence of war; and to yet many other factors. There is no doubt that many of these events can induce a business expansion or contraction. The persistent problem, however, is that none of the so-called underlying causes itself displays an inherent cyclicality—much less one with a periodicity of eight to ten years.

THE GREAT DEPRESSION

The Great Depression was probably the most traumatic economic episode in American life. GNP fell precipitously from $104 billion in 1929 to $56 billion in 1933. Unemployment rose from 1.5 million to 12.8 million: one person in every four in the labor force was out of work. Residential construction fell by 90 percent; nine million savings accounts were lost as banks closed their doors. Eighty-five thousand businesses failed. Wages fell to 5 cents an hour in sawmills, 6 cents in brick and tile manufacturing, 7½ cents in general contracting. As the stock market crashed, $30 billion in financial assets vanished. By 1932 nearly one in five of all Detroit schoolchildren was officially registered as seriously undernourished.

What caused the Great Depression? To this day we do not have a wholly convincing account. In part it was, of course, the consequence of a general decline in capital formation: investment expenditures fell by 88 percent from 1929 to 1933. But underlying this collapse were a number of contributory factors. Farm incomes had been steadily falling for years. The distribution of income was worsening, with profits booming at the same time that wage income was basically unchanged. Compounding and aggravating these weaknesses in the economy was a devastating collapse in credit. Whole structures of companies, pyramided one atop the other, fell like so many houses of cards when the stock market fell. And to worsen matters still further, the monetary authorities pursued policies of "prudence" and "caution" that unwittingly weakened the economy still further.

Can another Great Depression devastate the economy? Most economists would doubt it. Most bank accounts are today insured by the Federal Deposit Insurance Corporation, so that the wholesale wiping out of household assets would not happen again. The stock market, although still subject to wide swings, is unlikely to drag households or businesses into insolvency, because stocks can no longer be bought on the thin "margins" (partial payments) characteristic of the 1930s. Most important of all, the sheer size of government expenditure today makes a total collapse almost impossible. Moreover, if a severe depression were to begin, government would pursue policies of expansion either unknown or unthinkable in those days of laissez-faire economics. We will be studying all these matters shortly.

Then how do we explain cycles? Economists today no longer seek a single explanation of the phenomenon in an exogenous (external) cyclical force. Rather, they tend to see cycles as our own eye first saw them on the growth curve, *as variations in the rate of growth that tend to be induced by the dynamics of the growth process itself.*

FROM CAPACITY TO UTILIZATION

With this change in focus we bring into play a different set of concepts. In our survey of the long-term growth of GNP we were essentially dealing with the slow expansion of the *capacity* of the economy to produce goods and services. Now, however, as we concentrate on the immediate problems of boom and recession, it is not so much the capacity of the economy but *the degree of utilization* of the economy that becomes all-important. Hence, just as in microeconomics, when long-term price changes depended more on supply considerations than on demand considerations, and short-run price fluctuations depended more on demand shifts than supply shifts, so in dealing with the flow of total output, the potential supply of GNP was the main concern for long-run analysis, whereas in seeking to understand the short-run changes in GNP, changes in demand will be of primary interest.

Nevertheless, even in the determination of long-run prices, we will remember that demand was always present as one of the "blades of the scissors," as Alfred Marshall put it. So, too, in dealing with short-run changes in GNP, we see that supply is always present as one of the fundamental forces that determines how large output will actually be. It is, however, the *short-run forces of supply* that will occupy us in studying fluctuations of GNP. We will learn about them in this chapter, setting the stage for a much more extended examination of the forces of demand in the chapters to come.

THE SHORT-RUN SUPPLY OF GNP

What do we mean by the short-run supply forces for GNP? Let us first understand what we do *not* mean. A short-run supply function does not mean the relation between the quantity of GNP and its "price," as it might if we were talking about the short-run supply function for shoes. Nor does it mean the long-run changes in labor force or capital stock or productivity, which we learned about in our last chapter.

What does it mean? The idea is simple enough. The short-run supply function of GNP *tells us about the degree to which we utilize the existing capacity for production of our economy.* It tells us how much we can increase GNP in the short run by varying the degree of use of our existing labor and capital supplies; and it tells us how much GNP may fall if we fail to make use of these supplies.

Unemployment

That last point opens up the first obvious avenue for study. The supply of GNP that our stock of resources can deliver will certainly depend on the degree to which the productive capacity of labor and capital is used—or conversely, the degree to which labor and capital is unemployed and unutilized.

Usually when we think of unemployment we picture it as a kind of residual—the total labor force minus the number who are actually at work. If we look back at Fig. 3·6, we can see the colored band that represents this residual, a band that expanded to terrifying dimensions in the Great Depression (when one of every *four* members of the labor force was unable to find work) and that almost disappeared in the war years from 1942 to 1944.

AN ELASTIC LABOR FORCE

But when we look more closely into the actual phenomenon of unemployment we discover something quite surprising. It is that "unemployment" is not simply the difference between the number of people working and a fixed labor force, but the difference between the number working and an elastic, changeable labor force. Moreover we also discover that the size of the labor force is directly affected by the number of jobs, increasing as employment increases, shrinking as it falls.

The result is seemingly paradoxical. It is that employment and unemployment can both rise and fall at the same time, something that would be impossible if the labor force itself were fixed.

Table 4·2, on the next page, shows this curious phenomenon.

Notice that between 1969 and 1970, employment and unemployment *both* rose. The same phenomenon appeared between 1966 and 1967. How can this be?

The answer to the apparent paradox lies in the short-run responsiveness of the labor supply to the ease of finding work. In good times when jobs are plentiful, more youths

TABLE 4 · 2
Labor Force 1966–1972

| | SHORT-RUN CHANGES (IN MILLIONS) | | | | | | |
	1966	1967	1968	1969	1970	1971	1972
Number in civilian labor force	75.8	77.3	78.7	80.7	82.7	84.1	86.5
Civilian employment	72.9	74.4	75.9	77.9	78.6	79.1	81.7
Unemployment	2.9	3.0	2.8	2.8	4.1	5.0	4.8

and women will seek work. The whole labor force will then temporarily expand; and since not all of it may find work, both employment and unemployment may show increases. The reverse is true in a year of recession. What happens then is that many will be discouraged by bad times and "withdraw" from the labor force, remaining in school or in the household. As a result, the number of unemployed will then be smaller than if the larger labor force of a boom year had continued actively looking for work.

MEANING OF UNEMPLOYMENT

The concept of a variable participation rate for labor in the short run helps to elucidate the meaning of unemployment.

Clearly, unemployment is not a static condition, but one that varies with the *short-run participation rate* itself. Technically, the measure of unemployment is determined by a household-to-household survey conducted each month by the Bureau of the Census among a carefully selected sample.* An "unemployed" person is thereupon defined not merely as a person without a job—for perhaps such a person does not *want* a job—but as someone who is "actively" seeking work but is unable to find it. Since, however, the number of people who will be seeking work

will rise in good times and fall in bad times, figures for any given period must be viewed with caution.

As employment opportunities drop, unemployment will not rise by an equivalent amount. Some of those looking for work when job opportunities are plentiful will withdraw from the labor force and become part of *hidden unemployment*. When job opportunities expand, these "hidden unemployed" will reenter the labor force, so that unemployment will not fall as fast as employment rises. Thus the ups and downs in the measured unemployment rate reflect the state of the economy, but the swings are not as large as they would be if the term "unemployment" measured the hidden unemployed.

WORKING HOURS

Like short-run participation rates, *hours of labor are also sensitive to the ease of finding work*. As jobs become more available, hours of work per employee tend to lengthen. This occurs partly because employees are able to work overtime, or even to "moonlight," taking on a second job to augment their incomes. It also occurs because employers find it cheaper to lengthen hours, even at overtime rates, than to hire and train new employees.

These cautions by no means invalidate the statistics of unemployment, but they

*Sampling is an important statistical tool. If you would like to learn more about it, consult Section IV, Chapter 18.

warn us against taking those statistics at face value. In appraising the seriousness of a given rate of unemployment, the economist first looks at participation rates and hours of work, and then at unemployment rates, before he judges what fraction of the "long-run" potential labor supply is being utilized.

CAPACITY UTILIZATION

Is there a counterpart to unemployment affecting capital? There is—up to a point. We call it the rate of *capacity utilization.* This rate measures the relation between the maximum output that could be attained with a given capital stock and the actual output that is being produced by this stock. We usually use this rate for manufacturing industries, since adequate statistics for capacity output do not exist for many industries, such as construction or agriculture. But when we hear, for example, that steel plants are running at, say, 90 percent of capacity, the unused 10 percent is the capital counterpart of unemployment.

What about the elasticity of supply of capital? Does the stock of capital respond to economic conditions, in the way that the labor force does? To a certain extent it does. When demand is brisk, old plant destined for scrapping may be used for a time. Land that was taken out of cultivation can be brought back. Decayed buildings can be pressed into temporary service. Therefore there is a certain elasticity in the stock of capital, comparable to that of labor. Because the measurement of this flexibility of capital supply is so difficult, however, we do not make use of this elasticity when we speak of capital utilization.

CAPITAL OUTPUT RATIOS

There is a closely related concept that links short-term fluctuations in labor productivity with short-term fluctuations in capital productivity. (See box, "Measuring Productivity," Chapter 3.) Just as we can speak of a long-run productivity of labor, in terms of the relation between labor inputs and labor outputs, so there are, as we know, long-run trends in the productivity of capital. We can describe this productivity as the ratio between capital and output—*the amount of capital that it requires to create a unit of output.*

In the long run, this *capital-output* ratio changes only slowly as technology increases the productive power of capital. But in the short run, capital-output ratios are capable of sharp fluctuations much like those of labor. The amount of output that a "unit" of capital—say a factory or a machine—produces can swing sharply from month to month or year to year, especially if the factory or machine is underutilized and then brought up to "rated" capacity, or if it is pushed beyond the output rate it was designed for.

THE AGGREGATE PRODUCTION FUNCTION

Our discussion of the elasticity of supply of labor and capital has helped us understand how we can vary the amount of GNP we produce from our historically determined stock of capital and population. As the degree of utilization or employment changes, so will the amount of output that our factors of production turn out.

Now we must ask a larger question about this variable capacity to produce. Can we construct a supply curve for GNP as a whole, in the short run? We can indeed, and we call such a curve an *aggregate production function.* As the words suggest, it expresses the total supply capabilities of the economy as we alter the degree of utilization of all factors in it.

What does such an aggregate production function look like? Figure 4·4 shows us three possibilities.*

First, a technical note. You will see that we have put output on the horizontal axis and input on the vertical axis. In microeconomics, we generally put output on the vertical axis and input on the horizontal. This is simply a convention, but it explains why the curves turn in different directions than they would in microanalysis.

more output as we add inputs; in Panel III, less and less.

ECONOMIES OF SCALE

What accounts for these different shapes? The answer is not, as we might think, the law of variable proportions, because we are varying all factor inputs, not just one. Nor is the reason the law of increasing cost, because we are not shifting from one kind of output to

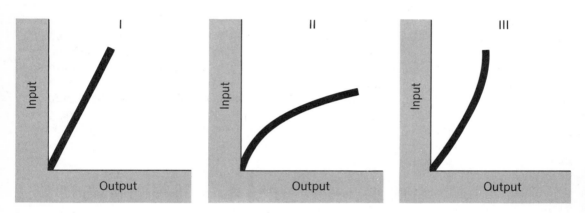

FiGURE 4 · 4
Possible production functions

Second, let us look at the three curves. In Panel I we depict a production function that gives us a constant proportional increase in output as we add "bundles" of labor and capital, let us say ½ percent more output for each 1 percent more in combined inputs. In Panel II, we get proportionally more and

another. Rather, the constraint that determines the shape of the curve has to do with *economies of scale.* As we add more and more of all inputs, we might encounter economies of size, or beyond a certain scale of output, diseconomies of size.

Which of the three curves actually portrays the production function of the United States? The curve is probably a combination of all three. If we were to begin from a very low level of output, we would likely enjoy economies of scale at first. Then after a "nor-

*We depict the curves for simplicity's sake without calibrating the graph. Usually production functions are graphed on log-log paper to show the rates of change of inputs and outputs, rather than their amounts.

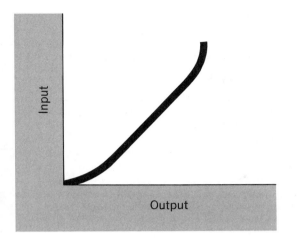

FIGURE 4 · 5
The aggregate production function

FIGURE 4 · 6
Shifts in the production function

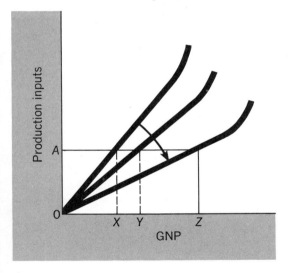

production function we might encounter dis-economies of scale (or we might simply run out of the highest-quality factors and be forced to resort to lower grade, relatively unproductive factors). Thus our aggregate production function looks like Fig. 4·5. We will be mainly interested in its upper portions.

We should note, however, that the slope of an aggregate production function need not remain fixed. As the productivity of all factors increases over time, we can attain the same total output with a smaller bundle of inputs, or what is the same thing, more output from the same bundle of inputs. This results in a clockwise shift in the production function as shown in Fig. 4·6.

Note that as our productivity grows, OA inputs give us larger and larger GNPs: first OX, then OY, then OZ.

AGGREGATE SUPPLY CURVE

The aggregate production function gives us what we set out to discover—a comprehension of the supply curve for GNP.* When we speak of the changing slope of such a production function, we are of course dealing in long-run time periods; but even in the short run we can think of the supply curve as *tending* downward as the productivity of labor and capital gradually increase.

What the aggregate production function therefore shows is how much GNP the economy can produce as it varies its inputs. It thereby gives us half of the information we need to arrive at a determination of the year-to-year, or month-to-month, fluctuations in GNP. We now know something about the shape of supply. The next problem is to discover what the demand for GNP will be.

mal" level of production were reached, we would enter a long stretch of constant returns to scale. At the very upper end of the

*Another means of studying total output is called input-output analysis. This is explained in a special supplement to this chapter.

KEY WORDS

CENTRAL CONCEPTS

Business cycles

1. We turn now from growth to fluctuations in growth called *business cycles*. A typical business cycle has four phases: expansion, an upper turning point, contraction, and a lower turning point.

Degree of utilization

2. Business cycles introduce us to the concept of the *degree of utilization* of the economy. We are interested now in the relation between factor inputs and GNP in the short run, rather than in long-run growth trends.

Short-run participation rates

3. Business cycles and degree of utilization introduce us to the idea of *unemployment* and *underutilization*. Here we note that the labor force is not a fixed number, but varies in size as the number of available jobs changes; i.e., there are changes in short-run *participation rates*.

Unemployment

4. As a result of flexible participation rates, the idea of *unemployment* becomes complex. *Unemployment reflects changes in the number of people looking for work, as well as changes in the number of available jobs.* Hours of labor are also responsive to demand.

Capital output ratios

5. Capital stock can also be *underutilized* and *capital output* ratios can change, as the stock of capital is left idle or pushed beyond its normal design capacity.

Aggregate production function

6. An *aggregate production function is the economy's supply curve.* It shows us the increase in the output of a given selection of goods if we increase inputs with "bundles" of capital and labor. Up to the point of "full employment and utilization," production functions tend to be straight lines, meaning that each proportionate increase in bundles of inputs yields an unchanging proportionate increase in output. We call this *constant returns to scale.*

Constant returns to scale

7. The slope of the production function will move downward as the productivity of the inputs changes.

QUESTIONS

1. How can employment and unemployment increase at the same time?

2. If there were a severe shortage of labor, what would the probable effect be on the length of the work week? The work year?

3. Can you think of some mechanism that would produce regular business cycles? How about the tendency of most capital goods to wear out in about ten years? Assuming that capital goods were originally bought in a "bunched" fashion, could that produce a wavelike pattern? How about cycles in birth rates? (Or do you suppose these are *caused* by business cycles?)

4. What is meant by an aggregate production function? How is it different from a production possibility curve?

5. Under what conditions would an aggregate production function show an increasing slope? A decreasing slope?

6. What does it mean when we state that the U.S. economy mainly has a straight-line aggregate production function, at least up to "capacity utilization"?

7. Draw a series of aggregate production functions for an economy in which pollution problems were becoming an ever more burdensome problem.

Special Supplement on Input-Output

Input-output is another means of understanding the production function. It is an analytical procedure developed during the last two decades under the leadership of Wassily Leontieff of Harvard University, who won the Nobel prize for his efforts.

Input-output analysis is an effort to clarify the way the economy literally fits together in terms of the flows of goods from one producer to another or from the last producer to the final buyer. In our normal aggregative way of looking at GNP, we do not see the immensely complex interaction of production flows down the various "stages" of production. All these flows are ignored as we concentrate on *final* production. Input-output analysis concentrates on *all* production, final or intermediate. It thereby gives us a much more detailed understanding of the linkages of output than we can get from normal GNP analysis.

Input-output analysis begins by classifying production into basic inputs or industries. Today the Department of Commerce operates with an input-output table that lists 87 different industries, such as livestock and livestock products, ordnance and accessories, household appliances, amusements. These 87 industries are listed one below the other. Then the output of each industry is placed in a "cell" or "cells" corresponding to the industries to which it is sold. An actual input-output table or *matrix* is too large to be shown here. Instead, Table 4·3 gives us a look at a model of such a matrix for an extremely simple hypothetical economy.

What is such a matrix good for? First, let us read across the rows of the table, to trace where output goes. For example, of the total wheat crop of 600 (thousand bushels), 100 are kept back to sow next year's crop, none go to the machine or auto industry, and 500 are used for food (and sold to labor). Machines have a different pattern. Forty machines are produced. Ten are used in harvesting wheat, 5 are used in making more machines (machine tools), 25 go to the auto industry, none are sold to labor. Automobiles are sold to wheat farms (trucks), used by the machinery and auto industry, as trucks or vehicles for salesmen, and sold in large numbers to consumers. Labor is used by all producers, including labor itself (barbers, lawyers, teachers).

This shows us the flow of production "horizontally" through the economy. But we can also use the table to trace its "vertical" distribution. That is, we can see that the production of 600 "units" of wheat (last figure in the top row) required *inputs* (the column under wheat) of 100 units of wheat, 10 machines, 5 automobiles (trucks), and 20 units of labor. To make 40 machines, it takes no wheat, 5 machines, 10 autos, and 30 units of labor. The production of 68 automobiles needs 25 machines, 3 cars, and 60 labor units. To "produce" 120 "units" of labor—to feed and sustain that much labor—takes 500 units of wheat, 50 cars, 10 units of personal services.

Thus our input-output analysis enables us to penetrate deeply into the interstices of the economy. But more than that, it *enables us to calculate production requirements* in a way that far exceeds in accuracy any previously known

TABLE 4·3

	Wheat	Machines	Automobiles	Labor	Total
Wheat (000 bushels)	100	0	0	500	600
Machines (units)	10	5	25	0	40
Automobiles (units)	5	10	3	50	68
Labor (000 man-years)	20	30	60	10	120

method. Suppose, for example, that the economy wanted to double its output of autos. Forget for a moment about economies of scale. To begin with, we can see that it will need 25 more machines, 3 additional autos, and 60 more units of labor.

But that is only a list of its *direct demands*. There is also a long series of *indirect demands*. For when the auto industry buys five additional machines, the machine industry will have to increase its output by one-eighth. This means it will need one-eighth more inputs of machines, autos, and labor. But in turn this sets up still further requirements. To "produce" more labor will require more outputs of wheat and cars. To produce more wheat will require still further output of machines and autos. Thus a whole series of secondary, indirect demands spread out through the economy, each generating still further demands.

Input-output analysis uses a technique known as *matrix algebra* to sum up the total effects of any original change. This is not a subject that we will explore here. It is enough to understand how the matrix enables us to calculate production requirements, very much in the manner of an aggregate production function, but in finer detail.

We should note one difficulty with input-output analysis. When we took our example of doubling auto output, we assumed that there would be no changes in the proportions of inputs required to double output and that the input "mixes" for the other industries would be unaffected by increases in their outputs. This assumption of *fixed production coefficients* is not in accord with reality. Increases in output, such as a doubling of auto output, not only usually lead to economies of scale, but may also result from wholly new techniques. Input-output analysis has no way of handling or predicting these kinds of changes. At best it gives us a picture of the production requirements of an economy under the assumption that production methods and products are fixed, although we know they are not.

Nonetheless, no more powerful tool has yet been developed to examine the interactions of the economic system. Input-output analysis is used more and more, not only by government planners or economists, but by large corporations that want to calculate how changes in various sectors of the economy affect demand for their products. Input-output tables enable them to do this because they show the indirect as well as direct demands that economic changes generate.

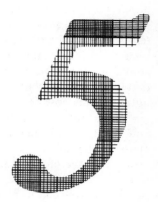

The Demand
for Output

So far, we have talked about GNP from three points of view. First we familiarized ourselves with the actual process of production itself—the interaction of the factors of production and the accumulated wealth of the past as they cooperated to bring a flow of output into being. Next we examined the forces that swelled that volume of output over time, mainly the increase in skills and capital equipment and technology that are responsible for our long-term trend of growth. Then we looked into the immediate causes of short-run fluctuations of output, from the point of view of supply, acquainting ourselves with the idea of a supply curve of GNP that we call the aggregate production function.

Now let us turn to the vital question of demand—to the forces that induce the factors of production to generate output. In particular, we want to look into the question of fluctuations of demand that, together with fluctuations in supply, will determine the actual amount of GNP produced at any moment.

Output and Demand

Let us start with a basic question—at once very simple and surprisingly complex. *How do we know that there will be enough demand to buy the amount of output that the factors produce?* Once we understand that, we will be well on the way to unlocking the puzzle of macroeconomies.

The question leads us to understand a fundamental linkage between demand and output. For how does output actually come into existence? Any businessman will give you the answer. He will tell you that the crucial factor enabling him to run his business is *demand* or *purchasing power;* that is, the presence of buyers who are willing and able to buy some good or service at a price he is willing to accept.

But how does demand or purchasing power come into existence? If we ask any buyer, he will tell us that his dollars come to him because they are part of his *income* or his cash receipts. But where, in turn, do the dollar receipts or incomes of buyers come from? If we inquire again, most buyers will tell us that they have money in their pockets because in one fashion or another they have contributed to the process of production; that is, because they have helped to make the output that is now being sold.

Thus output is generated by demand—and demand is generated by output! Our quest for the motive force behind the flow of production therefore leads us in a great circle through the market system. Here is the circular flow approached from a macro perspective. We can see this in Fig. 5·1.

At the top of the circlè we see payments flowing from households to firms or government units (cities, states, federal agencies, etc.), thereby creating the demand that brings forth production. At the bottom of the circle, we see more payments, this time flowing from firms or governments back to households, as

businesses hire the services of the various factors in order to carry out production. Thus we can see that there is a constant re-generation of demand as money is first spent by the public on the output of firms and governments, and then in turn spent by firms and governments for the services of the public.

AN ECONOMIC MODEL

Let us begin by examining this chain of payments and receipts as a model of the macro system.

Our model, to begin with, will be a very simple one. We must simplify it, at first, by ruling out some of the very events to which we will later turn as the climax of our study. For instance, we shall ignore changes in *people's tastes,* so that we can assume that

FIGURE 5 · 1
The circular flow, view II

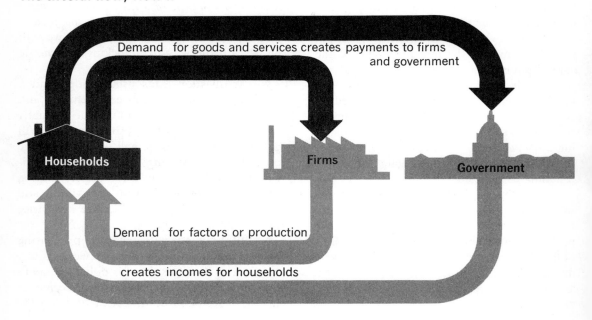

everyone will regularly buy the same kinds of goods. We shall ignore differences in the *structure of firms* or *markets,* so that we can forget about differences in competitive pressures. We shall rule out *population growth* and, even more important, *inventive progress,* so that we can deal with a very stable imaginary world. For the time being, we will exclude even *saving* and *net investment* (although of course we must permit replacement investment), so that we can ignore growth. Later, of course, we are to be deeply concerned with just such problems of dynamic change. But we shall not be able to come to grips with them until we have first understood an economic world as "pure" and changeless as possible.

COST AND OUTPUT

The very abstract model we have created may seem too far removed from the real world to tell us much about its operation. But if we now go back to the circle of economic activity in which payments to firms, governments, and factors become their incomes, and in turn reappear on the marketplace as demand, our model will enable us to explain a very important problem. *It is how an economy that has produced a given GNP is able to buy it back.*

This is by no means a self-evident matter. Indeed, one of the most common misconceptions about the flow of economic activity is that there will not be enough purchasing power to buy everything we have produced—that somehow we are unable to buy enough to keep up with the output of our factories. So it is well to understand once and for all how an economy can sustain a given level of production through its purchases on the market.

We start, then, with an imaginary economy in full operation. We can, if we wish,

imagine ourselves as having collected a year's output, which is now sitting on the economic front doorstep looking for a buyer. What we must now see is whether it will be possible to *sell* this gross national product to the people who have been engaged in producing it. In other words, *we must ask whether enough income or receipts have been generated in the process of production to buy back all the products themselves.*

Costs and Incomes

How does production create income? Businessmen do not think about "incomes" when they assemble the factors of production to meet the demand for their product. They worry about *cost.* All the money they pay out during the production process is paid under the heading of *cost,* whether it be wage or salary cost, cost of materials, depreciation cost, tax cost, or whatever. Thus it would seem that the concept of cost may offer us a useful point of entry into the economic chain. For *if we can show how all costs become incomes,* we will have taken a major step toward understanding whether our gross national product can in fact be sold to those who produced it.

It may help us if we begin by looking at the kinds of costs incurred by business firms in real life. Since governments also produce goods and services, this hypothetical firm should be taken to represent government agencies as well as business firms. Both incur the same kinds of costs; only the labels differ.

Table 5·1, a hypothetical expense summary of General Output Company, will serve as an example typical of all business firms, large or small, and all government agencies. (If you examine the year-end statements of any business, you will find that their costs all fall into one or more of the cost categories shown.)

TABLE 5 · 1
General Output Company Cost Summary

Wages, salaries, and employee benefits	$100,000,000
Rental, interest, and profits payments	5,000,000
Materials, supplies, etc.	60,000,000
Taxes other than income	25,000,000
Depreciation	20,000,000
Total	$210,000,000

FACTOR COSTS AND NATIONAL INCOME

Some of these costs we recognize immediately as payments to factors of production. The item for "wages and salaries" is obviously a payment to the factor *labor*. The item "interest" (perhaps not so obviously) is a payment to the factor *capital*—that is, to those who have lent the company money in order to help it carry on its productive operation. The item for rent is, of course, a payment for the rental of *land* or natural resources from their owners.

Note that we have included profits with rent and interest. In actual accounting practice, profits are not shown as an expense. For our purposes, however, it will be quite legitimate and very helpful to regard profits as a special kind of factor cost going to entrepreneurs for their risk-taking function. Later we shall go more thoroughly into the matter of profits.

Two things strike us about these factor costs. First, it is clear that they represent payments that have been made to secure production. In more technical language, they are payments for factor inputs that result in commodity outputs. All the production actually carried on within the company or government agency, all the value it has added to the

economy has been compensated by the payments the company or the agency has made to land, labor, and capital. To be sure, there are other costs, for materials and taxes and depreciation, and we shall soon turn to these. But whatever production or assembly or distribution the company or agency has carried out during the course of the year has required the use of land, labor, or capital. Thus *the total of its factor costs represents the value of the total new output that General Output by itself has given to the economy.*

From here it is but a simple step to add up *all* the factor costs paid out by *all* the companies and government agencies in the economy, in order to measure the total new *value added* by all productive efforts in the year. This measure is called *national income*. As we can see, it is less than gross national product, for it does not include other costs of output; namely, certain taxes and depreciation.

FACTOR COSTS AND HOUSEHOLD INCOMES

A second fact that strikes us is that *all factor costs are income payments*. The wages, salaries, interest, rents, etc., that were costs to the company or agency were income to its recipients. So are any profits, which will accrue as income to the owners of the business.

Thus, just as it sounds, national income means the total amount of earnings of the factors of production within the nation. If we think of these factors as constituting the households of the economy, we can see that *factor costs result directly in incomes to the household sector.* Thus, if factor costs were the only costs involved in production, the problem of buying back the gross national product would be a very simple one. We should simply be paying out to households, as the cost of production, the very sum needed to buy GNP when we turned around to sell it. But this is not the case, as a glance at the General Output expense summary shows. There are other costs besides factor costs. How shall we deal with them?

COSTS OF MATERIALS

The next item of the expense summary is puzzling. Called payments for "materials, supplies, etc.," it represents all the money General Output has paid, not to its own factors, but to other companies for other products it has needed. We may even recognize these costs as payments for those intermediate products that lose their identity in a later stage of production. How do such payments become part of the income available to buy GNP on the marketplace?

Perhaps the answer is already intuitively clear. When General Output sends its checks to, let us say, U.S. Steel or General Electric or to a local supplier of stationery, each of these recipient firms now uses the proceeds of General Output's checks to pay its own costs.

(Actually, of course, they have probably long since paid their own costs and now use General Output's payment only to reimburse themselves. But if we want to picture our model economy in the simplest way, we can imagine U.S. Steel and other firms sending their products to General Output and waiting until checks arrive to pay their own costs.)

And what are those costs? What must U.S. Steel or all the other suppliers now do with their checks? The answer is obvious. They must now reimburse their own factors and then pay any other costs that remain.

Figure 5·2 may make the matter plain. It shows us, looking back down the chain of intermediate payments, that what constitutes material costs to one firm is made up of factor and other costs to another. Indeed, as we unravel the chain from company to company, it is clear that all the contribution to new output must have come from the contribution of factors somewhere down the line, and that *all the costs of new output—all the value added—must ultimately be resolvable into payments to land, labor, and capital.*

Another way of picturing the same thing is to imagine that all firms or agencies in the

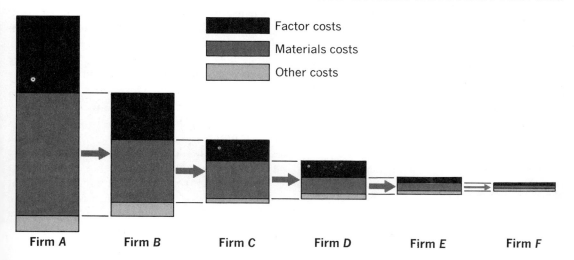

FIGURE 5 · 2
How materials costs become other costs

Factor costs

Materials costs

Other costs

Firm A   Firm B   Firm C   Firm D   Firm E   Firm F

country were bought up by a single gigantic corporation. The various production units of the new supercorporation would then ship components and semifinished items back and forth to one another, but there would not have to be any payment from one division to another. The only payments that would be necessary would be those required to buy the services of factors—that is, various kinds of labor or the use of property or capital—so that at the end of the year, the supercorporation would show on its expense summary only items for wages and salaries, rent, and interest (and as we shall see, taxes and depreciation), but it would have no item for materials cost.

We have come a bit further toward seeing how our gross national product can be sold. *To the extent that GNP represents new output made during the course of the year, the income to buy back this output has already been handed out as factor costs, either paid at the last stage of production or "carried along" in the guise of materials costs.*

But a glance at the General Output expense summary shows that entrepreneurs incur two kinds of costs that we have still not taken into account: taxes and depreciation. Here are costs employers have incurred that have not been accounted for on the income side. What can we say about them?

TAX COSTS

Let us begin by tracing the taxes that General Output pays, just as we have traced its materials payments.* In the first instance, its taxes will go to government units—federal, state, and local. But we need not stop there. Just as we saw that General Output's checks

*For simplicity, we also show government agencies as taxpayers. In fact, most government units do *not* pay taxes. Yet there will be hidden tax costs in the prices of many materials they buy. No harm is done by treating government agencies like taxpaying firms in this model.

to supplier firms paid for the suppliers' factor costs and for still further interfirm transactions, so we can see that its checks to government agencies pay for goods and services that these agencies have produced—goods such as roads, buildings, or defense equipment; or services such as teaching, police protection, and the administration of justice. General Output's tax checks are thus used to help pay for factors of production—land, labor, and capital—that are used in the *public sector.*

In many ways, General Output's payments to government units resemble its payments to other firms for raw materials. Indeed, if the government *sold* its services to General Output, charging for the use of the roads, police services, or defense protection it affords the company, there would be *no* difference whatsoever. The reason we differentiate between a company's payment to the public sector and its payments for intermediate products is important, however, and worth looking into.

The first reason is clearly that with few exceptions, the government does *not* sell its output. This is partly because the community has decided that certain things the government produces (education, justice, or the use of public parks, for instance) should not be for sale but should be supplied to all citizens without direct charge. In part, it is also because some things the government produces, such as defense or law and order, cannot be equitably charged to individual buyers, since it is impossible to say to what degree anyone benefits from—or even uses—these communal facilities. Hence General Output, like every other producer, is billed, justly or otherwise, for a share of the cost of government.

There is also a second reason why we consider the cost of taxes as a new kind of cost, distinct from factor payments. It is that when business firms have finished paying the factors, they have not yet paid all the sums that employers must lay out. *Some taxes, in other words, are an addition to the cost of production.*

INDIRECT VS. DIRECT TAXES

These taxes—so-called *indirect taxes*—are levied on the productive enterprise itself or on its actual physical output. Taxes on real estate, for instance, or taxes that are levied on each unit of output, regardless of whether or not it is sold (such as excise taxes on cigarettes), or taxes levied on goods sold at retail (sales taxes) are all payments that entrepreneurs must make as part of their costs of doing business.

Note that not all taxes collected by the government are costs of production. Many taxes will be paid, not by the entrepreneurs as an expense of doing business, but by the *factors* themselves. These so-called *direct* taxes (such as income taxes) are *not* part of the cost of production. When General Output adds up its total cost of production, it naturally includes the wages and salaries it has paid, but it does not include the taxes its workers or executives have paid out of their incomes. Such direct taxes transfer income from earners to government, but they are not a cost to the company itself.

In the same way, the income taxes on the profits of a company do *not* constitute a cost of production. General Output does not pay income taxes as a regular charge on its operations but waits until a year's production has taken place and then pays income taxes on the profits it makes *after* paying its costs. If it finds that it has lost money over the year, it will not pay any income taxes—although it will have paid other costs, including indirect taxes. *Thus direct taxes are not a cost that is paid out in the course of production and must be recouped, but a payment made by factors (including owners of the business) from the incomes they have earned through the process of production.*

TAXES AS COST

Thus we can see two reasons why taxes are handled as a separate item in GNP and are not telescoped into factor costs, the way materials costs are. One reason is that taxes are a payment to a *different sector* from that of business and thus indicate a separate stream of economic activity. But the second reason, and the one that interests us more at this moment, is that *certain taxes*—indirect taxes—*are an entirely new kind of cost of production, not previously picked up.* As an expense paid out by entrepreneurs, over and above factor costs (or materials costs), these tax costs must be part of the total selling price of GNP.

Will there be enough incomes handed out in the process of production to cover this item of cost? We have seen that there will be. The indirect tax costs paid out by firms will be received by government agencies who will use these tax receipts to pay income to factors working for the government. Any direct taxes (income taxes) paid by General Output or by its factors will also wind up in the hands of a government. Thus all tax payments result in the transfer of purchasing power from the private to the public sector, and when spent by the public sector, they will again become demand on the marketplace.

DEPRECIATION

But there is still one last item of cost. At the end of the year, when the company is totting up its expenses to see if it has made a profit for the period, its accountants do not stop with factor costs, material costs, and indirect taxes. If they did, the company would soon be in serious straits. In producing its goods, General Output has also used up a certain amount of its assets—its buildings and equipment—and a cost must now be charged for this wear and tear if the company is to be able to preserve the value of its physical plant intact. If it did not make this cost allowance, it would have failed to include all the resources that were used up in the process of production, and it would therefore be overstating its profits.

Yet, this cost has something about it clearly different from other costs that General Output has paid. Unlike factor costs or taxes or materials costs, depreciation is not paid for by check. When the company's accountants make an allowance for depreciation, all they do is make an entry on the company's book, stating that plant and equipment are now worth a certain amount less than in the beginning of the year.

At the same time, however, General Output *includes* the amount of depreciation in the price it intends to charge for its goods. As we have seen, part of the resources used up in production was its own capital equipment, and it is certainly entitled to consider the depreciation as a cost. Yet, it has not paid anyone a sum of money equal to this cost! How, then, will there be enough income in the marketplace to buy back its product?

REPLACEMENT EXPENDITURE

The answer is that in essence it has paid depreciation charges to itself. Depreciation is thus part of its gross income. Together with after-tax profits, these depreciation charges are called a business's *cash flow*.

A business does not *have to* spend its depreciation accruals, but normally it will, *to maintain and replace its capital stock.* To be sure, an individual firm may not replace its worn-out capital exactly on schedule. But when we consider the economy as a whole, with its vast assemblage of firms, that problem tends to disappear. Suppose we have 1,000 firms, each with machines worth $1,000 and each depreciating its machines at $100 per year. Provided that all the machines were

bought in different years, this means that in any given year, about 10 percent of the capital stock will wear out and have to be replaced. It's reasonable to assume that among them, the 1,000 firms will spend $100,-000 to replace their old equipment over a ten-year span.*

This enables us to see that insofar as there is a steady stream of replacement expenditures going to firms that make capital goods, there will be payments just large enough to balance the addition to costs due to depreciation. As with all other payments to firms, these replacement expenditures will, of course, become incomes to factors, etc., and thus can reappear on the marketplace.

ANOTHER VIEW OF COSTS AND INCOMES

Because it is very important to understand the relationship between the "selling price" of GNP and the amount of income available to buy it back, it may help to look at the matter from a different point of view.

This time let us approach it by seeing how the economy arranges things so that consumers and government and business, the three great sectors of final demand, are provided with enough purchasing power to claim the whole of GNP. Suppose, to begin with, that the economy paid out income only to its factors and priced its goods and services accordingly. In that case, consumers could purchase the entire value of the year's output,

---

*But what if the machines *were* all bought in one year or over a small number of years? Then replacement expenditures will *not* be evenly distributed over time, and we may indeed have problems. This takes us into the dynamics of prosperity and recession, to which we will turn in due course. For the purpose of our explanatory model, we will stick with our (not too unrealistic) assumption that machines wear out on a steady schedule and that aggregate replacement expenditures therefore also display a steady, unfluctuating pattern.

but business would be unable to purchase any portion of the output to replace its worn-out equipment. (Also it raises the awkward question of how we would pay factors working for the government, since government agencies would have very little income.)

That would obviously lead to serious trouble. Hence we must arrange for business to have a claim on output and for government factors to be paid for their services. The latter is simple. By imposing direct (income) taxes on factors, we divert income from the private to the public sector. And by imposing indirect taxes on output, we price output above its factor cost, thus making it impossible for consumers to claim the entire output.

In exactly the same way, business also reserves a claim on output by pricing its products to include a charge for depreciation. By so doing, it again reduces the ability of consumers to buy back the entire output of the economy, while it gives business the purchasing power to claim the output it needs (just as taxes give purchasing power to government). Now, after paying direct and indirect taxes and depreciation, the consumer is finally free to spend all the remainder of

accrue to government and business, but also as the means by which the output of the economy is made available to two important claimants besides private households.

THE THREE STREAMS OF EXPENDITURE

Our analysis is now essentially complete. Item by item, we have traced each element of cost into an income payment, so that we now know there is enough income paid out to buy back our GNP at a price that represents its full cost. Perhaps this was a conclusion we anticipated all along. After all, ours would be an impossibly difficult economy to manage if somewhere along the line purchasing power dropped out of existence, so that we were always faced with a shortage of income to buy back the product we made. But our analysis has also shown us something more unexpected. We are accustomed to thinking that all the purchasing power in the economy is received and spent through the hands of "people"—usually meaning households. Now we can see that this is not true. There is not only one, but there are *three* streams of incomes and costs, all quite distinct from one another although linked by direct taxes).

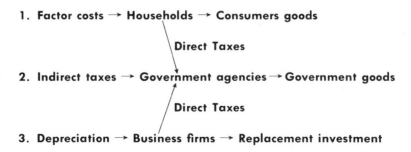

his income without danger of encroaching on the output that must be reserved for public activity and for the replacement of capital.

In other words, we can look at taxes and depreciation not merely as "costs" that the consumer has to pay or as "incomes" that

The one major crossover in the three streams is the direct taxes of households and business firms that go to governments. This flow permits governments to buy more goods and services than could be purchased with indirect taxes alone.

THE THREE FLOWS

To help visualize these three flows, imagine for an instant that our money comes in colors (all of equal value): black, orange, and brown. Now suppose that firms always pay their factors in orange money, their taxes in brown money, and their replacement expenditures in black money. In point of fact, of course, the colors would soon be mixed. A factor that is paid in orange bills will be paying some of his orange income for taxes; or a government agency will be paying out brown money as factor incomes; or firms will be using black dollars to pay taxes or factors, and brown or orange dollars to pay for replacement capital.

But at least in our mind we could picture the streams being kept separate. A brown tax dollar paid by General Output to the Internal Revenue Service for taxes could go from the government to another firm, let us say in payment for office supplies, and we can think of the office supply firm keeping these brown dollars apart from its other receipts, to pay its taxes with. Such a brown dollar could circulate indefinitely, from government agencies to firms and back again, helping to bring about production but never entering a consumer's pocket! In the same way, a black replacement expenditure dollar going from General Output to, let us say, U.S. Steel could be set aside by U.S. Steel to pay for *its* replacement needs; and the firm that received this black dollar might, in turn, set it aside for its own use as replacement expenditure. We could, that is, imagine a circuit of expenditures in which black dollars went from firm to firm, to pay for replacement investment, and never ended up in a pay envelope or as a tax payment.

There is a simple way of explaining this seemingly complex triple flow. Each stream indicates the existence of a *final taker* of gross national product: consumers, government, and business itself.* Since output has final claimants other than consumers, we can obviously have a flow of purchasing power that does not enter consumers' or factors' hands.

The Completed Circuit of Demand

The realization that factor-owners do not get paid incomes equal to the total gross value of output brings us back to the central question of this chapter: can we be certain that we will be able to sell our GNP at its full cost? Has there surely been generated enough purchasing power to buy back our total output?

*We continue to forget about net exports until Chapter 9. We can think of them perfectly satisfactorily as a component of gross private investment.

We have thus far carefully analyzed and answered half the question. *We know that all costs will become incomes to factors or receipts of government agencies or of firms making replacement items.* To sum up again, factor costs become the incomes of workers, managements, owners of natural resources and of capital; and all these incomes together can be thought of as comprising the receipts of the household sector. Tax costs are paid to government agencies and become receipts of the government sector. Depreciation costs are initially accrued within business firms, and these accruals belong to the business sector. As long as worn-out capital is regularly replaced, these accruals will be matched by equivalent new receipts of firms that make capital goods.

THE CRUCIAL ROLE OF EXPENDITURES

What we have not yet established, however, is that these sector receipts will become sector expenditures. That is, we have not demonstrated that all households will now *spend* all their incomes on goods and services, or that government units will necessarily *spend* all their tax receipts on public goods and services, or that all firms will assuredly *spend* their depreciation accruals for new replacement equipment.

What happens if some receipts are not spent? The answer is of key importance in understanding the operation of the economy. A failure of the sectors to spend as much money as they have received means that some of the costs that have been laid out will *not* come back to the original entrepreneurs. As a result, they will suffer losses. If, for instance, our gross national product costs $1 trillion to produce but the various sectors spend only $900 billion in all, then some entrepreneurs will find themselves failing to sell all their output. Inventories of unsold goods will begin piling up, and businessmen will soon be worried about overproducing. The natural thing to do when you can't sell all your output is to stop making so much of it, so that businesses will begin cutting back on production. As they do so, they will also cut back on the number of people they employ. As a result, businessmen's costs will go down; but so will factor incomes, for we have seen that costs and incomes are but opposite sides of one coin. As incomes fall, the expenditures of the sectors might very well fall further, bringing about another twist in the spiral of recession.

This is not yet the place to go into the mechanics of such a downward spiral of business. But the point is clear. *A failure of the sectors to bring all their receipts back to the marketplace as demand can initiate profound economic problems. In the contrast between an unshakable equality of output and incomes on the one hand and the uncertain connection between incomes and expenditures on the other, we have come to grips with one of the most important problems in macroeconomics.*

THE CLOSED CIRCUIT

We shall have ample opportunity later to observe exactly what happens when incomes are not spent. Now let us be sure that we understand how the great circle of the economic flow is closed when the sectors *do* spend their receipts. Figure 5·3 shows how we can trace our three streams of dollars through the economy and how these flows suffice to buy back GNP for its total cost. For simplicity, we assume that there are no direct taxes.

We can trace the flow from left to right. We begin on the left with the bar representing the total cost of our freshly produced GNP. As we know, this cost consists of all the factor costs of all the firms and government units in the nation, all the indirect tax costs incurred during production, and all the depreciation charges made during production. The bar also shows us the amount of money demand our economy must generate in order to buy back its own output.

FROM GNP TO GNI

The next bars show us the transmutation of costs into sector receipts for householders, government units, and business firms (who retain their own depreciation accruals). This relationship between costs and sector receipts is one of *identity*—all costs *must* be receipts. Hence we use the sign ≡ to indicate that this is a relation of identities—of definitional differences only. If we use GNI to stand for gross national income (the gross incomes of all the sectors), then:

$$GNP \equiv GNI$$

That is an identity to be remembered—and *understood!*

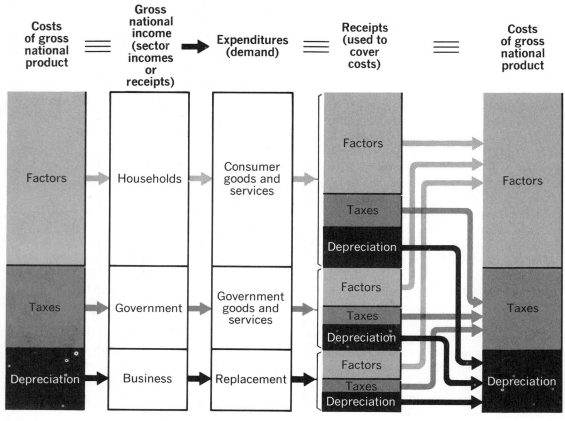

FIGURE 5 · 3
The circular flow, view III

INCOMES AND EXPENDITURES

Thereafter we notice the crucial link. We assume that each sector dutifully spends all its receipts, as it is supposed to. Our household sector buys the kinds of goods and services householders do in fact buy—consumption goods and services. Our government sector buys government goods and services, and our business sector buys replacement investment. This time we use an arrow (→) because this is emphatically *not* a relationship of identity. Our sectors may not spend all their income. Later we will see what happens if they don't.

Now note the next bar. Here we see what happens to these expenditures when they are received by the firms that make consumer goods or by the firms or individuals who make goods and services bought by governments or by the manufacturers of capital equipment. Each of these recipients will use the money he has received to cover factor payments, taxes, and depreciation for his own business. (What we show in our diagram are not these costs for each and every firm but the aggregate costs for all firms selling to each sector.)*

We are almost done. It remains only to aggregate the sector costs; that is, to add up all the factor costs, all the taxes, and all the depreciation accruals of *all* firms and government agencies—to reproduce a bar just like the one we started with. A circle of production has been completed. Firms and government units have received back, on the marketplace, a sum just large enough to cover their initial costs, including their profits for risk. The stage is set for another round of production, similar to the last.

GNP as a Sum of Costs and a Sum of Expenditures

Our bar graph also enables us to examine again the concept of gross national product, for now we can see that GNP can be looked at in one of two ways. We can think of measuring a year's gross national product as a *sum of all the costs incurred to make a year's output:* factor costs, indirect taxes, and depreciation. Or we can think of measuring the same GNP as the *sum of the expenditures that bought this output;* that is, consumption expenditure, government expenditure, and gross private investment expenditure. Since the final output is one and the same, we can see that the two methods of computing its value must also be the same.

TWO WAYS OF MEASURING GNP

An illustration may make it easier to grasp this identity of the two ways of measuring GNP. Suppose once again that we picture the

*Recall that for ease of exposition we are treating government agencies like firms and therefore show them as taxpayers.

economy as a gigantic factory from which the flow of production emerges onto a shipping platform, each item tagged with its selling price. There the items are examined by two clerks. One of them notes down in his book the selling price of each item and then analyzes that price into its cost (as income) components; factor cost (including profit), indirect taxes, and depreciation. The second clerk keeps a similar book in which each item's selling price is also entered, but his job is to note which sector—consumer, government, business investment, or export—is its buyer. Clearly, at the end of the year, the two clerks must show the same value of total output. But whereas the books of the first will show that total value separated into various costs, the books of the second will show it analyzed by its "customers"; that is, by the expenditures of the various sectors.

But wait! Suppose that an item comes onto the shipping platform without an order waiting for it! Would that not make the sum of costs larger than the sum of expenditures?

The answer will give us our final insight into the necessary equality of the two measures of GNP. For what happens to an item that is not bought by one of the sectors? It will be sent by the shipping clerk into inventory *where it will count as part of the business investment of the economy!* Do not forget that increases in inventory are treated as investment because they are a part of output that has not been consumed. In this case it is a very unwelcome kind of investment; and if it continues, it will shortly lead to changes in the production of the firm. Such dynamic changes will soon lie at the very center of our attention. In the meantime, however, *the fact that unbought goods are counted as investment*—as if they were "bought" by the firm that produced but cannot sell them—establishes the absolute identity of GNP measured as a sum of costs or as a sum of expenditures.

GNP AND GNI

To express the equality with the conciseness and clarity of mathematics, we can write, as we know:

$$GNP \equiv GNI$$

We already know that:

$$GNP \equiv C + I + G + X$$

and

$$GNI \equiv F + T + D$$

where C, I, G, and X are the familiar categories of expenditure, and F, T, and D stand for factor costs (income to land, capital, and labor), indirect taxes, and depreciation. Therefore, we know that:

$$C + I + G + X \equiv F + T + D$$

It is important to remember that these are all accounting identities, true by definition. The *National Income and Product Accounts,* the official government accounts for the economy, are kept in such a manner as to make them true.* As the name implies, these accounts are kept in two sets of "books," one on the products produced in the economy and one on the costs of production, which we know to be identical with the incomes generated in the economy. Since both sets of accounts are measuring the same output, the two totals must be equal.

NNP AND NATIONAL INCOME

It is now easy to understand the meaning of two other measures of output. One of these is called *net national product* (NNP). As the name indicates, it is exactly equal to the gross national product minus depreciation. GNP is

*There is a special supplement on these accounts at the end of this chapter.

used much more than NNP, since the actual measures of depreciation are very unreliable. The other measure, national income, we have already met. It is *GNP minus both depreciation and indirect taxes.* This makes it equal to the sum of factor costs only. Figure 5·4 should make this relationship clear. The aim of this last measure is to identify the net income that actually reaches the hands of factors of production. Consequently, the measure is sometimes called the *national income at factor cost.*

THE CIRCULAR FLOW

The "self-reproducing" model economy we have now sketched out is obviously still very far from reality. Nevertheless, the particular kind of unreality that we have deliberately constructed serves a highly useful purpose. An economy that regularly and dependably buys back everything it produces gives us a kind of bench mark from which to begin our subsequent investigations. We call such an economy, whose internal relationships we have outlined, an economy in *stationary equilibrium,* and we denote the changeless flow of costs into business receipts, and receipts back into costs, a *circular flow.*

We shall return many times to the model of a circular flow economy for insights into a more complex and dynamic system. Hence it is well that we summarize briefly two of the salient characteristics of such a system.

1. A circular flow economy will never experience a "recession."

Year in and year out, its total output will remain unchanged. Indeed, the very concept of a circular flow is useful in showing us that an economic system can maintain a given level of activity *indefinitely,* so long as all the sectors convert all their receipts into expenditures.

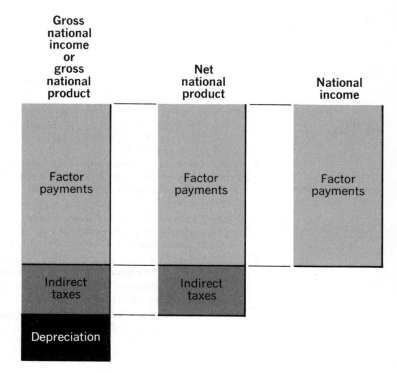

FIGURE 5 · 4
GNP, NNP, and NI

2. A circular flow economy also will never know a "boom."

That is, it will not grow, and its standard of living will remain unchanged. That standard of living may be high or low, for we could have a circular flow economy of poverty or of abundance. But in either state, changelessness will be its essence.

THE GREAT PUZZLE

What we have demonstrated in this chapter is an exceedingly important idea. There *can* always be enough purchasing power generated by the process of output to buy back that output.

Yet we all know, from our most casual acquaintance with economics, that in fact there is not always enough purchasing power

around, or that on occasions there is too much purchasing power. With too little, we have slumps and recessions; with too much, booms and inflation.

Hence the circular flow sets the stage for the next step in our study of macroeconomics. If there *can be* the right amount of purchasing power generated, why isn't there? Or to put the question more perplexingly: if there *can be* enough purchasing power to buy *any* size output, small or large, what determines how large purchasing power will actually be, and therefore how large output will actually be?

These questions point the way for the next stage of our investigation. We must study the workings of demand much more realistically than heretofore, by removing some of the assumptions that were necessary to create a model of a circular flow system.

KEY WORDS

CENTRAL CONCEPTS

Output and demand

1. A great *circle of payments and receipts constantly renews the demand* that keeps the economy going. Income is pumped out to the participants in the production process, who then spend their incomes to buy the output they have helped to make, thereby returning money to the firms that again pump it out.

Model

2. We seek to elucidate this circle by constructing a *model*—an economy stripped of everything that is not essential to the process we seek to understand. Our model simplifies and therefore highlights the relationships that underlie the macroeconomic process.

Costs

3. We use our model to show *how an economy can in fact buy back all of its own output*—how enough demand can be created to keep the economy going. To do so, we must show that *every item of cost to business firms can become demand* for them on the marketplace.

Factor payments

4. The first item of costs is *factor payments* (wages, rent, profits, interest). These payments for factor services are *the source of household income*. In turn, households can spend their incomes for *consumption goods*.

Indirect taxes

5. *Indirect taxes* are costs paid by firms to government agencies. In turn, these agencies spend their tax receipts for *government purchases*.

(Note that direct taxes—income taxes—are not a cost of production, but a levy imposed on factors after they have been paid.)

Direct taxes

6. *Depreciation costs* are costs incurred by *businesses* for the wear and tear of capital. They are accrued by business firms, who, in turn, are able to use them to purchase *replacement investment*.

7. *Materials costs* are payments to other firms. Ultimately, they can all be broken down into factor costs, indirect tax costs, and depreciation costs.

Depreciation

8. *The total value of output (GNP) can be seen not only as a sum of expenditures on different kinds of output* ($C + I + G + X$), *but as a sum of costs* ($F + T + D$), or gross incomes incurred in making this output. This gives us the important identity:

Material costs

$$\text{GNP} \equiv \text{GNI}$$

GNP ≡ GNI

9. *All costs thus become sector receipts:* factor costs become household incomes; indirect tax costs become government receipts; depreciation costs become business receipts. In turn, *these sector receipts can be returned to the market as new expenditures* (demand).

10. This gives us *three streams of cost—income—expenditure (demand)*:

Sector receipts

       Cost   Income   Expenditure

1. Factor costs→Households→Consumer goods
                (Direct taxes)

Three streams of GNP

2. Indirect taxes→Government agencies→Government goods
                (Direct taxes)

3. Depreciation→Business firms→Replacement investment

Expenditure

11. *The key linkage is that between receipts and expenditure. All costs must become receipts. But not all receipts need necessarily be spent.*

12. When all receipts are spent, then we have a perfect *circular flow*. In such a situation, the economy generates an unchanging flow of demand and therefore experiences neither boom, recession, nor growth.

Circular flow

QUESTIONS

1. How can a model elucidate reality when it is deliberately stripped of the very things that make reality interesting?

2. Why do we need a model to show that an economy can buy back its own production?

3. What are factor costs? What kinds of factor costs are there? To what sector do factor costs go?

4. What are direct taxes? What are indirect taxes? Which are considered part of production costs? Why?

5. To whom are materials costs paid? Why are they not part of the sum total of costs in GNP?

6. What is depreciation? Why is it a part of costs? Who receives the payments or accruals made for depreciation purposes?

7. Show in a carefully drawn diagram how costs become income or receipts of the different sectors.

8. Show in a second diagram how the incomes of the various sectors can become expenditures.

9. Why is the link between expenditure and receipt different from that between receipt and expenditure?

10. What is meant by a circular flow economy? Why does such an economy have neither growth nor fluctuation?

11. Explain the two different ways of looking at GNP and write the simple formula for each. Why is GNP the same thing as GNI?

12. Can we have demand without expenditure?

Supplement on the National Income and Product Accounts

The official accounts of the U.S. economy, the National Income and Product Accounts, illustrate all of the strengths and weaknesses of economic statistics. These statistics are published every quarter, but in the July issue of the *Survey of Current Business* (a publication of the U.S. Department of Commerce) a detailed set of accounts is given for the previous year. We will examine only the most basic tables. The official accounts present thousands of different numbers in dozens of formats as different ways of examining the economy. Any good economist should become familiar with these tables.

As we know, there are two prime ways of viewing the economy in the circular flow. One can look at costs (or *incomes*) or at *outputs*. Table 5·2 presents broad categories of each of these accounts. To avoid the confusion of calling the same number two different things—the gross national product and the gross national income or costs—the National Income and Product Accounts do not use the term gross national income, but refer to the sum of both columns as the gross national product.

Many of the terms in the table are now familiar to us. But let us examine a few that need special attention.

First, note (on the output side) that *change in inventories*, not inventories, enters the GNP. Since GNP measures goods and services produced during a given year, it takes into account goods that have been made and put into inventory only during that year. Goods held over in inventory from last year do not count.

What happens, then, if we sell goods out of last year's inventory and do not replace them? From the point of view of overall output, this is exactly the same as if a business firm did not replace its worn-out capital. By convention, we count this diminution in the level of our capital

TABLE 5 · 2
The National Income and Product Accounts: 1973

Output		Income	
Personal consumption expenditures	804.0	1. Compensation of employees	785.2
Durable goods	130.8	2. Proprietors income	84.2
Nondurable goods	335.9	3. Rental income	25.1
Services	337.3	4. Corporate profits and inventory valuation	
Gross private domestic investment	202.1	adjustment	109.4
Nonresidential structures and		5. Net interest	50.4
equipment	136.2	6. National income	1054.3
Residential structures	58.0	7. Indirect business taxes and nontax liability	117.8
Change in inventories	8.0	8. Business transfer payments	4.9
Net exports of goods and services	5.8	9. Statistical discrepancy	2.9
Exports	102.0	10. Minus: subsidies less current surplus of	
Imports	96.2	government enterprises	0.4
Government purchases	277.1	11. Net national product	1179.5
Federal	106.6	12. Capital consumption allowances	109.6
defense	73.9	13. Gross national (income) product	1289.1
nondefense	32.7		
State and local	170.5		
Gross national product	1289.1		

stock as a fall in the total value of output. Hence, the item "change in inventories" is the only item on the product side of GNP that can have a negative value. We cannot produce less than zero consumers goods or government output, but we can produce less goods for inventories than we need to maintain their levels.

The first strange term on the income side is the *inventory valuation adjustment* (no. 4 on the list). Remember than the GNP accounts attempt to measure incomes that are produced this year. If a corporation made a good last year but did not sell it, it will add that good to its inventories. If the good is actually sold this year when prices and costs have risen, measured corporate profits will be higher than they would have been if the good had been produced in the year in which it was sold. The good is sold for this year's higher prices, but the cost of making it is last year's lower cost. As a result, measured profits are higher because of production undertaken in the past. If we are trying to measure the profits that are produced this year, we must subtract these extra profits; and that is what the "valuation adjustment" attempts to do. (If prices and costs were falling, we would make a similar adjustment to increase this year's true profits.)

Indirect business taxes (no. 7) are already known to us. They are the sales and excise taxes (gas taxes, liquor taxes, etc.) that are assessed on the value of some products. *Nontax liabilities* (no. 7) refer to the public fees (licences, etc.) that are collected from businesses. *Business transfer payments* (no. 8) are corporate gifts to nonprofit institutions, consumer bad debts, and a few other minor payments.

For the moment, let's skip the statistical discrepancy and move on to *subsidies less current surplus of government enterprises* (no. 10). This entry refers to the profits and losses of TVA, state liquor stores, and other such government businesses. When the government loses money on one of its enterprises, these losses must be subtracted from the other income flows, because a loss means that incomes have been paid out, but no corresponding product has been produced.* If the losses were not subtracted, the gross national

product would not equal the gross national income.

This loss is an example of a true but misleading number. The loss occurs because some activities that the ordinary individual would not consider a business are counted as a business. The agriculture support programs of the federal government are such a "business." When the government pays the farmer $2.00 for a bushel of corn and then sells it for $1.50, it incurs a loss. The purpose is to raise farm incomes through subsidies, but this shows up in the GNP accounts as though it were an accidental loss. Most government businesses that are designed to make money do in fact make money.

Subtracting subsidies less surpluses is just a convention. One could just as easily add surpluses less subsidies. In the former case you are subtracting a positive number; in the latter case you are adding a negative number.

Depreciation Charges in the National Income and Product Accounts

The charges for *capital consumption allowances* (no. 12) illustrate the care that must be used in interpreting any economic statistics. Real economic depreciation is a measure of how fast capital is wearing out, but depreciation charges are also very important in determining the profits on which taxes are levied. Depreciation charges are subtracted from gross corporate income to obtain taxable profits. Income taxes are levied only on profits, not upon depreciation charges.

Since World War II the federal government has repeatedly lowered business income taxes by raising the allowable depreciation charges, thereby lowering taxable profits. While the statutory corporate profit tax rate has remained constant at approximately 50 percent, the effective tax rate (tax collections as a percent of gross corporate income) has fallen from 39 percent in 1953 to 27 percent in 1973, because allowable depreciation has grown so rapidly.

Tax allowances for depreciation are now so large that they are far above real economic depreciation. Yet the GNP accounts use the tax laws rather than actual studies of real depreciation to estimate depreciation charges in the National Ac-

---

*If a private business loses money, this shows up in negative corporate profits or proprietor's income. Thus, this is really a government counterpart to these private income categories.

counts. Why? There is a law stating that the U.S. Treasury must adjust depreciation charges (which enter into the calculation of taxable profits) to reflect real economic depreciation. To have the U.S. Department of Commerce use different estimates of real economic depreciation would be to accuse the U.S. Treasury of illegal actions. As a result, the two must use identical measures of depreciation—those allowed by the tax code, and not necessarily those called for by economic analysis. The net national product is consequently not a very accurate measure of what it is intended to measure—the output of goods and services that can be used after restoring our national capital to its previous level.

Now for the *statistical discrepancy* (no. 9). As we have seen, theoretically the gross national product must equal the gross national income. In practice, however, if you gave one group of statisticians the task of estimating the gross national product and another the task of estimating the gross national income, they would not come up with identical numbers. Why? Each side of the accounts is subject to measurement errors, and there is no reason why the errors should be identical. The statistical discrepancy is an estimate of these errors. Since the GNP and the GNI must be equal, we add a term (positive or negative) to the income side of the accounts to make them equal. The statistical discrepancy is simply the number that will make the final sum of both sides of the accounts the same.

Production of GNP

We have examined only the most basic table of GNP; and as we have said, there are dozens more. One of them is worth looking at. It shows who *produces* GNP, rather than who buys it or who earns it.

TABLE 5 · 3
Production of GNP, 1973

Private gross national product	1141.6
Business	1090.9
Farm	47.7
Nonfarm	1043.2
Households and institutions	41.1
Rest of the world	9.6
Gross government product	147.5

NOTE: Institutions are nonprofit private institutions such as universities and hospitals. They are added together with households, since neither attempts to earn profits. The *household* production of GNP includes the services of domestic servants and others.

Notice also that in this table, consumption and investment disappear, since all sectors—farms, households, governments, etc.—both consume and invest.

Many other tables are to be found in the Department of Commerce publications, including tables that show in much finer detail the large figures that appear on these tables. For anyone doing research on the activity of the economy, the annual July issue of the *Survey of Current Business* is indispensable. But before using these tables, one must understand the problems and pitfalls we have discussed in this introduction to the U.S. Income and Product Accounts.

Saving and
Investment

LET US RETURN FOR A MOMENT to our original perspective, an aerial view of the economic flow. We will remember that we could see the workings of the economy as an interaction between the factors of production and their environment, culminating in a stream of production—some private, some public—that was used in part for consumption and in part for the replacement or the further building up of capital. In our model of a circular flow economy we saw how such an economy can be self-sustaining and self-renewing, as each round of disbursements by employers found its way into a stream of purchasing power just large enough to justify the continuation of the given scale of output.

The Meaning of Saving

Yet we all know that such a circular flow is a highly unreal depiction of the world. In-

deed, it omits the most important dynamic factor of real economic life—the steady accumulation of new capital (and the qualitative change in the nature of the capital due to technology) that characterizes a *growing* economy. What we must now investigate is the process by which society adds each year to its stock of real wealth—and the effect of this process on the circuit of production and purchasing.

We begin by making sure that we understand a key word in this dynamic analysis—*saving*. We have come across saving many times by now in this book, and so we should be ready for a final mastery of this centrally important economic term. In Chapter 1, "Wealth and Output," we spoke of saving in *real* terms as the act by which society relinquished resources that might have been used for consumption, thereby making them available for the capital-building stream of output. Now we must translate that underlying real meaning of saving into terms corresponding with the buying and selling, paying and receiving discussed in the preceding chapter.

What is saving in these terms? It is very simply *not spending all or part of income for consumption goods or services.** It should be very clear then why saving is such a key term. In our discussion of the circular flow, it became apparent that expenditure was the critical link in the steady operation of the economy. If saving is not-spending, then it would seem that saving could be the cause of just that kind of downward spiral of which we caught a glimpse in our preceding chapter.

And yet this clearly is not the whole story. We also know that the act of investing—of spending money to direct factors into the production of capital goods—requires an act of saving; that is, of not using that same money to direct those factors instead into the production of consumers goods. *Hence, saving is clearly necessary for the process of investment.* Now, how can one and the same act be necessary for economic expansion and a threat to its stability? This is a problem that will occupy us during much of the coming chapters.

GROSS VS. NET SAVING

It will help us understand the problem if we again have recourse to the now familiar diagram of the circular flow. But this time we must introduce into it the crucial new fact of net saving. Note *net* saving. Quite unnoticed, we have already encountered saving in our circular flow. In our model economy, when business made expenditures for the replacement of capital, it used money that *could* have been paid in dividends to stockholders or in additional compensation to employees. Before a replacement expenditure was made, someone had to decide not to allocate that money for dividends or bonuses. Thus, there is a flow of saving—that is, of nonconsumption—even in the circular flow.

But this saving is not *net* saving. Like the regular flow of replacement investment itself, the flow of saving that finances this replacement serves only to maintain the existing level of capital wealth, not to increase it. Hence, just as with investment, we reserve the term *net saving* for saving that makes possible a rise in the total of our capital assets.

Gross and net saving are thus easy to define. *By gross saving we mean all saving, both for replacement and for expansion of our capital assets, exactly like gross investment. By net saving, we mean any saving that makes possible an increase in the stock of capital, again exactly as in the definition of net investment.*

We have already seen that an economy can maintain a circular flow when it saves only as much as is needed to maintain its capital. But now suppose that it saves more than that, as is shown in Fig. 6·1. Here householders save a portion of their incomes, over and above the amount saved by business to insure the maintenance of its assets.*

---

*Note "for consumption goods or services." Purchasing stocks or bonds or life insurance is also an act of saving, even though you must spend money to acquire these items. What you acquire, however, are assets, not consumption goods and services. Some acts of spending are difficult to classify. Is a college education, for instance, a consumption good or an investment? As we know, it is probably better thought of as an investment, even though in the statistics of GNP it is treated as consumption.

*Figure 6·1 represents all net saving as occurring in households, but it should be emphasized that a large fraction of this household savings actually takes place in corporations. When a corporation saves money, it is retaining earnings in the name of its owners—individuals who belong to households. Corporate saving can be thought of as household saving, since it ultimately belongs to households, but it is not directly under the control of households in the same sense that personal savings is under their control. We will discuss corporate saving in a later chapter.

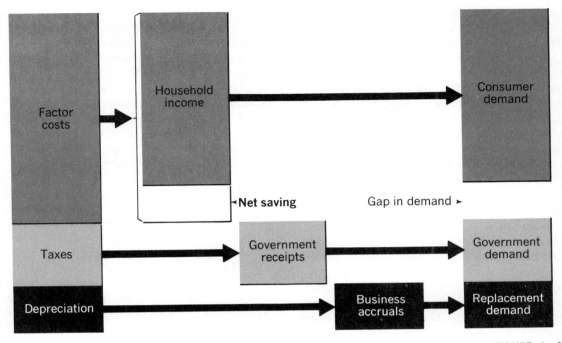

FIGURE 6 · 1
The demand gap

THE DEMAND GAP

What we see is precisely what we would expect. *There is a gap in demand introduced by the deficiency of consumer spending.* This means that the total receipts of employers who make consumer goods will be less than the total amounts they laid out. It begins to look as if we were approaching the cause of economic recession and unemployment.

Yet, whereas we have introduced net saving, we have forgotten about its counterpart, net investment. Cannot the investment activity of a growing economy in some way close the demand gap?

THE DILEMMA OF SAVING

This is indeed, as we shall soon see, the way out of the dilemma. But before we trace the way investment compensates for saving, let us draw some important conclusions from the analysis we have made up to this point.

1. Any act of saving, in and by itself, creates a gap in demand, a shortage of spending. Unless this gap is closed, there will be trouble in the economic system, for employers will not be getting back as receipts all the sums they laid out.

2. If the gap is caused by saving that is implicit in depreciation, it can be closed by replacement expenditures. But if it is caused by net saving, over and above the flow needed to maintain the stock of capital, it will require net investment to be closed.

3. The presence of a demand gap forces us to make a choice. If we want a dynamic, investing economy, we will have to be prepared to cope with the problems that net saving raises. If we want to avoid these problems, we can close the gap by urging consumers or corporations not to save. Then we would have a dependable circular flow, but we would no longer enjoy economic growth.

The Offset to Savings

How, then, shall we manage to make our way out of the dilemma of saving? The previous diagram makes clear what must be done. If a gap in demand is due to the savings of households, then *that gap must be closed by the expanded spending of some other sector.* There are only two other such sectors: government or business. Thus in some fashion or other, the savings of one sector must be "offset" by the increased activity of another.

But how is this offset to take place? How are the resources that are relinquished by consumers to be made available to entrepreneurs in the business sector or to government officials? In a market economy there is only one way that resources or factors not being used in one place can be used in another. Someone must be willing and able to hire them.

Whether or not government and business *are* willing to employ the factors that are not needed in the consumer goods sector is a very critical matter, soon to command much of our attention. But suppose that they are willing. How will they be able to do so? How can they get the necessary funds to expand their activity?

INCREASING EXPENDITURE

There are six principal methods of accomplishing this essential increase in expenditure.

1. The business sector can increase its expenditures by *borrowing* the savings of the public through the sale of new corporate bonds.

2. The government sector can increase its expenditures by *borrowing* savings from the other sectors through the sale of new government bonds.

3. The business sector can increase its expenditures by attracting household savings into partnerships, new stock, or other *ownership or equity.*

4. Both business and government sectors can increase expenditures by *borrowing* additional funds from commercial banks.*

5. The government sector can increase its expenditures by *taxing* the other sectors

6. Both business and government sectors can increase their expenditures by drawing on *accumulated past savings,* such as unexpended profits or tax receipts from previous years.

The first four methods above have one attribute that calls them especially to our attention. They give rise to *claims* that reveal from whom the funds have been obtained and to whom they have been made available, as well as on what terms. Bonds, corporate or government, show that savings have been borrowed from individuals or banks or firms by business and government units. Shares of stock reveal that savings have been obtained on an equity (ownership) basis, as do new partnership agreements. Borrowing from banks gives rise to loans that also represent the claims of one part of the community against another.

We can note a few additional points about claims, now that we see how many of them arise in the economy. First, many household savings are first put into banks and insurance companies—so-called financial intermediaries—so that the transfer of funds from households to business or government may go through several stages; e.g., from household to insurance company and then from insurance company to corporation.

Second, not *all* claims involve the offsetting of savings of one sector by expenditures of another. Many claims, once they have arisen, are traded back and forth and bought and sold, as is the case with most stocks and bonds. These purchases and sales involve the *transfer of existing claims,* not the creation of new claims.

---

*Actually, they are borrowing from the public through the means of banks. We shall learn about this in Chapter 13.

Finally, not every new claim necessarily involves the creation of an asset. If A borrows $5 from B, bets it on the races, and gives B his note, there has been an increase in claims, but no new asset has been brought into being to match it.

PUBLIC AND PRIVATE CLAIMS

Now let us look at Fig. 6·2. This time we show what happens when savings are made available to the business sector by direct borrowing from households. Note the claim (or equity) that arises.

If the government were doing the borrowing, rather than the business sector, the diagram would look like Fig. 6·3, p. 86. Notice that the claim is now a government bond.

We have not looked at a diagram showing business or government borrowing its funds from the banking system. (This process will be better understood when we take up the problem of money and banking, in Chapter 13.) The basic concept, however, although more complex, is much the same as above.

COMPLETED ACT OF OFFSETTING SAVINGS

There remains only a last step, which must now be fully anticipated. We have seen how it is possible to offset the savings in one

FIGURE 6 · 2
"Transfer" of savings to business

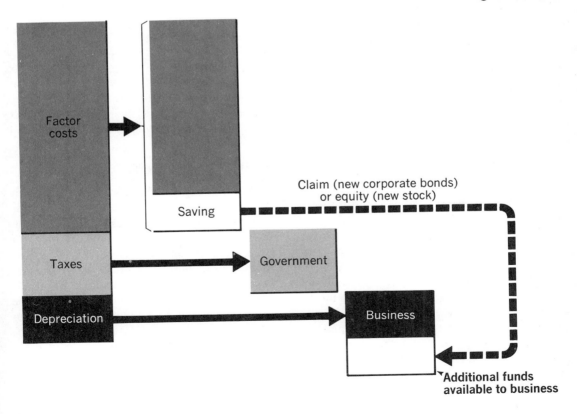

Factor costs

Saving

Claim (new corporate bonds) or equity (new stock)

Taxes

Government

Depreciation

Business

Additional funds available to business

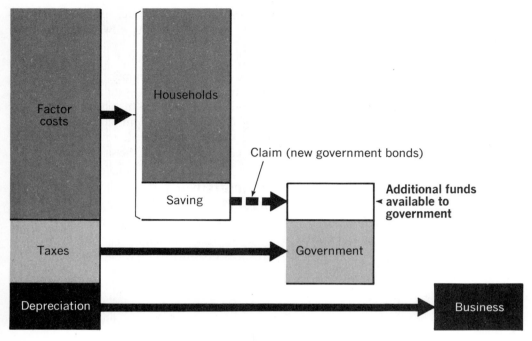

FIGURE 6·3
"Transfer" of savings to government

sector, where they were going to cause an expenditure gap, by increasing the funds available to another sector. It remains only to *spend* those additional funds in the form of additional investment or, in the case of the government, for additional public goods and services. The two completed expenditure circuits now appear in Fig. 6·4.

While Fig. 6·4 is drawn so that the new investment demand or new government demand is exactly equal to net saving, it is important to understand that there is nothing in the economic system guaranteeing that these demands will exactly equal net saving. The desire for new investment or new government goods and services may be either higher or lower than new saving. The need to regulate these new demands so that they will equal net savings is an important objective of *fiscal*

and monetary policies, a problem we will study later.

INTERSECTORAL OFFSETS

We shall not investigate further at this point the differences between increased public spending and increased business investment. What we must heed is the crucial point at issue: *if saving in any one sector is to be offset, some other sector (or sectors) must spend more than its income. A gap in demand due to insufficient expenditure in one sector can be compensated only by an increase in demand—that is, in expenditure—of another.*

Once this simple but fundamental point is clearly understood, much of the mystery of macroeconomics disappears, for we can then begin to see that an economy in move-

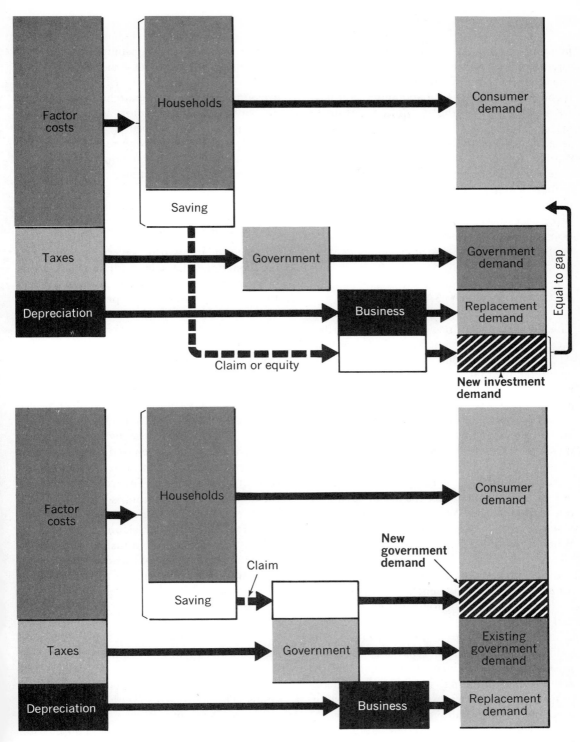

FIGURE 6 · 4
Two ways of closing the demand gap

ment, as contrasted with one in a stationary circular flow, is one in which sectors must *cooperate* to maintain the closed circuit of income and output. In a dynamic economy, we no longer enjoy the steady translation of incomes into expenditure which, as we have seen, is the key to an uninterrupted flow of output. Rather, we are faced with the presence of net saving and the possibility of a gap in final demand. Difficult though the ensuing problems are, let us not forget that net saving is the necessary condition for the accumulation of capital. *The price of economic growth, in other words, is the risk of economic decline.*

REAL AND MONEY SAVING

This central importance of saving in a growing economy will become a familiar problem. At this juncture, where we have first encountered the difficulties it can pose, we must be certain that we understand two different aspects that saving assumes.

One aspect, noticed in our initial overview of the economy, is the decision to relinquish *resources* that can be redeployed into capital-building. This is the real significance of saving. But this "real" aspect of saving is not the way we encounter the act of saving in our ordinary lives. We think of saving as a *monetary* phenomenon, not a "real" one. When we save, we are conscious of not using all our incomes for consumption, but we scarcely, if ever, think of releasing resources for alternative employments.

There is a reason for this dichotomy of real and money saving. In our society, with its extraordinary degree of specialization, the individuals or institutions that do the actual saving are not ordinarily those that do the actual capital-building. In a simple society, this dichotomy between saving and investing need not, and usually does not, occur. A farmer who decides to build new capital—for example, to build a barn—is very much

aware of giving up a consumption activity—the raising of food—in order to carry out his investment. So is an artisan who stops weaving clothing to repair his loom. Where the saver and the investor are one and the same person, there need be no "financial" saving, and the underlying real phenomenon of saving as the diversion of activity from consumption to investment is immediately apparent.

SAVERS AND INVESTORS

In the modern world, savers and investors are sometimes the same individual or group—as in the case of a business management that spends profits on new productive capacity rather than on higher executive salaries. More often, however, savers are not investors. Certainly householders, though very important savers, do not personally decide and direct the process of capital formation in the nation. Furthermore, the men and materials that households voluntarily relinquish by not using all their incomes to buy consumers goods have to be physically transferred to different industries, often to different occupations and locations, in order to carry out their investment tasks. This requires funds in the hands of the investors, so that they can tempt resources from one use to another.

Hence we need an elaborate system for directly or indirectly "transferring" money saving into the hands of those who will be in a position to employ factors for capital construction purposes. Nevertheless, underlying this complex mechanism for transferring purchasing power remains the same simple purpose that we initially witnessed. Resources that have been relinquished from the production of consumption goods or services are now employed in the production of capital goods. Thus, *saving and investing are essentially real phenomena,* even though it may take a great deal of financial manipulation to bring them about.

A final important point. *The fact that the decisions to save and the decisions to invest are lodged in different individuals or groups alerts us to a basic reason why the savings-investment process may not always work smoothly.* Savers may choose to consume less than their total incomes at times when investors have no interest in expanding their capital assets. Alternatively, business firms may wish to form new capital when savers are interested in spending money only on themselves. This separation of decision-making can give rise to situations in which savings are not offset by investment or in which investment plans race out ahead of savings capabilities. In our next chapters we will be investigating what happens in these cases.

Transfer Payments and Profits

We have talked about the transfer of purchasing power from savers to investors, but we have not yet mentioned another kind of transfer, also of great importance in the overall operation of the economy. This is the transfer of incomes from sector to sector (and sometimes within sectors).

TRANSFERS

As we already know, income transfers (called *transfer payments*) are a very useful and important means of reallocating purchasing power in society. Through transfer payments, members of the community who do not participate in production are given an opportunity to enjoy incomes that would otherwise not be available to them. Thus Social Security transfer payments make it possible for the old or the handicapped to be given an "income" of their own (not, to be sure, a currently *earned* income), or unemployment benefits give purchasing power to those who cannot get it through employment.

Not all transfers are in the nature of welfare payments, however. The distribution of money *within* a household is a transfer payment. So is the payment of interest on the national debt.* So is the grant of a subsidy to a private enterprise, such as an airline, or of a scholarship to a college student. Any income payment that is not earned by selling one's productive services on the market falls in the transfer category.

It may help to understand this process if we visualize it in our flow diagram. Figure 6·5, p. 90, shows two kinds of transfers. The upper one, from government to the household sector, shows a typical transfer of incomes, such as veterans' pensions or Social Security; the transfer below it reflects the flow of income that might be illustrated by a payment to agriculture for crop support. Transfers *within* sectors, such as household allowances, are not shown in the diagram.

One thing we may well note about transfers is that they can only *rearrange* the incomes created in the production process; they cannot increase those incomes. Income, as we learned in the last chapter, is inextricably tied to output—indeed, income is only the financial counterpart of output.

Transfer payments, on the other hand, are a way of arranging individual claims to production in some fashion that strikes the community as fairer or more efficient or more decorous than the way the market process allocates them through the production process. As such, transfer payments are an indispensable and often invaluable agency of social policy. But it is important to understand that no amount of transfers can, in itself, increase the total that is to be shared. That can happen only by raising output itself.

---

*As we know, the payment of interest on corporate debt is not considered a transfer payment, but a payment to a factor of production. Actually, much government interest should also be thought of as a factor payment (for the loan of capital for purposes of public output); but by convention, all government interest is classified as a transfer payment.

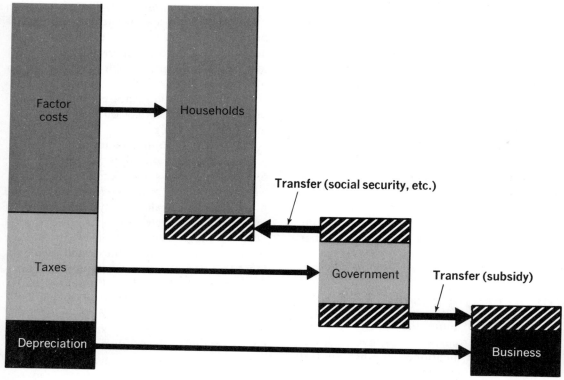

FIGURE 6 · 5
Transfer payments

TRANSFER PAYMENTS AND TAXES

We have mentioned, but only in passing, another means of transferring purchasing power from one sector to another: taxation. Heretofore, however, we have often spoken as though all government tax receipts were derived from indirect taxes that were added onto the cost of production.

In fact, this is not the only source of government revenue. Indirect taxes are an important part of state and local revenues, but they are only a minor part of federal tax receipts. Most federal taxes are levied on the incomes of the factors of production or on the profits of businesses after the other factors have been paid.

Once again it is worth remembering that the government taxes consumers (and businesses) because it is in the nature of much government output that it cannot be *sold.* Taxes are the way we are billed for our share —rightly or wrongly figured—of government production that has been collectively decided upon. As we can now see, taxes—both on business and on the household sector—also finance many transfer payments. That is, the government intervenes in the distribution process to make it conform to our politically expressed social purposes, taking away some incomes from certain individuals and groups, and providing incomes to others. Figure 6·6 shows what this looks like in the flow of GNP. (Note that the business sector is drawn with profits, as our next section will explain.)

As we can see, the exchanges of income between the household and the government sectors can be very complex. Income can flow from households to government units via taxation, and return to the household sector via transfer payments; and the same two-way flows can take place between government and business.

PROFITS AND DEMAND

The last diagram has already introduced a new element of reality in our discussion. Taxes on business *income* presuppose that businesses make *profits*. Let us see how these profits fit into the savings-investment process.

During our discussion of the circular flow, we spoke of profits as a special kind of factor cost—a payment to the factor *capital*. Now we can think of profits not merely as a factor cost (although there is always a certain element of risk-remuneration in profits), but as a return to especially efficient or forward-thinking firms who have used the investment process to introduce new products or processes ahead of the run of their industries. We also know that profits accrue to powerful firms who exact a semimonopolistic return from their customers.

FIGURE 6 · 6
Transfers and income taxes

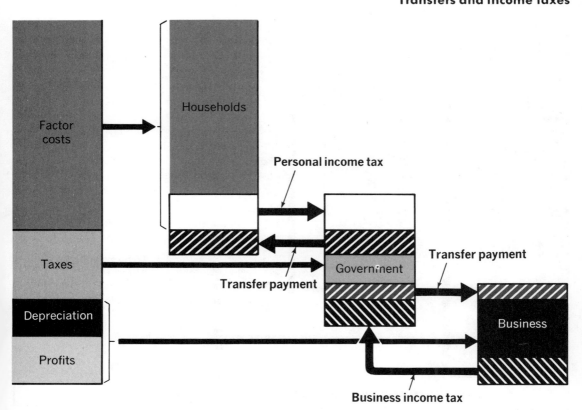

What matters in our analysis at this stage is not the precise explanation we give to the origin of profits, but a precise explanation of their role in maintaining a "closed-circuit" economy in which all costs are returned to the marketplace as demand. A commonly heard diagnosis for economic maladies is that profits are at the root of the matter, in that they cause a "withdrawal" of spending power or income from the community. If profits are "hoarded," or kept unspent, this can be true. In fact, however, profits are usually spent in three ways. They may be

1. Distributed as income to the household sector in the form of dividends or profit shares, to become part of household spending

2. Spent by business firms for new plant and equipment

3. Taxed by the government and spent in the public sector

All three methods of offsetting profits appear in Fig. 6·7.

Thus, we can see that profits need not constitute a withdrawal from the income stream. Indeed, unless profits are adequate, businesses will very likely not invest enough to offset the savings of the household sector. They may, in fact, even fail to make normal replacement expenditures, aggravating the demand gap still further in this way.

Thus the existence of profits, far from being deflationary—that is, far from causing a fall in income—is, in fact, essential for the

FIGURE 6 · 7
Profits in the circular flow

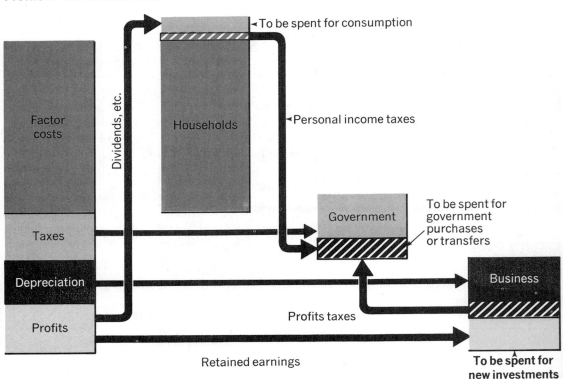

maintenance of a given level of income or for an advance to a higher level. Nonetheless, there is a germ of truth in the contentions of those who have maintained that profits can cause an insufficiency of purchasing power. *For unless profits are returned to the flow of purchasing power as dividends that are spent by their recipients or as new capital expenditures made by business or as taxes that lead to additional public spending, there will be a gap in the community's demand.* Thus we can think of profits just as we think of saving— an indispensable source of economic growth or a potential source of economic decline.

SAVING, INVESTMENT, AND GROWTH

We are almost ready to leave our analysis of the circle of production and income and to proceed to a much closer study of the individual dynamic elements that create and close demand gaps. Before we do, however, it is well that we take note of one last fact of the greatest importance. In offsetting the savings of any sector by investment, we have closed the production and income circuit, much as in the stationary circular flow, but there is one crucial difference from the circular flow. Now we have closed the flow by diverting savings into the creation of *additional* capital. Unlike the stationary circular flow where the handing around of incomes did no more than to maintain unchanged the original configuration of the system, in our new dynamic saving-and-investing model *each closing of the circuit results in a quantitative change— the addition of a new "layer" of capital.*

Hence, more and more physical wealth is being added to our system; and thinking back to our first impressions of the interaction of wealth and population, we would expect more and more productiveness from our human factors. With complications that we shall have to deal with in due course, *growth* has entered our economic model.

KEY WORDS

Saving

Demand gap

Inter-sectoral cooperation

CENTRAL CONCEPTS

1. The critical element missing from the concept of the circular flow is *saving.* The key question is how an economy can buy back all its output when some of its receipts are saved rather than returned to the market through expenditure.

2. Saving poses a dilemma. On one hand, it breaks the circular flow and creates a *demand gap.* On the other hand, if there is *no saving,* there can be *no investment.*

3. The answer to the dilemma is that *saving,* although essential for growth, *must be offset by additional expenditure.* This means that another sector must spend more than its income.

4. In six main ways, a sector can spend more than its income:
   • The *business sector can borrow* from the household sector.
   • The *government sector can borrow* from the household sector.
   • The *business sector* can attract household savings into *equities.*
   • Business and government can borrow from the *commercial banks.*
   • Governments can *tax* other sectors.
   • Business and government can spend *past savings.*

Real saving

5. Although saving involves money, it is essentially a "real" process (as is investment). That is, its real meaning is that resources are released from consumption. The acts of releasing resources (saving) and the acts of employing them (investment) are usually performed by different groups in modern society.

Transfer payments

6. *Transfer payments*, from one sector to another or within one sector, play an important part in *redistributing* income, but do not increase the total GNP.

7. Profits can be returned to the expenditure flow by being: (1) paid out as dividends, etc., to the household sector, where they can be used for consumption; (2) spent by business firms for new investment; or (3) taxed by the government and spent by it.

Profits and expenditure

8. Saving thus requires investment to assure that all payments will be returned to the market as demand. Note, however, that the process of *investment adds to capital* and thereby increases productivity. Saving and investment are therefore an integral part of the *process of growth*.

Growth

QUESTIONS

1. What do we mean by a demand gap? Show diagrammatically.

2. How is a demand gap filled by business investment? Show diagrammatically.

3. Why is saving indispensable for growth?

4. Can we have planned business investment without saving? Saving without planned business investment?

5. Draw carefully a diagram that shows how savings can be offset by government spending.

6. How is it possible for a sector to spend more than its income? How does it get the additional money?

7. What is a transfer payment? Draw diagrams of transfers from government to consumers, from government to business. Is charity a transfer? Is a lottery?

8. Diagram the three ways in which profits can be returned to the expenditure flow. What happens if they are not?

9. Why is a problem presented by the fact that those who make the decision to invest are not the same people?

10. In what way is a stationary circular flow economy different from an economy that saves and invests?

Consumption Demand

With a basic understanding of the crucial role of expenditure and of the complex relationship of saving and investment behind us, we are in a position to look more deeply into the question of the determination of gross national product. For what we have discovered heretofore is only the *mechanism* by which a market economy can sustain or fail to sustain a given level of output through a circuit of expenditure and receipt. Now we must try to discover the *forces* that dynamize the system, creating or closing gaps between income and outgo. What causes a demand for the goods and services measured in the GNP? Let us begin to answer that question by examining the flow of demand most familiar to us—consumption.

The Household Sector

Largest and in many respects most important of all the sectors in the economy is that of the nation's households—that is, its families and single-dwelling individuals (the two categories together called consumer units) considered as receivers of income and transfer payments or as savers and spenders of money for consumption.

How big is this sector? In 1973 it comprised some fifty-one million families and some fourteen million independent individuals who collectively gathered in $1,025 billion in income and spent $828 billion.* As Fig.

*The Department of Commerce has recently redefined some categories of the national income accounts, and the word *consumption* today applies, strictly speaking, only to personal expenditures for goods and services. Included in total consumer spending, however, are sizeable amounts for interest (mainly on installment loans) and for remittances abroad, neither of which sums are included in the amount for goods and services. The proper nomenclature for the total of consumer spending (goods and services plus interest and remittances) is now *personal outlays*. We shall, however, continue to use the simpler term, *consumption*, although our figures will be those for personal outlays.

Note, also, that the compilation of these figures is a time-consuming process in which earlier estimates are frequently subject to revision. Hence, figures for the components of consumption or, for that matter, for almost all magnitudes in the economic process are apt to vary slightly in successive printed statistics until, eventually, the "final" figures are arrived at. Note our caution about preliminary data in Chapter 18, p. 284.

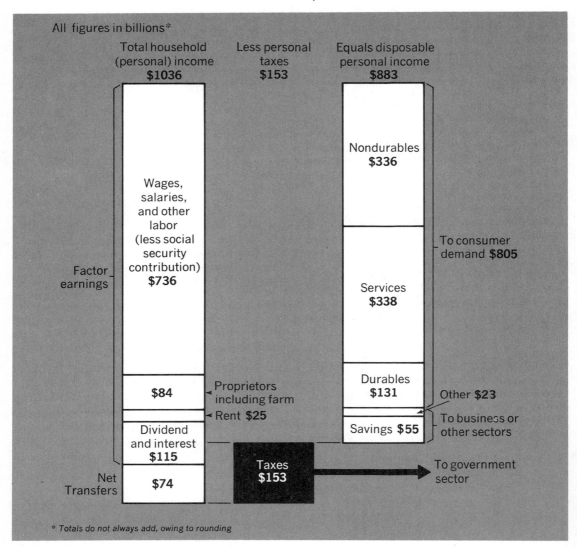

FIGURE 7 · 1
Consumption sector 1973

7·1 shows, the great bulk of receipts was from factor earnings, and transfer payments played only a relatively small role. As we can also see, we must subtract personal tax payments from household income (or *personal income* as it is officially designated) before we get *disposable personal income*—income actually available for spending. It is from disposable personal income that the crucial choice is made to spend or save.

Much of this chapter will focus on that choice.

SUBCOMPONENTS OF CONSUMPTION

Finally we note that consumer spending itself divides into three main streams. The largest of these is for *nondurable* goods, such as food and clothing or other items whose economic life is (or is assumed to be) short. Second largest is an assortment of expenditures we call consumer *services,* comprising things such as rent, doctors' or lawyers' or barbers' ministrations, theater or movie admissions, bus or taxi or plane transportation, and other purchases that are not a physical good but work performed by someone or some equipment. Last is a substream of expenditure for consumer *durable* goods, which, as the name suggests, include items such as cars or household appliances whose economic life is considerably greater than that of most nondurables. We can think of these goods as comprising consumers' physical capital.

There are complicated patterns and interrelations among these three major streams of consumer spending. As we would expect, consumer spending for durables is extremely volatile. In bad times, such as 1933, it has sunk to less than 8 percent of all consumer outlays; in the peak of good times in the early 1970s, it came to nearly double that. Meanwhile, outlays for services have been a steadily swelling area for consumer spending in the postwar economy. As a consequence of the growth of consumer buying of durables and of services, the relative share of the consumer dollar going to "soft goods" has been slowly declining. It is interesting to note, for example, that between 1960 and 1972 consumer spending for food and tobacco fell from 30 percent of all consumption to 22 percent, and that expenditures for apparel fell from 12 percent to 10 percent. Conversely, consumer spending on recreation and foreign travel and remittances climbed from 6 percent to more than 7 percent.

CONSUMPTION AND GNP

These internal dynamics of consumption are of the greatest interest to someone who seeks to project consumer spending patterns into the future—perhaps as an aid to merchandis-ing. But here we are interested in the larger phenomenon of the relationship of consumption as a whole to the flow of gross national product.

Figure 7·2 shows us this historic relationship since 1929. Certain things stand out.

1. Consumption spending is by far the largest category of spending in GNP.

Total consumer expenditures—for durable goods such as automobiles or washing machines, for nondurables like food or clothing, and for services such as recreation or medical care—account for approximately two-thirds of all the final buying in the economy.

2. Consumption is not only the biggest, but the most stable of all the streams of expenditure.

Consumption, as we have mentioned, is *the* essential economic activity. Unless there is a total breakdown in the social system, households will consume some bare minimum. Further, it is a fact of common experience that even in adverse circumstances, households seek to maintain their accustomed living standards. Thus consumption activities constitute a kind of floor for the level of overall economic activity. Investment and government spending, as we shall see, are capable of sudden reversals; but the streams of consumer spending tend to display a measure of stability over time.

3. Consumption is nonetheless capable of considerable fluctuation as a proportion of GNP.

Remembering our previous diagrams, we can see that this proportionate fluctuation must reflect changes in the relative importance of investment and government spending. And indeed this is the case. As investment spending fell in the Depression, consumption bulked relatively larger in GNP; as government spending increased during the war,

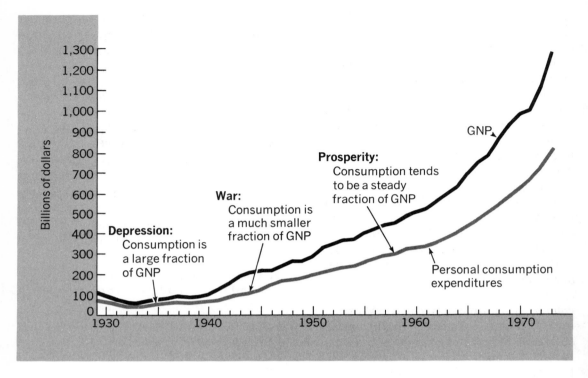

FIGURE 7 · 2
Consumption and GNP, current prices

consumption bulked relatively smaller. The changing *relative* size of consumption, in other words, reflects broad changes in *other* sectors rather than sharp changes in consuming habits.

4. Despite its importance, consumption alone will not "buy back" GNP.

It is well to recall that consumption, although the largest component of GNP, is still *only* two-thirds of GNP. Government buying and business buying of investment goods are essential if the income-expenditure circuit is to be closed. During our subsequent analysis it will help to remember that consumption expenditure by itself does not provide the only impetus of demand.

Saving in Historic Perspective

This first view of consumption activity sets the stage for our inquiry into the dynamic causes of fluctuations in GNP. We already know that the saving-investment relationship lies at the center of this problem, and that much saving arises from the household sector. Hence, let us see what we can learn about the saving process in historic perspective.

We begin with Fig. 7·3, showing the relationship of household saving to disposable income—that is, to household sector incomes after the payment of taxes.

What we see here are two interesting facts. First, during the bottom of the Great

Depression there were *no* savings in the household sector. In fact, under the duress of unemployment, millions of households were forced to *dissave*—to borrow or to draw on their old savings (hence the negative figure for the sector as a whole). By way of contrast, we notice the immense savings of the peak war years when consumers' goods were rationed and households were urged to save. Clearly, then, the *amount* of saving is capable of great fluctuation, falling to zero or pable of great fluctuation, falling to zero or to negative figures in periods of great economic distress and rising to as much as a quarter of income during periods of goods shortages.

In Fig. 7·4, p. 100, we are struck by another fact. However variable the amounts, the savings *ratio* shows a considerable stability in "normal" years. This steadiness is particularly noteworthy in the postwar period. From 1950 to the present, consumption has ranged between roughly 92 to 95 percent

FIGURE 7 · 3
Saving and disposable income

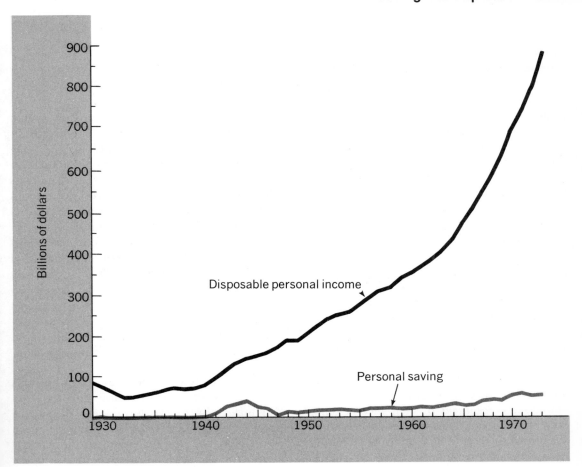

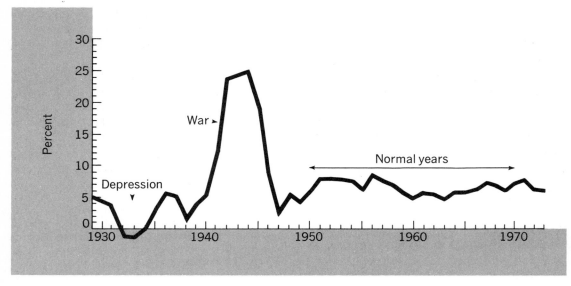

FIGURE 7 · 4
Saving as percent of disposable income

of disposable personal income—which is, of course, the same as saying that savings have ranged roughly between 8 percent and 5 percent. If we take the postwar period as a whole, *we can see that in an average year we have consumed a little more than 94 cents of each dollar of income and that this ratio has remained fairly constant even though our incomes have increased markedly.*

LONG-RUN SAVINGS BEHAVIOR

This stability of the long-run savings ratio is an interesting, important phenomenon and something of a puzzling one, for we might easily imagine that the savings ratio would rise over time. Statistical investigations of cross sections of the nation show that rich families tend to save not only larger amounts, but larger *percentages* of their income, than poor families do. Thus as the entire nation has grown richer and as families have moved from lower income brackets to higher ones, it

seems natural to suppose that they would also take on the higher savings characteristics that accompany upper incomes.

Were this so, the economy would face a very serious problem. In order to sustain its higher levels of aggregate income, it would have to invest an ever larger *proportion* of its income to offset its growing ratio of savings to income. As we shall see in our next chapter, investment is always a source of potential trouble because it is so much riskier than any other business function. If we had to keep on making proportionally larger investments each year to keep pace with our proportionally growing savings, we should live in an exceedingly vulnerable economic environment.

Fortunately, we are rescued from this dangerous situation, because our long-run savings ratio, as we have seen, displays a reassuring steadiness. In fact, there has been no significant upward trend in the savings ratio for the nation's households since the

SHORT-RUN VS. LONG-RUN SAVINGS BEHAVIOR

How do we reconcile the stability of the long-run savings ratio with the fact that statistical studies always reveal that rich families save a larger percentage of their incomes than do poor families? As the nation has moved, en masse, into higher income brackets, why has it not also saved proportionately more of its income?

The explanation for the long-run stability of savings behavior revolves around the importance of *relative* incomes, or "keeping up with the Joneses", in consumption decisions. If a family earned $11,000 in 1940, it was a wealthy family with an income far above the average. It could save a large fraction of its income and still have more than other families in the community had to spend on consumption. By 1973 the family with an $11,000 annual income was simply an average family. To keep up with consumption standards of other families in the community, it needed to spend a large fraction of its income. As a result, the savings rates for families with $11,000 gradually fell over time as the families changed from wealthy to average.

The same relative income effect is seen in the savings rates of black families. For any given income level, the average black family saves more than the average white family. Since black family incomes are lower than white family incomes, any given income has a higher relative position among blacks than it does among whites. To keep up with their peer group, whites must consequently spend more than blacks.

As a result of these and still other motivations, savings behavior in the long run differs considerably from that in the short run. Over the years, American households have shown a remarkable stability in their rate of overall savings. Its importance has already been mentioned. In a shorter period of time, however—over a few months or perhaps a year—households tend to save higher fractions of increases in their incomes than they do in the long run. The very great importance of this fact we shall subsequently note.

---

mid-1800s, and there may have been a slight downward trend.*

The Consumption-Income Relationship

What we have heretofore seen are some of the historical and empirical relationships of consumption and personal saving to income. We have taken the trouble to investigate these relationships in some detail, since they are among the most important causes of the gaps that have to be closed by investment. But the statistical facts in themselves are only a halfway stage in our macroeconomic investigation. Now we want to go beyond the facts to a generalized understanding of the behavior that gives rise to them. Thus our next task is to extract from the facts certain behavioral *relationships* that are sufficiently regular and dependable for us to build into a new dynamic model of the economy.

If we think back over the data we have examined, one primary conclusion comes to mind. This is the indisputable fact that the *amount* of saving generated by the household sector depends in the first instance upon the income enjoyed by the household sector. Despite the stability of the savings ratio, we have seen that the dollar volume of saving in the economy is susceptible to great variation, from negative amounts in the Great Depression to very large amounts in boom times.

*Economists maintain a certain tentativeness in their assertions about long-run trends, since the statistical foundation on which they are based is inevitably subject to some error and uncertainty.

Now we must see if we can find a systematic connection between the changing size of income and the changing size of saving.

PROPENSITY TO CONSUME

There is indeed such a relationship, lying at the heart of macroeconomic analysis. We call it the *consumption function* or, more formally, the *propensity to consume,* the name invented by John Maynard Keynes, the famous English economist who first formulated it in 1936.* What is this "propensity" to consume? It means that the relationship between consumption behavior and income is sufficiently dependable so that we can actually *predict* how much consumption (or how much saving) will be associated with a given level of income.

We base such predictions on a *schedule* that enables us to see the income-consumption relationship over a considerable range of variation. Table 7·1 is such a schedule, a purely hypothetical one, for us to examine.

TABLE 7 · 1
A Propensity to Consume Schedule

BILLIONS OF DOLLARS		
Income	Consumption	Savings
$100	$80	$20
110	87	23
120	92	28
130	95	35
140	97	43

One could imagine, of course, innumerable different consumption schedules; in one society a given income might be accompanied by a much higher propensity to consume (or propensity to save) than in another. But the

*More about Keynes in the box on p. 150. Note that his name is pronounced "Kanes," not "Keenes."

basic hypothesis of Keynes—a hypothesis amply confirmed by research—was that the consumption schedule in all modern industrial societies had a particular basic configuration, despite these variations. The propensity to consume, said Keynes, reflected the fact that on the average, men tended to increase their consumption as their incomes rose, but not by as much as their income increased. In other words, as the incomes of individuals rose, so did both their consumption *and their savings.*

Note that Keynes did not say that the proportion of saving rose. We have seen how involved is the dynamic determination of savings ratios. Keynes merely suggested that in the short run, the *amount* of saving would rise as income rose—or to put it conversely again, that families would not use *all* their increases in income for consumption purposes alone. It is well to remember that these conclusions hold in going down the schedule as well as up. Keynes' basic "law" implies that when there is a decrease in income, there will be some decrease in the *amount of saving,* or that a family will not absorb a fall in its income entirely by contracting its consumption.

What does the consumption schedule look like in the United States? We will come to that shortly. First, however, let us fill in our understanding of the terms we will need for our generalized study.

AVERAGE PROPENSITY TO CONSUME

The consumption schedule gives us two ways of measuring the fundamental economic relationship of income and saving. One way is simply to take any given level of income and to compute the percentage relation of consumption to that income. This gives us the *average propensity to consume.* In Table 7·2, using the same hypothetical schedule as before, we make this computation.

TABLE 7·2
Calculation of the Average Propensity to Consume

BILLIONS OF DOLLARS		Consumption divided by income (Average propensity to consume)
Income	Consumption	
$100	$80	.80
110	87	.79
120	92	.77
130	95	.73
140	97	.69

The average propensity to consume, in other words, tells us how a society at any given moment divides its total income between consumption and saving. It is thus a kind of measure of long-run savings behavior, for households divide their incomes between saving and consuming in ratios that reflect established habits and, as we have seen, do not ordinarily change rapidly.

MARGINAL PROPENSITY TO CONSUME

But we can also use our schedule to measure another very important aspect of saving behavior: the way households divide *increases*

(or decreases) in income between consumption and saving. This *marginal propensity to consume* is quite different from the average propensity to consume, as the figures in Table 7·3 (still from our original hypothetical schedule) demonstrate.

Note carefully that the last column in Table 7·3 is designed to show us something quite different from the last column of the previous table. Take a given income level—say $110 billion. In Table 7·2 the average propensity to consume for that income level is .79, meaning that we will actually spend on consumption 79 percent of our income of $110 billion. But the corresponding figure

TABLE 7·3
Calculation of the Marginal Propensity to Consume

BILLIONS OF DOLLARS			Change in consumption	Marginal propensity to consume = Change in consumption ÷ change in income
Income	Consumption	Change in income		
$100	$80	—	—	—
110	87	$10	$7	.70
120	92	10	5	.50
130	95	10	3	.30
140	97	10	2	.20

opposite $110 billion in the marginal propensity to consume table (7·3) is .70. This does *not* mean that out of our $110 billion income we somehow spend only 70 percent, instead of 79 percent, on consumption. It *does* mean that we spend on consumption only 70 percent *of the $10 billion increase* that lifted us from a previous income of $100 billion to the $110 billion level. The rest of that $10 billion increase we saved.

As we know, much of economics, in micro- as well as macroanalysis, is concerned with studying the effects of *changes* in economic life. It is precisely here that marginal concepts take on their importance. When we speak of the average propensity to consume, we relate all consumption and all income from the bottom up, so to speak, and thus we call attention to behavior covering a great variety of situations and conditions. But when we speak of the marginal propensity to consume, we are focusing only on our behavior toward *changes* in our incomes. Thus the marginal approach is invaluable, as we shall see, in dealing with the effects of short-run fluctuations in GNP.

A SCATTER DIAGRAM

The essentially simple idea of a systematic, behavioral relationship between income and consumption will play an extremely important part in the model of the economy we shall soon construct. But the relationships we have thus far defined are too vague to be of much use. We want to know if we can extract from the facts of experience not only a general dependence of consumption on income, but a *fairly precise method of determining exactly how much saving will be associated with a given amount of income.*

Here we reach a place where it will help us to use diagrams and simple equations rather than words alone. So let us begin by transferring our conception of a propensity

to consume schedule to a new kind of diagram directly showing the interrelation of income and consumption.

The *scatter diagram* (Fig. 7·5) shows precisely that. Along the vertical axis on the left we have marked off intervals to measure total consumer expenditure in billions of dollars; along the horizontal axis on the bottom we measure disposable personal income, also in billions of dollars. The dots tell us, for the years enumerated, how large consumption and income were. For instance, if we take the dot for 1966 and look directly below it to the horizontal axis, we can see that disposable personal income for that year was roughly $510 billion. The same dot measured against the vertical consumption axis tells us that consumption for 1966 was a little more than $475 billion. If we now divide the figure for consumption by that for income, we get a value of 93.1 percent for our propensity to consume. If we subtract that from 100, our propensity to save must have been 6.9 percent.*

Returning to the diagram itself, we notice that the black line which "fits" the trend of the dots does not go evenly from corner to corner. If it did, it would mean that each amount of income was matched by an *equal* amount of consumption—in other words, that there was no saving. Instead, the line leans slightly downward, indicating that as income goes higher, consumption also increases, but not by quite as much.

Does the chart also show us our marginal propensity to consume? Not really. As we know, our short-run savings propensities are higher than our long-run propensities. This chart shows our "settled" position, from

---

*It is difficult to read figures accurately from a graph. The actual values are: disposable income, $512 billion; consumption, $479 billion; average propensity to consume, 93.4 percent.
For more information on "fitting" a line to such a graph, see Chapter 18, section VII.

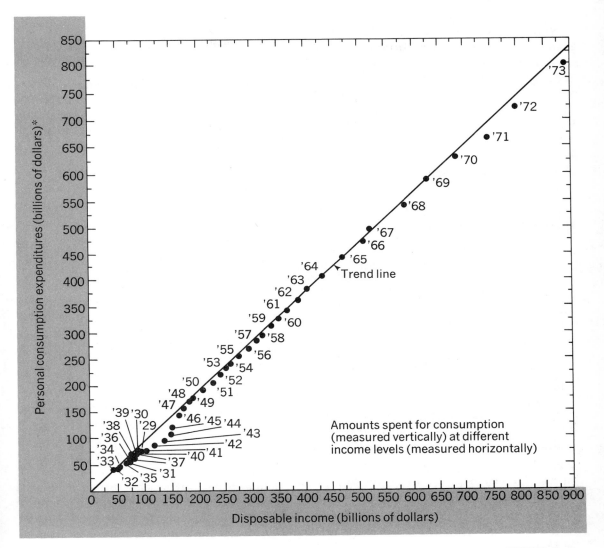

Amounts spent for consumption
(measured vertically) at different
income levels (measured horizontally)

FIGURE 7 · 5
United States' propensity to consume, 1929–1973

year to year, after the long-run, upward drift of spending has washed out our marginal (short-run) savings behavior.

Nevertheless, if we look at the movement from one dot to the next, we get some notion of the short-run forces at work. Dur-

ing the war years, for instance, as the result of a shortage of many consumer goods and a general exhortation to save, the average propensity to consume was unusually low. That is why the dots during those years form a bulge below the trend line. After the war, we can also see that the marginal propensity to consume must have been very high. As a matter of fact, for a few years, consumption actually rose faster than income, as people used their wartime savings to buy things that were unavailable during the war. Between 1946 and 1947, for example, disposable income rose by some $9.8 billion, but personal outlays rose by almost $18 billion! By 1950, however, the consumption-income relationship was back to virtually the same ratio as during the 1930s.

IN SIMPLE MATHEMATICS

There is another way of reducing to short-hand clarity the propensity to consume. For obviously, what we are looking for is a functional relationship between income (Y), the independent variable, and consumption (C), the dependent variable. In the mathematical language now familiar to us, we write

$$C = f(Y)$$

and we want to discover what f looks like.

Highly sophisticated and complex formulas have been tried to "fit" values of C and Y. Their economics and their mathematics both are beyond the scope of this book. But we can at least get a clearer idea of what it means to devise a *consumption function* by trying to make a very simple one ourselves. If we look at Fig. 7·5 on p. 106, we can see that during the Depression years, at very low levels of income, around $50 billion, consumption was just as large as income itself. (In some years it was actually bigger; as we have seen, there was net dissaving in 1933.) Hence, we might hypothesize that a consumption function for the United States might have a fixed value representing this "bottom," plus some regular fraction designating the amount of income that would be saved for all income over that amount.

A GENERALIZED CONSUMPTION FUNCTION

This is a very important hypothesis. It enables us to describe the consumption function as an amount that represents rock-bottom consumption, to which we add additional consumption spending as income rises. If a is the "bottom," and subsequent spending out of additional income is $b(Y)$, where b represents this spending "propensity," we can now write the consumption function as a whole as:

$$C = a + b(Y)$$

We have seen that a is $50 billion, and we know that our actual spending propensity, b, is about 94 percent. Therefore, we can get a *very rough* approximation of consumption by adding $50 billion to 94 percent of our disposable income over $50 billion. In 1973, for example, disposable income was $883 billion. If we add $50 billion to .94 (883 − 50), we get $833. Actual consumption in 1973 was $828 billion.*

Let the reader be warned, however, that devising a reliable consumption function is much more difficult than this simple formula would indicate. The process of translating economics into *econometrics*—that is, of finding ways to represent abstract theoretical relationships in terms of specific empirical relations—is a very difficult one. Nonetheless, even our simple example gives one an idea of what the economist and the econometrician hope to find: a precise way of expressing functional interrelations (like those between consumption and income), so that the relations will be useful in making predictions.

*Would you like to know a little more about the mathematics of the consumption function? Look at Chapter 18, Section V.

INDIVIDUAL VERSUS AGGREGATE CONSUMPTION

Here an important warning is in order. The consumption function should not be taken as a representation of individual consumption patterns. Individual preferences vary enormously, and a wide variety of random factors causes individuals to purchase different commodities at different times. But the task of predicting the consumption expenditures of a large group of people is much easier than the task of predicting the consumption of any individual in the group. The random factors that make individual predictions difficult average out in a large group. Some individuals will spend more than we would predict on the basis of their income, but others will spend less.

AGE

In addition to random disturbances, systematic factors other than incomes influence consumption. Age is a critical variable. When individuals marry and establish households of their own they are confronted with the need to acquire many consumer durables. As a result, young families are apt to have low or even negative savings rates—they consume more than they earn by using installment payments. When individuals reach middle age, they have already incurred those expenditures necessary to raise a family and are starting to think about retirement. Their consumption propensities fall, and their savings propensities rise.

If the age distribution of the population were changing rapidly, the marginal propensity to consume would not be as stable and constant as it is. Age can be ignored only in the aggregate, since the age distribution of the population does not change rapidly.

PASSIVITY OF CONSUMPTION

Throughout this chapter we have talked of the dynamics of consuming and saving. Now it is important that we recall the main conclusion of our analysis, *the essential passivity of consumption as an economic process.* Consumption spending, we will recall, is a function of income. This means it is a *dependent* variable in the economic process, a factor that is acted *on*, but that does not itself generate spontaneous action.

To be sure, it is well to qualify this assertion. We have earlier paid special attention to the long-term stability of the national savings ratio and pointed out that one cause of this stability was a general upward tendency of consumption, as families "learned" to spend their rising incomes. This dynamic, although slow-acting, behavioral trend has exerted a strong background force on the trend of the economy. Then, too, there have been occasions, the most famous being the years just following World War II, when consumption seemed to generate its own momentum and—as we have seen—raced out ahead of income. But this was a period when wants were intense, following wartime shortages, and when huge amounts of wartime savings were available to translate those wants into action. During the normal course of things, no matter how intense "wants" may be, consumers ordinarily lack the spendable cash to translate their desires into effective demand.

This highlights an extremely important point. Wants and appetites *alone* do not drive the economy upward; if they did, we should experience a more impelling demand in depressions, when people are hungry, than in booms, when they are well off. Hence the futility of those who urge the cure of depressions by suggesting that consumers should buy more! There is nothing consumers

CONSUMER CREDIT

What about consumer credit, someone will ask. Aren't many families in debt up to their ears? Doesn't the ability to buy "on time" enable consumers as a group to spend *more* than their incomes?

Consumer credit indeed enables families to spend a larger amount than they earn as incomes or receive as transfers, for short periods of time. Nonetheless, consumers do not use credit to spend more than their total receipts: *some* consumers do, but consumers as a group do not. We know this is true because the *value of all consumption spending includes purchases that are made on credit*, such as cars or many other kinds of items bought on household loans or on installment. But this total spending is still less than the total receipts of the consumer sector. Thus there is net household saving, even though purchases are made on credit.

Would there be more saving if there were no credit? In that situation, many families would put income aside until they had accumulated enough to buy cars, refrigerators, houses, and other big items. During the period that they were saving up to buy these goods, their savings rates would certainly be higher than if they had consumer credit at their disposal. But after they had bought their "lumpy" goods, their savings rates would again fall, perhaps below the level of a consumer credit economy, which tempts us to buy lumpy items and to perform our saving through installment payments.

As a result, we would expect to find high savings rates in an economy where desires for lumpy items were increasing but where consumer credit was not available. Economists cite this as one explanation of the fact that Japanese families have savings rates that are more than three times as high as American families, even though Japanese incomes are lower. In Japan you cannot "buy now, pay later"; so you save now and buy later.

would rather do than buy more, if only they could. Let us not forget, furthermore, that consumers are at all times being cajoled and exhorted to increase their expenditures by the multibillion dollar pressures exerted by the advertising industry.

The trouble is, however, that consumers cannot buy more unless they have more incomes to buy with. It is true, of course, that for short periods they can borrow or they may temporarily sharply reduce their rate of savings; but each household's borrowing capacity or accumulated savings are limited, so

that once these bursts are over, the steady habitual ways of saving and spending are apt to reassert themselves.

Thus it is clear that in considering the consumer sector we study a part of the economy that, however ultimately important, is not in itself the source of major changes in activity. Consumption mirrors and, as we shall see, can magnify disturbances elsewhere in the economy, but it does not initiate the greater part of our economic fortunes or misfortunes.

KEY WORDS

Consumption

Disposable income

CENTRAL CONCEPTS

1. Consumption is the largest source of economic activity, and accordingly the largest absolute source of demand within the economy. Nonetheless, *consumption alone will not create enough demand to buy all of the nation's output.*

2. Consumption in absolute amounts is capable of wide fluctuations, but *the relation of consumption to disposable income is relatively stable.*

<table>
<tr><td>

Consumption function

</td><td>

3. Over the long run (since the mid-1800s), *the fraction of disposable income that has been saved seems to have been more or less unchanged.* This has prevented the economy from facing the problem of a growing proportion of saving. In the short run, the ratio of saving to increases in income is apt to be higher than over the long run.

</td></tr>
<tr><td>

Schedule

</td><td>

4. We call the relation between saving and disposable income the *consumption function*. We can represent this function (relationship) in a *schedule* showing the division of disposable income, at different levels of income, between consumption and saving.

5. The consumption schedule shows that the *amount of consumption rises as income rises, but not by as much as income.* Therefore the amount of saving also rises as income rises.

</td></tr>
</table>

Consumption function

Schedule

Average propensity to to consume

Marginal propensity to consume

$C = a + b(Y)$
"Bottom"

3. Over the long run (since the mid-1800s), *the fraction of disposable income that has been saved seems to have been more or less unchanged.* This has prevented the economy from facing the problem of a growing proportion of saving. In the short run, the ratio of saving to increases in income is apt to be higher than over the long run.

4. We call the relation between saving and disposable income the *consumption function*. We can represent this function (relationship) in a *schedule* showing the division of disposable income, at different levels of income, between consumption and saving.

5. The consumption schedule shows that the *amount of consumption rises as income rises, but not by as much as income.* Therefore the amount of saving also rises as income rises.

6. From the consumption schedule we can derive two ratios. One shows us the relation between the *total income* and the *total consumption* of any period. We call this the *average propensity to consume*. The other shows us the relationship between the *change in income and the change in consumption* between two periods. This is called the *marginal propensity to consume*.

7. The average propensity to consume shows us how people behave with regard to consumption and saving over the *long run*. The marginal propensity to consume shows us how they behave over the *short run*.

8. Consumption is generally regarded as a *passive economic force*, rather than an initiating active one. It is acted on by changes in income. Thus we generalize the force of consumption by saying that it is a *function of income:* $C = a + b(Y)$, where a is the "bottom" and b is the marginal propensity to consume.

QUESTIONS

1. What are the main components of consumption? Why are some of these components more dynamic than others?

2. "The reason we have depressions is that consumption isn't big enough to buy the output of all our factories." What is wrong with this statement?

3. What do you think accounts for the relative stability of the savings ratio over the long run? Would you expect the savings ratio in the short run to be relatively stable? Why or why not?

4. What is meant by the consumption function? Could we also speak of a savings function? What would be the relation between the two?

5. Suppose that a given family had an income of $8,000 and saved $400. What would be its average propensity to consume? Could you tell from this information what its marginal propensity to consume was?

6. Suppose the same family now increased its income

to $9,000 and its saving to $500. What is its new average propensity to consume? Can you figure out the family's marginal propensity to consume?

7. Draw a scatter diagram to show the following:

Family income	Savings
$4,000	$ 0
5,000	50
6,000	150
7,000	300
8,000	500

From the figures above, calculate the average propensity to consume at each level of income. Can you calculate the marginal propensity to consume for each jump in income?

8. How do you read $S = f(Y)$? From what you know of the propensity to consume, how would you describe the relation of S to Y?

9. Why can't we cure depressions by urging people to go out and spend?

Investment Demand

IN STUDYING THE BEHAVIOR of the consumption sector, we have begun to understand how the demand for GNP arises. Now we must turn to a second source of demand—investment demand. This requires a shift in our vantage point. As experienced consumers, we know about consumption, but the activity of investing is foreign to most of us. Worse, we are apt to begin by confusing the meaning of investment, as a source of demand for GNP, with "investing" in the sense familiar to most of us when we think about buying stocks or bonds.

INVESTMENT: REAL AND FINANCIAL

We had best begin, then, by making certain that our vocabulary is correct. *Investing, or investment, as the economist uses the term in describing the demand for GNP, is an activity that uses the resources of the community to maintain or add to its stock of physical capital.*

Now this may or may not coincide with the purchase of a security. When we buy an ordinary stock or bond, we usually buy it from someone who has previously owned it, and therefore our personal act of "investment" becomes, in the economic view of things, merely a *transfer* of claims without any direct bearing on the creation of new wealth. A pays B cash and takes his General Output stock; B takes A's cash and doubtless uses it to buy stock from C; but the transactions between A and B and C in no way alter the actual amount of real capital in the economy. Only when we buy *newly issued* shares or bonds, and then only when their proceeds are directly allocated to new equipment or plant, does our act of personal financial investment result in the addition of wealth to the community. In that case, A buys his stock directly (or through an investment banker) from General Output itself, and not from B. A's cash can now be spent by General Output for new capital goods, as presumably it will be.

Thus, much of investment, as economists

see it, is a little-known form of activity for the majority of us. This is true not only because real investment is not the same as personal financial investment, but because the real investors of the nation usually act on behalf of an institution other than the familiar one of the household. The unit of behavior in the world of investment is typically the business *firm,* just as in the world of consumption it is the household. Boards of directors, chief executives, or small-business proprietors are the persons who decide whether or not to devote business cash to the construction of new facilities or to the addition of inventory; and this decision, as we shall see, is very

different in character and motivation from the decisions familiar to us as members of the household sector.

The Investment Sector in Profile

Before we begin an investigation into the dynamics of investment decisions, however, let us gain a quick acquaintance with the sector as a whole, much as we did with the consumption sector.

Figure 8·1 gives a first general impression of the investment sector in a recent year. Note that the main source of gross

FIGURE 8 · 1

Business sector 1973

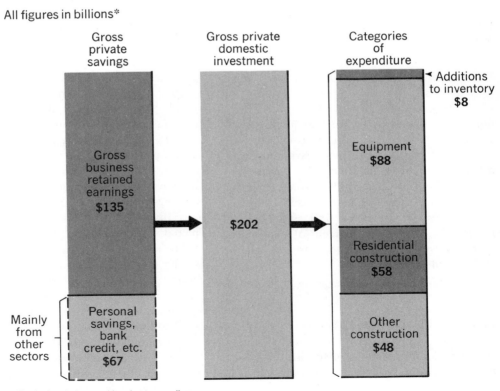

All figures in billions*

Gross private savings

Gross private domestic investment

Categories of expenditure

◄ Additions to inventory $8

Gross business retained earnings $135

$202

Equipment $88

Residential construction $58

Mainly from other sectors

Personal savings, bank credit, etc. $67

Other construction $48

* Totals do not always add, owing to rounding

private domestic investment expenditure is the retained earnings of business; that is, the expenditures come from depreciation accruals or from profits that have been kept in the business. However, as the next bar shows, gross investment *expenditures* are considerably larger than retained earnings. The difference represents funds that business obtains in several ways.

1. It may draw on cash (or securities) accumulated out of retained earnings or depreciation accruals of previous years.

2. It may obtain savings from the household sector by direct borrowing or by sale of new issues of shares of stock or indirectly via insurance companies or savings banks or pension funds, and so on.

3. It may borrow from commercial banks.

4. The difference also represents investment in housing, which is not typically financed by corporate earnings but by consumers, borrowing from banks.

The last two sources of funds we will not fully understand until we reach Chapter 13 when we study the money mechanism. But our chart enables us to see that most gross investment is financed by business itself from its *internal* sources—retained earnings plus depreciation accruals—and that external sources play only a secondary role. In particular, this is true of new stock issues, which, during most of the 1960s and early 1970s, raised only some 3 to 8 percent of the funds spent by the business sector for new plant and equipment.

CATEGORIES OF INVESTMENT

From the total funds at its disposal, the business sector now renews its worn-out capital and adds new capital. Let us say a word concerning some of the main categories of investment expenditure.

1. Inventories

At the top of the expenditure bar in Fig. 8·1, we note an item of $8.0 billion for *additions to inventory.* Note that this figure does not represent total inventories, but only *changes* in inventories, upwards or downwards. If there had been no change in inventory over the year, the item would have been zero, even if existing inventories were huge. Why? Because those huge inventories would have been included in the investment expenditure flow of *previous* years when they were built up.

Additions to inventories are capital, but they need not be additions to capital *goods.* Indeed, they are likely to include farm stocks, consumer goods, and other items of all kinds. Of course, these are goods held by business, and not by consumers. But that is the very point. We count inventory additions as net investment because they are output that has been produced but that has not been consumed. In another year, if these goods pass from the hands of business into consumers' hands, and inventories decline, we will have a negative figure for net inventory investment. This will mean, just as it appears, that we are consuming goods faster than we are producing them—that we are disinvesting.

Inventories are often visualized as completed TV sets sitting in some warehouse. While some inventories are completed goods sitting in storage, most are in the form of goods on display in stores, half-finished goods in the process of production, or raw materials to be used in production. When a steel company adds to its stock of iron ore, it is adding to its inventories.

Investments in inventory are particularly significant for one reason. Alone among the investment categories, inventories can be *rapidly* used up as well as increased. A positive figure for one year or even one calendar quarter can quickly turn into a negative figure the next. *This means that expenditures for inventory are usually the most volatile element of any in gross national product.* A glance at Fig. 8·2 shows a particularly dramatic instance of how rapidly inventory spending can change. In the second quarter of 1960, we were *disinvesting* in inventories at an annual rate of almost $5 billion. Two quarters later, we were building up inventories—*investing* in inventories—by roughly the same amount. Thus, within a span of six months, there was a swing of almost $10 billion in spending. Rapid inventory swings, although not quite of this magnitude, are by no means uncommon.

As we shall see more clearly later, this volatility of investment has much significance for business conditions. Note that while inventories are being built up, they serve as an offset to saving—that is, some of the resources released from consumption are used by business firms to build up stocks of inventory capital. But when inventories are being "worked off," we are actually making the demand gap bigger. As we would expect, this can give rise to serious economic troubles.

2. Equipment

The next item in the expenditure bar (Fig. 8·1) is more familiar: $88 billion for *equipment*. Here we find expenditures for goods of a varied sort—lathes, trucks, generators,

FIGURE 8 · 2
Inventory swings and GNP

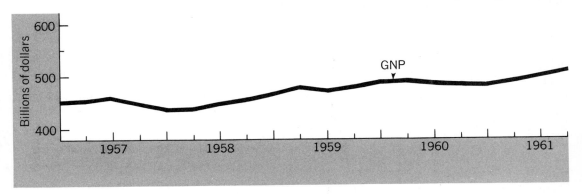

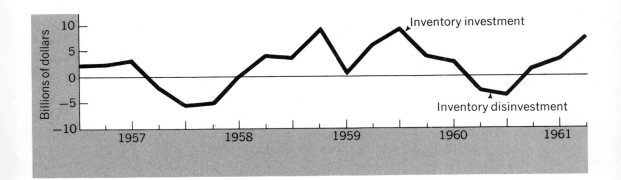

computers, office typewriters.* The total includes both *new equipment* and *replacement equipment,* and we need a word of caution here. Exactly what does it mean to "replace" a given item of equipment? Suppose we have a textile loom that cost $100,000 and that is now on its last legs. Is the loom "replaced" by spending another $100,000, regardless of what kind of machine the money will buy? What if loom prices have gone up and $100,000 no longer buys a loom of the same capacity? Or suppose that prices have remained steady but that owing to technological advance, $100,000 now buys a loom of double the old capacity.

From an economic perspective, *replacement is the dollar amount that would be necessary to buy the same productive capacity.* But this is an amount that is seldom known with great accuracy. It may not be possible to buy new equipment with exactly the same productive capacity as old equipment. Often businesses replace whole factories rather than individual pieces of equipment. These new factories are likely to have very different configurations of equipment as well as different productive capacities. Such problems make the definition of "replacement" an accountant's headache and an economist's nightmare. At the moment there isn't even a generally accepted estimate of replacement investment. We need not involve ourselves deeper in the question, but we should note the complexities introduced into a seemingly simple matter once we leave the changeless world of stationary flow and enter the world of invention and innovation.

3. Construction—residential

Our next section on the expenditure bar (Fig. 8·1) is total *residential construction.* Why do we include this $58 billion in the investment sector when most of it is repre-

sented by new houses that householders buy for their own use?

Part of the answer is that most houses are built by business firms, such as contractors and developers, who put up the houses *before* they are sold. Thus the original expenditures involved in building houses typically come from businessmen, not from households. Later, when the householder buys a house, he takes possession of an existing asset, and his expenditure does not pump new incomes into the economy but only repays the contractor who *did* contribute new incomes.

Actually, this is a somewhat arbitrary definition, since, after all, businessmen own *all* output before consumers buy it. However, another reason for considering residential construction as investment is that, unlike most "consumer goods," houses are typically maintained as if they were capital goods. Thus their durability also enters into their classification as investment goods.

Finally, we class housing as investment because residential purchases "behave" very much like other items of construction. Therefore it simplifies our understanding of the forces at work in the economy if we classify residential construction as an investment expenditure rather than as a consumer expenditure.

4. Other construction—plant

Last on the bar, $48 billion of *other construction* is largely made up of the "plant" in "plant and equipment"—factories and stores and private office buildings and warehouses. (It does not, however, include public construction such as roads, dams, harbors, or public buildings, all of which are picked up under government purchases.) It is interesting to note that the building of structures, as represented by the total of residential construction plus other private construction, accounts for over half of all investment expenditure, and this total would be further swelled

*But *not* typewriters bought by consumers. Thus the same good can be classified as a consumption item or an investment item, depending on the use to which it is put.

if public construction were included herein. This accords with the dominant role of structures in the panorama of national wealth we first encountered in Chapter 1. It tells us, too, that swings in construction expenditure can be a major lever for economic change.

Investment in Historic Perspective

With this introduction behind us, let us take a look at the flow of investment, not over a single year, but over many years.

In Fig. 8·3, several things spring to our notice. Clearly, investment demand is not nearly so smooth and unperturbed a flow of spending as consumption. Note that gross investment in the depths of the Depression virtually disappeared—that we almost failed to *maintain,* much less add to, our stock of wealth. (Net investment was, in fact, a negative figure for several years.) Note also investment was reduced during the war years as private capital formation was deliberately limited through government allocations.

Two important conclusions emerge from this examination of investment spending:

FIGURE 8 · 3
Gross private domestic investment, 1929–1973

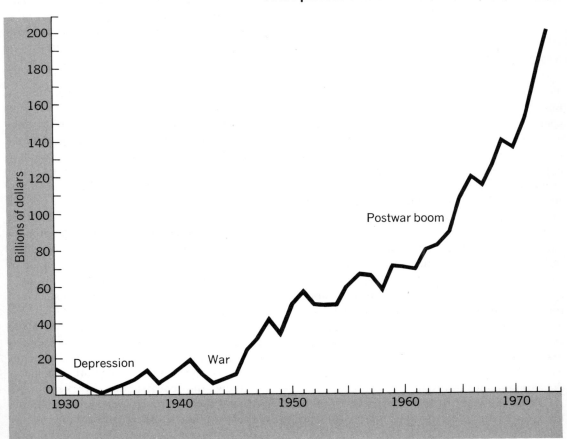

First, as we have already seen, investment spending contains a component—net additions to inventory—that is capable of drastic, sudden shifts. This accounts for much of the wavelike movement of the total flow of investment expenditure.

Second, investment spending as a whole is capable of more or less total collapses, of a severity and degree that are never to be found in consumption.

The prime example of such a collapse was, of course, the Great Depression. From 1929 to 1933, while consumption fell by 41 percent, investment fell by *91 percent,* as we can see in Fig. 8·3. Similarly, whereas consumption rose by a little more than half from 1933 to 1940, investment in the same period rose by *nine times.*

IMPORTANCE OF INVESTMENT

This potential for collapse or spectacular boom always makes investment a source of special concern in the economic picture. But even the tendency toward inventory fluctuations, or toward milder declines in other capital expenditures, is sufficient to identify investment as a prime source of economic instability. As we have said before, there is often a tendency among noneconomists to equate all buying in the economy with consumer buying. Let us never lose sight of the fact that the maintenance of, and addition to, capital is also a part of GNP spending and that a considerable part of the labor force depends for its livelihood on the making of investment goods. At the bottom of the Great Depression in 1933, it was estimated that one-third of total unemployment was directly associated with the shrinkage in the capital goods industry.

We shall want to look more closely into the reasons for the sensitivity of investment spending. But first a question must surely have occurred to the reader. For all its susceptibility to change, the investment sector is, after all, a fairly small sector. In 1973, total expenditures for gross private domestic investment came to only about one-seventh of GNP, and the normal year-to-year variation in investment spending in the 1960s and 1970s is only about 1 to 2 percent of GNP. To devote so much time to such small fluctuations seems a disproportionate emphasis. How could so small a tail as investment wag so large a dog as GNP?

The Multiplier

The answer lies in a relationship of economic activities known as the *multiplier.* The multiplier describes the fact that *additions to spending (or diminutions in spending) have an impact on income that is greater than the original increase or decrease in spending itself.* In other words, even small increments in spending can *multiply* their effects (whence the name).

It is not difficult to understand the general idea of the multiplier. Suppose that we have an island community whose economy is in a perfect circular flow, unchanging from year to year. Next, let us introduce the stimulus of a new investment expenditure in the form of a stranger who arrives from another island (with a supply of acceptable money) and who proceeds to build a house. This immediately increases the islanders' incomes. In our case, we will assume that the stranger spends $1,000 on wages for construction workers, and we will ignore all other expenditures he may make. (We also make the assumption that these workers were previously unemployed, so that the builder is not merely taking them from some other task.)

Now the construction workers, who have had their incomes increased by $1,000, are very unlikely to sit on this money. As we know from our study of the marginal pro-

INTENDED AND UNINTENDED

INVENTORY INVESTMENT

Changes in inventories reflect both the desires of firms and their planning errors. *Investment in inventories can therefore be intended or unintended.* If an automobile manufacturer expects to sell 1 million cars and is disappointed in this expectation, actual sales will lag behind expected sales. Since production was planned on the basis of expected sales, it will exceed actual sales until production can be readjusted to the new sales levels. Autos built but not sold will be added to inventories. In this case, inventories go up not because the firm wanted more inventories, but because it made a mistake.

If actual sales exceed expected sales, the reverse will happen. Inventories fall. But again, the firm did not lower inventories because lower inventories were more profitable, but by mistake. Low inventories can be extremely unprofitable. If certain models are not available or in limited supply, the auto maker will find that he is losing potential sales to a competitor that can give the consumer the kind of car he wants at the time he wants it.

These unintended changes in inventories enter into the statistics of GNP, just as do intended changes in inventories. But they obviously have very different significances regarding future economic behavior.

---

pensity to consume, they are apt to save some of the increase (and they may have to pay some to the government as income taxes), but the rest they will spend on additional consumption goods. Let us suppose that they save 10 percent and pay taxes of 20 percent on the $1,000 they get. They will then have $700 left over to spend for additional consumer goods and services.

But this is not an end to it. The sellers of these goods and services will now have received $700 over and above their former incomes, and they, too, will be certain to spend a considerable amount of their new income. If we assume that their family spending patterns (and their tax brackets) are the same as the construction workers, they will also spend 70 percent of their new incomes, or $490. And now the wheel takes another turn, as still *another* group receives new income and spends a fraction of it—in turn.

CONTINUING IMPACT OF RESPENDING

If the newcomer then departed as mysteriously as he came, we would have to describe the economic impact of his investment as constituting a single "bulge" of income that gradually disappeared. The bulge would consist of the original $1,000, the secondary $700, the tertiary $490, and so on. If everyone continued to spend 70 percent of his new income, after ten rounds all that would remain by way of new spending traceable to the original $1,000 would be about $38. Soon, the impact of the new investment on incomes would have virtually disappeared.

But now let us suppose that after our visitor builds his house and leaves, another visitor arrives to build another house. This time, in other words, we assume that the level of investment spending *continues* at the higher level to which it was raised by the first expenditure for a new house. We can see that the second house will set into motion precisely the same repercussive effects as did the first, and that the new series of respendings will be added to the dwindling echoes of the original injection of incomes.

In Fig. 8·4, we can trace this effect. The succession of colored bars at the bottom of the graph stands for the continuing injec-

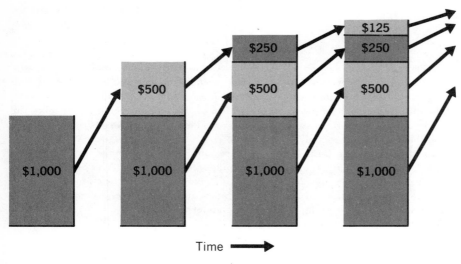

FIGURE 8 · 4
The multiplier

tions of $1,000 as new houses are steadily built. (Note that this means the level of new investment is only being maintained, not that it is rising.) Each of these colored bars now generates a series of secondary, tertiary, etc., bars that represent the respending of income after taxes and savings. In our example we

have assumed that the respending fraction is 50 percent.

Let us now examine the effects of investment spending in a generalized fashion, without paying attention to specific dollar amounts. In Fig. 8·5, we see the effects of a single, *once-and-for-all* investment expendi-

FIGURE 8 · 5
Once-over and continuing effects of investment

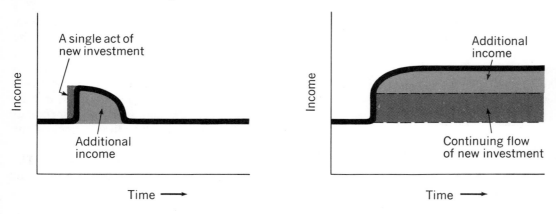

ture (the stranger who came and went), contrasted with the effects of a *continuing* stream of investment.

Our diagrams show us three important things:

1. A single burst of investment creates a bulge of incomes larger than the initial expenditure, but a bulge that disappears.

2. A continuing flow of investment creates a new higher permanent level of income, larger than the investment expenditures themselves.

3. A continuing flow of new investment creates a higher income level that gradually levels out.

the total addition to income due to the respending of that $1,000 is $3,000, we have a multiplier of 3; if the total addition is $2,000, the multiplier is 2.

What determines how large the multiplier will be? The answer depends entirely on our marginal consumption (or, if you will, our marginal saving) habits—that is, on how much we consume (or save) out of each dollar of additional income that comes to us. Let us follow two cases below. In the first, we will assume that each recipient spends only one-half of any new income that comes to him, saving the rest. In the second case, he spends three-quarters of it and saves one-quarter.

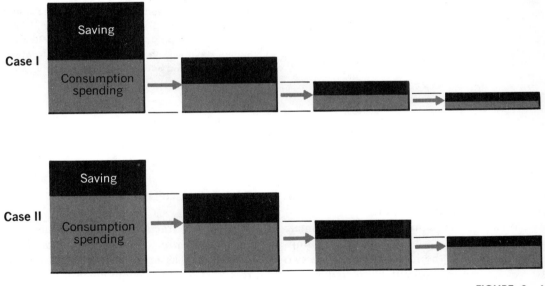

FIGURE 8·6
Comparison of two multipliers

MARGINAL PROPENSITY TO SAVE

We can understand now that *the multiplier is the numerical relation between the initial new investment and the total increase in income.* If the initial investment is $1,000 and

It is very clear that the amount of income that will be passed along from one receiver to the next will be much larger where the marginal propensity to consume is higher. In fact, we can see that the total amount of new incomes (total amount of boxes above)

MATHEMATICS FOR THE CURIOUS

How do we know that the multiplier will be 4, if the marginal propensity to save is ¼ ? Most of us "intuitively" see that the sum of respending hinges on the savings fraction, and we take on faith the simple formula that tells us how to calculate that sum by taking the reciprocal of the mps and multiplying it by the change in spending.

But some students may want to go beyond faith, to understanding. Here is a simple mathematical demonstration that the multiplier formula is "really" true.

What we are trying to get at, with the multiplier formula, is the *sum of a series*, in which an initial term is multiplied again and again by some number that is less than 1 (and greater than 0). Suppose the initial term is $10 and the number-less-than-one is .8. Then we want to know the sum of the following problem:

$$10 + .8(10) + .8[.8(10)]....$$

This is the same as if we wrote:

$$10 + .8(10) + .8^2(10) + .8^3(10) ... + ...8^n(10)$$

If we think of .8 as designating the marginal propensity to consume, we are looking for the sum of an initial new expenditure of $10, of which $8 will be spent in the first round (.8 × $10); $6.40 ($.8^2$ × $10) in the second round; $5.12 ($.8^3$ × $10) in the third, and so on. From the textbook, we "know" that this sum is found by taking the mps, which is .2, or $\frac{1}{5}$, and multiplying the original expenditure by its reciprocal. Thus, $10 × 5 = $50. Now let's prove it.

We can restate our multiplier series in simple algebra by calling the initial term a and the number-less-than-one (.8 above) b. Then the series looks like this:

$$a + b \cdot a + b^2 \cdot a ... + ...b^n \cdot a$$

where b^n stands for the fraction spent on the last (nth) round.

Suppose we call the sum of this series S. Now we are going to perform a truly magical (but perfectly legitimate) mathematical trick. We will first write the formula we have just described, and below it we will write the *same* formula, after we have multiplied both sides of the equation by b.

must be mathematically related to the proportion that is spent each time.

What is this relationship? The arithmetic is easier to figure if we use not the consumption fraction, but the *saving fraction* (the two are, of course, as intimately related as the first slice of cake and the remaining cake). If we use the saving fraction, the *sum of new incomes is obtained by taking the reciprocal of* (i.e., inverting, or turning upside down) *the fraction we save.* Thus, if we save ½ our income, the total amount of new incomes generated by respending will be ½ inverted, or 2—twice the original increase in income. If we save ¼, it will be the reciprocal of ¼ or 4 times the original change.

BASIC MULTIPLIER FORMULA

We call the fraction of new income that is saved the *marginal propensity to save* (often abbreviated as mps). As we have just seen, this fraction is the complement of an already familiar one, the marginal propensity to consume. If our marginal propensity to consume is 80 percent, our marginal propensity to save must be 20 percent; if our mpc is three-quarters, our mps must be one-quarter. In brief, mps + mpc ≡ 1.

Understanding the relationship between the marginal propensity to save and the size of the resulting respending fractions allows us to state a very simple (but very important)

$$S = a + b \cdot a + b^2 \cdot a \ldots + \ldots b^n a$$
$$b \cdot S = \quad b \cdot a + b^2 \cdot a \ldots + \ldots \quad b^{n+1} \cdot a$$

We have strung out the second equation so that terms such as $b \cdot a$ lie underneath their counterparts in the first equation.

Now we subtract the second equation from the first. All the terms that are under one another just disappear. This leaves us:

$$S - b \cdot S = a - b^{n+1} \cdot a$$

Next we factor out S on the left side, giving us $S(1 - b)$, and divide both sides by $(1 - b)$. The result:

$$S = \frac{a - b^{n+1} \cdot a}{(1 - b)}$$

We are almost at the end. Now we examine what happens as the exponent n approaches infinity. Remember that by definition b is a number less than 1, so that with each successive increase in the exponent, b becomes *smaller*. Thus we can assume that the final term approaches zero, as its exponent approaches infinity. That is to say, it "vanishes." This is very convenient because it leaves us with the much simpler formula:

$$S = \frac{a}{1 - b}$$

Do you see the connection with the multiplier? The term b was the fraction (.8) by which we constantly multiplied the initial sum ($10). *Thus this fraction was exactly like the marginal propensity to consume!* Therefore, $1 - b$ must be the difference between 1 and the mpc (or .2). We know this is the mps. Therefore we can write mps in place of $1 - b$; and while we are about it, we can write $10, or ΔI, or any other number in place of a.

Hence our formula becomes translated into economic terms and looks like this:

$$S = \frac{\Delta I}{\text{mps}}$$

The term S stood for the sum of the series. An economist will call it ΔY since this is the sum of the additional incomes generated by each round of spending.

ΔY is therefore $10 \div .2 (or $50). And that is why the formula below is *really* true.

formula for the multiplier:

change in income = multiplier × change in investment

Since we have just learned that the multiplier is determined by the reciprocal of the marginal propensity to save, we can write:

$$\text{multiplier} = \frac{1}{\text{mps}}$$

If we now use the symbols we are familiar with, plus a Greek letter Δ, delta, that means "change in," we can write the important economic relationship above as follows:

$$\Delta Y = \frac{1}{\text{mps}} \times \Delta I$$

Thus, if our mps is $1/4$ (meaning, let us not forget, that we save a quarter of increases in income and spend the rest), then an increase in investment of $1 billion will lead to a total increase in incomes of $4 billion

$$\$4 \text{ billion} = \frac{1}{1/4} \times \$1 \text{ billion}$$

Note that the multiplier is a complex or *double* fraction:

it is $\dfrac{1}{1/4}$ and *not* $\dfrac{1}{4}$.

If the mps is $\frac{1}{10}$, $1 billion gives rise to incomes of $10 billion; if the mps is 50 percent, the billion will multiply to $2 billion. And if mps is 1? This means that the entire increase in income is unspent, that our island construction workers tuck away (or find taxed away) their entire newly earned pay. In that case, the multiplier will be 1 also, and the impact of the new investment on the island economy will be no more than the $1,000 earned by the construction workers in the first place.

LEAKAGES

The importance of the size of the marginal savings ratio in determining the effect that additional investment will have on income is thus apparent. Now, however, we must pass from the simple example of our island economy to the more complex behavioral patterns and institutional arrangements of real life. The average propensity to save (the ratio of saving to disposable income) runs around 6 to 7 percent. In recent years, the *marginal* propensity to save (the ratio of additional saving to increases in income) figured over the period of a year has not departed very much from this figure. If this is the case, then, following our analysis, the multiplier would be very high. If mps were even as much as 10 percent of income, a change in investment of $1 billion would bring a $10 billion change in income. If mps were nearer 6 percent—the approximate level of the average propensity to save—a change of $1 billion would bring a swing of over $16 billion. Were this the case, the economy would be subject to the most violent disturbances whenever the level of spending shifted.

In fact, however, the impact of the multiplier is greatly reduced because the successive rounds of spending are damped by factors other than personal saving. One of them we have already introduced in our imaginary

island economy. This is the tendency of *government taxation* to "mop up" a fraction of income as it passes from hand to hand. This mopping-up effect of taxation is in actuality much larger than that of saving. For every dollar of change in income, federal taxes will take about 30 cents, and state and local taxes another 6 cents.

Another dampener is the tendency of respending to swell *business savings* as well as personal incomes. Of each dollar of new spending, perhaps 10 cents goes into business profits, and this sum is typically saved, at least for a time, rather than immediately respent.

Still another source of dampening is the tendency of consumers and businesses to increase purchases from abroad as their incomes rise. These rising *imports* divert 3 to 4 percent of new spending to foreign nations and accordingly reduce the successive impact of each round of expenditure.

All these withdrawals from the respending cycle are called *leakages,* and the total effect of all leakages together (personal savings, business savings, taxes, and imports) is to reduce the overall impact of the multiplier from an impossibly large figure to a very manageable one. The combined effect of all leakages brings the actual multiplier in the United States in the 1970s to a little more than 2 over a period of 2 years.*

To be sure—and this is very important—all these leakages *can* return to the income stream. Household saving can be turned into capital formation; business profits can be invested; tax receipts can be disbursed in gov-

---

*In dealing with the multiplier equation ($\Delta Y = \frac{1}{mps} \times \Delta I$), we can interpret mps to mean the total withdrawal from spending due to all leakages. This brings mps to around $\frac{1}{2}$, and gives us a multiplier of 2.

It is interesting to note that the leakages all tend to increase somewhat in boom times and to decline in recessions, which results in a slightly larger multiplier in bad times than in good.

ernment spending programs; and purchases from foreign sellers can be returned as purchases *by* foreigners. What is at stake here is the regularity and reliability with which these circuits will be closed. In the case of ordinary income going to a household, we can count with considerable assurance on a "return expenditure" of consumption. In the case of the other recipients of funds, the assurance is much less; hence we count their receipts as money that has leaked out of the expenditure flow, for the time being.

THE DOWNWARD MULTIPLIER

The multiplier, with its important magnifying action, rests at the very center of our understanding of economic fluctuations. Not only does it explain how relatively small stimuli can exert considerable upward pushes, but it also makes much clearer than before how the failure to offset a small savings gap can snowball into a serious fall in income and employment.

For just as additional income is respent to create still further new income, a loss in income will not stop with the affected households. On the contrary, as families lose income, they cut down on their spending, although the behavior pattern of the propensity to consume schedule suggests that they will not cut their consumption by as much as their loss in income. Yet each reduction in consumption, large or small, lessens to that extent the income or receipts of some other household or firm.

We have already noted that personal savings alone do not determine the full impact of the multiplier. This is even more fortunate on the way down than on the way up. If the size of the multiplier were solely dependent on the marginal propensity to save, an original fall in spending would result in a catastrophic contraction of consumption through the economy. But the leakages that cushion the upward pressure of the multiplier also cushion its downward effect. As spending falls, business savings (profits) fall, tax receipts dwindle, and the flow of imports declines. We shall discuss this cushioning effect when we look into the government sector.

All of these leakages now work in the direction of mitigating the repercussions of the original fall in spending. The fall in business profits means that less will be saved by business and thus less withdrawn from respending; the decline in taxes means that more money will be left to consumers; and the drop in imports similarly releases additional spending power for the domestic market. Thus, just as the various leakages pulled money away from consumption on the way up, on the way down they lessen their siphoning effect and in this way restore purchasing power to consumers' hands. As a result, in the downward direction as in the upward, the actual impact of the multiplier is about 2, so that a fall in investment of, say, $5 billion will lower GNP by $10 billion.

THE MULTIPLIER AND INVESTMENT

Even with a reduced figure, we can now understand how a relatively small change in investment can magnify its impact on GNP. If the typical year-to-year change in investment is around $10 billion to $20 billion, a multiplier of 2 will produce a change in GNP of $20 billion to $40 billion, by no means a negligible figure. In addition, as we shall shortly see, the multiplier may set up repercussions that feed back onto investment. But more of that momentarily. First let us make three final points in regard to the multiplier.

1. Other multipliers

We have talked of the multiplier in connection with changes in investment spending. *But we must also realize that any original change in any spending has a multipler effect.*

We have used investment as the "trigger" for the multiplier because it is, in fact, a component of spending that is likely to evidence *large* and *sudden* changes. But an increase in foreigners' purchases of our exports has a multiplier effect, as does an increase in government spending or a decrease in taxes, or a spontaneous increase in consumption itself due to, say, a drop in the propensity to save. Any stimulus to the economy is thus not confined to its original impact, but gives a series of successive pushes to the system until it has finally been absorbed in leakages. We shall come back to this important fact in our next chapter.

2. Idle resources

Finally, there is a very important proviso to recognize, although we will not study its full significance until Chapter 14. This is the important difference between an economy with idle resources—unemployed labor or unused machines or land—and one without them.

For *it is only when we have idle resources that the responding impetus of the multiplier is useful.* Then each round of new expenditure can bring idle resources into use, creating not only new money incomes but *new production and employment.* The situation is considerably different when there are no, or few, idle men or machines. Then the expenditure rounds of the multiplier bring higher money incomes, but these are not matched by increased real output.

In both cases, the multiplier exerts its leverage, bringing about an increase in total expenditure larger than the original injection of new spending. In the case without idle resources, however, the results are solely *inflationary,* as the increased spending results in higher incomes and higher prices, but not in higher output. In the case where idle resources exist, we can avoid this mere "money" multiplication and enjoy a rise in output as a result of our increased spending. Indeed, we can even speak of the *employment*

multiplier in situations where there is considerable unemployment, meaning by this the total increase in employment brought about by a given increase in spending. We shall return in subsequent chapters to a fuller scrutiny of the difference between the case of idle and of fully employed resources, but we must bear the distinction in mind henceforth.

3. The importance of time lags

Last we must distinguish between the multiplier as a mathematical relationship and the multiplier in real life.

In equations, the multiplier is "instantaneous." If investment rises by $10 billions and the multiplier is 2, we "instantly" have a $20 billion rise in output. In actuality, the successive "rounds" of spending display very important *time lags.* Investment expenditures of $10 billion will first show up as increased sales of businesses. Businesses usually will draw down on inventories rather than immediately increasing production (and factor incomes), to hedge against the possibility that the increase is only temporary. This leads to a smaller increase in incomes, other than profits, than might be expected. And for the same hedging reason, businesses are unlikely at first to use their additional profits to pay higher incomes or to finance new investment.

Moreover, incomes that do go to consumers are also not instantaneously spent. One recent study has shown that families spent only 66 cents out of each dollar of new income in the first three months during which they received that income. Only gradually did their spending propensities build up to "normal." And even when they *did* spend their additional incomes, the businesses that enjoyed larger sales were again likely to display the cautious hedging attitudes we have described. That is another reason why the multiplier, 2 years after an investment increase, is in fact only about 2.

KEY WORDS

Investment

Instability

Inventories

Multiplier

Marginal propensity to save

$$\Delta Y = \frac{1}{mps} \times \Delta I$$

Leakages

Downward multiplier

Full employment

Time lags

CENTRAL CONCEPTS

1. The investment sector is made up not of households and their activities, but of *business firms adding to their capital assets.* By and large, these additions to business capital are financed out of *internal funds* (retained earnings and depreciation accruals) rather than from external sources (borrowing or new equities). The main categories of investment expenditure are additions to inventory, new equipment, residential housing, and other construction, mainly plant.

2. The main characteristic of all investment expenditure is its *potential instability.* In times of serious recession, net investment can virtually cease. Even in ordinary times, inventory investment is capable of drastic changes.

3. Changes in investment (or in any other kind of spending) are given larger economic impact because of the *multiplier effect.* This arises because incomes received from a new investment (or any other source) are *partly respent*, giving rise to additional new incomes which, in turn, are respent.

4. A single "burst" of investment creates a bulge in incomes that disappears over time; but a *continuing level of new investment creates a continuing higher level of new incomes.*

5. The size of the multiplier depends on the fraction of additional income spent for consumption by each new recipient. *The more the spending* (or the less the saving) *the greater will be the multiplier.*

6. *We calculate the multiplier by taking the reciprocal of the marginal propensity to save.* This gives us the important formula:

$$\Delta Y = \frac{1}{mps} \times \Delta I \text{ (change in income } = \text{ multiplier } \times \text{ change in investment)}$$

7. The *size of mps is determined by leakages.* There are four main leakages:
   - Saving
   - Taxation
   - Business profits
   - Imports

   Total leakages in the U.S. amount to about one-half of increases in income. Therefore the U.S. multiplier is about 2.

8. *Each of these leakages takes money out of the "automatic" respending circuit of consumption.* Money going into leakages *can* return to the economy via additional investment, but it does not do so as reliably as money that stays in the consumption flow.

9. Magnifying the effects on income of a fall in investment, the *multiplier works downward,* as well as upward.

10. The multiplier will have very different economic effects, depending on whether or not the economy is *fully employed.*

11. The multiplier acts *over time*, not instantaneously.

QUESTIONS

1. If you buy a share of stock on the New York Stock Exchange, does that always create new capital? Why, or why not?

2. Why are additions to inventory so much more liable to rapid fluctuation than are other kinds of investment?

3. Why do we face the possibility of a total collapse of investment, but not of consumption?

4. Draw a diagram showing the multiplier effect of a $1,000 expenditure when the marginal propensity to save is one-tenth. Draw a second diagram, showing the effect when the marginal propensity to consume is nine-tenths. Are the diagrams the same?

5. Compare two multiplier diagrams: one where the marginal propensity to save is one-quarter; the other where it is one-third. The *larger* the saving ratio, the larger or smaller the multiplier?

6. Calculate the impact on income if investment rises by $10 billion and the multiplier is 2. If the multiplier is 3. If it is 1.

7. Income is $500 billion; investment is $50 billion. The multiplier is 2. If inventories decline by $10 billion, what happens to income?

8. Draw a diagram showing what happens to $1 billion of new investment given the following leakages: mps 10 percent; marginal taxation 20 percent; marginal propensity to import 5 percent; marginal addition to business saving 15 percent. What will be the size of the second round of spending? the third? the final total?

9. If the marginal propensity to consume is three-quarters, what is the size of the marginal propensity to save? If it is five-sixths? If it is 70 percent?

10. What is the formula for the multiplier?

The Motivation
of Investment

THE INHERENT INSTABILITY OF INVESTMENT, and the multiplier repercussions that arise from changes in investment, begin to give us an understanding of the special importance of the business sector in determining the demand for GNP. In our next chapter we shall look into equally special characteristics of government demand before assembling the demand functions of all the sectors, to match them against the supply of GNP.

But before we proceed to that goal, we must learn something further about the nature of investment demand—in particular, about the motivations that give rise to it— for if we compare the underlying behavioral drives that impel consumption and investment, we can see a fundamental difference of the greatest significance.

UTILITY VS. PROFIT

Consumption demand, we remember, is essentially directed at the satisfaction of the individual—at providing him with the "utili-ties" of the goods and services he buys. An increasingly affluent society may not be able to say that consumer expenditure is any longer solely geared to necessity, but at least it obeys the fairly constant promptings of the cultural and social environment, with the result that consumer spending, in the aggregate, fluctuates relatively little, except as income fluctuates.

A quite different set of motivations drives the investment impulse. Whether the investment is for replacement of old capital or for the installation of new capital, the ruling consideration is not apt to be the personal use or satisfaction that the investment yields to the owners of the firm. Instead, the touchstone of investment decisions is *profit*.

Figure 9·1 (p. 128) shows corporate profits since 1929 and their division into retained earnings, dividends, and taxes. What is strikingly apparent, of course, is the extreme fluctuation of profits between prosperity and recession. Note that corporations as a whole lost money in the depths of the De-

HAVE CORPORATE PROFITS CHANGED?

Have corporate profits changed as a percent of GNP? The answer is not easily given, since the federal government has chosen to reduce corporation income taxes by increasing depreciation allowances rather than lowering nominal tax rates. (See supplement on National Income and Product Accounts at the end of Chap. 5.) In 1929, corporate gross cash flow (profits plus depreciation allowances) amounted to 12.4 percent of GNP; in 1947, they amounted to 11.4 percent, from 1965 to 1972 they averaged 10.9 percent.

Profits after tax were 8.3 percent of GNP in 1929, 8.7 percent in 1947, and fell to 5.4 percent from 1965 to 1972. Thus it appears that corporate profits have been falling as a share of the total economy, at least over the last decade or two. This does not mean that profit rates of every corporation have necessarily fallen: some have; some have not. And we should note that corporate profits have, of course, increased sharply as a percent of GNP from their level in the early 1900s, but the percentage increased because corporations themselves were not a dominant form of business organization until after World War I.

FIGURE 9 · 1
Profits, taxes, and dividends

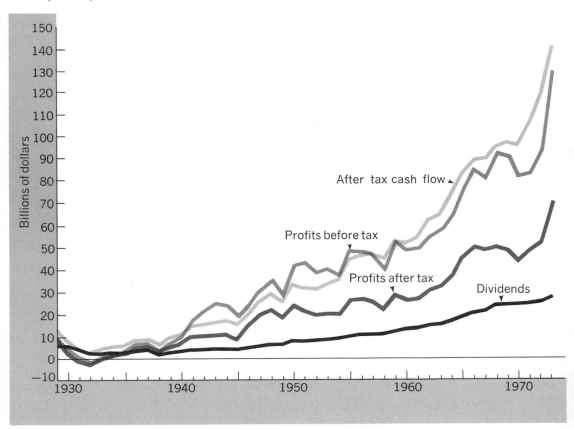

pression years, but that even in the lush postwar period, the swings from year to year have been considerable (compare 1958 and 1959).

EXPECTATIONS

The chart shows us how corporate profits looked to businessmen when the books were tallied at the end of each year. But the results of his last year's operation, although very important, is not the main thing that motivates a businessman to invest. Primarily, he is interested in the profits he expects from *next year's* operations. His view is never backward, but always forward.

Note the important stress on *expectations*. One firm may be enjoying large profits on its existing plant and equipment at the moment; but if it anticipates no profits from the sale of goods that an *additional* investment would make possible, the firm will make no additions to capital. Another firm may be suffering current losses; but if it anticipates a large profit from the production of a new good, it may launch a considerable capital expenditure.

There is a sound reason for this anticipatory quality of investment decisions. Typically, the capital goods bought by investment expenditures are expected to last for years and to pay for themselves only slowly. In addition, they are often highly specialized. If capital expenditures could be recouped in a few weeks or months, or even in a matter of a year or two, or if capital goods were easily transferred from one use to another, they would not be so risky and their dependence on expectations not so great. But it is characteristic of most capital goods that they *are* durable, with life expectancies of ten or more years, and that they tend to be limited in their alternative uses, or to have no alternative uses at all. You cannot spin cloth in a steel mill or make steel in a cotton mill.

The decision to invest is thus always forward-looking. Even when the stimulus to build is felt in the present, the calculations that determine whether or not an investment will be made necessarily concern the flow of income to the firm in the future. These expectations are inherently much more volatile than the current drives and desires that guide the consumer. Expectations, whether based on guesses or forecasts, are capable of sudden and sharp reversals of a sort rare in consumption spending. Thus in its orientation to the future we find a main cause for the volatility of investment expenditures.

Induced and Autonomous Investment

One kind of profit expectation, and the investment that stems from it, derives from *an observed rise in current consumption spending,* as a result of higher incomes.

Many business firms decide to invest because they must expand their capacity to maintain a given share of a growing market. Real estate developers who build to accommodate an already visible suburban exodus, or supermarkets that build to serve a booming metropolis, or gas stations that must be built to serve a new highway, or additions to manufacturing capacity that must be made because existing facilities cannot keep up with demand—these are all examples of what we call *induced investment.*

THE ACCELERATION PRINCIPLE

When rising incomes and consumption lead to induced investment, the relationship is called the *acceleration principle* or the *accelerator.* The name springs from the fact that the amount of induced investment depends upon the rate of growth of the economy. An economy that is not growing has no induced

TABLE 9·1
A Model of the Accelerator

Year	Sales	Existing capital	Needed capital (2 × sales)	Replacement investment	Induced new investment (2 × addition to sales)	Total investment
1	$100	$200	$200	$20	—	$20
2	120	200	240	20	$40	60
3	130	240	260	20	20	40
4	135	260	270	20	10	30
5	138	270	276	20	6	26
6	140	276	280	20	4	24
7	140	280	280	20	—	20
8	130	280	260	—	—	0
9	130	260	260	20	—	20

investment. Also, an economy that has un-utilized capacity will not have induced investment.

Table 9·1 is a model that explains this phenomenon. It shows us an industry whose sales rise for six years, then level off, and finally decline. We assume it has no unused equipment and that its equipment wears out every ten years. Also, we will make the assumption that the capital-output ratio (see p. 55) in this industry is 2; that is, it requires a capital investment of $2 to produce a flow of output of $1.

Now let us see the accelerator at work.

In our first view of the industry, we find it in equilibrium with sales of, let us say, 100 units, capital equipment valued at 200 units, and regular replacement demand of twenty units, or 10 percent of its stock of equipment. Now we assume that its sales rise to 120 units. To produce 120 units of goods, the firm will need (according to our assumptions) 240 units of capital.' This is 40 units more than it has, so it must order them. Note that its demand for capital goods now shoots from 20 units to 60 units: 20 units for replace-ment as before, and 40 new ones. Thus investment expenditures *triple*, even though sales have risen but 20 percent!

Now assume that in the next year sales rise further, to 130 units. How large will our firm's investment demand be? Its replacement demand will not be larger, since its new capital will not wear out for ten years. And the amount of new capital needed to handle its new sales will be only 20 units, not 40 as before. Its total investment demand has *fallen* from 60 units to 40.

What is the surprising fact here? It is that *we can have an actual fall in induced investment, though sales are still rising!* In fact, as soon as the *rate of increase* of consumption begins to fall, *the absolute amount* of induced investment declines. Thus a slowdown in the rate of improvement in sales can cause an absolute decline in the orders sent to capital goods makers. This helps us to explain how weakness can appear in some branches of the economy while prosperity seems still to be reigning in the market at large.

Now look at what happens to our model in the eighth year, when we assume that sales slip back to 130. Our existing capital (280 units) will be greater by 20 units than our needed capital. That year the industry will have no new orders for capital goods and may not even make any replacements, because it can produce all it needs with its old machines. Its orders to capital goods makers will fall to zero, even though its level of sales is 30 percent higher than at the beginning. The next year, however, if sales remain steady, it will again have to replace one of its old machines. Its replacement demand again jumps to 20. No wonder capital goods industries traditionally experience feast or famine years!

There is, in addition, an extremely important point to bear in mind about the accelerator. *Its upward leverage usually takes effect only when an industry is operating at or near capacity.* When an industry is not near capacity, it is relatively simple for it to satisfy a larger demand for its goods by raising output on its underutilized equipment. Thus, unlike the multiplier, which yields its effects on output only when we have unemployed resources, the accelerator yields its effects only when we do *not* have unemployed capital.

AUTONOMOUS INVESTMENT

Not all investment is induced by prior rises in consumption. A very important category of investment is that undertaken in the expectation of a profit to be derived from a *new* good or a *new* way of making a good. This type of investment is usually called *autonomous* investment.

In autonomous investment decisions, prior trends in consumption have little or nothing to do with the decision to invest. This is particularly the case when new technologies provide the stimulus for investment. Then the question in the minds of the man-

agers of the firm is whether the new product will create *new* demand for itself.

Technological advance is not, however, the only cause for autonomous investment, and therefore we cannot statistically separate autonomous from induced investment. With some economic stimuli, such as the opening of a new territory or shifts in population or population growth, the motivations of both autonomous and induced investment are undoubtedly present. Yet there is a meaningful distinction between the two, insofar as induced investment is sensitive and responsive to sales, whereas autonomous investment is not. This means that induced investment, by its nature, is more foreseeable than autonomous investment.

At the same time, both spontaneous and induced investments are powerfully affected by the overall investment "climate"—not alone the economic climate of confidence, the level and direction of the stock market, etc., but the political scene, international developments, and so on. Hence it is not surprising that investment is often an unpredictable component of GNP, and thus a key "independent" variable in any model of GNP.

BUSINESS CYCLES AGAIN

Perhaps you noticed a wavelike movement in the investment induced by changing consumption. Our understanding of the accelerator, combined with the multiplier, now enables us to gain a much deeper insight into the mechanism of the *business cycle*.

Let us assume that some stimulus, such as an important industry-building invention, has begun to increase investment expenditures. We can easily see how such an initial impetus can generate a cumulative and self-feeding boom. As the multiplier and accelerator interact, the first burst of investment stimulates additional consumption, the additional consumption induces more investment,

THE STOCK MARKET AND INVESTMENT

How does the stock market affect business investment? There are two direct effects. One is that the market has traditionally served as a general barometer of the expectations of the business-minded community as a whole. We say "business-minded" rather than "business," because the demand for and supply of securities mainly comes from securities dealers, stockbrokers, and the investing public, rather than from nonfinancial business enterprises themselves. When the market is buoyant, it has been a signal to business that the "business climate" is favorable, and the effect on what Keynes called the "animal spirits" of executives has been to encourage them to go ahead with expansion plans. When the market is falling, on the other hand, spirits tend to be dampened, and executives may think twice before embarking on an expansion program in the face of general pessimism.

This traditional relationship is, however, greatly lessened by the growing power of government to influence the trend of economic events. Businessmen once looked to the market as the key signal for the future. Today they look to Washington. Hence, during the past decade when the stock market has shown wide swings, business investment in plant and equipment has remained basically steady. This reflects the feelings of corporate managers that government policy will keep the economy growing, whatever "the market" may think of events.

A second direct effect of the stock market on investment has to do with the ease of issuing new securities. One of the ways in which investment is financed is through the issuance of new stocks or bonds whose proceeds will purchase plant and equipment. When the market is rising, it is much easier to float a new issue than when prices are falling. This is particularly true for certain businesses—A.T. & T. is a prime example—that depend heavily on stock issues for new capital rather than on retained earnings.

and this in turn reinvigorates consumption. Meanwhile, this process of mutual stimulation serves to lift business expectations and to encourage still further expansionary spending. Inventories are built up in anticipation of larger sales. Prices "firm up," and the stock market rises. Optimism reigns. A boom is on.

What happens to end such a boom? There are many possible reasons why it may peter out or come to an abrupt halt. It may simply be that the new industry will get built, and thereafter an important stimulus to investment will be lacking. Or even before it is completed, wages and prices may have begun to rise as full employment is neared, and the climate of expectations may become wary. (Businessmen have an old adage that "what goes up must come down.") Meanwhile, per-

haps tight money will choke off spending plans or make new projects appear unprofitable.

Or investment may begin to decline because consumption, although still rising, is no longer rising at the earlier *rate* (the acceleration principle in action). We have already noticed that the action of the accelerator, all by itself, could give rise to wave-like movements in total expenditure. The accelerator, of course, never works all by itself, but it can exert its upward and downward pressures within the flux of economic forces and in this way give rise to an underlying cyclical impetus.

It is impossible to know in advance what particular cause will retard spending—a credit shortage, a very tight labor market, a saturation of demand for a key industry's products (such as automobiles). But it is all too easy to see how a hesitation in spending can turn into a general contraction. Perhaps warned by a falling stock market, perhaps by a slowdown in their sales or an end to rising profits, businessmen begin to cut back. Whatever their initial motivation, what follows thereafter is much like the preceding expansion, only in reverse. The multiplier mechanism now breeds smaller rather than larger incomes. Downward revisions of expectations reduce rather than enhance the attractiveness of investment projects. As consumption decreases, unemployment begins to rise. Inventories are worked off. Bankruptcies become more common. We experience all the economic and social problems of a recession.

But just as there is a "natural" ceiling to a boom, so there is a more or less "natural" floor to recessions.* The fall in inventories, for example, will eventually come to an end: for even in the severest recessions, merchants and manufacturers must have *some* goods on their shelves and so must eventually begin stocking up. The decline in expenditures will lead to easy money, and the slack in output will tend to a lower level of costs: and both of these factors will encourage new investment projects. Meanwhile, the countercyclical effects of government fiscal policy will slowly make their effects known. Sooner or later, in other words, expenditures will cease falling, and the economy will tend to "bottom out."

The Determinants of Investment

The profit expectations that guide investment decisions are largely unpredictable. But there exists one influence on investment decisions

*In retrospect, the tremendous and long-lasting collapse of 1929 seems to have been caused by special circumstances having to do mainly with speculation and monetary mismanagement.

that seems to offer a more determinable guide. This is the influence of the *rate of interest* on the investment decisions of business firms.

INTEREST COSTS

The rate of interest should offer two guides to the investing firm. If the businessman must borrow capital, a higher rate of interest makes it more expensive to undertake an investment. For huge firms that target a return of 15 to 20 percent on their investment projects, a change in the interest rate from 7 to 8 percent may be negligible. But for certain kinds of investment—notably utilities and home construction—interest rates constitute an important component of the cost of investment funds. To these firms, the lower the cost of borrowed capital, the more the stimulus for investment. The difference in *interest costs* for $1 million borrowed for twenty years at 7 percent (instead of 8 percent) is $200,000, by no means a negligible sum. Since construction is the largest single component of investment, the interest rate therefore becomes an important influence on the value of total capital formation.

A second guide is offered to those businessmen who are not directly seeking to borrow money for investment, but who are debating whether to invest the savings (retained earnings) of their firms. This problem of deciding on investments introduces us to an important idea: the discounting of future income.

DISCOUNTING THE FUTURE

Suppose that someone gave you an ironclad promise to pay you $100 a year hence. Would you pay him $100 *now* to get back the same sum 365 days in the future? Certainly not, for in parting with the money you are suffering an *opportunity cost* or a cost that can be measured in terms of the opportunities that your action (to pay $100 now) has foreclosed for you. Had the going rate of interest been 5 percent, for example, you could have loaned your $100 at 5 percent and had $105 at the end of the year. Hence, friendship aside, you are unlikely to lend your money unless you are paid something to compensate you for the opportunities you must give up while you are waiting for your money to return. Another way of saying exactly the same thing is that we arrive at the *present value* of a specified sum in the future by discounting it by some percentage. If the discount rate is 5 percent, the present value of $100 one year in the future is $100 ÷ 1.05, or approximately $95.24.

This brings us back to our businessman who is considering whether or not to make an investment. Suppose that he is considering investing $100,000 in a machine that he expects to earn $25,000 a year for 5 years, over and above all expenses, after which it will be worthless. Does this mean that the expected profit on the machine is therefore $25,000—the $125,000 of expected earnings less the $100,000 of original cost? No, it does not, for the expected earnings will have to be discounted by some appropriate percentage to find their present value. Thus the first $25,000 to be earned by the machine must be reduced by some discount rate; and the second $25,000 must be discounted *twice* (just as $100 to be repaid in *two* year's time will have to yield the equivalent of *two* years' worth of interest); the third $25,000, three times, etc.*

*The formula for calculating the present value of a flow of future income that does not change from year to year is:

$$\text{Present value} = \frac{R}{(1 + i)} + \frac{R}{(1 + i)^2} + \ldots + \frac{R}{(1 + i)^n}$$

where R is the annual flow of income, i is the interest rate, and n is the number of years over which the flow will last.

Clearly, this process of discounting will cause the present value of the expected future returns of the machine to be less than the sum of the undiscounted returns. If, for example, its returns are discounted at a rate of 10 percent, the businessman will find that the present value of a five-year flow of $25,000 per annum comes not to $125,000 but to only $94,700. This is *less* than the actual expenditure for the machine ($100,000). Hence, at a discount rate of 10 percent, the businessman would not undertake the venture.

On the other hand, if he used a discount rate of 5 percent, the present value of the same future flow would be worth (in round numbers) $109,000. In that case, the machine *would* be a worthwhile investment.

INTEREST RATES AND INVESTMENT

What rate should our businessman use to discount his future earnings? Here is where the rate of interest enters the picture. Looking out at the economy, the businessman sees that there is a whole spectrum of interest rates, ranging from very low rates on bonds (usually government bonds) where the element of risk is very small, to high rates on securities of the same maturity (that is, coming due in the same number of years) where the risk is much greater, such as "low-grade" corporate bonds or mortgages. Among this spectrum of rates, there will be a rate at which *he* can borrow—high or low, depending on his credit worthiness in the eyes of the banking community. By applying that rate he can discover whether the estimated future earning from his venture, properly discounted, is actually profitable or not.

MARGINAL EFFICIENCY OF INVESTMENT

There is still another way in which the interest rate should help determine the volume of investment, although it is really only another

GOVERNMENT AND INDIVIDUAL INVESTMENT

Does the process of discounting earnings and comparing them with costs apply to public investment or to individuals investing in, say, education?

It may. A government contemplating an investment in roads, parks, or police stations does not expect to show a financial profit, but it does expect a flow of benefits—a kind of *social profit*. These benefits can often be roughly measured in terms of their financial worth, and the public institution can then compare the discounted value of these expected benefits against their costs.

In similar fashion, an individual contemplating a personal investment, such as acquiring a new skill, may make a similar calculation. He estimates the future increase in earnings that he expects from his training, discounts this sum, and compares it with the cost of undertaking the investment. Of course, individuals do not always act with the precision of "economic man." Nonetheless, the idea of discounting future returns helps give analytic clarity to the reason why a 20-year-old person will willingly accept the cost of becoming a doctor or an engineer, whereas a 55-year-old will not. For the younger person, the investment is expected to pay off (quite aside from the pleasures of the increased skills themselves). For the older person, it is not. An older person may go to school for pleasure, but not for profit.

version of the same idea. The businessman can calculate the rate of discount that would just suffice to make a particular investment pay. *This rate is called the marginal efficiency of investment.* In our illustration above, we saw that over a five-year period, a rate of 10 percent proved the machine to be unprofitable and that one of 5 percent made it show an expected profit. There must be some rate, between these two, that would just make the discounted value of the expected returns equal the cost of the $100,000 machine; if we figure it out, the rate turns out to be approximately 8 percent.*

*How did we arrive at the figure of 8 percent? By using the formula in the preceding footnote and solving for the value of i (the discount rate) that would make the sum of the terms on the right—the discounted future earnings—just equal to the *cost* of the machine, which we put on the left. The mathematics is a bit complicated, but the idea is not. Clearly, if we expect an investment to yield very high returns (R in the formula), it will have a very high marginal efficiency—that is, it will take a very high discount rate (i in the formula) to bring the sum of future earnings down to the level of cost. On the other hand, if the investment is expected to give only small returns, it will have a low marginal efficiency, for only a low discount rate will keep the discounted value of future earnings from falling below costs.

What has this to do with the rate of interest? The answer is that the businessman very likely has a choice among different investment projects from which he anticipates different returns. Suppose he ranks those projects, as we have in Fig. 9·2, starting with the most profitable (A) and proceeding to the least profitable (G). How far down the list should he go? The rate of interest gives the answer. Suppose the rate (for projects of comparable risk) is shown by *OX*. Then all his investment projects whose marginal efficiency is higher than *OX* (investments A through D) will be profitable, and all those whose marginal efficiency falls below *OX* (E through G) will be discarded or at least postponed.

Note that if the interest rate falls, more investments will be worthwhile; and that if it rises, fewer will be. As the figure on the right shows in generalized form, a fall in the rate of interest (e.g., from *OX* to *OY*) induces a rise in the quantity of investment (from *OC* to *OG*).

Increases in autonomous investment or induced investment can be represented as the

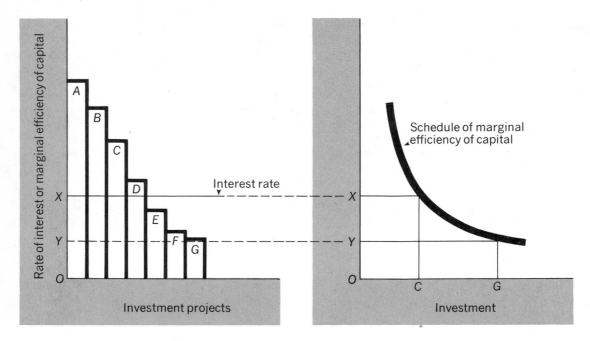

FIGURE 9 · 2
Marginal efficiency of capital

marginal efficiency of capital schedule shift-ing to the right. New opportunities, either arising from the development of new goods and services or because of increasing sales of old goods, mean that a given amount of cap-ital can earn a higher rate of return or that more investment will occur at any given rate of interest. Draw in a new marginal efficiency curve in Fig. 9·2 and prove this to yourself.

Thus, whether we figure interest as a cost or as a guideline against which we measure the expected returns of a capital investment, we reach the important conclusion that *low interest rates should encourage investment spending*—or in more formal language, that *investment should be inversely related to the rate of interest.* To be sure, the fact that a given investment, such as project *B* above, has a marginal efficiency higher than the in-

terest rate is no guarantee that a business ac-tually will undertake it. Other considerations —perhaps political, perhaps psychological— may deter management, despite its encour-aging calculations. But assuredly a business will not carry out a project that yields less than the interest rate, because it can make more profit by lending the money, at the same degree of risk, than by investing it.

THE INTEREST RATE PUZZLE

Perhaps the reader will have remarked on a certain cautionary tone in this discussion of the effect of interest rates on investment. We have spoken of the effects that changing in-terest rates *should have* on business invest-ment, as an opportunity cost or as a money payment or as a guideline against which to measure the marginal efficiency of investment.* We have not spoken of the effect that interest rates *do* have, because extensive empirical investigations have failed to disclose the effects we would expect.

Here we come to another puzzle in economics—an area in which our analysis, based on what rational profit-maximizing entrepreneurs should do, fails to square with what we find they actually do. Let us take a moment to explore this intriguing and unsolved problem.

THE INVESTMENT FUNCTION

We are now familiar with the consumption function, that relates income to consumption. If our analysis is to be believed, there should also be an *investment function* relating investment to the rate of interest. That is, we should be able to specify that for each percentage point fall in interest, investment rises by such-and-such a percent. We would expect the function to show a curve like the hypothetical one in Fig. 9·3.

In fact, when econometricians first began to inquire into the interest-investment relationship, they found exactly this kind of relation between interest rates and residential construction. As they expected, when it became cheaper to borrow or take out a mortgage, home-building increased. But to their consternation, when they investigated the relation between interest rates and plant and equipment investment, no such relationship appeared. Worse, the data seemed to show a "wrong" relationship: when interest rates went up, plant and equipment investment also went up! Figure 9·4 shows the kind of relation that research established between

*Economists also speak of the marginal efficiency of *capital*. Technically speaking, this is a somewhat different concept. But the two terms are often used interchangeably.

plant and equipment investment (shown as a proportion of GNP) and interest rates, *i*.

THE ELUSIVE INTEREST-RATE INVESTMENT FUNCTION

Did this mean that our theory is wrong in some fundamental sense? Econometricians

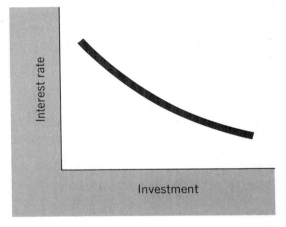

FIGURE 9·3
The hypothetical interest— investment function

FIGURE 9·4
The econometric interest— investment function

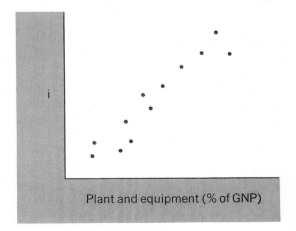

have tried a number of ways to make it come out right. One method was to correct the money rate of interest to the *real rate of interest*. The real rate of interest is the money rate reduced by the rate of inflation. If you get 5 percent on a savings bank deposit, but prices rise by 5 percent, your real interest return is zero. So too if businessmen could borrow at 8 percent, but prices rose by 5 percent, their real interest cost was only 3 percent. Unhappily, when money interest rates were corrected for inflation, the expected investment function still did not appear.

Numerous other attempts have also been made to "specify" an investment function that would reconcile the observed phenomenon of investment perversely rising with interest rates. Econometricians have struggled to incorporate after-tax profit rates and many other possible influences into their investment function term, but all to no avail. *No reliable interest rate—investment function has yet been devised.* Good investment functions have been found for explaining and predicting plant and equipment investment in terms of the rate of growth of the economy, the degree of capacity utilization, and the rate of return on capital investments; but the econometricians who build these functions have not been able to include interest rates in the expected manner.

OTHER EXPLANATIONS

Is there no way, then, of explaining a phenomenon that seems to fly in the face of common sense as well as theory? One plausible explanation has been advanced. Historically, interest rates rise during periods of rapid growth. This happens for two reasons. During these periods, the demand curve for *induced* investment shifts to the right. Therefore, even if higher interest rates tend to discourage autonomous investment, this

effect may be overridden by the accelerator taking hold elsewhere.

Second, periods of rapid growth push economies toward full employment. Governments thereupon deliberately raise interest rates through the money mechanism to try to cool off the economy. In this complex of cross currents we can have the curious parallel of higher interest rates and higher investment in plant and equipment, but we can see that the influence of interest rates alone is difficult—even impossible—to isolate. Therefore we continue to assume that *if* we could isolate those effects, they would show the negatively sloped investment function we use in economic theory. We make this assumption because it accords with the premises of maximization, and because we believe we can explain away the seeming disconfirmation of our theory in real life. Nevertheless, the interest rate—investment relationship remains something of a puzzle and a source of discomfiture to economists.

The Export Sector

Before we go on to the problem of public demand, we must mention, if only in passing, a sector we have so far largely overlooked. This is the foreign sector, or more properly the sector of net exports.

If we lived in Europe, South America, or Asia, we could not be so casual in our treatment of foreign trade, for this sector constitutes the very lifeline of many, perhaps even most, countries. Our own highly self-sustained economy in which foreign trade plays only a small quantitative (although a much more important qualitative) role in generating total output is very much the exception rather than the rule.*

---

*International currency problems, however, can play a very important role in our economic affairs.

In part, it is the relatively marginal role played by foreign trade in the American economy that allows us to treat it so cavalierly. But there is also another problem. The forces that enter into the flows of international trade are much more complex than any we have heretofore discussed. Not alone the reactions of American consumers and firms, but those of foreign consumers and firms must be taken into account. Thus comparisons between international price levels, the availability of foreign or domestic goods, credit and monetary controls, exchange rates —a whole host of other such considerations

FIGURE 9 · 5
Exports, imports, and net exports

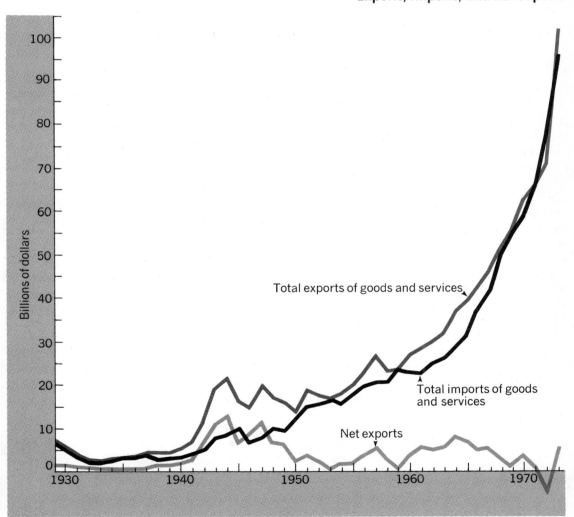

—lie at the very heart of foreign trade. To begin to unravel these interrelationships, one must study international trade as a subject in itself. Nevertheless, we should try to understand the main impact of foreign trade on the demand for GNP, even if we cannot yet investigate the forces and institutions of foreign trade as thoroughly as we might like.

IMPACT OF FOREIGN TRADE

We must begin by repeating that our initial overview of the economic system, with its twin streams of consumption and investment, was actually incomplete. It portrayed what we call a "closed" system, an economy with no flows of goods or services from within its borders to other nations, or from other nations to itself.

Yet such flows must, of course, be taken into account in computing our national output. Let us therefore look at a chart that shows us the main streams of goods and services that cross our borders, as well as a table of the magnitudes in our benchmark years (see Fig. 9.5, p. 139).

First a word of explanation. Exports show the total value of all goods and services we sold to foreigners. Imports show the total value of all goods and services we bought from foreigners. Our bottom line shows the net difference between exports and imports, or the difference between the value of the goods we sold abroad and the value we bought from abroad. This difference is called *net exports,* and it constitutes the net contribution of foreign trade to the demand for GNP.

If we think of it in terms of expenditures, it is not difficult to see what the net contribution is. When exports are sold to foreigners, their expenditures add to American incomes. Imports, on the contrary, are expenditures that we make to other countries (and hence that we do not make at home). If we add the foreign expenditures made here and subtract the domestic expenditures made abroad, we will have left a net figure that will show the contribution (if any) made by foreigners to GNP.

THE EXPORT MULTIPLIER

What is the impact of this net expenditure on GNP? It is much the same as net private domestic investment. If we have a rising net export balance, we will have a net increase in spending in the economy.

Conversely, if our net foreign trade balance falls, our demand for GNP will decline, exactly as if the demand for domestic investment fell. Thus, even though we must defer for a while a study of the actual forces at work in international trade, we can quickly include the effects of foreign trade on the level of GNP by considering the net trade balance as a part of our investment demand for output.

One point in particular should be noted. If there is a rise in the net demand generated by foreigners, this will have a *multiplier effect,* exactly as an increase in investment will have. Here is, in fact, the parable of an individual visiting an island (p. 116) come to life. Additional net foreign spending will generate new incomes which will generate new buying; and decreased net foreign spending will diminish incomes, with a similar train of secondary and tertiary effects.

KEY WORDS

Expectations

Induced investment

Autonomous investment

Acceleration principle

Business cycles

Rate of Interest

Discounting future income

Marginal efficiency of investment

Investment function

Export multiplier

Real rate of interest

Export sector

CENTRAL CONCEPTS

1. The motivation for investment expenditure is not personal use or satisfaction, but *expected profit*. Note that investment is always geared to forward profit expectations rather than to past or present results.

2. We distinguish between two kinds of investment motivation. When investments are made to meet an expected demand arising from present or clearly indicated changes in consumption, we speak of *induced investment*. When investment is stimulated by developments (such as inventions) that have little relation to existing trends, we speak of *autonomous investment*.

3. Induced investment is subject to the *acceleration principle*, which describes how a given increase in C can give rise to a proportionally larger increase in *I*. The acceleration principle also shows us that the absolute level of induced investment can fall, even though the level of C is still rising. Thus it helps explain the onset of recessions. Note that the acceleration principle "takes hold" only when an industry is at or near full utilization.

4. The interaction of the multiplier and the accelerator helps elucidate the mechanism of *business cycles*.

5. The rate of interest should affect investment in two ways. (1) It directly affects *the cost of investment* and (2) it gives us a rate (for investments with risks similar to the one we are contemplating) that allows us to calculate whether the *discounted future returns of our investment are greater than its cost.*

6. We can also discover the rate of discount that just makes the expected returns on an investment equal to its cost. This rate is called the *marginal efficiency of investment*. Unless the marginal efficiency of investment is greater than the rate of interest, an investment will not be undertaken.

7. Note that whether we consider interest as a cost or a guideline against which to compare the marginal efficiency of capital, *the lower the interest rate, the larger the* volume of investment should be.

8. The *investment function* is highly complex. It depends partly on changes within *the system, such as the accelerator, and partly on changes in "external" events, above all those affecting expected profits.*

9. Efforts to discover an investment function have not shown that plant and equipment spending declines when interest rises, although housing construction does. Corrections for the *real rate of interest*, and for other possible causes, have failed to give us an expected negatively sloped investment function.

10. It is possible to explain this anomaly in terms of the *crosscurrents* that affect interest and investment during a boom. The induced investment during a boom causes a rise in the price of money. The actions of government also deliberately raise interest rates to lessen inflation. In these circumstances it is impossible to detect the actual effect of the rate on plant and equipment spending. We assume that our negatively sloped function is correct because it makes sense, but we cannot demonstrate it in fact.

11. The *export sector* affects the demand for GNP by any excess of exports, or foreign purchases, over imports, or purchases from foreigners. It is therefore very similar to investment demand as an influence on the level of GNP. We can speak of an *export multiplier* exactly as we have spoken of an investment multiplier.

QUESTIONS

1. Discuss the difference in the motivation of a consumer buying a car for pleasure and the same person buying a car for his business.

2. Which of the following are induced and which autonomous investment decisions: a developer builds homes in a growing community; a city enlarges its water supply after a period of water shortage; a firm builds a laboratory for basic research; an entrepreneur invests in a new gadget.

3. What is the basic idea of the acceleration principle? Describe carefully how the acceleration principle helps explain the instability of investment.

4. What is meant by "discounting" the value of an expected return? If the rate of interest were 10 percent, what would be the *present value* of $100 due a year hence? What would be its present value two years hence? (HINT: the first year's discounted value has to be discounted a *second time*.)

5. Assume that it costs 7 percent to borrow from a bank. What is the minimum profit that must be expected from an investment before it becomes worthwhile? Could we write that $I = f(r)$ where r stands for the rate of interest? What would be the relation between a change in r and I? Would $I = f(r)$ be a complete description of the motivation for investment? Why should future costs as well as profits be discounted?

6. If inflation is proceeding at 3 percent a year and the banks charge 7 percent for loans, what is the real rate of interest? What is meant by this "real" rate?

7. Why doesn't the accelerator work when there is idle equipment? What significance does this have for the flow of investment as the economy moves from a position of underutilization to one of high utilization?

8. Do you think it is valid to assume that the investment function is negatively related to interest rates, even though we can't show this statistically?

9. Explain how exports stimulate income. Does this mean that imports are bad? Are savings bad?

Government Demand

WE TURN NOW TO THE LAST OF THE MAIN sources of demand for GNP—the government. As before, we should begin by familiarizing ourselves with its long historical profile. Figure 10·1 (p. 144) at once shows the signal fact that will underlie the discussion in this chapter. It is that up to 1940 the government was almost insignificant as a source of economic demand. More important, the New Deal (1933–1940) and the postwar era marked a turning point in the *philosophy* of government, from a passive to an active force in macroeconomic affairs. In Europe, government has played a substantial economic role for a longer period; but in Europe as well as America, the deliberate *public management* of demand is a modern phenomenon on which this chapter will focus.

Government in the Expenditure Flow

Before we begin our analysis, let us take a closer look at a recent year, to help us fit the government sector into the flow of national expenditure. Figure 10·2 (p. 145) has the familiar bars of our flow diagram. Note that indirect taxes, totaling some $118 billion in 1973, amounted to almost 10 percent of the value of GNP. As can be seen, however, income taxes on households and businesses are much more important than indirect taxes in providing total government revenues. (What the diagram does not show is that about two-thirds of the indirect taxes are state and local in origin: property taxes, excise taxes, motor vehicle and gasoline taxes, and others. Income taxes and Social Security contributions constitute about nine-tenths of the income of the federal government.)

On the expenditure side, we see that state and local purchases of goods and services are more important than federal purchases in providing public demand; however, since two-thirds of all transfer payments are federal in origin, total federal *expenditures* (as contrasted with purchases of goods and services) run about one-fifth higher than all state and local expenditures.

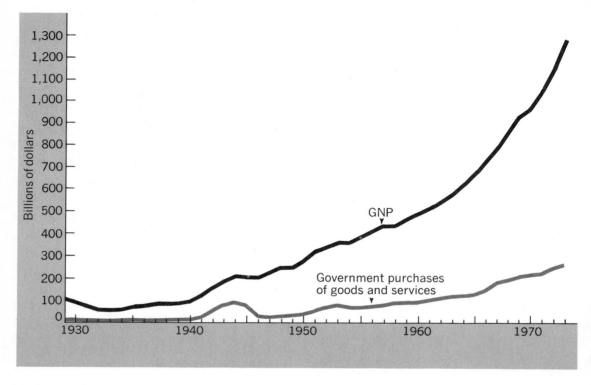

FIGURE 10 · 1
GNP and the government sector

Finally, it is worth reminding ourselves of the different significance and impact of public purchases and transfers. Public purchases of goods and services, whether they originate with local or federal government, require the use of land, labor, and capital. They thus contribute to GNP. Transfer payments, on the other hand, do not increase output. They are simply a reallocation of income, from factors to various groups of the community in the business sector or the household sector. Transfers, therefore, do not require new production and therefore do not add to GNP.

GOVERNMENT SECTOR IN HISTORICAL PERSPECTIVE

How large does the public sector bulk in the total flow of GNP? Let us again try to put a perspective into our answer by observing the trend of government purchases over the years.

We have already pointed out the striking change from prewar to postwar years. The government sector, taken as a whole, has changed from a very small sector to a very large one. In 1929, total government purchases of goods and services were only half of total private investment spending; in 1973, total government purchases were almost 40 percent *larger* than private investment. *In terms of its contributions to GNP, government is now second only to consumption.*

Thus, the public sector, whose operation we will have to examine closely, has become a major factor in the economy as a whole. Let us begin by learning to distinguish carefully among various aspects of what we call "government spending." As we shall see, it is very easy to get confused between "expenditures" and "purchases of goods and services"; between federal spending and total government spending (which includes the states and localities); and between war and nonwar spending.

1. Government expenditures vs. purchases of goods and services

When we speak of government spending, we must take care to specify whether we mean total *expenditures of the government,* which include transfer payments, or *purchases of goods and services by the government,* which represent only actual economic activity performed for, and bought by, the government. In the latter category we include all "production" that owes its existence to public demand, whether from federal, state, or local

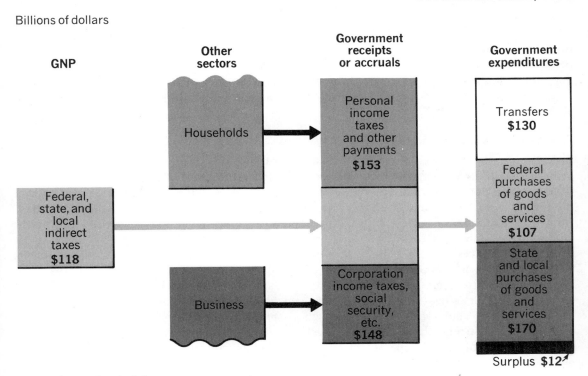

FIGURE 10 · 2
Government sector, 1973

Billions of dollars

Tax breakdown partly estimated

agencies; in the former we include activities performed for the government *plus* transfer payments made by government, at all levels, as part of the redistribution of income. Thus, under "purchases" we include items such as arms and education and police and roads; under "expenditures" we count all these plus Social Security; interest on the debts of localities, states, and the federal government; welfare; and other such transfers.

The distinction is important in terms of the relative bulk of what we call government spending. The purchases of goods and services by all government agencies amounted in 1973 to about $277 billion (of which, as Fig. 10·2 shows, the federal governmen accounted for just over $100 billion). *The term "G" in our GNP equation stands for these total purchases.* The larger "expenditure" category came to $407 billion. Thus government purchases were the direct cause of the production of about 21 percent of GNP itself, whereas government expenditures amounted in all to not quite one-third of GNP. Remember that a rise in transfers does not increase GNP, so that you must be careful not to use "expenditures" and "purchases" indiscriminately.

2. Federal vs. state and local spending

In dealing with the public sector we must also be careful to distinguish between expenditures or purchases that originate with the federal government and those that stem from state and local agencies. As we noted in Fig. 10·2, state and local spending for goods and services is *larger* than federal purchasing. This is the consequence of the rise of an urbanized, motorized, education-minded society that has imposed vast new burdens on state and local authorities: the supervision of vehicular traffic alone requires the employment of roughly one out of every ten state and local employees, and the support of education now runs to $65 billion a year. These have been increasing during the last decade, and now, annual state and local spending for such goods and services runs about 60 percent ahead of federal purchases.

On the other hand, federal expenditures, *including transfers,* make *total* federal spending larger than total state-and-local spending. In 1973, for example, federal expenditures, including transfers such as Social Security, interest on the debt, various subsidies, grants to the states, etc., brought total federal outlays of all kinds to more than double the amount it spent for goods and services alone.

3. Welfare vs. warfare

Most of the rise in federal purchases of goods and services is the result of our swollen armaments economy, a problem so important that we will look into it separately in a supplement to this chapter. Defense spending in 1973 amounted to about 30 percent of our federal expenditures of all kinds including transfers, and to a much larger fraction—not quite 75 percent—of federal purchases of goods and services. In contrast, note that federal purchases of nonwar goods and services as a percent of GNP are actually smaller than in the prewar days and have shown only a slight rise during the last decade.

Meanwhile, social welfare expenditures of all kinds and of all government agencies (federal, state, and local), including such payments as Social Security, health and medical programs, public education, public housing, welfare assistance, etc., have risen from about 10 percent of GNP in the mid-1930s to about 19 percent today. This is not a large percentage by international standards. In 1971 (the last year for which I have comparative figures) at least 4 other nations spent a higher proportion of their GNP on education than we did. Other social welfare spending (excluding education) amounted to about 13 percent of our GNP, compared with an average of more than 15 percent among the in-

PUBLIC AND PRIVATE BUYING

It is important to realize that government buying can be divided into consumption and investment expenditures, just as private expenditures are. In 1972, for example, governments—federal, state, and local—spent $56 billion for structures and durable goods such as roads, schools, parks, sewage disposal plants and the like, as well as $69 billion on manpower training programs and education to upgrade human skills. These are all *public investment* programs.

Governments also spend large sums on *public consumption*; that is, on providing goods that are enjoyable or necessary for the public at large. Streets are swept, zoos operated, bombers flown, criminals caught.

Why do we separate government consumption and investment from private consumption and investment? The immediate answer is that the money is spent by some government agency rather than by a household or a firm. But there is a deeper reason behind this. It is that a *political decision* has been made to put certain types of expenditures into the hands of the public authorities.

This decision varies from nation to nation. Some countries, like the U.S., have private airlines. Others, such as most of the nations of Europe, have public airlines. In the old days, roads were private; today roads are public, although occasionally one finds a privately owned road. (Note, by the way, that we could not utilize our private consumption of automobile travel unless we simultaneously "consumed" the public road on which we travel.) All nations provide public defense, justice, administration; most provide some public health; a few provide public entertainment. Ideology draws the line, not only between socialist and capitalist governments, but within socialist and capitalist governments: there is a large private agricultural sector in Yugoslavia, a very small one in Russia; many municipally owned power stations in Europe; far fewer here.

What is important to realize is that government expenditure is not a form of economic activity different from consumption or investment. It is the same kind of economic activity, undertaken collectively, through a public agency, rather than privately.

TABLE 10 · 1
Federal Nondefense Purchases

Selected years	1929	1933	1940	1960–65	1966	1967	1968	1969	1970	1971	1972	1973
Percent of GNP	1.0*	3.0*	4.0	2.1	2.2	2.3	2.5	2.5	2.4	2.5	2.6	2.6

*Estimated.

dustrialized nations of Europe. It is noteworthy that in 1971 the average monthly Social Security check per married couple came to just over $132; in Scandinavian countries the payments, compared to average earnings, were roughly twice as generous as ours.

The Main Tasks of Government

The forms and functions of government spending are so complex that it may help us if we now step back and simplify the picture. Basically the federal government has three major economic functions. Measured in terms of expenditures, its largest responsibility lies in the conduct of *international affairs.* Here we find expenditures for defense, foreign aid, veterans' expenditures, military research including space exploration. In 1972 this absorbed 41 percent of all federal spending.

Second, the federal government writes checks in the form of *transfer payments* to individuals and businesses. Here are the farm subsidies, subsidies for the merchant marine, and the very large outflow for Social Security and other welfare. In all, this adds up to another 42 percent of federal expenditure.

Third, the federal government writes checks, in the form of *grants-in-aid* to states and local governments. This accounts for 15 percent of federal outlays. The remainder of federal spending—2 percent—represents direct federal government operating costs and various miscellaneous functions.

It will help us review the main outlines of government spending if we look at Fig. 10·3. The first chart shows us the strikingly different *sources of funds* that flow to the federal and to state and local governments. Note the much heavier reliance of the federal government on income taxes, and the corresponding dependence of state and local governments on indirect taxes. The middle chart shows us the difference in the division of activity between federal and other governments by kinds of payments. But this table obscures a still more basic division, which we see in the third chart. Here we contrast the functions of federal and state and local governments. Now the importance of the three main functions of the federal government clearly emerges.

The Economics of the Public Sector

So far we have been mainly concerned with problems of a definitional kind—in finding out what the government does. Now we want to examine the public sector from a different angle; namely, its unique *economic* character. And here the appropriate place to begin seems to be in the difference in *motivations* that guide public, as contrasted with private, spending.

We recall that the motivations for the household sector and the business sector are lodged in the free decisions of their respective units. Householders decide to spend or save their incomes as they wish, and we are able to construct a propensity to consume schedule only because there seem to be spending and saving patterns that emerge spontaneously from the householders themselves. Similarly, business firms exercise their own judgments on their capital expenditures, and as a result we have seen the inherent variability of investment decisions.

But when we turn to the expenditures of the public sector, we enter an entirely new area of motivation. It is no longer fixed habit or profit that determines the rate of spending, but *political decision*—that is, the collective will of the people as it is formulated and expressed through their local, state, and federal legislatures and executives.

As we shall soon see, this does not mean that government is therefore an entirely unpredictable economic force. There are regularities and patterns in the government's economic behavior, as there are in other sectors. Yet the presence of an explicit political will that can direct the income or outgo of the sector *as a whole* (especially its federal component) gives to the public sector a special significance. *This is the only sector whose expenditures and receipts are open to deliberate control.* We can exert (through public action) very important influences on the behavior of households and firms. But we cannot directly alter their economic activity in the manner that is open to us with the public sector.

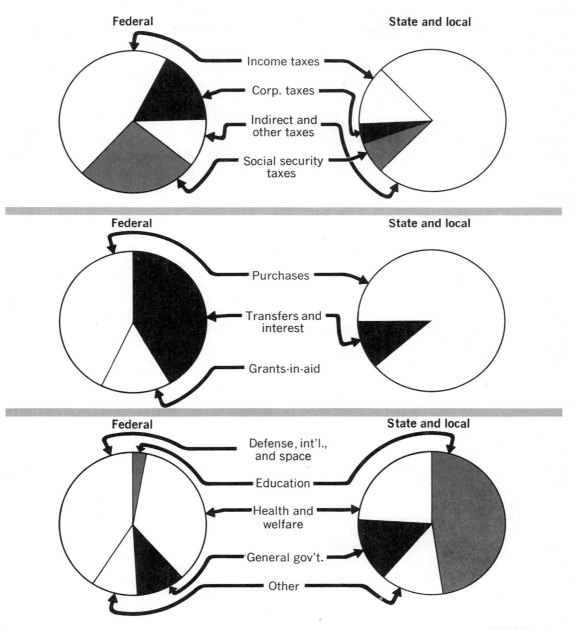

Income taxes

Corp. taxes

Indirect and
other taxes

Social security
taxes

Federal   State and local

Purchases

Transfers and
interest

Grants-in-aid

Federal   State and local

Defense, int'l.,
and space

Education

Health and
welfare

General gov't.

Other

FIGURE 10 · 3
Federal, state, and local finances

JOHN MAYNARD KEYNES

Few economists have left so deep a mark on their own times as John Maynard Keynes, and few have roused such passions, pro and con. It is difficult now, when (as a famous conservative economist has said) "We are all Keynesians," to recall the impact of Keynes's seminal book, *The General Theory of Employment, Interest, and Money*, when it appeared in 1936. Yet there were debates in the halls of academe in which voices shook and faces became empurpled over questions such as whether or not savings and investment were equal, as Keynes *defined* them to be! (We shall come to that question shortly.)

What made Keynes so controversial? Partly it was the economic philosophy that lay half explicit, half implicit in his great book—a philosophy of active government intervention. In a period when the reigning philosophy in many circles was still laissez faire, this was reason enough for Keynes's disturbing impact.

But perhaps another reason was Keynes's personality. Inordinately gifted, he was successful at a dozen things: a brilliant mathematician, a major diplomat, a great collector of modern French art, a dazzlingly skillful investor and speculator—here was one theoretical economist who *did* make a lot of money—a fascinating speaker, a consummate stylist. Keynes was not one to wear these talents modestly, and his wit was savage. Sir Harry Goshen, chairman of a Scottish bank, once deplored a Keynesian proposal and urged that things should be allowed to take "their natural course." "Is it more appropriate to smile or rage at these artless sentiments?" Keynes asked. "Best perhaps to let Sir Harry take *his* natural course."

FISCAL POLICY

The deliberate use of the government sector as an active economic force is a relatively new conception in economics. Much of the apparatus of macroeconomic analysis stems essentially from the work of John Maynard Keynes during the Great Depression. At that time his proposals were regarded as extremely daring, but they have become increasingly accepted by both major political parties. Although the bold use of the economic powers of the public sector is far from commanding unanimous assent in the United States today, there is a steadily growing consensus in the use of fiscal policy—that is, the deliberate utilization of the government's taxing and spending powers—to help insure the stability and growth of the national economy.

The basic idea behind modern fiscal policy is simple enough. We have seen that economic recessions have their roots in a failure of the business sector to offset the savings of the economy through sufficient investment. If savings or leakages are larger than intended investment, there will be a gap in the circuit of incomes and expenditures that can cumulate downward, at first by the effect of the multiplier, thereafter, and even more seriously, by further decreases in investment brought about by falling sales and gloomy expectations.

But if a falling GNP is caused by an inadequacy of expenditures in one sector, our analysis suggests an answer. Could not the insufficiency of spending in the business sector be offset by higher spending in another sector, the public sector? Could not the public sector serve as a supplementary avenue for the "transfer" of savings into expenditure?

As Fig. 10·4 shows, a demand gap can indeed be closed by "transferring" savings to the public sector and spending them. The diagram shows savings in the household sector partly offset by business investment and partly by government spending. It makes clear that at least so far as the mechanics of the economic flow are concerned, the public sector can serve to offset savings or other leakages equally as well as the private sector.

How is the "transfer" accomplished? It can be done much as business does it, by offering bonds that individuals or institutions may buy with their savings. Unlike business, the government cannot offer stock, for it is not run as a profit-making enterprise. However, government has a source of funds quite different from business; namely, *taxes. In effect, government can "commandeer" purchasing power in a way that business cannot.*

TAXES, EXPENDITURES, AND GNP

We shall look more carefully into the question of how the government can serve as a kind of counterbalance for the private economy. But first we must discover something about the normal behavior of the public sector; for despite the importance of political decisions in determining the action of the public sector, and despite the multiplicity of government units and activities, *we can nonetheless discern "propensities" in government spending and receiving*—propensities that play their compensating role in the economy quite independently of any direct political intervention.

The reason for these propensities is that both government income and government outgo are closely tied to private activity. Government receipts are derived in the main from taxes, and taxes—direct or indirect—

FIGURE 10 · 4
Public expenditure and the demand gap

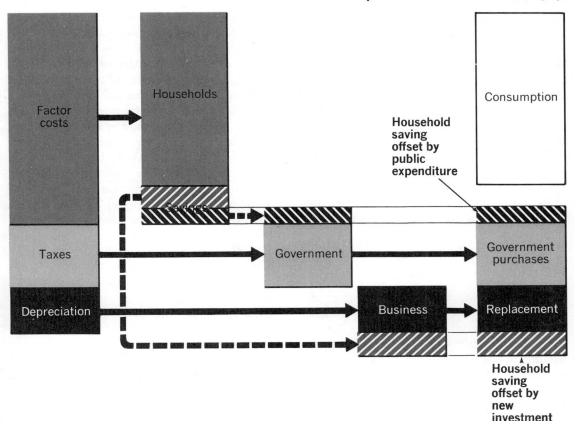

tend to reflect the trend of business and personal income. In fact, we can generalize about tax payments in much the same fashion as we can about consumption, describing them as a predictable function of GNP. To be sure, this assumes that tax *rates* do not change. But since rates change only infrequently, we can draw up a general schedule that relates tax receipts and the level of GNP. The schedule will show not only that taxes rise as GNP rises, but that they rise *faster* than GNP.

Why faster? Largely because of the progressive structure of the federal income tax. As household and business incomes rise to higher levels, the percentage "bite" of income taxes increases. Thus as incomes rise, tax liabilities rise even more. Conversely, the tax bite works downward in the opposite way. As incomes fall, taxes fall even faster, since households or businesses with lowered incomes find themselves in less steep tax brackets.

Government expenditures also show certain "propensities," which is to say, *some government spending is also functionally related to the level of GNP.* A number of government programs are directly correlated to the level of economic activity in such a way that spending *decreases* as GNP *increases,* and vice versa. For instance, unemployment benefits are naturally higher when GNP is low or falling. So are many welfare payments at the state and local level. So, too, are disbursements to farmers under various agricultural programs.

AUTOMATIC STABILIZERS

All these automatic effects taken together are called the *automatic stabilizers* or the *built-in stabilizers* of the economy. What they add up to is an automatic government counterbalance to the private sector. As GNP falls because private spending is insufficient, taxes decline even faster and public expenditures grow, thereby automatically causing the government sector to offset the private sector to some extent. In similar fashion, as GNP rises, taxes tend to rise even faster and public expenditures decline, thereby causing the government sector to act as a brake.

The public sector therefore acts as an automatic compensator, even without direct action to alter tax or expenditure levels, pumping out more public demand when private demand is slowing and curbing public demand when private demand is brisk.

How effective are the built-in stabilizers? It is estimated that the increase in transfer payments plus the reduction in taxes offset about 35¢ of each dollar of original decline in spending. Here is how this works. Suppose that private investment were to fall by $10 billion. If there were no stabilizers, household spending might fall by another $10 billion (the multiplier effect), causing a total decline of $20 billion in incomes.

The action of the stabilizers, however, will prevent the full force of this fall. First, the reduction in incomes of both households and firms will lower their tax liabilities. Since taxes take about 35¢ from each dollar, the initial drop of $10 billion in incomes will reduce tax liabilities by about $3.5 billion. Most of this—let us say $3 billion—is likely to be spent. Meanwhile some public expenditures for unemployment insurance and farm payments will rise, pumping out perhaps $1 billion into the consumption sector, all of which we assume to be spent by its recipients.

Thus, the incomes of firms and households, having originally fallen by $10 billion, will be offset by roughly $4 billion— $1 billion in additional transfer incomes and $3 billion in income spent by households because their taxes are lower. As a result, the decline in expenditure will be reduced from $10 billion to about $6 billion (actually $6.5 billion, according to the calculations of the

Council of Economic Advisers). The multiplier will then indeed affect this net reduction in spending, so that total incomes in the economy will fall by twice as much, or $13 billion in all. But this is considerably less than the fall of $20 billion that would otherwise have taken place.

This is certainly an improvement over a situation with no stabilizers. Yet if the drop in investment is not to bring about some fall in GNP, it will have to be *fully* compensated by an equivalent increase in government spending or by a fall in taxes large enough to induce an equivalent amount of private spending. This will require public action more vigorous than that brought about automatically. Indeed, it requires that the government take on a task very different from any we have heretofore studied, the task of "demand management," or acting as the *deliberate* balancing mechanism of the economy.*

Demand Management

How does the government manage demand? It has three basic alternatives. It can

1. *increase or decrease expenditures*

2. *raise or lower taxes*

3. *alter its monetary policy*

We have already looked into the mechanics of the first option in Fig. 10·4, where we showed that government expenditure fills a demand gap exactly like private expenditure. It follows that a decrease in government

---

*Although we should note that different kinds of private and public spending programs may have different multipliers if they go to different spending groups. A government public works program that uses unskilled labor is apt to have a larger initial repercussion on GNP than a private investment project in computers. Additional transfer expenditures may also have initial multiplier effects different from direct purchases of goods and services. And finally, different tax structures will cause changes in GNP to affect private spending differently.

spending will also create a decrease in final demand, just as a drop in the spending of any other sector.

Our diagram did not show the direct effect of tax changes, simply because it is difficult to draw such a diagram clearly. But it is not difficult to understand the effect of a tax change. When the government lowers taxes it diminishes the transfer of income from households or firms into the public sector. Households and firms therefore have more income to spend. Contrariwise, in raising taxes, a government withdraws spending power from households and firms. As a result, we can expect that private spending will fall.

OFFSETS AND REPERCUSSIONS

The direct effects of changes in expenditures and taxes are thus easy to picture. (We will postpone for a few chapters the use of monetary policy, but we can already anticipate that the purpose of monetary policy is also to induce households or firms to spend more or less money, much as changes in taxes.

A few cautions are in order, however. When government expenditures or taxes are changed, the government wants to raise or lower total demand by a certain amount. Therefore the fiscal authorities must take into account the repercussions that their own policies may have. For example, an increase in government expenditures financed by borrowing may bring about a rise in private expenditures because the announcement of a policy of higher spending may spur businessmen into taking more aggressive investment action. If that is the case, government spending plus additional private spending may raise total demand by more than the government originally desired! At the other extreme, it is possible that the announcement of a government spending program may "scare off" business spending. This was probably the case in the early days of the New Deal, although it is much less likely to happen today, when business has come to welcome most government spending.

TIME LAGS

Second, there is a long delay between the adoption of a new tax or expenditure policy and the realization of its effects. Increased expenditures or new tax proposals have to move through Congress, often a time-consuming process. In addition, if expenditures require capital construction, it may take months, even years, before spending really gets rolling. Thus by the time the new expenditures begin to give their boosting effect, the economic situation may have changed in a way that makes those expenditures unwelcome. So, too, with expenditure cuts. It takes a long time to turn off most government programs. By the time the spending ceases, we may wish it were still with us!

Some economists have therefore suggested that we should have "stockpiles" of approved expenditure projects and "standby" authority to permit the President to raise or lower tax rates, within stated limits, in order to speed up the process of demand management. Other countries have successfully used such expenditure "stockpiles" as a means of accelerating the demand management process, and the last several U.S. administrations have sought—so far in vain— for executive power to adjust tax rates. Most economists would probably favor both proposals, but neither is yet an actuality. As a result, *very long time lags must be taken into account in the normal process of demand management.*

TAX CUTS VS. EXPENDITURES

Which of these two methods of managing demand—taxes or spending—is preferable?

The question basically asks us which we need more: public goods or private goods. But there are a number of technical economic criteria that we must also bear in mind.

First, tax cuts and expenditures tend to favor different groups. Tax cuts benefit those who pay taxes, and expenditures benefit those who receive them. This simple fact reveals a good deal about the political and economic pros and cons of each method. Tax cuts help well-to-do families and are of little direct benefit to poor families whose incomes are so low that they pay little or no income taxes. Expenditure programs *can* benefit these disadvantaged groups or areas—for example, by slum clearance in specific cities, training programs, or simply higher welfare payments. Expenditure programs can also help special groups, such as military or road contractors, or middle-income families who usually benefit from housing programs.

The difference, then, is that tax programs have a widespread impact, whereas expenditure programs tend to have a concentrated impact: *tax cuts or increases are diffused across the economy, exerting their influences on different income strata, whereas expenditure programs are often concentrated geographically or occupationally.* (Some expenditure programs, such as Social Security or medical aid, can have a broad "horizontal effect" as well.)

Second, *expenditure programs tend to be more reliable as a means of increasing demand, whereas tax programs tend to be effective in decreasing demand.* The reason is clear enough. If the government wishes to increase final demand and chooses to lower taxes, it makes possible a higher level of private spending, but there is no guarantee that firms or households will in fact spend all their tax savings. Indeed, the marginal propensity to consume leads us to be quite certain that firms and households will not spend all their tax reductions, at least for a time. Thus if the government wants to increase demand by say $7 billion, it may have to cut taxes by about $10 billion.

On the other hand, tax increases are a very reliable method of decreasing demand. Individuals or firms *can* "defy" tax increases and maintain their former level of spending by going out and borrowing money or by spending their savings, but it is unlikely they will do so. If the government tries to hold back total demand by cutting its own expenditure programs, however, there is the chance that firms and individuals will undo the government's effort to cut demand by borrowing and spending more themselves.

There is no magic formula that will enable us to declare once and for all what policy is best for demand management. It is often impossible to raise taxes for political reasons, in which case a decrease in expenditures is certainly the next best way to keep total demand from rising too fast. So too, it may be impossible to push through a program of public expenditure because public opinion or congressional tempers are opposed to spending. In that case, a tax cut is certainly the best available way to keep demand up if the nation is threatened with a recession.

GOVERNMENT-MADE CYCLES

Thus the management of demand is fraught with difficulties. One of them stems from the fact that by virtue of its size, government is itself the source of much economic instability. Government is not just a "balance wheel" in the economy, but a primary source of demand; and when that demand changes, we are likely to experience booms or recessions.

For example, the recessions of 1954 and 1957–1958 were both caused by cuts in military spending. No other government (or private) spending rose to fill the gap, and the economy suffered a decline as a result. Again, a recession was "made in Washington" in 1960–1961, when the Eisenhower administration tried to balance the federal government's budget by cutting expenditures. Not surprisingly, total demand fell and the economy slumped. Yet another instance arose in 1969–1970, when the Nixon administration tried to curb inflation by trimming government spending. Once again the economy responded by slowing down its growth—alas, without curing its inflationary ills.

FISCAL DRAG

We shall return at length to the problem of inflation, but let us pursue a little further the difficulties of managing demand. One of these is the problem known as *fiscal drag,* a problem that arises from the same mechanism that gives rise to the automatic stabilizers. We have seen that most taxes depend on the level of income and that the federal government tends to increase its tax collections faster than income grows. As a result, if the government maintains a more or less "do nothing" policy, it will gradually collect more and more taxes, while its expenditures remain constant.

This would lead to a chronic, rising surplus in the federal budget. What this surplus means, in macroeconomic terms, is that the government is taking income away from the household and business sectors and failing to spend it. Hence such a surplus could seriously hold back the economy from attaining its maximum output. Thus the government may have to declare a "fiscal dividend" by cutting taxes or increasing expenditures, if it is to prevent a slowdown.

RUOs

Still another problem of demand management is exactly the converse of the one we have just mentioned. It has been called RUOs, or *relatively uncontrollable outlays.* This problem refers to the fact that certain kinds of expenditure gather a momentum of their own and defy sensible management. Military outlays were for many years sacrosanct, and they steadily rose, whatever their economic consequences. So were farm supports. More recently, Social Security expenditures have been rising more rapidly than the growth of GNP, because Social Security payments have become an important political issue.

Under the influence of RUOs, the federal budget can run badly into deficit, even though considerations of demand management would call for a cut in government spending. For example, in 1970 we incurred a federal deficit of $13 billion, and in 1971 a deficit of $22 billion—not because of deliberate planning to offset demand gaps elsewhere, but largely because we could not turn off certain spigots of government spending. According to a study made by the Brookings Institution, such relatively uncontrollable outlays now constitute over 70 percent of the federal budget, and their importance is going up, not down.

GRANTS-IN-AID

A different problem of demand management relates to the fiscal aid the federal government gives to the states, so-called grants-in-aid. Grants-in-aid have risen from $12.7 billion in 1966 to $42 billion in 1973, and they may rise further. *Because grants-in-aid encourage state and local spending, they are one of the most important macroeconomic instruments controlled by the federal government.*

Grants-in-aid are of three kinds. *Categorical grants* are made for specifically designated purposes; for example, grants for highway expenditure. *Block grants* are designated not for specific purposes but for broad categories of purpose; an example is a grant for "educational purposes." *Unrestricted grants* may be used for any purpose. The controversial plan to distribute a fixed percentage of federal revenue to states and localities under a "revenue-sharing" plan is, in part, such an unrestricted grant.

The distinction among these types of grants is clearer from a legal than from an economic point of view. Consider a locality that was going to build a new road. If it receives a categorical grant for that purpose, the community can use revenues, formerly intended for road building, for another purpose: a categorical grant has become in fact an unrestricted grant. So, too, a block grant for education may free up some funds formerly intended for education but that can now be spent in another area. The "catch" in these grants is that the federal government often attaches a matching provision to its grant, so that the locality has to spend some of its revenues on, say, roads or education, to qualify for federal aid. Thus a promise of $1 in federal aid for a given purpose may induce state and local authorities to undertake programs that lead to a much larger increase in total expenditure than the federal outlay.

REVENUE SHARING

The Nixon administration strongly urged that many categorical grants be replaced by a system of automatic *revenue sharing.* Proponents of this plan stress two advantages. One is that the federal government is a much more effective taxgatherer than the states or cities. By sharing its revenues with states and localities it will give them spending abilities they could not otherwise enjoy. Second, the plan accords with the general philosophy of those who would like to see economic power deconcentrated and brought back toward local government.

Opponents of the plan fear that the more-or-less unrestricted granting of funds may lead to state and local tax cuts instead of to additional state and local spending. These cuts may occur because states tend to compete with one another for new industry, each state trying to keep its taxes lower than its neighbors. When all states do this, no one gains a competitive advantage, but the result is too little spending for domestic purposes. The danger is that the assurance of federal aid will take the pressure off states and localities, who will use their revenue shares to cut down on local taxation, thereby cutting down as well on local programs. Proponents of revenue sharing reply that the share of revenue going to each state can be determined by formulas that will reward states for making a strong local tax effort. Opponents then charge that this will benefit rich states that can afford higher taxes and penalize poor ones that cannot.

To these complex considerations, there must be added another. Grants-in-aid and revenue sharing force us to confront the difficult question of what level of government should make various expenditure and tax decisions. There is disagreement over which functions are best "reserved" for the federal government (e.g., highways?); over how much intervention the federal government should have in economic activities traditionally reserved for the states (education?); and over what sorts of strictly local programs should be aided by categorical grants (such as local police forces). These are matters for political determination, but their effects on the level and distribution of public demand can be very considerable.

THE RESPONSIBILITY OF PUBLIC DEMAND

All these considerations point out how difficult it is to conduct demand management as smoothly in practice as in textbooks. There was a time, not too long ago, when economists talked rather glibly of "fine-tuning" the economy. That was in the first flush of triumph of the *idea* of managed demand, before the hard realities of fiscal drag and RUOs and other problems had been fully faced. Economists are a good deal more modest in their claims these days.

Nevertheless, the basic idea of using the government as a balancing mechanism for the economy remains valid, however difficult it may be to realize the perfect balance in fact. It is valid because the federal sector is the only sector whose operations we can collectively control. There is no way for business to determine how much it should spend as a sector, no way for consumers to concert their activity. More important, even if there were such a way, business and consumer actions might not accord with the needs of the macroeconomy. Only the public sector can act consciously on behalf of the public interest; only the public sector can attempt to reconcile the needs of all groups. However exasperating or inefficient or clumsy public demand management may be, it remains a major accomplishment, both in theory and fact, of twentieth-century economics.

KEY WORDS

Government purchases vs. government expenditures

CENTRAL CONCEPTS

1. The *public sector* derives its income from three main sources: indirect taxes (mainly for state and local governments), personal income taxes, and corporate taxes. Expenditures for *goods and services* are roughly equally divided between federal government and state and local government, but the federal government is the larger source of *transfer expenditures*.

Fiscal policy

Automatic
stabilizers

Demand
management

Expenditures

Taxes

Monetary policy

Time lags

Expenditures vs.
tax cuts

Fiscal drag

RUOs

Grants-in-aid

2. Comparing 1970 with the 1920s, we find that the public sector has grown considerably as a proportion of GNP. Federal purchases have grown largely for defense purposes. Total expenditures have grown because of much larger defense spending and, in recent years, larger spending for welfare, including such items as education, social security, and welfare assistance.

3. The critical differentiating factor between the public and the private sectors is that the public sector can be deliberately employed as an instrument of *national economic policy*.

4. The use of government spending and taxing to achieve economic stability is called *fiscal policy*. *Automatic stabilizers* lessen the momentum of booms and cushion the impact of recessions. The stabilizers arise from the progressive incidence of income taxation, from expenditure programs geared to unemployment, and so on.

5. The effort to use the government as a balance wheel in the economy is called *demand management*. Demand management uses three main instruments. It seeks to

   • raise or lower aggregate demand by altering the *level of public expenditures*
   • influence aggregate demand by raising or lowering *taxes*
   • affect final demand through *monetary policy*

6. Demand management is complicated for many reasons. One of them is that changes in expenditures or taxes may induce augmenting or offsetting changes in the private sector. A second difficulty is that long *time lags* occur between policy and its implementation.

7. It is difficult to choose categorically between expenditures and taxes as a preferred means of control. Tax changes tend to benefit or hurt taxpayers and are of little immediate concern to the nonincome-taxpaying poor. Expenditures can be focused on special groups or areas. *Generally speaking, tax increases are more effective than expenditure decreases as a means of reducing demand; and expenditure increases are surer than tax cuts as a method of increasing demand.*

8. Other difficulties of demand management are the threat of *fiscal drag*, the problem of *relatively uncontrollable outlays* (RUOs), and the use of *grants-in-aid*. Grants-in-aid, in particular, are an important tool of demand management, but they present many problems with regard to the effect of various grant-in-aid programs and the desirable location of political decision over different kinds of economic activity.

QUESTIONS

1. What are the main differences between the public and the private sectors? Are these differences economic or political?

2. Show in a diagram how increased government expenditure can offset a demand gap. Show also how decreased government taxation can do the same.

3. What is meant by the automatic stabilizers? Give an example of how they might work if we had an increase in investment of $20 billion and the multiplier were 2; and if the increase in taxes and the decrease in public expenditure associated with the boom in investment were $3 billion and $1 billion, respectively.

4. What do you consider a better way of combating a mild recession—tax cuts or higher expenditures? Why? Suppose we had a deep recession, then what would you do?

5. In what sorts of economic conditions should the government run a surplus?

6. Suppose the government cuts taxes by $10 billion and also cuts its expenditures by the same amount. Will this stimulate the economy? Suppose it raises its expenditures and also raises taxes? Would this be a good antirecession policy?

Special Supplement on the Military Subeconomy

The Department of Defense (DOD) is the largest planned economy outside the Soviet Union. Its property—plant and equipment, land, inventories of war and other commodities—amounts to over $200 billion, equal to about 7 percent of the assets of the entire American economy. It owns 39 million acres of land, roughly an area the size of Hawaii. It rules over a population of more than 3 million—direct employees or soldiers —and spends an "official" budget of roughly $75 billion, a budget three-quarters as large as the entire gross national product of Great Britain.

This makes the DOD richer than any small nation in the world and, of course, incomparably more powerful. That part of its assets represented by nuclear explosives alone gives it the equivalent of six tons of TNT for every living inhabitant of the globe, to which must be added the awesome military power of its "conventional" weapons. The conventional explosives dropped in Indochina *before* the extension of the war to Laos amounted to well over 3 million tons, or 50 percent *more* than the total bomb tonnage dropped on all nations in both European and Pacific theaters during World War II.

The DOD system embraces both people and industry. In the early 1970s the people included, first, some 2.5 million soldiers deployed in more than 2,000 bases or locations abroad and at home, plus another half million civilians located within the United States and abroad. No less important are some 2 million civilian workers who are directly employed on war production, in addition to a much larger number employed in the secondary echelon of defense-related output. This does not include still further millions who owe their livelihood to the civilian services they render to the military. Symptomatic of the pervasive influence of military spending is the rise in unemployment in Connecticut to 8.1 percent of the labor force when a first small effort was made in 1971 to cut back on military output. What would be the effect of a major contraction in defense spending is a problem we will have to defer for later consideration, but no one denies that such a major contraction—*unless counteracted by*

vigorous expansion of civilian spending—could plunge this country into a severe depression.

The Web of Military Spending

The web of DOD expenditures extends to more areas of the economy than one might think. One expects Lockheed Aircraft, with 88 percent of its sales to the government, to be a ward of the DOD, which explains why the government agreed to rescue the company from bankruptcy in 1971 with an enormous advance of funds. One does not expect the DOD to show up (from 1960 to 1967) as the source of some 44 percent of the revenues of Pan Am or to be, through its Post Exchange (PX) system, the third largest marketing chain in the country, just after Sears and the A&P; or to be a major factor in the housing industry, spending more for military housing between 1956 and 1967 than the total spent by the federal government on all other public housing.

All in all, some 22,000 firms are prime contractors with the DOD, although the widespread practice of subcontracting means that a much larger number of enterprises—perhaps 100,000 in all—look to defense spending for a portion of their income. Within the main constituency, however, a very few firms are the bastion of the DOD economy. The hundred largest defense contractors supply about two-thirds of the $40-odd billion of manufactured deliveries; and within this group, an inner group of ten firms by themselves accounted for 30 percent of the total. Incidentally, many of these largest contractors owe not only their sales to the military economy, but a considerable portion of their capital as well. As of 1967, defense contractors used $2 billion worth of government-owned furniture and office machines, $4.7 billion worth of government-owned materials, and over $5 billion worth of government plant and equipment, on all of which they were allowed to make profits just as if they were using their own property.

The military establishment, as the largest single customer in the economy, not only supports a central core of industry but also penetrates that core with 2,072 retired military officers who were employed in 1969 by the 95 biggest contractors (the 10 largest firms averaging 106 officers each). Meanwhile, the establishment has a powerful political arm as well. In the early 1970s the DOD employed more than 300 lobbyists on Capitol Hill and (a conservative estimate) some 2,700 public relations men in the U.S. and abroad. This close political relationship undoubtedly has some bearing on the Pentagon's requests for funds being given, until recently, only the most cursory congressional inspection, leading among other things to cost "overruns" of $24 billion on 38 weapons systems.

This is not to say, of course, that the United States does not need a strong defense capability today. But there is no question that the Pentagon subeconomy—some would say "substate"—has become a major element in, and a major problem for, American capitalism. Indeed, the questions it raises are central: how important is this subeconomy to our economic vitality? How difficult would it be to reduce? Can our economy get along without a military subsector?

Military Dependency

Let us begin by reviewing a few important facts.

At the height of the Vietnam War in 1968, more than 10 percent of our labor force was employed in defense-related work. As the Vietnam War gradually decelerated, this percentage fell to about 7 percent. Defense expenditures, meanwhile, dropped from their peak of nearly $80 billion to just under $75 billion in 1973.

These global figures do not, however, give a clear picture of the strategic position of defense spending within the economy. For the problem is that war-related spending and employment are not distributed evenly across the system but are bunched in special areas and industries. In a survey made in 1967, the Defense Department found that 72 employment areas depended on war output for 12 percent or more of their employment and that four-fifths of these areas were communities with labor forces of less than 50,000. This concentration of defense activity is still a fact of economic life in the mid 1970s. The impact of a cutback on these middle-sized communities can be devastating.

In addition, defense-employment is concen-trated among special skills as well as in a nucleus of defense-oriented companies. In the late 1960s, about one scientist or engineer out of every five in private industry was employed on a defense-related job. Thirty-eight percent of all physicists depended on war-work. Twenty-five percent of all sheet-metal workers, the same proportion of pattern-makers, and 54 percent of all airplane mechanics worked on defense projects. These proportions have declined, but "defense" is still a major employer of these skills. And as we have already remarked, there is a core of companies dependent on military spending for their very existence. These are not usually the largest companies in the economy (for whom, on the average, defense receipts amount to about 10 percent of total revenues) but the second echelon of corporations: of 30 companies with assets in the $250 million to $1 billion range, 6 depended on war spending for half their incomes, and 7 depended on it for a quarter of theirs.

Thus a cutback in defense spending will be felt very sharply in particular areas, where there may be no other jobs available, or among occupational groups who have no alternative employment at equivalent pay or in companies that are "captives" of the DOD. Such companies and areas naturally lobby hard for defense expenditure on which their livelihood depends. So do their representatives in Congress. It is this interweaving of economic and political interests that makes the problem of defense cutbacks so difficult.

Conversion Possibilities

Yet a cutback is not economically impossible. What is needed is a program of retraining, relocation, income support, and conversion aid that will cushion the inevitable shock of a decline in military spending. In 1971 the National Urban Coalition estimated that we would need to spend about $4 billion over two years to move and retrain the bulk of the personnel who would be displaced if we cut our military budget by one third (in real terms) by 1976.

The sum is not large compared with the saving in national resources that would thereby be affected. *What is crucial, economically, is that the decline in war-related spending be offset by* increases *in peace-related spending, to be sure that the overall level of demand would remain high enough to act as a magnet, attracting the displaced workers to other jobs.* The Coalition therefore proposes a broadscale attack on many social problems that would raise total (local, state, and federal) government expenditures on goods and services by over 50 percent to assure that the conversion would in fact be a smooth one.

Could such a vast conversion actually be carried out? At this juncture it is important to point out that there is no insuperable *economic* problem posed by conversion, whatever the political or psychological problems. After World War II, defense spending fell from 37.5 percent of GNP (compared with only 7.4 percent today) to 6.6 percent in the short space of two years. During this period 10 million men and women were demobilized from the armed forces and added to the labor force. Yet unemployment from 1947 to 1949 rose only from 3.6 percent of the labor force to 5.5 percent. Clearly the problem today is much less formidable than it was then.

Opportunity Cost of Armaments

The difference between the two periods is that post-World War II conversion was largely the result of a hugh pent-up civilian demand. Today there is no evidence of unfilled consumer needs. The Vietnam War did not impose shortages on the American people. Thus, unless we were willing to undertake an ambitious program of public spending or tax cuts the conversion will almost certainly generate severe unemployment—and consequent political pressures to maintain military spending.

Meanwhile, it is clear that the armaments economy is not only costing us a vast sum of money, but is also weighing heavily on the Russians. The annual military expenditure of the U.S. and the U.S.S.R. together amounts to about two-thirds of the entire output of the billion peoples of Latin America, Southeast Asia, and the Near East. If we add in the arms expenditures of the rest of the world, we reach the total of more than $50 for every inhabitant of the globe. Not only

is this an opportunity cost of tragically large dimensions, if we consider the uses to which those resources might otherwise be applied, but even in terms of a strictly military calculus, much of it is *total waste, since neither side has been able to gain a decisive advantage despite its enormous expenditures.*

The Prisoners' Dilemma

How does such a senseless course commend itself to national governments? Needless to say, the answers lie deep in the web of political, economic, and social forces of our times. But analytical reasoning can nonetheless throw some light on the matter by unraveling a peculiar situation involving two prisoners, each of whom knows something about the other and who are being interrogated separately. If *both* prisoners remain silent, both will get very light terms, since the evidence against each is not conclusive. If one prisoner squeals on the other, he will get off scot-free as a reward for turning state's evidence, while the other prisoner gets a heavy term. But if *both* prisoners squeal, both will get severe terms, convicted by each other's testimony.

Now, if the two prisoners could confer—and more important, if they trusted each other absolutely—they would obviously agree that the strategy of shared silence was the best for each. But if the prisoners are separated or unsure of each other's trustworthiness, each will be powerfully tempted to rat on the other in order to reduce his own sentence. As a result, since the two are equally tempted, the outcome is likely to end in *both* sides ratting—and in both sides getting heavy punishment. Thus the pursuit of individual "self-interest" lures the two prisoners into a strategy that penalizes them both.

Something very like a Prisoners' Dilemma afflicts the nations of the world, especially the two superpowers, America and Russia. Although a policy of limited arms spending would clearly be to their mutual best advantage, their distrust of each other leads each to try to get ahead of the other. This state of mutual suspicion is then worsened when special interest groups in each nation deliberately play on the fears of the public. The end result is that both spend vast sums on armaments that yield them no advantage, while the world (including them) suffers an opportunity cost on an enormous scale. Only with a frank and candid exploration of shared gains and losses can both prisoners hope to get out of their dilemma. Prospects for a massive conversion of the U.S. arms economy may hinge on our understanding of this central military and political reality of our time.

Sources: Seymour Melman, *Pentagon Capitalism* (New York: McGraw Hill, 1970); Leonard Rodberg and Derek Sherer, *The Pentagon Watchers* (Garden City: Doubleday, 1970); Adam Yarmolinsky, *The Military Establishment* (New York: Harper, 1971); *Economic Report of the President* (1971).

Deficit Spending

UP TO THIS MOMENT, we have been analyzing the public sector in terms of its effect on the demand for GNP. Now we are going to take a brief but necessary respite from our systematic examination of the various sources of demand for output. The use of the public sector as a source of deliberate demand management poses a question that we must understand before we can comfortably resume our inquiry. This is the question of the government debt.

Any government that uses its budget as a stabilizing device must be prepared to spend more than it takes in in taxes. On occasion it must purposefully plan a budget in which outgo exceeds income, leaving a negative figure called a *deficit*.

That raises a problem that alarms and perplexes many people. Like a business or consumer, the government cannot spend money it does not have. Therefore it must *borrow* the needed funds from individuals, firms, or banks in order to cover its deficit. Deficit spending, in other words, means the spending of borrowed money, money derived from the sale of government bonds.

DEFICITS AND LOSSES

Can the government safely run up a deficit? Let us begin to unravel this important but perplexing question by asking another: can a private business afford to run up a deficit?

There is one kind of deficit that a private business *cannot* afford: a deficit that comes from spending more money on current production than it will realize from its sale. This kind of deficit is called a *business loss;* and if losses are severe enough, a business firm will be forced to discontinue its operations.

But there is another kind of deficit, although it is not called by that name, in the operations of a private firm. This is an excess of expenditures over receipts brought about by spending money on *capital assets.* When the American Telephone and Telegraph Company or the Exxon Corporation uses its own savings or those of the public to build a new plant and new equipment, it does not show a "loss" on its annual statement to stockholders, even though its total expenditures on current costs and on capital may have been greater than sales. Instead, expenditures are divided into two kinds, one relating current costs to current income, and the other relegating expenditures on capital goods to an entirely separate "capital account." Instead of calling the excess of expenditures a deficit, they call it investment.*

DEBTS AND ASSETS

Can A.T.&T. or Exxon afford to run deficits of the latter kind indefinitely? We can answer the question by imagining ourselves in an economic landscape with no disturbing changes in technology or in consumers' tastes, so that entrepreneurs can plan ahead with great safety. Now let us assume that in this comfortable economy, Exxon decides to build a new refinery, perhaps to take care of the growing population. To finance the plant, it issues new bonds, so that its new asset is matched by a new debt.

Now what about this debt? How long can Exxon afford to have its bonds outstanding?

The answer is—forever!

Remember that we have assumed an economy remaining changeless in tastes and techniques, so that each year the new refinery can turn out a quota of output, perfectly confident that it will be sold; and each year it can set aside a reserve for wear and tear, perfectly confident that the refinery is being properly depreciated. As a result, each year the debt must be as good as the year before— no better and no worse. The bondholder is sure of getting his interest, steadily earned, and he knows that the underlying asset is being fully maintained.

Admittedly, after a certain number of years the new factory will be worn out. But if our imaginary economy remains un-

changed and if depreciation accruals have been properly set aside, when the old plant gives out, an identical new one will be built from these depreciation reserves. Meanwhile, the old debt, like the old plant, will also come to an end, for debts usually run for a fixed term of years. The Exxon Corporation must now pay back its debtholders in full. But how? The firm has accumulated a reserve to buy a new plant, but it has not accumulated a second reserve to repay its bondholders.

Nevertheless, the answer is simple enough. When the bonds come due in our imaginary situation, the Exxon Corporation issues *new* bonds equal in value to the old ones. It then sells the new bonds and uses the new money it raises to pay off the old bondholders. When the transaction is done, a whole cycle is complete: both a new refinery and a new issue of bonds exist in place of the old. Everything is exactly as it was in the first place. Furthermore, as long as this cycle can be repeated, such a debt could safely exist in perpetuity! And why not? Its underlying asset also exists, eternally renewed, in perpetuity.

REAL CORPORATE DEBTS

To be sure, not many businesses are run this way, for the obvious reason that tastes and techniques in the real world are anything but changeless. Indeed, there is every reason to believe that when a factory wears out it will *not* be replaced by another costing exactly as much and producing just the same commodity. Yet, highly stable businesses such as the Exxon Corporation or A.T.&T. do, in fact, continuously "refund" their bond issues, paying off old bonds with new ones, and never "paying back" their indebtedness as a whole. A.T.&T., for instance, actually increased its total indebtedness from $1.1 billion in 1929 to $24.1 billion in 1972. Exxon ran up its debt from $170.1 million in 1929 to

---

*Investment does not *require* a "deficit," since it can be financed out of current profits. But many expanding companies do spend more money on current and capital account than they take in through sales and thereby incur a "deficit" for at least a part of their investment.

$2.7 billion in 1973. And the credit rating of both companies today is as good as, or better than, it was in 1929.

Thus some individual enterprises that face conditions of stability similar to our imaginary situations do actually issue bonds "in perpetuity," paying back each issue when it is due, only to replace it with another (and, as we have seen, *bigger*) issue.

TOTAL BUSINESS DEBTS

Most strong individual businesses can carry their debts indefinitely, and the business sector *as a whole* can easily do so. For although individual businesses may seek to retire their debts, as we look over the whole economy we can see that as one business extinguishes its debt, another is borrowing an even larger sum. Why larger? Because the *assets* of the total business sector are also steadily rising.

Table 11·1 shows this trend in the growth of corporate debt.*

Note that from 1929 through 1940, corporate debt *declined.* The shrinkage coincided with the years of depression and slow recovery, when additions to capital plant were small. But beginning with the onset of the postwar period, we see a very rapid increase in business indebtedness, an increase that continues down to our present day.

If we think of this creation of debt (and equity) as part of the savings-investment process, the relationship between debts and assets should be clear. Debts are claims, and we remember how claims can arise as the financial counterpart of the process of real capital formation. Thus, rising debts on capital account are a sign that assets are also increasing. It is important to emphasize the *capital account.* Debts incurred to buy capital assets are very different from those incurred to pay current expenses. The latter have very little close connection with rising wealth, whereas when we see that debts on corporate capital account are rising, we can take for granted that assets are probably rising as well. The same is true, incidentally, for the ever-rising total of consumer debts that mirror a corresponding increase in consumers' assets. As our stock of houses grows, so does our total mortgage debt; as our personal inventories of cars, washing machines, and other appliances grow, so does our outstanding consumer indebtedness.

GOVERNMENT DEFICITS

Can government, like business, borrow "indefinitely"? The question is important enough to warrant a careful answer. Hence,

TABLE 11·1
Corporate Net Long-Term Debt*

Year	1929	1933	1940	1950	1966	1967	1968	1969	1970	1971	1972
Billions of dollars	47	48	44	60	231	258	286	324	360	402	447

*Maturity over one year.

*We do not show the parallel rise in new equities (shares of stock), since changes in stock market prices play so large a role here. We might, however, add a mental note to the effect that business issues new stock each year, as well as new bonds. During the 1960s and early 1970s, net new stock issues have ranged from about $2 to $9 billion per annum.

let us begin by comparing government borrowing and business borrowing.

One difference that springs quickly to mind is that businesses borrow in order to acquire productive assets. That is, matching the new claims on the business sector is additional real wealth that will provide for larger output. From this additional wealth, business will also receive the income to pay interest on its debt or dividends on its stock. But what of the government? Where are its productive assets?

We have already noted that the government budget includes dams, roads, housing projects, and many other items that might be classified as assets. During the 1960s, federal expenditures for such civil construction projects averaged about $5 billion a year. Thus the total addition to the gross public debt during the 1960s (it rose from roughly $239 billion in 1960 to $470 billion in 1973) could be construed as merely the financial counterpart of the creation of public assets.

Why is it not so considered? Mainly because, as we have seen, the peculiar character of public expenditures leads us to lump together all public spending, regardless of kind. In many European countries, however, public capital expenditures are sharply differentiated from public current expenditures. If we had such a system, the government's deficit on capital account could then be viewed as the public equivalent of business's deficit on capital account. Such a change might considerably improve the rationality of much discussion concerning the government's deficit.

SALES VS. TAXES

But there is still a difference. Private capital enhances the earning capacity of a private business, whereas most public capital, save for such assets as toll roads, does not "make money" for the public sector. Does this constitute a meaningful distinction?

We can understand, of course, why an individual business insists that its investment must be profitable. The actual money that the business will pay out in the course of making an investment will almost surely not return to the business that spent it. A shirt manufacturer, for instance, who invests in a new factory cannot hope that the men who build that factory will spend all their wages on his shirts. He knows that the money he spends through investment will soon be dissipated throughout the economy, and that it can be recaptured only through strenuous selling efforts.

Not quite so with a national government, however. Its income does not come from sales but from taxes, and those taxes reflect the general level of income of the country. Thus any and all that government lays out, just because it enters the general stream of incomes, redounds to the taxing capacity or, we might say, the "earning capacity" of government.

How much will come back to the government in taxes? That depends on two main factors: the impact of government spending on income via the multipler, and the incidence and progressivity of the tax structure. Under today's normal conditions, the government will recover about half or a little more of its expenditure.* But in any event, note that the government does not "lose" its money in the way that a business does. Whatever goes into the income stream is always *available* to the government as a source of taxes; but whatever goes into the income stream is not necessarily available to any single business as a source of sales.

This reasoning helps us understand why federal finance is different from state and local government finance. An expenditure made by New York City or New York State is apt to be respent in many other areas of the country. Thus taxable incomes in New

---

*We can make a rough estimate of the multipler effect of additional public expenditure as 2 and of the share of an additional dollar of GNP going to federal taxes as about $\frac{1}{3}$ (see page 152). Thus $1 of public spending will create $2 of GNP, of which 65¢ will go back to the federal government.

York will not, in all probability, rise to match local spending. As a result, *state and local governments must look on their finances much as an individual business does.* The power of full fiscal recapture belongs solely to the federal government.

The National Debt

INTERNAL AND EXTERNAL DEBTS

This difference between the limited powers of recoupment of a single firm and the relatively limitless powers of a national government lies at the heart of the basic difference between business and government deficit spending. It helps us understand why the government has a capacity for financial operation that is inherently of a far higher order of magnitude than that of business. We can sum up this fundamental difference in the contrast between the *externality of business debts* and the *internality of national government debts.*

What do we mean by the externality of business debts? We simply mean that business firms owe their debts to someone distinct from themselves—someone over whom they have no control—whether this be bondholders or the bank from which they borrowed. Thus, to service or to pay back its debts, business must transfer funds from its own possession into the possession of outsiders. If this transfer cannot be made, if a business does not have the funds to pay its bondholders or its bank, it will go bankrupt.

The government is in a radically different position. Its bondholders, banks, and other people or institutions to whom it owes its debts belong to the same community as that whence it extracts its receipts. In other words, the government does not have to transfer its funds to an "outside" group to pay its bonds. It transfers them, instead, from some members of the national community over which

it has legal powers (taxpayers) to other members of the *same* community (bondholders). The contrast is much the same as that between a family that owes a debt to another family, and a family in which the husband has borrowed money from his wife; or again between a firm that owes money to another, and a firm in which one branch has borrowed money from another. *Internal debts do not drain the resources of one community into another, but merely redistribute the claims among members of the same community.*

PROBLEMS OF A NATIONAL DEBT

A government cannot always borrow without trouble, however. Important and difficult problems of money management are inseparable from a large debt. More important, the people or institutions from whom taxes are collected are not always exactly the same people and institutions to whom interest is paid, so that servicing a government debt often poses problems of *redistribution of income.* For instance, if all government bonds were owned by rich people and if all government taxation were regressive (i.e., proportionately heavier on low incomes), then servicing a government debt would mean transferring income from the poor to the rich. Considerations of equity aside, this would also probably involve distributing income from spenders to savers and would thereby intensify the problem of closing the savings gap.

In addition, a debt that a government owes to foreign citizens is *not* an internal debt. It is exactly like a debt that a corporation owes to an "outside" public, and it can involve payments that can cripple a nation. Do not forget that the internality of debts applies only to *national* debts held as bonds by members of the same community of people whose incomes contribute to government revenues.

PERPETUAL PUBLIC DEBTS

Can a national government therefore have a perpetual debt? We have seen that it can. To be sure, the debt must be constantly refunded, much as business refunds its debts, with new issues of bonds replacing the old. But like the business sector, we can expect the government debt in this way to be maintained indefinitely.

Will our public debt grow forever? That depends largely on what happens to our business debts and equities. If business debts and equities grow fast enough—that is, if we are creating enough assets through investment—there is no reason why government debts should grow. Government deficits, after all, are designed as *supplements* to deficits. The rationale behind public borrowing is that it will be used only when the private sector is not providing enough expenditure to give us a large enough GNP to provide reasonably full employment.

Nonetheless, the prospect of a rising national debt bothers many people. Some day, they say, it will have to be repaid. Is this true? It may aid us to think about the problem if we try to answer the following questions:

1. Can we afford to pay interest on a rising debt?

The capacity to expand debts, both public and private, depends largely on the willingness of people to lend money, and this willingness in turn reflects their confidence that they will be paid interest regularly and

will have their principal returned to them when their bonds are due.

We have seen how refunding can take care of the repayment problem. But what about interest? With a private firm, this requires that interest costs be kept to a modest fraction of sales, so that they can easily be covered. With government, similar financial prudence requires that interest costs stay well within the taxable capacity of government. The figures in Table 11·2 give us some perspective on this problem today.

It can be seen that interest is a much higher percentage of federal revenues than of corporate revenues. But there is a reason for this. Corporations are supposed to maximize their revenues; the government is not supposed to maximize its tax income. Hence we must also judge the size of the federal interest cost in comparison with the size of GNP, the total tax base from which the government can draw. Finally, we should know that interest as a percentage of all federal receipts has remained very steady in recent years, and it is actually much lower than in the 1920s, when interest costs amounted to about 20 to 30 percent of the federal budget.

2. Can we afford the burden of a rising debt?

What is the "burden" of a debt? For a firm, the question is easy to answer. It is the *interest cost* that must be borne by those who owe the debt. Here, of course, we are back to the externality of debts. *The burden of a debt is*

TABLE 11·2
Debt and Interest Costs

	Net interest ($ billions)	Interest as proportionate cost
Nonfinancial corporations (1973)	$18.8	2.8 percent of gross corporate revenues
Federal government (1973)	14.4	5.5 percent of receipts 1.1 percent of GNP

the obligation it imposes to pay funds from one firm or community to another.

But we have seen that there is no such cost for an internal debt, such as that of a nation. The *cost* of the debt—that is, the taxes that must be levied to pay interest—becomes *income* to the very same community, as checks sent to bondholders for their interest income. Every penny that the debt costs our economy in taxes returns to our economy as income.

The same is also true of the principal of the debt. The debts we owe inside the nation we also *own* inside the nation—just as the I.O.U. a husband owes his wife is also an I.O.U. owned by the family; or, again, just as an amount borrowed by Branch A of a multibranch firm is owed to Branch B of the same firm.

There is a further point here. Internal debts are debts that are considered as financial *assets* within the "family." Nobody within A.T.&T. considers its debts to be part of the assets of the firm, but many thousands of people in the U.S. consider the country's debts to be their assets. Indeed, everyone who owns a government bond considers it an asset. Thus in contrast to external debts, paying back an internal debt does not "lift a burden" from a community, because no burden existed in the first place! When a corporation pays off a debt to a bank, it is rid of an obligation to an outside claimant on its property. But when a husband pays his wife, the *family* is no richer, any more than the *firm* is better off if one branch reimburses another. So, too, with a nation. If a national debt is repaid, the national economy is not rid of an obligation to an outside claimant. We would be rid only of obligations owed to one another.

REAL BURDENS

This is not to say—and the point is important—that government spending is costless. Consider for a moment the main cause of

government spending over the past fifty years: the prosecution of three wars. There was surely a terrific cost to these wars in lives, health, and (in economic terms) in the use of factors of production to produce guns instead of butter. But note also that all of this cost is irrevocably and unbudgeably situated in the past. The cost of all wars is borne during the years when the wars are fought and must be measured in the destruction that was then caused and the opportunities for creating real wealth that were then missed. The debt inherited from these wars is no longer a "cost." Today it is only an instrument for the transfer of incomes within the American community.

So, too, with debts incurred to fight unemployment. The cost of unemployment is also borne once and for all at the time it occurs, and the benefits of the government spending to combat unemployment will be enjoyed (or if the spending is ill-advised, the wastes of spending will be suffered) when that spending takes place. Afterward, the debt persists as a continuing means of transferring incomes, but the debt no longer has any connection to the "cost" for which it was incurred.

Costs, in other words, are *missed opportunities,* potential well-being not achieved. Debts, on the other hand (when they are held within a country) only transfer purchasing power and do not involve the nation in giving up its output to anyone else.

INDIRECT EFFECTS

Does this mean that there are no disadvantages whatsoever in a large national debt?

We have talked of one possible disadvantage, that of transferring incomes from spenders to savers, or possibly of transferring purchasing power from productive groups to unproductive groups. But we must pay heed to one other problem. This is the problem a rising debt may cause indirectly, but none-

PERSONAL DEBTS AND PUBLIC DEBTS

In view of the fact that our national debt today figures out to approximately $2,200 for every man, woman, and child, it is not surprising that we frequently hear appeals to "common sense," telling us how much better we would be without this debt, and how our grandchildren will groan under its weight.

Is this true? We have already discussed the fact that internal debts are different from external debts, but let us press the point home from a different vantage point. Suppose we decided that we would "pay off" the debt. This would mean that our government bonds would be redeemed for cash. To get the cash, we would have to tax ourselves (unless we wanted to roll the printing presses), so that what we would really be doing would be transferring money from taxpayers to bondholders.

Would that be a net gain for the nation? Consider the typical holder of a government bond —a family, a bank, or a corporation. It now holds the world's safest and most readily-sold paper asset from which a regular income is obtained. After our debt is redeemed, our families, banks, and corporations will have two choices: (1) they can hold cash and get *no* income, or (2) they can invest in other securities that are slightly *less* safe. Are these investors better off? As for our grandchildren, it is true that if we pay off the debt they will not have to "carry" its weight. But to offset that, neither will they be carried by the comfortable government bonds they would otherwise have inherited. They will also be relieved from paying taxes to meet the interest on the debt. Alas, they will be relieved as well of the pleasure of depositing the green Treasury checks for interest payments that used to arrive twice a year.

theless painfully, *if it discourages private investment*.

This could be a very serious, real cost of government debts, were such a reaction to be widespread and long-lasting. It may well be (we are not sure) that the long drawn-out and never entirely successful recovery from the Great Depression was caused, to a considerable extent, by the adverse psychological impact of government deficit spending on business investment intentions. Business did not understand deficit spending and interpreted it either as the entering wedge of socialism (instead of a crash program to save capitalism) or as a wastrel and a harebrained economic scheme. To make matters worse, the amount of the government deficit (at its peak $4 billion), while large enough to frighten the business community, was not big enough to begin to exert an effective leverage on total demand, particularly under conditions of widespread unemployment and financial catastrophe.

Today, however, it is much less likely that deficit spending would be attended by a drop in private spending. A great deal that was new and frightening in thought and practice in the 1930s is today well-understood and tested. World War II was, after all, an immense laboratory demonstration of what public spending could do for GNP. The experience of recent years gives good reason to believe that deficit spending in the future will not cause a significant slowdown in private investment expenditure.

THE PUBLIC SECTOR AGAIN IN PERSPECTIVE

We have spent enough time on the question of the debt. Now we must ask what is it that close examination of the problems of government finance reveals, making them look so different from what we expect. The answer is largely that we think of the government as if it were a firm or a household, when it is actually something else. *The government is a sector;* and if we want to think clearly about it, we must compare it, not to the maxims and activities of a household or a firm, but to those of the entire consumer sector or the entire business sector.

Then we can see that the government sector plays a role not too dissimilar from that of the business sector. We have seen how businesses, through their individual decisions to add to plant and equipment, act in concert to offset the savings of consumers. The government, we now see, acts in precisely the same way, except that its decisions, rather than reflecting the behavior of innumerable entrepreneurs in a search for profit, reflect the deliberate political will of the community itself.

Persons who do not understand the intersectoral relationships of the economy like to say that business must "live within its income" and that government acts irresponsibly in failing to do so. These critics fail to see that business does *not* live within its income, but borrows the savings of other sectors and thus typically and normally spends more than it takes in from its sales alone. By doing so, of course, it serves the invaluable function of providing an offset for saving that would otherwise create a demand gap and thereby precipitate a downward movement in economic activity.

Once this offsetting function is understood, it is not difficult to see that government, as well as business, can serve as a "spender" to offset savings, and that in the course of doing so, both government and business typically create new assets for the community.

PUBLIC AND PRIVATE ASSETS

Finally, we have seen something else that gives us a last insight into government spending. We have seen that the creation of earning assets is indispensable for business, because each asset constitutes the means by which an individual business seeks to recoup its own investment spending. But with the government, the definition of an "earning asset" can properly be much larger than with a business firm. The government does not need its assets to make money for itself directly, for the government's economic capability arises from its capacity to tax *all* incomes. So far as government is concerned, then, all that matters is that savings be turned into expenditures, and thereby into taxable incomes.

As a result, government can and should be motivated—even in a self-interested way—by a much wider view of the economic process than would be possible or proper for a single firm. Whereas a firm's assets are largely its capital goods, the assets of a nation are not only capital wealth but the whole productive capacity of its people. Thus government expenditures that redound to the health or well-being or education of its citizens are just as properly considered asset-building expenditures as are its expenditures on dams and roads.

KEY WORDS

Deficits

Government borrowing

Government debt

Assets and debts

Internal vs. external debts

Redistribution

Debt burden

CENTRAL CONCEPTS

1. The use of the government budget as a deliberate antirecession instrument leads to *deficits*. These deficits are financed by *government borrowing* and hence lead to government debt.

2. The government debt can be thought of in the same way as much private debt: as the *financial counterpart of assets.*

3. *All debts, as long as their underlying assets are economically productive, can be maintained indefinitely* by being refunded when they come due.

4. In a *progressive and growing economy, debts increase as assets rise.* Debts are only a way of financing the growth in assets.

5. National governments have the power of fiscal recapture of any money spent by them—a power not available to state governments or even to the largest businesses. Hence national governments are in a fundamentally different position regarding the safety of their domestically-held debts. This difference is expressed in the concept of *internal debts* versus *external ones.*

6. Domestically-held national debts do not lead to bankruptcy. They do present important and difficult problems of *monetary management*, and they can also result in the *redistribution of income*. These are *real burdens* of the debt.

7. *Repaying the debt would not lift a burden from the economy.* Taxes would decrease (because the debt need no longer be serviced), but income would also decrease (because interest would no longer be paid). Former government bondholders would have to find another acceptable financial asset.

8. The confusion with which the public debt is often viewed arises from a failure to understand that *the government is not a "household" but a sector*, fully comparable to the business sector in its intersectoral operations.

QUESTIONS

1. In what ways is a government deficit comparable to business spending for investment purposes? In what ways is it not?

2. If the government is going to go into debt, does it matter if it spends money for roads or for relief? For education or for weapons? Is there any connection between the use to which government spending is put and *the economic analysis of deficit spending*? Think hard about this: suppose you could show that some spending increased the productivity of the country and that other spending didn't. Would that influence your answer?

3. What is meant by the internality of debts? Is the debt of New York State internal? The debt of a country like Israel?

4. What relation do debts generally have to assets? Can business debts increase indefinitely? Can a family's? Can the debt of all consumers?

5. What are the real burdens of a national debt?

6. Trace out carefully all the consequences of paying back the national debt.

7. How would you explain to someone who is adamantly opposed to socialism that government deficit spending was (a) safe and (b) not necessarily "socialistic"? Or do you think it is not safe and that it is socialistic?

The Determination of GNP

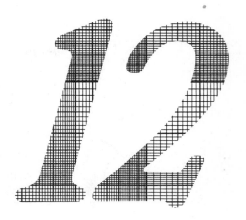

WE HAVE REACHED THE DESTINATION toward which we have been traveling for many chapters. We are finally in a position to understand how the forces of supply and demand determine the actual level of GNP that confronts us in daily life—"the state of the economy" that affects our employment prospects, our immediate well-being, our state of satisfaction or dissatisfaction with the way things are going. To repeat what we have earlier said, we are not interested now in the "historical" level of gross national product—the height to which the underlying processes of growth have carried us—but in the degree of utilization of that total capacity, the fluctuations of "good times and bad times" that we worry about from one year to the next.

THE SUPPLY OF GNP

As we know, that short-run level of GNP is determined by the outcome of two opposing tendencies of supply and demand, just as the level of prices and quantities in a marketplace is "set" by the counterplay of these forces. In Chapter 4 we summed up the short-run supply of GNP in terms of an aggregate production function, and Fig. 12·1 (next page) refreshes our memory of that function. *It shows us the rising curve of total potential output available to us from utilizing larger and larger quantities of labor and capital.* Note that the curve finally reaches a maximum—technically when every man and woman is working to the exhaustion point.

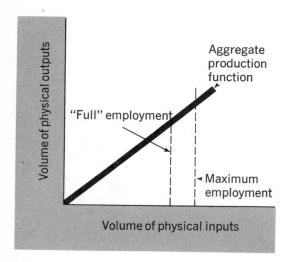

FIGURE 12 · 1
The production function

The normal level of "full" employment is well below that maximum.

THE DEMAND FOR GNP

Now what of the demand function? How much physical output will the factors of production buy as we vary output from levels where employment is very low to levels of full employment?

We will postpone for a moment a detailed discussion of the demand function, to emphasize one aspect. Unlike a curve showing quantities demanded and prices, this demand curve will *slope upward* since we are relating quantities demanded and *incomes*. This enables us to draw a generalized demand curve for all output, which we show in Fig. 12·2 (right).

EMPLOYMENT AND EQUILIBRIUM

Like the market for any single good or service, the market for all goods and services will find its equilibrium where the total quan-

tity of goods demanded equals that supplied. But now we must note something of paramount importance. While the economy will automatically move to this equilibrium point, the *point need not bring about the full employment of the factors of production, particularly labor*. In Fig. 12·2, the economy at equilibrium produces a GNP indicated by GNP_e, which corresponds with an employment of inputs given by I_e.

It could very well be, however, that if all factors of production were fully employed, inputs would be I_F. If they *were* all employed, a "full employment" GNP_F would be produced. *Thus, even though the economy is in equilibrium, it will not necessarily be at a point of full employment.* All we can say about the equilibrium point—exactly as in a market for goods and services—is that it is a level of output toward which the system will move, and from which it will not budge unless the supply curve or the demand curve shifts. It is not necessarily the *right* level—in this case, the level that results in "full" (or even high) employment. It may indeed be a very unsatis-

FIGURE 12 · 2
Supply and demand for physical output

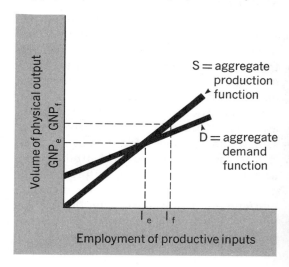

factory level, such as that in the Great Depression.

From Employment to Expenditure

Up to this point, our analysis has been in physical terms—units of inputs (employment) and units of output (actual production). Now we want to analyze the supply and demand for GNP in ordinary money terms, as the dollar value of inputs and the dollar value of outputs. This will enable us to speak of the determination of GNP in terms of *the supply* and *demand for output.*

THE SUPPLY OF INCOMES

What do we mean by the supply of output? We no longer mean the actual physical volume of output at different levels of employment, but the dollar value of that output. And here is where the identity GNP ≡ GNI comes into play in a surprising way. For if we recall Chapter 5 (p. 71) we know that each and every output will give rise to a sum of incomes that is exactly equal with (identical to) the value of that output. If we now translate that identity into graphical form, we can see that the supply curve of output must be identical with the supply curve of incomes. It will therefore have a 45° slope, as shown in Fig. 12·4. By convention we call this the *supply curve of income,* but we can see that it is also a supply curve of the value of output.

Figure 12·3 shows us why the line is a 45° slope. The axes of the graph are GNI and GNP. If output is at point Y along the GNP (output) axis, the corresponding point on the income axis must be at point X where OY = OX. This is also true of points Y' and X', Y'' and X'', and so on.

From these points, it is easy to draw a

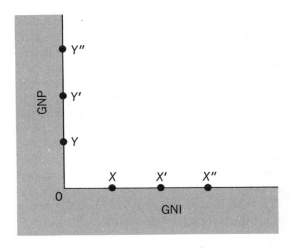

FIGURE 12 · 3
Identity of GNI and GNP

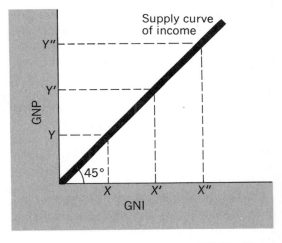

FIGURE 12 · 4
Supply curve of income

supply curve of income that relates GNP and GNI.

REAL AND MONEY GNP

This 45° line has a special characteristic that we should clearly understand. No matter what the shape of the aggregate production function in real terms—whether we are dealing with a highly efficient or very inefficient economy—the supply curve of *income* will always be a 45° slope. This is because the supply curve of income tells us only that there will always be a supply of incomes equal to the value of output (GNI ≡ GNP), whereas the supply curve of real goods and services looks "behind" the *value* of output and income to the measurement of *quantities* of output and the *quantities* of inputs. Thus the 45° line represents a definitional, rather than a functional, relationship.

THE DEMAND CURVE FOR OUTPUT

If the supply curve of income always has the same slope, why do we bother with it? The answer is that it enables us to highlight the crucial role played by the volume of expenditures in bringing about the equilibrium level of GNP. We can see this if we now add a demand curve for output to our 45° diagram. This is a curve that will be made up of the demands of the various sectors of the economy—households, business, and government. It is therefore a curve that sums up the demand function for consumption, investment, and public expenditure.

In the determination of GNP, the 45° supply curve plays a passive role very much like a totally inelastic (vertical) supply curve. In both cases, demand plays the active role in establishing the outcome—of GNP on the one hand, price on the other. But in both cases, supply is a necessary consideration: the other blade of scissors.

Now in real life, as we know, the demand functions of the business and government sectors are exceedingly complex. But in this schematic representation of how supply and demand bring a given money value of GNP into being, we can ignore those difficulties and simply assume that the demand

functions for *G* and *I* are "given" for any moment, although they will certainly shift up or down over time. The crucial demand function then becomes the expenditure of the household sector. And here we have an important clue. From our study of the propensity to consume, we know that this function starts at a "bottom" and slopes upward. Moreover, the upward slope is determined by the marginal propensity to consume, which is less than 1. Therefore the slope must be less than 45°.

We can now put together these components to form a demand function for total output. If we follow steps 1 through 4 in Fig. 12·5, p. 177, we can see how the demand side of GNP emerges. Figure 12·6 then combines the supply and the demand curves into a graph that shows us the forces that establish an equilibrium level for GNP.

This equilibrium, let us remember, tells us the money value of GNP brought about by the flow of demand against supply. It might, for example, indicate that this equilibrium value of GNP was $1.5 trillion. It does *not* tell us whether $1.5 trillion is a *good* size for GNP, any more than an equilibrium price of $20 for a commodity tells us whether that is a good or bad price from the viewpoint of buyers, producers, or the economy at large. We will spend a number of later chapters discussing problems such as inflation, employment, and growth, all of which critically examine the social usefulness of whatever GNP supply and demand have established.

THE CIRCULAR FLOW

Before we can discuss these problems, however, we must be sure we understand the nature of the GNP-establishing process, just as we must understand how a market works before we can get into issues of social policy connected with a market. Let us therefore take another step and connect our supply-

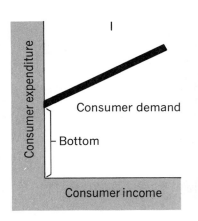

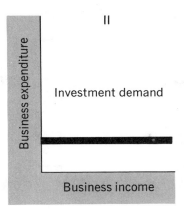

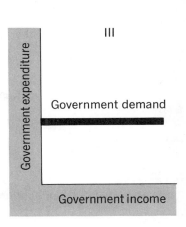

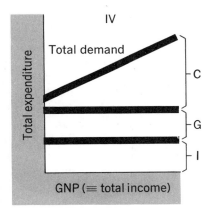

FIGURE 12 · 5
The components of the demand for GNP

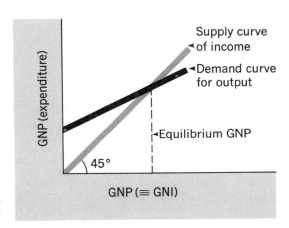

FIGURE 12 · 6
Supply and demand for GNP

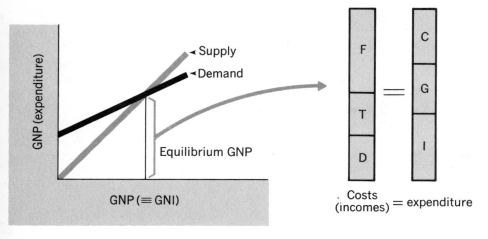

Costs (incomes) = expenditure

FIGURE 12 · 7
Equilibrium GNP

demand equilibrium for GNP with our previous discussion of the circular flow. In Fig. 12·7, let us take out a thin slice of output at equilibrium and examine it under a magnifying glass.

As always, GNP can be analyzed into its component factor, indirect tax, and depreciation costs $(F + T + D)$ and into its component expenditures or demands $(C + G + I)$. From our earlier discussion we recall that *all costs become incomes*. Therefore our supply curve of incomes must also represent the costs of that supply: we could relabel the GNI axis Gross National Cost. What we see in our diagram is that at equilibrium, total demand for GNP equals total cost for GNP, much like our circular flow (p. 72).*

THE DEMAND GAP

Now let us examine another slice of GNP that is above equilibrium, as in Fig. 12·8.

*But not exactly like our circular flow. We are now dealing with an economy that has saving and investing, profits and losses. Therefore we must think of the cost category "depreciation" (D) as including profits, and the expenditure category "investment" (I) as including net investment as well as replacement. We also continue to forget about exports, for simplicity.

Here the cost of GNP is represented by OA. It is composed of $F + T + D$, and as we know, it is *identical* with the incomes that are the other side of all costs. Thus OA is the cost of GNP measured in terms of gross national income. But now the demand for GNP, OB, is less than OA. The difference consists of the demand gap, with which we are familiar.

If we had taken a slice below equilibrium, what would have been the situation? Now the demand curve lies above the supply curve. That is, total expenditures would have been larger than total costs ($\equiv$ incomes). *We would have had a demand surplus, rather than a demand gap.* You might try drawing such a slice and seeing what the relation of $F + T + D$ would be to $C + G + I$.

THE MOVEMENT TO EQUILIBRIUM

Now let us trace the forces that would push GNP toward the position of equilibrium. At the level of GNP that lies above equilibrium, entrepreneurs and public agencies would have paid out larger sums as costs ($\equiv$ incomes) than they would receive back as sales ($\equiv$ demand). Sales would be below the level

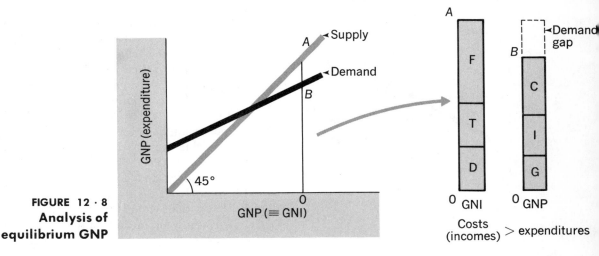

FIGURE 12 · 8
Analysis of
equilibrium GNP

of expectations that led to the employment of the factors in the first place. The first result would be a piling up of unsold inventories. Quickly, however, production plans would be revised downward. Fewer factors would be employed. With the fall in employment, incomes would fall, and as incomes fell, so would demand.

The analysis is exactly reversed if GNP is below equilibrium. Now demand ($C + G + I$) is greater than costs or incomes ($F + T + D$). Entrepreneurs will meet this extra demand out of inventories, and they will begin to plan for higher output, hiring more factors, and embarking on investment programs, thereby raising costs and incomes.

Note that in both cases, demand does not change as rapidly as income. In the first case it does not fall as fast as income; in the second it rises more slowly than income. This is the result of the marginal propensity to consume, which, as we have seen, reflects the unwillingness of households to raise or lower their consumption spending as much as any change in their incomes.

Assuming for the moment that G and I remain unchanged, we can see that as the employment of factors increases or decreases, the

total demand must come closer to total costs or incomes. *If there is a demand gap, income will fall more rapidly than demand, and the gap will close. If there is a demand surplus, income will rise faster than demand and the surplus will gradually disappear.* In both cases, the economy will move toward equilibrium.

THE MOVEMENT OF EQUILIBRIUM

If we now introduce changes in G and I, we can see that *the equilibrium point itself may move.* As the economy enters a downward spiral, investment spending may fall, outbalancing the supportive action of the automatic stabilizers. If this is the case, then the equilibrium level of GNP will move leftward, and the recession may not halt until we reach a very low level of GNP. This is, in fact, exactly what happens when a severe recession causes investment to fall, and the economy does not "bottom out" until GNP has fallen substantially, bringing with it considerable unemployment. Figure 12·9 (p. 180) shows us this process schematically.

Let us begin at a level of GNP indicated by output *OA*. A demand gap exists, and the level of output begins to fall toward *OB*,

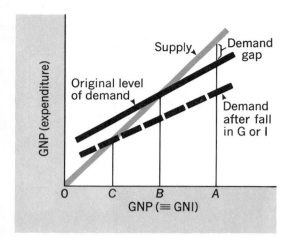

FIGURE 12 · 9
A change in equilibrium GNP

which is an equilibrium level at the *original level of demand.* But now the fall in GNP adversely affects *I* as well as *C,* so that the demand schedule for output shifts downward to the dotted line. Hence the economy will not settle at output *OB* but will continue downward until *OC,* where once again the demand for output equals the supply of output.

THE EXPANSION PROCESS

Just the opposite course of events helps us explain an upward movement. Suppose our economy "began" in equilibrium at output *OC,* following a severe recession. Now let us suppose that a rise in demand takes place. This could be the consequence of a burst of autonomous investment or simply the result of brighter expectations or the consequence of deficit spending or any combination. If you will extend the line at *OC* up to the new demand curve (the upper line, this time), you can see that demand for output ($C + I + G$) is now larger than the costs of output ($F + T + D$).

As a result, entrepreneurs will find their receipts rising. They will add factors, rehiring labor that has been let go during the recession and adding to their stock of inventories or equipment. The economy will begin to move toward the equilibrium depicted by output *OB.*

Once again, however, we must be careful not to imagine that the equilibrium point is fixed. As the economy moves so will autonomous investment and government spending and taxing. Hence the final equilibrium level may be less than, equal to, or greater than *OC,* depending on further shifts in the demand curve. But the *process* by which an equilibrium level of GNP is reached is always indicated by the relationship between the supply curve of GNI and the demand curve for GNP.

Another View of Equilibrium

LEAKAGES AND INJECTIONS

So far we have examined the determination of equilibrium by comparing the total supply of incomes and the total demand for goods and services at different levels of GNP. But there is another way of understanding the same idea, if we approach it from the familiar vantage point of savings and investment. We have seen that savings—or rather, all *leakages*—bring about potential demand gaps. We can now add a similar general category for *all increases in expenditure*—net investment, additional government spending, rising exports, or even a spontaneous jump in consumption—and call these *injections.* Equilibrium will then be determined by the interplay of these leakages and injections.

In Fig. 12·10, we show these injections as a solid band in Panel I. In Panel II, we show leakages as the triangle that represents the difference between incomes received (always the 45° line) and expenditure. (Note

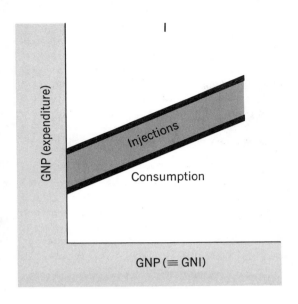

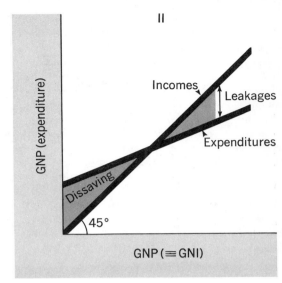

FIGURE 12·10
Injections and leakages

that below a certain level, there is *dissaving*—a kind of negative leakage—as consumers strive to maintain their living standards by spending more than their incomes, drawing on accumulated savings, or as businesses maintain their depreciation flows by drawing on previous years earnings.)

If we superimpose the two diagrams (see Fig. 12·11), we can see that the equilibrium level of GNP can be looked at not only as the point at which total demand ($C + I + G$) equals total incomes ($F + T + D$), but also as the point where total leakages (household savings, business savings, additional taxes, additional imports) just equal total injections.

At any GNP higher than the equilibrium, the flow of leakages will be larger than that of injections, and a demand gap will push GNP back toward equilibrium. At any point below equilibrium, the band of injections is wider than the triangle of leakages, and the economy will move in the other direction, "up" toward equilibrium. Do not

FIGURE 12·11
Equilibrium of GNP

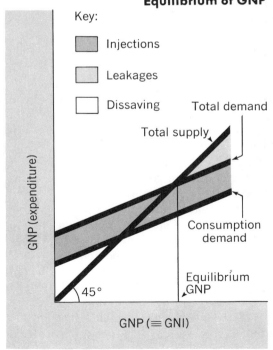

INTENDED AND
UNINTENDED S AND I

The careful reader may have noted that we speak of *intended* savings and *intended* investment as the critical forces in establishing equilibrium. This is because there is a formal balance between *all* saving and investment (or all leakages and all injections) at every moment in the economy.

This sounds very strange. Are there not demand gaps, when saving is not offset by investment? Have we not just shown a schedule in which S was not equal to I at every level of income? How then can saving and investment be identities?

The answer is unexpectedly simple. Both saving and investment are made up of *intended and unintended* flows. I may intend to save a great deal, but if my income falls, my actual savings may be very small. As an entrepreneur, I may intend to invest nothing this year; but if sales are poor, I may end up with an unintended investment in unsold inventories. Thus, through fluctuations in incomes, profits, and inventories, people are constantly saving and investing more or less than they intended. These unintended changes make *total* savings equal to (identical with) *total* investment, whereas obviously the intended portions of saving or investment may be unequal.

Economists speak of the difference between intended and unintended activities as *ex ante* and *ex post*. *Ex ante* means "looking forward;" *ex post* means "looking backward." *Ex ante* savings and investment (or leakages and injections) are usually not equal. But at each and every moment,

forget that the demand curve can always shift, moving equilibrium to the right or left.

SCHEDULES AND TIME

There is a problem inherent in diagrams such as these. One tends to interpret them as if they showed the movement of the economy over time—as if the horizontal axis read 1970, 1971, 1972, and so on. But this is not what the diagram is intended to show. As in the case of the determination of prices, we are trying to build a model to show the forces at work in *a given period of time*. Our diagrams refer to the crosscurrents during each and every moment of time for the economy. If we wanted to show time itself, we would have to introduce a whole ladder of demand and supply schedules showing the components of demand or supply at different dates. Such a diagram would he hopelessly complicated, so we must use our imaginations to portray time, and we must remember that in the graphs we abstract from time to reveal the underlying principles that are constantly at work determining the level of GNP.

SAVING AND INVESTMENT

Equilibrium is always a complicated subject to master, so let us fix the matter in our minds by going over the problem one last time. Suppose that we are going to predict the level of GNP for an island community by means of a questionnaire. To simplify our task, we will ignore government and exports, so that we can concentrate solely on consumption, saving, and investment.

We begin by interrogating the island's business community about their intentions for next year's investment. Now we know that some investment will be induced and that, therefore, investment will partly be a result of the island's level of income; but again for simplification, we assume that businessmen have laid their plans for next year. They tell us they intend to spend $30 million for new housing, plant, equipment, and other capital goods.

Next, our team of pollsters approaches a carefully selected sample of the island's householders and asks them what their consumption and savings plans are for the coming year. Here the answer will be a bit ex post savings and investment *will* be equal because someone will have been stuck with higher or lower inventories or greater or lesser saving than he intended ex ante.

The strict balance between the formal accounting meanings of saving and investment and the tug-of-war between the active forces of *intended* saving and investment are sources of much confusion to students who ask why the terms are defined in this difficult way. In part we owe the answer to Keynes, who first defined S and I as identities. Since then the usage has become solidified because it is useful for purposes of national accounting.

For our purposes, we must learn to distinguish between the formal, ex post identity between total saving and investment (or between all leakages and all injections) and the active,

ex ante difference between *intended* savings and investment (or *intended* saving, *intended* imports, *intended* business saving, etc., and *intended* additional expenditures of all kinds).

What matters in the determination of GNP are the *actions* people are taking—actions that lead them to try to save or to invest or that make them struggle to get rid of unintended inventories or to build up desired inventories. These are the kinds of activities that will be moving the economy up and down in the never-ending "quest" for its equilibrium point. The fact that at each moment ex post savings and investment are identical from the viewpoint of the economy's balance sheet is important only insofar as we are economic accountants. As analysts of the course of future GNP, we concentrate on the inequality of ex ante, intended actions.

disconcerting. Reflecting on their past experience, our householders will reply: "We can't say for sure. We'd *like* to spend such-and-such an amount and save the rest, but really it depends on what our incomes will be." Our poll, in other words, will have to make inquiries about different possibilities that reflect the island's propensity to consume.

Now we tabulate our results, and find that we have the schedule in Table 12·1.

TABLE 12 · 1

Income	Consumption (in millions)	Saving	Investment
$100	$75	$25	$30
110	80	30	30
120	85	35	30

INTERPLAY OF SAVING AND INVESTMENT

If we look at the last two columns, those for saving and investment, we can see a powerful cross play that will characterize our model economy at different levels of income, for the forces of investment and saving will not be in balance at all levels. At some levels, the propensity to save will outrun the act of purposeful investment; at others, the motivations to save will be less than the investment expenditures made by business firms. In fact, our island model shows that at only one level of income—$110 million—will the saving and investment schedules coincide.

What does it mean when intended savings are greater than the flow of intended investment? It means that people are *trying* to save out of their given incomes a larger amount than businessmen are willing to invest. Now if we think back to the exposition of the economy in equilibrium, it will be clear what the result must be. The economy cannot maintain a closed circuit of income and expenditure if savings are larger than investment. This will simply give rise to a demand gap, the repercussions of which we have already explored.

But a similar lack of equilibrium results if intended savings are less than intended investment expenditure (or if investment spending is greater than the propensity to save).

183

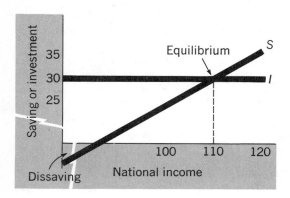

FIGURE 12 · 12
Saving and investment

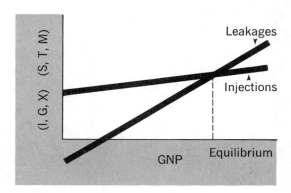

FIGURE 12 · 13
Leakages and injections

Now businessmen will be pumping out more than enough to offset the savings gap. The additional expenditures, over and above those that compensate for saving, will flow into the economy to create new incomes— and out of those new incomes, new savings.

Income and output will be stable, in other words, only when the flow of intended investment just compensates for the flow of intended saving. Investment and saving thus conduct a tug of war around this pivot point, driving the economy upward when intended investment exceeds the flow of intended saving; downward when it fails to offset saving.
In Fig. 12·12 we show this crosscurrent in schematic form. Note that as incomes fall very low, householders will *dissave*.

INJECTIONS VS. LEAKAGES

We can easily make our graph more realistic by adding taxes (T) and imports (M) to savings, and exports (X) and government spending to investment. The vertical axis in Fig. 12·13 now shows all leakages and injections. And just to introduce another feature of the real world, we will tilt the injection line upward, on the assumption that induced investment will be an important constituent of total investment. The leakages curve will

not be exactly the same shape as the savings curve, but it will reflect the general tendency of savings and imports and taxes to rise with income.

TWO DIAGRAMS, ONE SOLUTION

Our new diagram also enables us to see the connection between our first approach to equilibrium as the supply and demand for GNP, and our present analysis of equilibrium in terms of leakages and injections.

As Fig. 12·14 shows, the injections curve and the leakages curve in our previous diagram are exactly those we have already encountered in Fig. 12·11.

Notice that the shaded triangle showing leakages is transposed to the second diagram. There it looks "flatter" only because we now ignore consumption and therefore put the leakage triangle on a horizontal base instead of a sloping one. Our "fixed" injection schedule is also exactly the same in both diagrams, although once again, in the lower figure it is "flatter" because it no longer sits on a sloping C line. Now it should be obvious why the equilibrium intersection point must be at the same figure on the GNP axis of both diagrams.

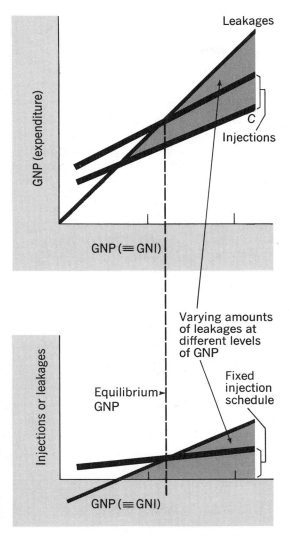

FIGURE 12 · 14
Two methods of showing equilibrium

vestment, government spending, or exports resulted in larger changes in GNP because the additions to income were respent, creating still more new incomes. Further, we remember that the size of the multiplier effect depended on the marginal propensity to consume, the marginal propensity to tax, and the marginal propensity to buy imports as GNP rises. Now it remains only to show how this basic analytic concept enters into the determination of equilibrium GNP.

Let us begin with the diagram that shows injections and leakages, and let us now draw a new line showing an increase in injections (Fig. 12·15). Notice that the increase in GNP is larger than the increase in injections. *This is the multiplier itself in graphic form.*

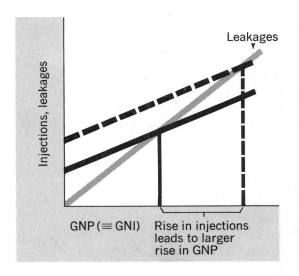

FIGURE 12 · 15
Multiplier in graphic form

The Multiplier

There remains only one part of the jigsaw puzzle to put into place. This is the integration of the *multiplier* into our analysis of the determination of GNP.

We remember that the essential point about the multiplier was that changes in in-

We can see exactly the same result in our diagram of the supply and demand for GNP. Notice how a rise in the demand for GNP (a rise in injections) leads to a larger rise in the output of GNP (see Fig. 12·16).

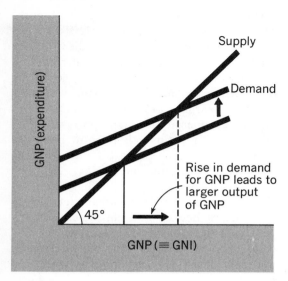

FIGURE 12 · 16
Multiplier and GNP

THE SLOPE OF THE LEAKAGE CURVE

Both diagrams also show that the relation between the original increase in injections and the resulting increase in GNP depends on the *slope* of the leakage line. Figure 12·17 shows

us two different injection-GNP relationships that arise from differing slopes.

Notice how the *same* increase in spending (from *OA* to *OB* on the injections axis) leads to a much smaller increase in panel I GNP (from *OX* to *OY*), where the leakage slope is high, than in panel II (from *OX'* to *OY'*), where the slope is more gradual.

Why is the increase greater when the slope is more gradual? The answer should be obvious. The slope represents the marginal propensity to save, to tax, to import—in short, all the marginal propensities that give rise to leakages. If these propensities are high—if there are high leakages—then the slope of the leakage curve will be high. If it is low, the leakage curve will be flat.

A LAST LOOK AT EQUILIBRIUM

Thus we finally understand how GNP reaches an equilibrium position after a change in demand. Here it is well to reiterate, however, that the word "equilibrium" does not imply a static, motionless state. Nor does it mean a desired state. We use the word only to denote the fact that *given* certain behavior

FIGURE 12 ·17
Two multipliers

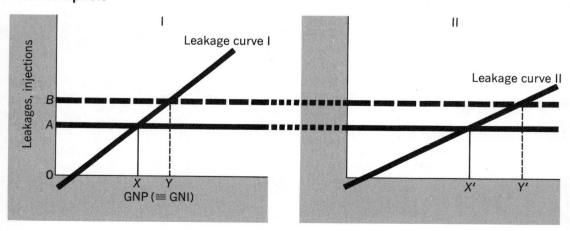

THE MULTIPLIER ONCE AGAIN

You can see the relation between our multiplier analysis and our graphical analysis by thinking about the following two examples.

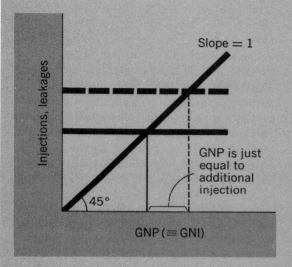

1. Suppose that the leakage fraction is 1; in other words, that we absorb *all* increases in income in additional savings, taxes, imports. What will the multiplier be? We know that the multiplier is 1/*mps*. If *mps* = 1, then the multiplier fraction will be 1, and the increase in income will be 1 times the injection. In graphical terms, this looks like the accompanying figure.

The leakage curve shows that each dollar of additional GNP leads to another dollar of leakage. Hence the increase in GNP arising from an increase in injections is exactly equal to the original increase in injections. The multiplier is unity.

2. Now suppose that the leakage fraction is .5. The multiplier, once again, is 1/.5 or 2. In the second figure, we show the same relationship in graphical terms.

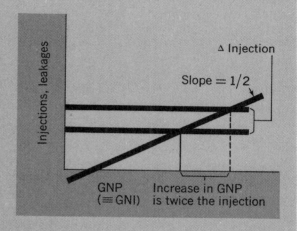

patterns, there will be a determinate point to which their interaction will push the level of income; and *so long as the underlying patterns of injections and leakages remain unchanged, the forces they exert will keep income at this level.*

In fact, of course, the flows of spending and saving are continually changing, so that the equilibrium level of the economy is constantly shifting, like a Ping-Pong ball suspended in a rising jet of water. Equilibrium can thus be regarded as a target toward which the economy is constantly propelled by the push-pull between leakages and injec-

tions. The target may be attained but momentarily before the economy is again impelled to seek a new point of rest. What our diagrams and the underlying analysis explain for us, then, is not a single determinate point at which our economy will in fact settle down, but the *direction* it will go in quest of a resting place, as the dynamic forces of the system exert their pressures.

THE PARADOX OF THRIFT

The fact that income must always move toward the level where the flows of intended saving and investment are equal leads to one of the most startling—and important—paradoxes of economics. This is the so-called paradox of thrift, a paradox that tells us that the *attempt to increase intended saving* may, under certain circumstances, lead to a *fall in actual saving.*

The paradox is not difficult for us to understand at this stage. An attempt to save, *when it is not matched with an equal willingness to invest or to increase government expenditure,* will cause a gap in demand. This means that businessmen will not be getting back enough money to cover their costs. Hence, production will be curtailed or costs will be slashed, with the result that incomes will fall. As incomes fall, savings will also fall, because the ability to save will be reduced. Thus, by a chain of activities working their influence on income and output, the effort to *increase* savings may end up with an actual *reduction* of savings.

This frustration of individual desires is perhaps the most striking instance of a common situation in economic life, the incompatibility between some kinds of individual behavior and some collective results. An individual farmer, for instance, may produce a larger crop in order to enjoy a bigger income; but if all farmers produce bigger crops, farm prices are apt to fall so heavily that farmers end up with less income. So too, a single family may wish to save a very large fraction of its income for reasons of financial prudence; but if all families seek to save a great deal of their incomes, the result—unless investment also rises—will be a fall in expenditure and a common failure to realize savings objectives. The paradox of thrift, in other words, teaches us that the freedom of behavior available to a few individuals cannot always be generalized to all individuals.*

---

*The paradox of thrift is actually only a subtle instance of that type of faulty reasoning called the fallacy of composition. The fallacy consists of assuming that what is true of the individual case must also be true of all cases combined. The flaw in reasoning lies in our tendency to overlook "side effects" of individual actions (such as the decrease in spending associated with an individual's attempt to save more, or the increase in supply when a farmer markets his larger crop) which may be negligible in isolation but which are very important in the aggregate.

KEY WORDS

CENTRAL CONCEPTS

Supply and
demand for GNP

1. The level of GNP is determined by the interplay of two forces—the (short-run) supply of GNP and the demand for GNP. The first is the aggregate production function; the second is the sum of the consumption, investment, and government demands for output.

Equilibrium GNP

2. *The equilibrium level of GNP need not correspond to full employment. Thus the fact that GNP is in equilibrium does not mean that it is at a socially satisfactory level.*

$GNP \equiv GNI$
$45°$ line

3. GNP is determined not only by the supply and demand for output, but *also by the interplay of the supply of income and the demand for GNP stemming from an expenditure of income. Since GNP $\equiv$ GNI, we can convert the aggregate supply function into a 45° line showing that all levels of GNP are matched by an identical GNI.*

Upward-sloping
demand curve

4. *We can also depict the demand for goods arising from the expenditure of income. This demand curve is made up of the demands of the various sectors. Generally it slopes upward, since it relates quantities demanded and incomes, not prices.*

Moreover, it does not begin at the origin, but at some level representing "the bottom"—the expenditures that would have to be made even if no output were made and no incomes earned.

The meaning of equilibrium

5. At equilibrium levels of GNP F+T+D (cash flow including profits) = C+I+G+X. At nonequilibrium levels there would be a demand gap, or a demand surplus.

Expenditures vs. costs

6. At levels of GNP other than equilibrium there will be forces that push GNP toward equilibrium. These forces arise because expenditures are greater than costs (or incomes), leading to a rise in GNP; or because expenditures are less than costs, leading to curtailment of production and a fall in GNP. *Equilibrium is reached because demand rises or falls less rapidly than income.*

Leakages Injections

7. *The simplest model of an economy in equilibrium is one in which intended S = intended I.* We can enlarge this model to include the equality of all intended *leakages* and *injections.*

Changing equilibrium

8. Equilibrium is not a static concept. Like the equilibrium price in a market, *equilibrium levels of GNP constantly change* as the forces of supply and demand change.

Slope of the curve of leakages

9. The multiplier shows us the relation between an increase in injections and the resulting increase in GNP. We can show it graphically as well as algebraically. In a graph, the *critical fraction* mps *is depicted by the slope of the leakage curve.*

Paradox of thrift

10. The desire to save can be frustrated by a failure of GNP to be high enough to permit households or businesses to save. Indeed, the attempt to save, by lowering expenditures, may actually drive income down and reduce the flow of saving. This is called the *paradox of thrift.*

QUESTIONS

1. Explain equilibrium in terms of the demand and supply for output, using an aggregate production function and a demand function for output. Why does the supply function begin at the origin? Why doesn't the demand function?

2. Draw an equilibrium diagram and indicate the volume of GNP it implies. Can you tell from the diagram if this is a full-employment GNP? What information would you need to draw in the various ranges of employment on the GNP axis?

3. Why is GNP an identity with GNI? Be sure you understand this.

4. Why does the "curve" of an identity always have a 45° slope? Demonstrate this by plotting a curve that relates the number of bachelors (horizontal axis) with the number of unmarried men (vertical axis).

5. Describe the "scenario" by which GNP is "pushed"

from a point above equilibrium back to equilibrium. Do the same for a GNP below equilibrium.

6. What are the components of the aggregate demand function? Can you write the function for the consumption portion of this total demand function? Can we write a plausible investment function? A government expenditure function? Is it reasonable to assume that these functions are "fixed" in the short-run period in which we are interested? Can we use an aggregate demand function, even though we do not know its precise shape, to highlight the process of adjustment of GNP?

7. Can you show why there is no demand gap at equilibrium? Remember: instead of "depreciation," use cash flow.

8. Now show how a shift in the demand function will bring about a new equilibrium point.

9. Draw a diagram showing the interplay of leakages

and injections, with injections as a layer of expenditures above consumption, and leakages as a triangle. Can you explain the triangle? How do you define the top line of the triangle? The bottom line? What is the difference?

10. Now show the interplay in the simplest form between savings and investment. Enlarge the saving/investment diagram to a leakage/injection diagram. Relate it to the diagram above.

11. Show how the multiplier affects the size of changes in GNP, according to the slope of the leakage curve. What does this slope represent? Relate the slope to the *mps*.

12. What is the paradox of thrift? Can you turn it upside down? Suppose no one wanted to save, and everyone tried to spend all his income. What would happen to total income? What would probably happen to saving?

13. Suppose that an economy turns out to have the following consumption and saving schedule (in billions):

Income	Saving	Consumption
$400	$50	$350
450	55	395
500	60	440
550	70	480
600	85	515

Now suppose that firms intend to make investments of $60 billion during the year. What will be the level of income for the economy? If investment rises to $85 billion, then what will be its income? What would be the multiplier in this case?

14. What is the difference between the 45° supply curve of income and the aggregate production function?

Money

13

WE HAVE ALMOST COMPLETED our analysis of the major elements of macroeconomics, and soon we can bring our analysis to bear on some major problems of the economy. But first there is a matter that we must integrate into our discussion. This is the role that money plays in fixing or changing the level of GNP, along with the other forces that we have come to know.

Actually, we have been talking about money throughout our exposition. After all, one cannot discuss expenditure without assuming the existence of money. But now we must look behind this unexamined assumption and find out exactly what we mean when we speak of money. This will entail two tasks. In this chapter we shall investigate the perplexing question of what money *is*—for as we shall see, money is surely one of the most sophisticated and curious inventions of human society. Then in our next chapter, once we have come to understand what currency and gold and bank deposits are and how they come into being, we will look into the effect that money has on our economic operations.

The Supply of Money

Let us begin, then, by asking—"What is money?" Coin and currency are certainly money. But are checks money? Are the deposits from which we draw checks money? Are savings accounts money? Stamps? Government bonds?

The answer is a somewhat arbitrary one. From the spectrum of possible candidates, we reserve the term *money* for those items used to make *payments*. This means that we include cash in the public's possession and checking accounts, because we pay for most things by cash or check. Surprisingly, it means that we do not usually count savings accounts, since we have to draw "money" *out* of our savings accounts, in the form of cash, or have it transferred to our checking account, if we want to use our savings accounts to make expenditures. So, too, we have to sell government bonds to get money.*

*Some economists do count savings accounts as money. By convention, cash plus checking accounts are called the M_1 measure of money; and M_1 plus savings accounts are called the M_2 measure of money.

CREDIT CARDS

Money serves as a mechanism for storing potential purchasing power and for actually purchasing goods and services. Since cash and personal checks are the principal means for making these purchases, money has come to be defined as cash outside banks plus checking accounts. But what about credit cards. Shouldn't they be considered money?

Credit cards clearly can be used to make purchases, so that they appear on the surface to have a vital attribute of money. But a moment's reflection shows that in fact they *substitute* for cash or checks in which payment is finally made. The moment you pay your credit card bill, or the moment the credit card company pays the local merchant, the credit card is replaced by standard money. *Thus credit cards play the role of money only to the extent that credit bills are unpaid!*

CURRENCY

Money, then, is mainly currency and checking accounts. In 1973, for example, our total money supply was $260 billion, of which $60 billion was currency in the hands of the public, and $200 billion was the total of checking accounts (or demand deposits, as they are also called).

Of the two kinds of "money," currency is the form most familiar to us. Yet there is a considerable mystery even about currency. Who determines how much currency there is? How is the supply of coins or bills regulated?

We often assume that the supply of currency is "set" by the government that "issues" it. Yet when we think about it, we realize that the government does not just hand out money, and certainly not coins or bills. When the government pays people, it is nearly always by check.

Then who does fix the amount of currency in circulation? You can answer the question by asking how you yourself determine how much currency you will carry. If you think about it, the answer is that you "cash" a check when you need more currency than you have, and you put the currency back into your checking account when you have more than you need.

What you do, everyone does. The amount of cash that the public holds at any time is no more and no less than the amount that it *wants* to hold. When it needs more—at Christmas, for instance—the public draws currency by cashing checks on its own checking accounts; and when Christmas is past, shopkeepers (who have received the public's currency) return it to their checking accounts.

Thus the amount of currency we have bears an obvious, important relation to the size of our bank accounts, for we can't write checks for cash if our accounts will not cover them.

Does this mean, then, that the banks have as much currency in their vaults as the total of our checking accounts? No, it does not. But to understand that, let us follow the course of some currency that we deposit in our banks for credit to our accounts.

BOOKKEEPING MONEY

When you put money into a commercial bank,* the bank does not hold that money for you as a pile of specially earmarked bills or as a bundle of checks made out to you from some payer. The bank takes notice of your deposit simply by crediting your "ac-

*A commercial bank is a bank that is empowered by law to offer checking services. It may also have savings accounts. A savings bank has only savings accounts and may not offer checking services.

In this role credit cards are not unique. Any unpaid bill or charge account is like money, in that you are able to purchase goods and services in exchange for your personal IOU. In a sense, each person is able to "print" money to the extent that he can persuade people to accept his IOUs. For most of us, that extent is very limited.

From an economist's point of view, the value of all outstanding trade credit (unpaid bills, unpaid charge accounts, or credit cards) *should* be considered money. It is not included in the official statistics for two reasons. First, it is difficult or impossible to figure how much trade credit is outstanding at any moment. Second, fluctuations in trade credit do not have a big impact on the economy. Ordinarily, the value of trade credit does not vary much, and therefore trade credit does not give rise to substantial changes in the effective money supply.

count," a bookkeeping page recording your present "balance." After the amount of the currency or check has been credited to you, the currency is put away with the bank's general store of vault cash and the checks are sent to the banks from which they came, where they will be charged against the accounts of the people who wrote them.

There is probably no misconception in economics harder to dispel than the idea that banks are warehouses stuffed with money. In point of fact, however, you might search as hard as you pleased in your bank, but you would find no money that was yours other than a bookkeeping account in your name. This seems like a very unreal form of money; and yet, the fact that you can present a check at the teller's window and convert your bookkeeping account into cash proves that your account must nonetheless be "real."

But suppose that you and all the other depositors tried to convert your accounts into cash on the same day. You would then find something shocking. There would not be nearly enough cash in the bank's till to cover the total withdrawals. In 1973, for instance, total demand deposits in the United States amounted to about $200 billion. But the total amount of coin and currency held by the banks was only $6.5 billion!

At first blush, this seems like a highly dangerous state of affairs. But second thoughts are more reassuring. After all, most of us put money into a bank because we do *not* need it immediately, or because making payments in cash is a nuisance compared with making them by check. Yet, there is always the chance—more than that, the certainty—that some depositors *will* want their money in currency. How much currency will the banks need then? What will be a proper reserve for them to hold?

FEDERAL RESERVE SYSTEM

For many years, the banks themselves decided what reserve ratio constituted a safe proportion of currency to hold against their demand deposits (the technical name for checking accounts). Today, however, most large banks are members of the Federal Reserve, a central banking system established in 1913 to strengthen the banking activities of the nation. Under the Federal Reserve System, the nation is divided into twelve districts, each with a Federal Reserve Bank owned (but not really controlled) by the member banks of its district. In turn, the twelve Reserve Banks are themselves coordinated by a seven-man Federal Reserve Board in Washington. Since the members of the board are appointed for fourteen-year terms, they constitute a body that has been purposely established as an independent, nonpolitical monetary authority.*

.One of the most important functions of the Federal Reserve Board is to establish reserve ratios for different categories of banks, within limits set by Congress. Historically these reserve ratios have ranged between 13 and 26 percent of demand deposits for city banks, with a somewhat smaller reserve ratio for country banks. Today, reserve ratios are determined by size, and they vary between 18 percent for the largest banks and 8 percent for the smallest. The Federal Reserve Board also sets reserve requirements for "time" deposits (the technical term for savings deposits). These range from 3 to 5 percent. Do not forget, however, that time deposits do not count—or directly serve—as "money."

THE BANKS' BANK

Yet here is something odd! We noticed that in 1973 the total amount of deposits was $200 billion and that banks' holdings of coin and currency were only $6.5 billion. This is much less than the 18 percent—or even 8 percent —reserve against deposits established by the Federal Reserve Board. How can this be?

The answer is that cash is not the only reserve a bank holds against deposits. Claims on other banks are also held as its reserve.

What are these claims? Suppose, in your account in Bank A, you deposit a check from someone who has an account in Bank B. Bank A credits your account and then presents the check to Bank B for "payment." By "payment" Bank A does not mean coin and currency, however. Instead, Bank A and Bank B settle their transaction at still *another*

bank where both Bank A and Bank B have their own accounts. These accounts are with the twelve Federal Reserve Banks of the country, where all banks who are members of the Federal Reserve System (and this accounts for banks holding most of the deposits in our banking system) *must* open accounts. Thus at the Federal Reserve Bank, Bank A's account will be credited, and Bank B's account will be debited, in this way moving reserves from one bank to the other.†

In other words, *the Federal Reserve Banks serve their member banks in exactly the same way as the member banks serve the public.* Member banks automatically deposit in their Federal Reserve accounts all checks they get from other banks. As a result, banks are constantly "clearing" their checks with one another through the Federal Reserve System, because their depositors are constantly writing checks on their own banks payable to someone who banks elsewhere. Meanwhile, *the balance that each bank maintains at the Federal Reserve—that is, the claim it has on other banks—counts, as much as any currency, as part of its reserve against deposits.*

In 1973, therefore, when demand deposits were $200 billion and cash in the banks only $6.5 billion, we would expect the member banks to have had heavy accounts with the Federal Reserve banks. And so they did —$33 billion in all. Thus, total reserves of the banks were $39.5 billion ($6.5 billion in cash plus $33 billion in Federal Reserve accounts), enough to satisfy the legal requirements of the Fed.

FRACTIONAL RESERVES

Thus we see that our banks operate on what is called a *fractional reserve system.* That is, a certain specified fraction of all demand deposits must be kept "on hand" at all times

---

*This has resulted, on occasion, in sharp clashes of viewpoint with the Treasury Department or the Bureau of the Budget where fiscal and economic policy is formulated by each administration. There is some disagreement over whether the nation is better served by a Federal Reserve that can impede an economic policy it disagrees with or one that is bound to assist the economic aims of each incumbent administration. Generally speaking, however, the Federal Reserve gives in to any strongly held view of the administration, although it is legally independent of the executive.

†When money is put into a bank account, the account is credited; when money is taken out, the account is debited.

in cash or at the Fed. The size of the minimum fraction is determined by the Federal Reserve, for reasons of control that we shall shortly learn about. It is *not* determined, as we might be tempted to think, to provide a "safe" backing for our bank deposits. For under *any* fractional system, if *all* depositors decided to draw out their accounts in currency and coin from all banks at the same time, the banks would be unable to meet the demand for cash and would have to close. We call this a "run" on the banking system. Needless to say, runs can be terrifying and destructive economic phenomena.*

Why, then, do we court the risk of runs, however small this risk may be? What is the benefit of a fractional banking system? To answer that, let us look into our bank again.

LOANS AND INVESTMENTS

Suppose its customers have given our bank $1 million in deposits and that the Federal Reserve Board requirements are 20 percent, a simpler figure to work with than the actual one. Then we know that our bank must at all times keep $200,000, either in currency in its own till or in its demand deposit at the Federal Reserve Bank.

But having taken care of that requirement, what does the bank do with the remaining deposits? If it simply lets them sit, either as vault cash or as a deposit at the Federal Reserve, our bank will be very "liquid," but it will have no way of making an income. Unless it charges a very high fee for its checking services, it will have to go out of business.

And yet there is an obvious way for the bank to make an income, while performing a valuable service. The bank can use all the cash and check claims it does not need for its

reserve to make *loans* to businessmen or families or to make financial *investments* in corporate or government bonds. It will thereby not only earn an income, but it will assist the process of business investment and government borrowing. Thus the mechanics of the banking system lead us back to the concerns at the very center of our previous analysis.

Inside the Banking System

Fractional reserves allow banks to lend, or to invest in securities, part of the funds that have been deposited with them. But that is not the only usefulness of the fractional reserve system. It works as well to help enlarge or diminish the supply of investible or loanable funds, as the occasion demands. Let us follow how this process works. To make the mechanics of banking clear, we are going to look at the actual books of the bank—in simplified form, of course—so that we can see how the process of lending and investing appears to the banker himself.

ASSETS AND LIABILITIES

We begin by introducing two basic elements of business accounting: *assets* and *liabilities*. Every student at some time or another has seen the balance sheet of a firm, and many have wondered how total assets always equal total liabilities. The reason is very simple. Assets are all the things or claims a business owns. Liabilities are claims against those assets—some of them the claims of creditors, some the claims of owners (called the Net Worth of the business). Since assets show everything that a business owns, and since liabilities show how claims against these selfsame things are divided between creditors and owners, it is obvious that the two sides of the balance sheet must always come to exactly the same total. The total of assets and the total of liabilities are an identity.

---

*A "run" on the banking system is no longer much of a threat, because the Federal Reserve could supply its members with vast amounts of cash. We shall learn how, later in this chapter.

T ACCOUNTS

Businesses show their financial condition on a *balance sheet* on which all items on the left side represent assets and all those on the right side represent liabilities. By using a simple two-column balance sheet (called a "T account" because it looks like a T), we can follow very clearly what happens to our bank as we deposit money in it or as it makes loans or investments.

EXCESS RESERVES

Now we recall from our previous discussion that our bank does not want to remain in this very liquid, but very unprofitable, position. According to the law, it must retain only a certain percentage of its deposits in cash or at the Federal Reserve—20 percent in our hypothetical example. All the rest it is free to lend or invest. As things now stand, however, it has $1 million in reserves—$800,000 more

ORIGINAL BANK

Assets	Liabilities
$1,000,000 (cash and checks)	$1,000,000 (money owed to depositors)
Total $1,000,000	**Total $1,000,000**

We start off with the example we have just used, in which we open a brand new bank with $1 million in cash and checks on other banks. Accordingly, our first entry in the T account shows the two sides of this transaction. Notice that our bank has gained an asset of $1 million, the cash and checks it now owns, and that it has simultaneously gained $1 million in liabilities, the deposits it *owes* to its depositors (who can, after all, take their money out any time).

As we know, however, our bank will not keep all its newly-gained cash and checks in the till. It may hang on to some of the cash, but it will send all the checks it has received, plus any currency that it feels it does not need, to the Fed for deposit in its account there. As a result, its T account will now look like this:

than it needs. Hence, let us suppose that it decides to put these *excess reserves* to work by lending that amount to a sound business risk. (Note that banks do not lend the excess reserves themselves. These reserves, cash and deposits at the Fed, remain right where they are. Their function is to tell the banks how much they may loan or invest.)

MAKING A LOAN

Assume now that the Smith Corporation, a well-known firm, comes in for a loan of $800,000. Our bank is happy to lend them that amount. But "making a loan" does not mean that the bank now pays the company in cash out of its vaults. Rather, *it makes a loan by opening a new checking account for the firm* and by crediting that account with $800,000.

ORIGINAL BANK

Assets		Liabilities	
Vault Cash	$ 100,000	Deposits	$1,000,000
Deposit at Fed	900,000		
Total	**$1,000,000***	**Total**	**$1,000,000**

*If you will examine some bank balance sheets, you will see these items listed as "Cash and due from banks." This means, of course, cash in their own vaults plus their balance at the Fed.

(Or if, as is likely, the Smith firm already has an account with the bank, it will simply credit the proceeds of the loan to that account.)

Now our T account shows some interesting changes.

serves are now sufficient to cover the Smith Corporation's account as well as the original deposit accounts. A glance reveals that all is well. We still have $1 million in reserves against $1.8 million in deposits. Our reserve

ORIGINAL BANK

Assets		Liabilities	
Cash and at Fed	$1,000,000	Original deposits	$1,000,000
Loan (Smith Corp.)	800,000	New deposit (Smith Corp.)	800,000
Total	**$1,800,000**	**Total**	**$1,800,000**

There are several things to note about this transaction. First, our bank's reserves (its cash and deposit at the Fed) have not yet changed. The $1 million in reserves are still there.

Second, notice that the Smith Corporation loan counts as a new asset for the bank because the bank now has a legal claim against the company for that amount. (The interest on the loan is not shown in the balance sheet; but when it is paid, it will show up as an addition to the bank's cash.)

Third, deposits have increased by $800,000. Note, however, that this $800,000 was not paid to the Smith firm out of anyone else's account in the bank. It is a new checking account, one that did not exist before. As a result, the supply of money is also up! More about this shortly.

THE LOAN IS SPENT

Was it safe to open this new account for the company? Well, we might see whether our re-

ratio is much higher than the 20 percent required by law.

It is so much higher, in fact, that we might be tempted to make another loan to the next customer who requests one, and in that way further increase our earning capacity. But an experienced banker shakes his head. "The Smith Corporation did not take out a loan and agree to pay interest on it just for the pleasure of letting that money sit with you," he explains. "Very shortly, the company will be writing checks on its balance to pay for goods or services; and when it does, you will need every penny of the reserve you now have."

That, indeed, is the case. Within a few days we find that our bank's account at the Federal Reserve Bank has been charged with a check for $800,000 written by the Smith Corporation in favor of the Jones Corporation, which carries its account at another bank. Now we find that our T account has changed dramatically to look like this:

ORIGINAL BANK

Assets		Liabilities	
Cash and at Fed	$ 200,000	Original deposits	$1,000,000
Loan (Smith Corp.)	800,000	Smith Corp. deposits	0
Total	**$1,000,000**	**Total**	**$1,000,000**

SECOND BANK

Assets		Liabilities	
Cash and at Fed	$800,000	Deposit (Jones Corp.)	$800,000
Total	**$800,000**	**Total**	**$800,000**

Let us see exactly what has happened. First, the Smith Corporation's check has been charged against our account at the Fed and has reduced it from $900,000 to $100,000. Together with the $100,000 cash in our vault, this gives us $200,000 in reserves.

Second, the Smith Corporation's deposit is entirely gone, although its loan agreement remains with us as an asset.

Now if we refigure our reserves we find that they are just right. We are required to have $200,000 in vault cash or in our Federal Reserve account against our $1 million in deposits. That is exactly the amount we have left. Our bank is now fully "loaned up."

EXPANDING THE MONEY SUPPLY

But the banking *system* is not yet fully loaned up. So far, we have traced what happened to only our bank when the Smith Corporation spent the money in its deposit account. Now we must trace the effect of this action on the deposits and reserves of other banks.

We begin with the bank in which the Jones Corporation deposits the check it has just received from the Smith Corporation. As the above T account shows, the Jones Corporation's bank now finds itself in exactly the same position as our bank was when we opened it with $1 million in new deposits, except that the addition to this "second generation" bank is smaller than the addition to the "first generation" bank.

As we can see, our second generation bank has gained $800,000 in cash and in deposits. Since it needs only 20 percent of this for required reserves, it finds itself with $640,000 excess reserves, which it is now free to use to make loans as investments. Suppose that it extends a loan to the Brown Company and that the Brown Company shortly thereafter spends the proceeds of that loan at the Black Company, which banks at yet a third bank. The following two T accounts show how the total deposits will now be affected.

As Fig. 13·1 makes clear, the process will not stop here but can continue from one bank to the next as long as any lending power

SECOND BANK
(after Brown Co. spends the proceeds of its loan)

Assets		Liabilities	
Cash and at Fed	$160,000	Deposits (Jones Corp.)	$800,000
Loan (to Brown Co.)	640,000	Deposits (Brown Co.)	0
Total	**$800,000**	**Total**	**$800,000**

THIRD BANK
(after Black Co. gets the check of Brown Co.)

Assets		Liabilities	
Cash and at Fed	$640,000	Deposit (Black Co.)	$640,000
Total	**$640,000**	**Total**	**$640,000**

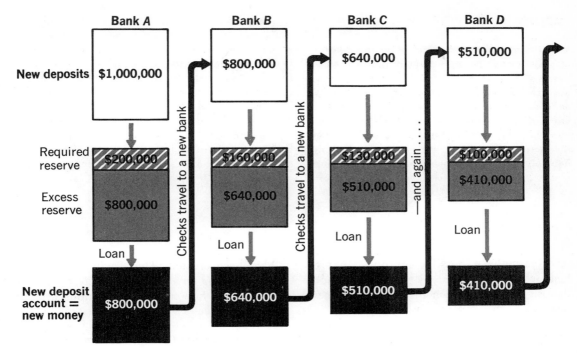

FIGURE 13 · 1
Expansion of the money supply

Expansion of the Money Supply

remains. Notice, however, that this lending power gets smaller and smaller and will eventually reach zero.

Expansion of the Money Supply

If we now look at the bottom of Fig. 13·1, we will see something very important. Every time any bank in this chain of transactions has opened an account for a new borrower, *the supply of money has increased.* Remember that the supply of money is the sum of currency outside the banking system (i.e., in our own pockets) plus the total of demand deposits. As our chain of banks kept opening new accounts, it was simultaneously expanding the total check-writing capacity of the economy. Thus, money has materialized, seemingly out of thin air.

Now how can this be? If we tell any banker in the chain that he has "created"

money, he will protest vehemently. The loans he made, he will insist, were backed at the time he made them by excess reserves as large as the loan itself. Just as we had $800,000 in excess reserves when we made our initial loan to the Smith Corporation, so every subsequent loan was always backed 100 percent by unused reserves when it was made.

Our bankers are perfectly correct when they tell us that they never, never lend a penny more than they have. Money is not created in the lending process because a banker lends money he doesn't have. *It is created because you and I generally pay each other by checks that give us claims against each other's bank.* If we constantly cashed the checks we exchanged, no new money would be created. But we do not. We deposit each other's checks in our own bank accounts; and in doing so, we give our banks more reserves than they need against the deposits we have just made. These new excess

MONEY AND DEBT

All this gives us a fresh insight into the question of what money is. We said before that it is whatever we use to make payments. But what do we use? The answer is a surprising one. We use *debts*—specifically, the debts of commercial banks. Deposits are, after all, nothing but the liabilities that banks owe their customers. Furthermore, we can see that one purpose of the banking system is to buy debts from other units in the economy, such as businesses or governments, in exchange for its own debts (which are money). For when a bank opens an account for a business to which it has granted a loan or when it buys a government bond, what else is it doing but accepting a debt that is *not* usable as money, in exchange for its deposit liabilities that *are* usable as money. And why is it that banks create money when they make loans, but you or I do not, when we lend money? Because we all accept bank liabilities (deposits) as money, but we do not accept personal or business IOUs to make payments with.

reserves make it possible for our banks to lend or invest, and thereby to open still more deposit accounts, which in turn lead to new reserves.

LIMITS ON THE EXPANSION

This all sounds a little frightening. Does it mean that the money supply can go on expanding indefinitely from a single new deposit? Wouldn't that be extremely dangerous?

It would of course be very dangerous, but there is no possibility that it can happen. For having understood how the supply of money can expand from an original increase in deposits, we may now understand equally well what keeps an expansion within bounds.

1. Not every loan generates an increase in bank deposits.

If our bank had opened a loan account for the Smith Corporation at the same time that another firm had paid off a similar loan, there would have been no original expansion in bank deposits. In that case, the addition of $800,000 to the Smith account would have been exactly balanced by a decline of $800,000 in someone else's account. Even if that decline would have taken place in a different bank, it would still mean that the nation's total of bank deposits would not have risen, and therefore no new money would

have been created. Thus, *only net additions to loans have an expansionary effect.* We will shortly see how such net additions arise in the first place.

2. There is a limit to the rise in money supply from a single increase in deposits.

As Fig. 13·1 shows, in the chain of deposit expansion each successive bank has a smaller increase in deposits, because each bank has to keep some of its newly gained cash or checks as reserve. Hence the amount of *excess* reserves, against which loans can be made, steadily falls.

Further, we can see that the amount of the total monetary expansion from an original net increase in deposits is governed by the size of the fraction that has to be kept aside each time as reserve. *In fact, we can see that just as with the multiplier, the cumulative effect of an increase in deposits will be determined by the reciprocal of the reserve fraction.* If each bank must keep one-fifth of its increased deposits as reserves, then the cumulative effect of an original increase in deposits, when it has expanded through the system, is five times the original increase. If reserves are one-fourth, the expansion is limited to four times the original increase, and so on.

If M is the money supply, D is net new deposits, and r is the reserve ratio, it follows that:

$$\Delta M = \frac{1}{r} \times \Delta D$$

Notice that this formula is exactly the same as that for the multiplier.*

3. The monetary expansion process can work in reverse.

Suppose that the banking system as a whole suffers a net loss of deposits. Instead of putting $1 million into a bank, the public takes it out in cash. The bank will now have too few reserves, and it will have to cut down its loans or sell its investments to gain the reserves it needs. In turn, as borrowers pay off their loans, or as bond buyers pay for their securities, cash will drain from other banks who will now find *their* reserves too small in relation to their deposits. In turn, they will therefore have to sell more investments or curtail still other loans, and this again will squeeze still other banks and reduce their reserves, with the same consequences.

Thus, just as an original expansion in deposits can lead to a multiple expansion, so an original contraction in deposits can lead to a multiple contraction. The size of this contraction is also limited by the reciprocal of the reserve fraction. If banks have to hold a 25 percent reserve, then an original fall of $100,000 in deposits will lead to a total fall of $400,000, assuming that the system was fully "loaned up" to begin with. If they had to hold a 20 percent reserve, a fall of $100,000 could pyramid to $500,000.

4. The expansion process may not be fully carried through.

We have assumed that each bank in the chain always lends out an amount equal to its excess reserves, but this may not be the case. The third or fifth bank along the way may have trouble finding a credit-worthy customer and may decide—for the moment,

anyway—to sit on its excess reserves. Or borrowers along the chain may take out cash from some of their new deposits and thereby reduce the banks' reserves and their lending powers. Thus the potential expansion may be only partially realized.

5. The expansion process takes time.

Like the multiplier process, the expansion of the money supply encounters many "frictions" in real life. Banks do not instantly expand loans when their reserves rise; bank customers do not instantly spend the proceeds of bank loans. The time lags in banking are too variable to enable us to make an estimate of how long it takes for an initial increase in new deposits to work its way through the system, but the time period is surely a matter of months for two or three "rounds."

WHY BANKS MUST WORK TOGETHER

There is an interesting problem concealed behind this crisscrossing of deposits that leads to a slowly rising level of the money supply. Suppose that an imaginary island economy was served by a single bank (and let us forget about all complications of international trade, etc.), and suppose that this bank, which worked on a 20 percent reserve ratio, was suddenly presented with an extra one million dollars worth of reserves—let us say newly mined pure gold. Our bank could, of course, increase its loans to customers. By how much? *By five million dollars!*

In other words, our island bank, all by itself, could use an increase in its reserves to create a much larger increase in the money supply. It is not difficult to understand why. Any borrower of the new five million, no matter where he spent his money on the island, would only be giving his checks to someone who also banked at the single, solitary bank. The whole five million, in other words, would stay *within* the bank as its

---

*Why is ΔM determined by multiplying ΔD by $1/r$? Same reason as the multiplier. See box on pp. 120–21.

deposits, although the identity of those depositors would, of course, shift. Indeed, there is no reason why such a bank should limit its expansion of the money supply to five million. As long as the "soundness" of the currency was unquestioned, such a bank could create as much money as it wanted through new deposits, since all of those deposits would remain in its own keeping.

The imaginary bank makes it plain why ordinary commercial banks *cannot* expand deposits beyond their excess reserves. Unlike the monopoly bank, they must expect to *lose* their deposits to other banks when their borrowers write checks on their new accounts. As a result they will also lose their reserves, and this can lead to trouble.

OVERLENDING

This situation is important enough to warrant taking a moment to examine. Suppose that in our previous example we had decided to lend the Smith Corporation not $800,000 but $900,000, and suppose as before that the Smith Corporation used the proceeds of that loan to pay the Jones Corporation. Now look at the condition of our bank after the Smith payment has cleared.

Our reserves would now have dropped to 10 percent! Indeed, if we had loaned the

One way that a bank may repair the situation is by borrowing reserves for a short period (paying interest on them, of course) from another bank that may have a temporary surplus at the Fed; this is called borrowing federal funds. Or a bank may quickly sell some of its government bonds and add the proceeds to its reserve account at the Fed. Or again, it may add to its reserves the proceeds of any loans that have come due and deliberately fail to replace these expired loans with new loans. Finally, a bank may borrow reserves directly from its Federal Reserve Bank and pay interest for the loan. We shall shortly look into this method when we talk about the role of the Federal Reserve in regulating the quantity of money.

The main point is clear. A bank is safe in lending only an amount that it can afford to lose to another bank. But of course one bank's loss is another's gain. That is why, by the exchange of checks, the banking system can accomplish the same result as the island monopoly bank, whereas no individual bank can hope to do so.

INVESTMENTS AND INTEREST

If a bank uses its excess reserves to buy securities, does that lead to the same multiplication effect as a bank loan?

ORIGINAL BANK

Assets		Liabilities	
Cash and at Fed	$ 100,000	Original deposits	$1,000,000
Loan (Smith Corp.)	900,000	Smith Corp. deposit	0
Total	**$1,000,000**	**Total**	**$1,000,000**

company $1,000,000 we would be in danger of insolvency.

Banks are, in fact, very careful not to overlend. If they find that they have inadvertently exceeded their legal reserve requirements, they quickly take remedial action.

It can. When a bank buys government securities, it usually does so from a securities dealer, a professional trader in bonds.* Its

*The dealer may be only a middleman, who will in turn buy from, or sell to, corporations or individuals. This doesn't change our analysis, however.

check (for $800,000 in our example) drawn on its account at the Federal Reserve will be made out to a dealer, who will deposit it in his bank. As a result, the dealer's bank suddenly finds itself with an $800,000 new deposit. It must keep 20 percent of this as required reserve, but the remainder is excess reserve against which it can make loans or investments as it wishes.

Is there a new deposit, corresponding to that of the businessman borrower? There is: the new deposit of the securities dealer. Note that in his case, as in the case of the borrower, the new deposit on the books of the bank has not been put there by the transfer of money from some other commercial bank. The $800,000 deposit has come into being through the deposit of a check of the Federal Reserve Bank, which is not a commercial bank. Thus it represents a new addition to the deposits of the private banking system.

Let us see this in the T accounts. After our first bank has bought its $800,000 in bonds (paying for them with its Federal Reserve checking account), its T account looks like this.

Here there are excess reserves of $640,000 with which additional investments can be made. It is possible for such new deposits, albeit diminishing each time, to remain in the financial circuit for some time, moving from bank to bank as an active business is done in buying government bonds.

YIELDS

Meanwhile, however, the very activity in bidding for government bonds is likely to raise their price, and thereby lower their rate of interest.

This is important to understand. A bond has a *fixed* rate of return and a stated face value. If it is a 4 percent, $1,000 bond, this means it will pay $40 interest yearly. If the bond now sells on the marketplace for $1,100, the $40 yearly interest will be less than a 4 percent return ($40 is only 3.6 percent of $1,100). If the price should fall to $900, the $40 return will be more than 4 percent ($40 is 4.4 percent of $900). Thus the *yield* of a bond varies inversely—in the other direction—from its market price.

ORIGINAL BANK

Assets		Liabilities	
Cash at Fed	$ 200,000	Deposits	$1,000,000
Government bonds	800,000		
Total	**$1,000,000**	**Total**	**$1,000,000**

As we can see, there are no excess reserves here. But look at the bank in which the seller of the government bond has deposited the check he has just received from our bank:

When the price of government bonds changes, all bond prices tend to change in the same direction. This is because all bonds are competing for investors' funds. If the yield on

SECOND BANK

Assets		Liabilities	
Cash	$800,000	New deposit of bond seller	$800,000
Total	**$800,000**	**Total**	**$800,000**

"governments" falls, investors will switch from governments to other, higher yielding bonds. But as they bid for these other bonds, the prices of these bonds will rise—and their yields will fall, too!

In this way, a change in yields spreads from one group of bonds to another. A lower rate of interest or a lower yield on government securities is quickly reflected in lower rates or yields for other kinds of bonds. In turn, a lower rate of interest on bonds makes loans to business look more attractive. Thus, sooner or later, excess reserves are apt to be channeled to new loans as well as new investments. Thereafter the deposit-building process follows its familiar course.

Controlling the Money Supply

We have now seen how a banking system can create money through the successive creation of excess reserves. But the key to the process is the creation of the *original* excess reserves, for without them the cumulative process will not be set in motion. We remember, for example, that a loan will not result in an increase in the money supply if it is offset by a decline in lending somewhere else in the banking system; neither will the purchase of a bond by one commercial bank if it is only buying a security sold by another. *To get a net addition to loans or investments, however, a banking system—assuming that it is fully loaned up—needs an increase in its reserves.* Where do these extra reserves come from? That is the question we must turn to next.

ROLE OF THE FEDERAL RESERVE

In our example we have already met one source of changes in reserves. When the public needs less currency, and it deposits its extra holdings in the banks, reserves rise, as we have seen. Contrariwise, when the public wants more currency, it depletes the banks'

holdings of currency and thereby lowers their reserves. In the latter case, the banks may find that they have insufficient reserves behind their deposits. To get more currency or claims on other banks, they will have to sell securities or reduce their loans. This might put a very severe crimp in the economy. Hence, to allow bank reserves to be regulated by the public's fluctuating demand for cash would seem to be an impossible way to run our monetary system.

But we remember that bank reserves are not mainly currency; in fact, currency is a relatively minor item. Most reserves are the accounts that member banks hold at the Federal Reserve. Hence, if these accounts could somehow be increased or decreased, we could regulate the amount of reserves—and thus the permissible total of deposits—without regard to the public's changing need for cash.

This is precisely what the Federal Reserve System is designed to do. Essentially, the system is set up to regulate the supply of money by raising or lowering the reserves of its member banks. When these reserves are raised, member banks find themselves with excess reserves and are thus in a position to make loans and investments by which the supply of money will increase further. Conversely, when the Federal Reserve lowers the reserves of its member banks, they will no longer be able to make loans and investments, or they may even have to reduce loans or get rid of investments, thereby extinguishing deposit accounts and contracting the supply of money.

MONETARY CONTROL MECHANISMS

How does the Federal Reserve operate? There are three ways.

1. Changing reserve requirements

It was the Federal Reserve itself, we will remember, that originally determined how much in reserves its member banks should hold against their deposits. Hence by changing that reserve requirement for a given level of deposits, it can give its member banks excess reserves or can create a shortage of reserves.

In our imaginary bank we have assumed that reserves were set at 20 percent of deposits. Suppose now that the Federal Reserve determined to lower reserve requirements to 15 percent. It would thereby automatically create extra lending or investing power for our *existing* reserves. Our bank with $1 million in deposits and $200,000 in reserves could now lend or invest an additional $50,000 without any new funds coming in from depositors. On the other hand, if requirements were raised to, say, 30 percent, we would find that our original $200,000 of reserves was $100,000 short of requirements, and we would have to curtail lending or investing until we were again in line with requirements.

Do not forget that these new reserve requirements affect *all* banks. Therefore, changing reserve ratios is a very effective way of freeing or contracting bank credit on a large scale. But it is an instrument that sweeps across the entire banking system in an undiscriminating fashion. It is therefore used only rarely, when the Federal Reserve Board feels that the supply of money is seriously short or dangerously excessive and needs remedy on a countrywide basis. For instance, in early 1973, the board raised reserve requirements one-half percent for all banks, partly to mop up excess reserves and partly to sound a general warning against what it considered to be a potentially dangerous inflationary state of affairs.

2. Changing discount rates

A second means of control uses interest rates as the money-controlling device. Recall that member banks that are short on reserves have a special privilege, if they wish to exercise it. They can *borrow* reserve balances

from the Federal Reserve Bank itself and add them to their regular reserve account at the bank.

The Federal Reserve Bank, of course, charges interest for lending reserves, and this interest is called the *discount rate.* By raising or lowering this rate, the Federal Reserve can make it attractive or unattractive for member banks to borrow to augment reserves. Thus in contrast with changing the reserve ratio itself, changing the discount rate is a mild device that allows each bank to decide for itself whether it wishes to increase its reserves. In addition, changes in the discount rate tend to influence the whole structure of interest rates, either tightening or loosening money.*

Although changes in the discount rate can be used as a major means of controlling the money supply and are used to control it in some countries, they are not used for this purpose in the U. S. The Federal Reserve Board does not allow banks to borrow whatever they would like at the current discount rate. The discount "window" is a place where a bank can borrow small amounts of money to smooth out short-run fluctuations in deposits and loans, but it is not a place where banks can borrow major amounts of money to expand their lending portfolios. As a result, the discount rate serves more as a signal of what the Federal Reserve would like to see happen than as an active force in determining the total borrowings of banks.

3. Open-market operations

Most frequently used, however, is a third technique called open-market operations. This technique permits the Federal Reserve Banks to change the supply of reserves by

---

*When interest rates are high, money is called tight. This means not only that borrowers have to pay higher rates, but that banks are stricter and more selective in judging the credit worthiness of business applications for loans. Conversely, when interest rates decline, money is called easy, meaning that it is not only cheaper but literally easier to borrow.

buying or selling U.S. government bonds on the open market.

How does this work? Let us suppose that the Federal Reserve authorities wish to increase the reserves of member banks. They will begin to buy government securities from dealers in the bond market; and they will pay these dealers with Federal Reserve checks.

Notice something about these checks: *they are not drawn on any commercial bank!* They are drawn on the Federal Reserve Bank itself. The security dealer who sells the bond will, of course, deposit the Fed's check, as if it were any other check, in his own commercial bank; and his bank will send the Fed's check through for credit to its own account, as if it were any other check. *As a result, the dealer's bank will have gained reserves, although no other commercial bank has lost reserves.* On balance, then, the system has more lending and investing capacity than it had before. In fact, it now has *excess* reserves, and these, as we have seen, will spread out through the system. *Thus by buying bonds, the Federal Reserve has, in fact, deposited money in the accounts of its members, thereby giving them the extra reserves that it set out to create.*

Conversely, if the authorities decide that member banks' reserves are too large, they will sell securities. Now the process works in reverse. Security dealers or other buyers of bonds will send their own checks on their own regular commercial banks to the Federal Reserve in payment for these bonds. This time the Fed will take the checks of its member banks and charge their accounts, thereby reducing their reserves. *Since these checks will not find their way into another commercial bank, the system as a whole will have suffered a diminution of its reserves.* By selling securities, in other words, the Federal Reserve authorities lower the Federal Reserve ac-

counts of member banks, thereby diminishing their reserves.*

ASYMMETRIC CONTROL

How effective are all these powers over the money supply? The Federal Reserve Board's capacity to control money is often compared to our ability to manipulate a string. If the Federal Reserve Board wishes to *reduce* the money supply, it can increase the discount rate or sell bonds. Sooner or later, this tends to be effective. If banks have free or excess reserves, they will not immediately have to reduce their lending portfolios; but eventually, by pulling on the string hard enough, the Fed can force a reduction in bank loans and the money supply.

The Federal Reserve Board's capacity to increase the money supply is not equally great. It can reduce reserve rates and buy bonds, but it cannot *force* banks to make loans if they do not wish to do so. Banks can, if they wish, simply increase their excess reserves. Normally, banks wish to make loans and earn profits; but if risks are high, they may not wish to do so. Such a situation occurred in the Great Depression. Banks

---

*Isn't this, some bright student will ask, really the same thing as raising or lowering the reserve ratio? If the Fed is really just putting money into member bank accounts when it buys bonds and taking money out when it sells them, why does it bother to go through the open market? Why not just tell the member banks that their reserves are larger or smaller?

Analytically, our student is entirely right. There is, however, cogent reason for working through the bond market. It is that the open-market technique allows banks to *compete* for their share of the excess reserves that are being made available or taken away. Banks that are good at attracting depositors will thereby get extra benefit from an increase in the money supply. Thus, rather than assigning excess reserves by executive fiat, the Fed uses the open market as an allocation device.

Finally, open-market operations allow the Fed to make very small changes in the money supply, whereas changes in reserve requirements would be difficult to adjust in very fine amounts.

piled up vast reserves rather than make loans, since the risks of defaults were too high to make most loans an attractive economic gamble. In terms of our analogy, the Federal Reserve Board can pull, but it cannot push on its string of controls.

STICKY PRICES

We are almost ready to look into the dynamics of money, in our next chapter, but we must examine a question that we have heretofore passed over in silence. We have taken for granted that we need a larger supply of money in order to expand output. But why should we? Why could we not grow just as well if the supply of money were fixed?

Theoretically we could. If we cut prices as we increased output, a given amount of money (or a given amount of expenditure) could cover an indefinitely large real output. Furthermore, as prices fell, workers would be content not to ask for higher wages (or would even accept lower wages), since in real terms they would be just as well or better off.

It is not difficult to spot the flaw in this argument. In the real world, prices of many goods cannot be cut easily. If the price of steel rose and fell as quickly and easily as prices on the stock exchange, or if wages went down without a murmur of resistance, or if rents and other contractual items could be quickly adjusted, then prices would be flexible and we would not require any enlargement of our money supply to cover a growing real output.

In fact, as we know, prices are extremely "sticky" in the downward direction. Union leaders do not look with approval on wage cuts, even when living costs fall. Contractual prices cannot be quickly adjusted. Many big firms administer their prices and carefully avoid price competition: note, for example, that the prices of many consumer items are printed on the package months before the item will be sold.

Thus we can see that a fixed supply of money would put the economy into something of a straitjacket. As output tended to increase, businessmen would need more money to finance production, and consumers would need more money to make their larger expenditures. If businessmen could get more money from the banks, all would be well. But suppose they could not. Then the only way a businessman could get his hands on a larger supply of cash would be to persuade someone to lend it to him, and his persuasion would be in the form of a higher rate of interest. But this rising interest rate would discourage other businessmen from going ahead with their plans. Hence the would-be boom would be stopped dead in its tracks by a sheer shortage of spending power.

A flexible money supply obviates this economic suffocation. The fact that banks can create money (provided that they have excess reserves) enables them to take care of businesses that wish to make additional expenditures. The expenditures themselves put additional money into the hands of consumers. And the spending of consumers in turn sends the enlarged volume of purchasing power back to business firms to complete the great flow of expenditure and receipt.

Paper Money and Gold

Finally, let us clear up one last mystery of the monetary system—the mystery of where currency (coin and bills) actually comes from and where it goes. If we examine most of our paper currency, we will find that it has "Federal Reserve Note" on it; that is, it is paper money issued by the Federal Reserve System. We understand, by now, how the public gets these notes: it simply draws them from its checking accounts. When it does so, the commercial banks, finding their supplies of vault cash low, ask their Federal Reserve district banks to ship them as much new cash as they need.

And what does the Federal Reserve Bank do? It takes packets of bills ($1 and $5 and $10) out of its vaults, *where these stacks of printed paper have no monetary significance at all,* charges the requisite amount against its member banks' balances, and ships the cash out by armored truck. So long as these new stacks of bills remain in the member banks' possession, they are still not money! But soon they will pass out to the public, where they will be money. Do not forget, of course, that as a result, the public will have that much *less* money left in its checking accounts.

Could this currency-issuing process go on forever? Could the Federal Reserve ship out as much money as it wanted to? Suppose that the authorities at the Fed decided to order a trillion dollars worth of bills from the Treasury mints. What would happen when those bills arrived at the Federal Reserve Banks? The answer is that they would simply gather dust in their vaults. *There would be no way for the Fed to "issue" its money unless the public wanted cash.* And the amount of cash the public could want is always limited by the amount of money it has in its checking accounts.

THE GOLD COVER

Are there no limitations on this note-issuing or reserve-creating process? Until 1967 there *were* limitations imposed by Congress, requiring the Federal Reserve to hold gold certificates equal in value to at least 25 percent of all outstanding notes. (Gold certificates are a special kind of paper money issued by the U.S. Treasury and backed 100

percent by gold bullion in Fort Knox.) Prior to 1964 there was a further requirement that the amount of gold certificates also be sufficient to give a 25 percent backing as well to the total amount of member bank deposits held by the Fed. Thus the legal obligation not to go beyond this 25 percent gold cover provided a strict ceiling on the amount of member bank reserves the Federal Reserve system could create or on the amount of notes it could ship at the request of its member banks.

All this presented no problem in, say, 1940, when the total of member bank reserves plus Federal Reserve notes came to only $20 billion, against which we held gold certificates worth almost $22 billion. Trouble began to develop, however, in the 1960s when a soaring GNP was accompanied by a steadily rising volume of both member bank reserves and Federal Reserve notes. By 1964, for example, member bank reserves had grown to $22 billion, and outstanding Reserve notes to nearly $35 billion. At the same time, our gold stock had declined to just over $15 billion. With $57 billion in liabilities ($22 billion in member bank reserves plus $35 billion in notes) and only $15 billion in gold certificates, the 25 percent cover requirement was clearly imperiled.

Congress thereupon removed the cover requirement from member bank reserves, leaving all our gold certificates available as "backing" for our Federal Reserve notes. But even that did not solve the problem. Currency in circulation continued to rise with a record GNP until it exceeded $40 billion in 1967. Our gold stock meanwhile continued to decline to $12 billion in that year and threatened to fall further. The handwriting on the wall indicated that the 25 percent cover could not long be maintained.

There were basically two ways out of the dilemma. One would have been to change the gold cover requirements from 25 percent to, say, 10 percent. That would have made our gold stock more than adequate to "back" our paper money (and our member bank deposits, too).*

The second way was much simpler. *It was simply to eliminate the gold cover entirely.* With very little fuss, this is what Congress did in 1967.

GOLD AND MONEY

Does the presence or absence of a gold cover make any difference? From the economist's point of view it does not. Gold is a metal with a long and rich history of hypnotic influence, so there is undeniably a psychological usefulness in having gold "behind" a currency. But unless that currency is 100 percent convertible into gold, *any* money demands an act of faith on the part of its users. If that faith is destroyed, the money becomes valueless; so long as it is unquestioned, the money is "as good as gold."

Thus the presence or absence of a gold backing for currency is purely a psychological problem, so far as the value of a domestic currency is concerned. But the point is worth pursuing a little further. Suppose our currency *were* 100 percent convertible into gold —suppose, in fact, that we used only gold coins as currency. Would that improve the operation of our economy?

A moment's reflection should reveal that it would not. We would still have to cope with a very difficult problem that our bank deposit money handles rather easily. This is the problem of how we could increase the supply of money or diminish it, as the needs of the economy changed. With gold coins as money, we would either have a frozen stock of money (with consequences that we shall trace in the next chapter), or our supply of money would be at the mercy of our luck in gold-mining or the currents of international trade that funneled gold into our hands or took it away. And incidentally, a gold currency would not obviate inflation, as many countries have discovered when the vagaries of international trade or a fortuitous discovery of gold mines increased their holdings of gold faster than their actual output.

MONEY AND BELIEF

As we cautioned at the outset, money is a highly sophisticated and curious invention.

---

*Actually, the gold never really backed our currency, since no American was legally permitted to buy gold bullion.

At one time or another nearly everything imaginable has served as the magic symbol of money: whales' teeth, shells, feathers, bark, furs, blankets, butter, tobacco, leather, copper, silver, gold, and (in the most advanced nations) pieces of paper with pictures on them or simply numbers on a ledger page. In fact, anything is usable as money, provided that there is a natural or enforceable scarcity of it, so that men can usually come into its possession only through carefully designated ways. Behind all the symbols, however, rests the central requirement of faith. Money serves its indispensable purposes as long as we believe in it. It ceases to function the moment we do not. Money has well been called "the promises men live by."

But the creation of money and the control over its supply is still only half the question. We have yet to trace how our money supply influences the flow of output itself—or to put it differently, how the elaborate institutions through which men promise to honor one another's work and property affect the amount of work they do and the amount of new wealth they accumulate. This is the subject to which our next chapter will be devoted.

KEY WORDS

Money

Deposits

Currency

Federal
Reserve Banks

Federal
Reserve System

Fractional
reserves

Excess reserves

Deposit creation

Loans

Reserve ratios

CENTRAL CONCEPTS

1. **Money is defined as whatever we use to make *payments*. As such, in modern economies, the most important constituents of money are *currency outside the banking system and demand deposits (checking accounts).***

2. **Currency flows into, and is drawn out of, checking accounts. The total amount of checking accounts, however, far exceeds the actual currency held in banks.**

3. **Banks are forced, by law, to hold reserves against stated fractions of their demand deposits. For most banks these reserves can be either in *vault cash* or in *accounts at a Federal Reserve Bank.***

4. **There are *twelve Federal Reserve Banks* that service their member banks exactly as the member banks service the public. The Reserve Banks are coordinated by a policy-making Board of Governors (Federal Reserve Board) in Washington. The Board is empowered to change reserve ratios for city or country banks, within legally established limits, and to take other actions to control the supply of money.**

5. **The function of the reserves established by the Federal Reserve Board is not to ensure the "safety" of the currency, but to provide a means of *controlling the supply of money*.**

6. **Any reserves of a commercial bank over and above those imposed by the Federal Reserve are called *excess reserves*. Commercial banks earn profits by lending or investing amounts equal to their excess reserves.**

7. **When a bank makes a loan, it opens an account in the name of the borrower. This account is a *net addition to total deposits and is therefore new money*. Thus bank lending can increase the supply of money. Investing in government bonds is also likely to lead to new demand deposits.**

8. **New deposits created by loans are typically drawn on by checks that go into other banks. Here they also give rise to excess reserves and to the possibility of *further deposit creation through more loans or investments*.**

9. **The total amount of new money that the banking system can create depends on the *reserve ratio*. The size of credit expansion is determined by the reciprocal of the reserve ratio.**

Credit expansion

10. It is only the banking *system* that can expand the money supply up to the limit imposed by the reciprocal of the reserve ratio. A single bank can lend only up to the amount that it is prepared to "lose." *Hence each individual bank lends only an amount that is fully covered by its excess reserves.*

Discount rate

11. The Federal Reserve System controls the ability of the banking system to expand the supply of money by *controlling the amount of its reserves*. It can do so in three ways:

● By changing *reserve ratios*

Monetary controls

● By changing the *discount rate*, as a "signal" to the banking community

● By *open-market operations*

Open-market operations

12. The most commonly used method is open-market operations. This is a means of controlling the size of reserves by *purchases and sales of government bonds on the open market*. When the Federal Reserve System buys bonds, it issues in payment its own checks, which enter the commercial banks and are added to their reserves. This gives the commercial banks excess reserves and enables them to make additional loans or investments. Selling bonds brings checks from commercial bank accounts to the Federal Reserve Banks, and thereby lowers the reserve accounts of member banks. This reduces their ability to make loans or investments. Fed powers are more effective in contracting than in expanding the money supply.

Sticky prices

13. A flexible money supply is needed because of *sticky prices*.

Gold "cover"

14. There is no longer any gold backing required behind member bank reserves or behind Federal Reserve notes. The amount or percentage of gold cover is essentially arbitrary. *Gold plays only a symbolic role in a national monetary system.* The true value of money ultimately reposes in the faith men have in it.

QUESTIONS

1. Why do we not count cash in the tills of commercial banks in the money supply? Why don't we include savings accounts?

2. When you deposit currency in a commercial bank, what happens to it? Can you ask for your particular bills again? If you demanded to see "your" account, what would it be?

3. What determines how much vault cash a bank must hold against its deposits? Would you expect this proportion to change in some seasons, such as Christmas? Do you think it would be the same in worried times as in placid times? In new countries as in old ones?

4. Is currency the main reserve of a bank? Do reserves ensure the safety of a currency? What function do they have?

5. What are excess reserves? Suppose a bank has $500,000 in deposits and that there is a reserve ratio of 30 percent imposed by law. What is its required reserve? Suppose it happens to hold $200,000 in vault cash or at its account at the Fed. What, if any, is its excess reserve?

6. If the bank above wanted to make loans or investments, how much would it be entitled to lend or invest?

7. Suppose its deposits increased by another $50,000. Could it lend or invest this entire amount? Any of it? How much?

8. If a bank lends money, it opens an account in the name of the borrower. Now suppose the borrower draws down his new account. What happens to the reserves of the lending bank? Show this in a T account.

9. Suppose the borrower sends his check for $1,000 to someone who banks at another bank. Describe what happens to the deposits of the second bank. If the reserve ratio is 20 percent, how much new lending or investing can it do?

10. If the reserve ratio is 20 percent, and the original addition to reserves is $1,000, what will be the total potential amount of new money that can be created by the banking system? If the ratio is 25 percent?

11. What is the difference between a banking system and a single competitive bank? Can a single bank create new money? Can it create more new money than an amount equal to its excess reserves? Can a banking system create more money than its excess reserves?

12. Suppose that a bank has $1 million in deposits, $100,000 in reserves, and is fully loaned up. Now suppose the Federal Reserve System lowers reserve requirements from 10 percent to 8 percent. What happens to the lending capacity of the bank?

13. If the discount rate rises from 5 percent to 6 percent, does that affect the willingness of banks to lend? How?

14. The Federal Reserve Banks buy $100 million in U.S. Treasury notes. How do they pay for these notes? What happens to the checks? Do they affect the reserves of member banks? Will buying bonds increase or decrease the money supply?

15. Now explain what happens when the Fed sells Treasury notes. Who buys them? How do they pay for them? Where do the checks go? How does payment affect the accounts of the member banks at the Federal Reserve Banks?

16. Why do you think gold has held such a place of prestige in the minds of men?

Money and the Macro System

14

IN OUR PRECEDING CHAPTER, we found out something about what money is and how it comes into being. Now we must turn to the much more complicated question of how money works—the level of output. What happens when the banks create or destroy deposits? Can we directly raise or lower incomes by altering the quantity of money? Can we control inflation or recession by using the monetary management powers of the Federal Reserve System? These extremely important questions will be the focus of discussion in this chapter.

The Quantity Theory of Money

QUANTITY EQUATION

One relation between money and economic activity must already have occurred to us. It is that the quantity of money must have something to do with *prices*. Does it not stand to reason that if we increase the supply of money, prices will go up, and that if we

decrease the amount of money, prices will fall?

Something very much like this belief lies behind one of the most famous equations (really identities) in economics. The equation looks like this:

$$MV \equiv PT$$

where

M = *quantity of money* (currency outside banks plus demand deposits)

V = *velocity of circulation,* or the number of times per period or per year that an average dollar changes hands

P = *the general level of prices,* or a price index

T = *the number of transactions made in the economy* in a year, or a measure of *physical output*

If we think about this equation, its meaning is not hard to grasp. What the quantity equation says is that the amount of ex-

penditure (*M* times *V*, or the quantity of money times the frequency of its use) equals the amount of *receipts* (*P* times *T*, or the price of an average sale times the number of sales). Naturally, this is an identity. In fact, it is our old familiar circular flow. What all factors of production receive (*PT*) must equal what all factors of production spend (*MV*).

Just as our GNP identities are true at every moment, so are the quantity theory of money identities true at every instant. They merely look at the circular flow from a different vantage point. And just as our GNP identities yielded useful economic insights when we began to inquire into the functional relationships within those identities, so the quantity theory can also shed light on economic activity if we can find functional relationships concealed within its self-evident "truth."

THE ASSUMPTIONS OF THE QUANTITY THEORY

To move from tautologies to operationally useful relationships, we need to make assumptions that lend themselves to investigation and evidence. In the case of the GNP $\equiv$ $C + G + I + X$ identity, for instance, we made a critical assumption about the propensity to consume, which led to the multiplier and to predictive statements about the influence of injections on GNP. In the case of $MV \equiv PT$, we need another assumption. What will it be?

The crucial assumptions made by the economists who first formulated the quantity theory were two: (1) the velocity of money—the number of times an average dollar was used per year—*was constant;* and (2) transactions (sales) *were always at a full-employment level.* If these assumptions were true, it followed that the price level was a simple function of the supply of money:

$$P = \frac{V}{T} \cdot M$$
$$P = kM$$

where k was a constant defined by V/T.

If the money supply went up, prices went up; if the quantity of money went down, prices went down. Since the government controlled the money supply, it could easily regulate the price level.

TESTING THE QUANTITY THEORY

Is this causal relation true? Can we directly manipulate the price level by changing the size of our stock of money?

The original inventors of the quantity equation, over half a century ago, thought this was indeed the case. And of course it *would* be the case if everything else in the equation held steady while we moved the quantity of money up or down. In other words, if the velocity of circulation, *V*, and the number of transactions, *T*, were fixed, changes in *M* would have to operate directly on *P*.

Can we test the validity of this assumption? There is an easy way to do so. Figure 14·1 shows us changes in the supply of money compared with changes in the level of prices.

A glance at Fig. 14·1 answers our question. Between 1929 and 1973, the supply of money in the United States increased over eightfold while prices rose only a little more than twofold. Clearly, something *must* have happened to *V* or to *T* to prevent the eightfold increase in *M* from bringing about a similar increase in *P*. Let us see what those changes were.

CHANGES IN V

Figure 14·2 gives us a first clue as to what is wrong with a purely mechanical interpre-

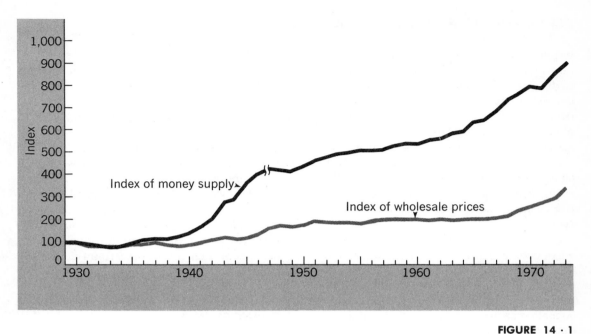

FIGURE 14 · 1
Money supply and prices

FIGURE 14 · 2
Money supply and velocity

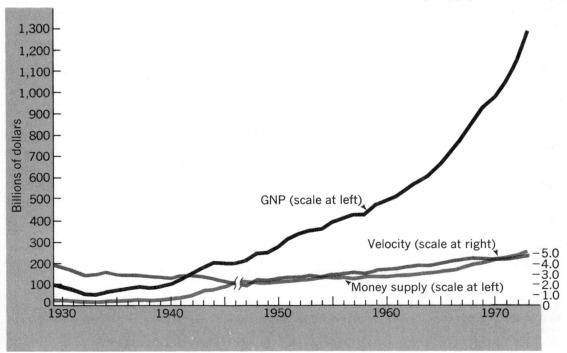

tation of the quantity theory. In it we show how many times an average dollar was used to help pay for each year's output.* We derive this number by dividing the total expenditure for each year's output (which is, of course, the familiar figure for GNP) by the actual supply of money—currency plus checking accounts—for each year. As the chart shows, the velocity of money fell by 50 percent between 1929 and 1946, only to rise again to the 1929 level over the postwar years.

We shall return later to an inquiry into why people spend money less or more quickly, but it is clear beyond question that they do. This has two important implications for our study of money. First, it gives a very cogent reason why we cannot apply the quantity theory in a mechanical way, asserting that an increase in the supply of money will *always* raise prices. For if people choose to spend the increased quantity of money more slowly, its impact on the quantity of goods may not change at all: whereas if they spend the same quantity of money more rapidly, prices can rise without any change in *M*.

Second and more clearly than we have seen, the variability of *V* reveals that money itself can be a destabilizing force—destabilizing because it enables us to do two things that would be impossible in a pure barter economy. We can:

1. *delay between receiving and expending our rewards for economic effort*

2. *spend more or less than our receipts by drawing on, or adding to, our cash balances*

*Note that final output is not quite the same as *T*, which embraces *all* transactions, including those for intermediate goods. But if we define *T* so that it includes only *transactions that enter into final output*, *PT* becomes a measure of gross national product. In the same way, we can count only those expenditures that enter into GNP when we calculate *MV*. It does no violence to the idea of the quantity theory to apply it only to final output, and it makes statistical computation far simpler.

The Classical economists used to speak of money as a "veil," implying that it did not itself play an active role in influencing the behavior of the economic players. But we can see that the ability of those players to vary the rate of their expenditure—to hang onto their money longer or to get rid of it more rapidly than usual—makes money much more than a veil. Money (or rather, people's wish to hold or to spend money) becomes an independent source of change in a complex economic society. To put it differently, the use of money introduces an independent element of uncertainty into the circular flow.*

CHANGES IN T

Now we must turn to a last and perhaps most important reason why we cannot relate the supply of money to the price level in a mechanical fashion. This reason lies in the role played by *T*; that is, by the volume of output.

Just as the early quantity theorists thought of *V* as essentially unvarying, so they thought of *T* as a relatively fixed term in the quantity equation. In the minds of nearly all economic theorists before the Depression, output was always assumed to be as large as the available resources and the willingness of the factors of production would permit. While everyone was aware that there might be minor variations from this state of full output, virtually no one thought they would be of sufficient importance to matter. *Hence the quantity theory implicitly assumed full employment or full output as the normal condition of the economy.* With such an assumption, it was easy to picture *T* as an unimpor-

*Technically, the standard economic definition of money is that it is both a means of exchange and a store of value. It is the latter characteristic that makes money a potentially disturbing influence.

tant term in the equation and to focus the full effect of changes in money on *P*.

The trauma of the Great Depression effectively removed the comfortable assumption that the economy "naturally" tended to full employment and output. At the bottom of the Depression, real output had fallen by 25 percent. Aside from what the Depression taught us in other ways, it made unmistakably clear that changes in the volume of output (and employment) were of crucial importance in the overall economic picture.

OUTPUT AND PRICES

How does our modern emphasis on the variability of output and employment fit into the overall question of money and prices? The answer is very simple, but very important. We have come to see that *the effect of more money on prices cannot be determined unless we also take into account the effect of spending on the volume of transactions or output.*

It is not difficult to grasp the point. Let us picture an increase in spending, perhaps initiated by businessmen launching a new investment program or by the government inaugurating a new public works project. These new expenditures will be received by many other entrepreneurs, as the multiplier mechanism spreads the new spending through the economy. But now we come to the key question. What will entrepreneurs do as their receipts increase?

It is at this point that the question of output enters. For if businessmen are operating factories or stores *at less than full capacity,* and if there is an *employable supply of labor available,* the result of their new receipts is almost certain to be an increase in output. That is, employers will take advantage of the rise in demand, to produce and sell more goods and services. They may also try to raise prices and increase their profits further; but *if their industries are reasonably competitive,* it is doubtful that prices can be raised very much. Other businessmen with idle plants will simply undercut them and take their business away. An example is provided by the period 1934 through 1940, when output increased by 50 percent while prices rose by less than 5 percent. The reason, of course, lay in the great amount of unemployed resources, making it easy to expand output without price increases.

PRICES AND EMPLOYMENT

Thus we reach a general conclusion of the greatest importance. *An increase in spending of any kind tends to result in more output and employment whenever there are considerable amounts of unemployed resources.* But this is no longer true when we reach a level of high employment or very full plant utilization. Now an increase in spending *cannot* quickly lead to an increase in output, simply because the resources for more production are lacking. The result, instead, will be a rise in prices, for no firm can lose business to competitors when competitors are unable to fill additional orders. Thus the corollary of our general conclusion is that *additional spending from any source is inflationary when it is difficult to raise output.*

FULL EMPLOYMENT VS. UNDEREMPLOYMENT

It is impossible to overstress the importance of this finding for macroeconomic *policy.* Policies that make sense when we are fully employed may make no sense when we are badly underemployed, and vice versa.

To spend more in the public or in the private sector is clearly good for an economy that is suffering from underutilized resources, but equally clearly inflationary and bad for an economy that is bumping up against the ceiling of output. Similarly, to balance budgets or run budget surpluses makes little sense when men are looking for work and businessmen are looking for orders, but it is the course of wisdom when there are no idle resources to absorb the additional expenditure.

One of the main differences between con-temporary economic thought and that of the past is precisely this sharp division between policies that make sense in full employment and those that make sense in conditions of underemployment. It was not that the economists of the past did not recognize the tragedy of unemployment or did not wish to remedy it. It was rather that they did not see how an economy could be in *equilibrium* even though there was heavy unemployment.

The dragging years of the Great Depression taught us not only that output could fall far below the levels of full utilization, but—and perhaps this was its most intellectually unsettling feature—that an economy could be plagued with unemployed men and machines for almost a decade and yet not spontaneously generate the momentum to reabsorb them. Today we understand this condition of unemployment equilibrium, and we have devised various remedial measures to raise the equilibrium point to a satisfactory level, including, not least, additional public expenditure. But this new understanding must be balanced with a keen appreciation of its relevance to the underlying situation of employment. Remedies for an underemployed economy can be ills for a fully employed one.

INFLATION AND PUBLIC FINANCE

We can see that the conclusion we have reached puts a capstone on our previous analysis of deficit spending. It is now possible to add a major criterion to the question of whether or not to use the public sector as a supplement to the private sector. That criterion is whether or not substantially "full" employment has been reached.

If the economy is operating at or near the point of full employment, additional net public spending will only add more MV to a situation in which T is already at capacity and where, therefore, P will rise. But note that this conclusion attaches to more than additional *public* spending. When full employment is reached, additional spending of any kind—public or private, consumption or investment—will increase MV and, given the ceiling on T, affect P.

A different conclusion is reached when there is large-scale unemployment. Now additional public (or private) spending will result not in higher prices, but in larger output and higher employment. Thus we cannot say that public spending in itself is "inflationary." Rather, we must see that *any kind of additional spending can be inflationary in a fully employed economy.*

Money and Expenditure

We have almost lost sight of our subject, which is not really inflation (we will come back to that in Chapter 15) but how money affects GNP. And here there is an important point. How does an increased supply of money get "into" GNP? People who have not studied economics often discuss changes in the money supply as if the government "put" money into circulation, mailing out dollar bills to taxpayers. The actual connection between an increase in M and an increase in MV is much more complex. Let us look into it.

INTEREST RATES AND THE TRANSACTIONS DEMAND FOR MONEY

From our previous chapter, we know the immediate results of an increased supply of money, whether brought about by open-market operations or a change in reserve ratios. *The effect in both cases is a rise in the lendable or investible reserves of banks.* Ceteris paribus, this will lead to a fall in interest rates as banks compete with one another in lending their additional unused reserves to firms or individuals.

As interest rates decline, some firms and individuals will be tempted to increase their borrowings. It becomes cheaper to take out a mortgage, to buy a car on an installment loan, to finance inventories. Thus, as we would expect, the demand curve for "spending money," like that for most commodities, slopes downward. As money gets cheaper, people want to "buy" (borrow) more of it. To put it differently, the lower the price of money, the larger the quantity demanded.

We speak of this demand curve for money to be used for expenditure as the *transactions demand for money*.

FINANCIAL DEMAND

But there is also another, quite separate source of the demand for money. This is the demand for money for *financial purposes*, to be held by individuals or corporations as part of their assets.

What happens to the demand for money for financial purposes as its price goes down? Financial demand also increases, although for different reasons. When interest rates are high, individuals and firms tend to keep their wealth as fully invested as possible, in order to earn the high return that is available. But when interest rates fall, the opportunity cost of keeping money idle is much less: if you are an investor with a portfolio of $10,000 and the rate of interest is 7 percent, you give up $700 a year if you are very "liquid" (i.e., all in cash); whereas if the interest rate is only 3 percent, your opportunity cost for liquidity falls to $300.

LIQUIDITY PREFERENCE

Economists call this increased willingness to be in cash as interest rates fall *liquidity preference*. The motives behind liquidity preferences are complex—partly speculative, partly precautionary. But they act in all cases to make us more and more willing or eager to be in cash when interest rates are low, and less and less willing when rates are higher. Thus the financial demand for cash, like the transactions demand, is a downward sloping demand curve.

We can now put together the two demand curves for money and add the supply curve of money—the actual stock of money available. The result looks like Fig. 14·3.

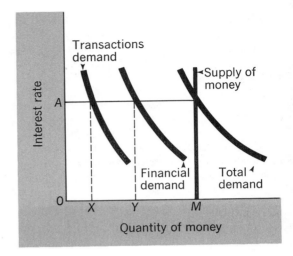

FIGURE 14·3
Transactions and financial demands for money

Our diagram shows us that at interest rate *OA*, there will be *OX* amount of money demanded for transactions purposes and *OY* amount demanded for liquidity purposes. The total demand for money will be *OM* (= *OX* + *OY*), which is just equal to the total supply.

CHANGING THE SUPPLY OF MONEY

Now let us suppose that the monetary authorities reduce the supply of money. We show this in Fig. 14·4. Now we have a curious situation. The supply of money has declined from *OM* to *OM'*. But notice that the demand curve for money shows that firms and individuals want to hold *OM*, at the given rate of interest *OA*. *Yet they cannot hold amount* OM, *because the monetary authorities have cut the supply to* OM'. What will happen?

The answer is very neat. As bank reserves fall, banks will "tighten" money—raise lending rates and screen loan applications more carefully. Therefore individuals and firms will be competing for a reduced supply of loans and will bid more for them. At the same time, individuals and firms will feel the pinch of reduced supplies of cash and will try to get more money to fulfill their liquidity desires. The easiest way to get more money is to sell securities, to get out of bonds and into cash. *Note, however, that selling securities does not create a single additional dollar of money. It simply transfers money from one holder to another. But it does change*

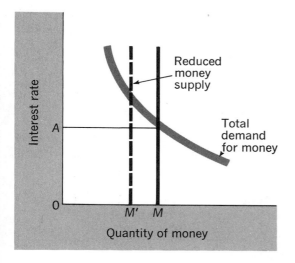

FIGURE 14 · 4
Reducing the supply of money

the rate of interest. As bonds are sold their price falls, and as the price of bonds falls, the interest yield on bonds rises (see p. 203).

Our next diagram (Fig. 14·5) shows what happens. As interest rates rise, the public is content to hold a smaller quantity of money. Hence a new interest rate, *OB,* will emerge, at which the public is *willing* to hold the money that there *is to hold.* The attempt to become more liquid ceases, and a new equilibrium interest rate prevails.

Suppose the authorities had increased the supply of money. In that case, individuals

and firms would be holding more money than they wanted at the going rate of interest. They would try to get out of money into bonds, sending bond prices up and yields

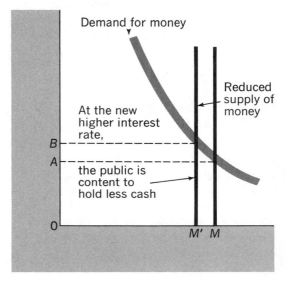

FIGURE 14 · 5
Determination of new equilibrium

FIGURE 14 · 6
Increasing the supply of money

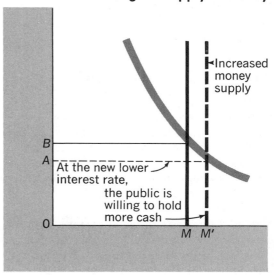

down. Simultaneously, banks would find themselves with extra reserves and would compete with one another for loans, also driving interest rates down. As interest rates fell, firms and individuals would be content to hold more money either for transactions or liquidity purposes, until a new equilibrium was again established. Fig. 14·6 shows the process at work.

THE DETERMINATION OF INTEREST RATES

This gives us the final link in our argument. We have seen that interest rates determine whether we wish to hold larger or smaller balances, either for transactions or financial (liquidity) purposes. But what determines the interest rate itself? We can now see that the *answer is the interplay of our demand for money and the supply of money.*

Our demand for money is made up of our transactions demand curve and our financial (liquidity) demand curve. The supply of money is given to us by the monetary authorities. The price of money—interest— is therefore determined by the demand for, and supply of, money, exactly as the price of any commodity is determined by the demand and supply for it.

MONEY AND EXPENDITURE

What our analysis enables us to see, however, is that once the interest rate is determined, it will affect the use to which we put a given supply of money. Now we begin to understand the full answer to the question of how changes in the supply of money affect GNP (and prices). Let us review the argument one last time.

1. Suppose that the monetary authorities want to increase the supply of money. They will lower reserve ratios or buy government bonds on the open market.

2. Banks will find that they have larger

reserves. They will compete with one another and lower lending rates.

3. Individuals and firms will also find that they have larger cash balances than they want at the going rate of interest. They will try to get rid of their extra cash by buying bonds, thereby sending bond yields down.

4. As interest rates fall, both as a result of bank competition and rising bond prices, the new, larger supply of money will find its way into use. *Part of it will be used for additional transactions purposes, as individuals and firms take advantage of cheaper money and increase their borrowings. Part of it will be used for larger financial balances, as the public's desire for liquidity grows with falling interest rates.*

THE PROCESS IN DIAGRAM

We can see the process very clearly in Fig. 14·7. We begin with *OM* money supply and

FIGURE 14 · 7
Using money for two purposes

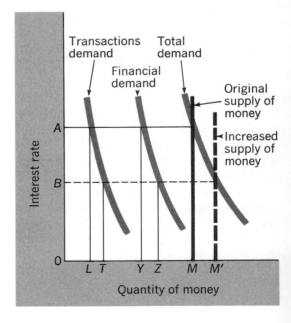

a rate of interest OA: as we can see, OL amount of money is held for liquidity purposes, and OY for transactions purposes. Now the stock of money is increased to OM'. The interest rate falls, for the reasons we now understand, until it reaches OB. At the new interest rate, liquidity balances have increased to OT, and transactions balances to OZ.

Exactly the same process would take place, in reverse, if the stock of money were decreased from OM' to OM. Can you see that the decreased supply of money will result partly in smaller transactions balances and partly in smaller liquidity balances? Do you understand that it is the higher rate of interest that causes the public to hold these smaller balances?

THE LIQUIDITY EFFECT

We have traced the circuitous manner in which a change in M "gets into" GNP. But there is yet another route that bypasses the rate of interest entirely. The "monetarist" school suggests that increases in M directly affect our spending habits, *even though interest rates remain unchanged.*

The monetarists suggest that changes in the supply of money directly affect our spending propensities because changes in the money supply alter our portfolios. A portfolio describes the way in which we hold our assets—in cash, savings accounts, checking accounts, various kinds of bonds, stocks, real estate, etc. When the money supply is altered, for example through open-market operations, the government is tempting the public to shift its portfolios into cash. But there is no reason to believe that the public wants this much cash; if it *had* wanted it, it would not have held the bonds (at their going rate of interest) in the first place. Therefore the public will seek to reduce its undesired cash holdings by buying real assets—cars, homes, inventories, and other things.

Most economists are willing to add this *liquidity effect* to the *interest rate effect,* so that monetary policy is believed to affect the economy both through its impact on the price of money and also directly through its impact on our portfolio preferences. What remains in doubt is the degree of influence that should be attributed to interest or to liquidity.

THE MODERN QUANTITY THEORY

We are now in a position to reformulate the quantity theory. Modern proponents of the theory recognize that economies do not always operate at full employment and that the velocity of money changes (we can see that liquidity preferences must be closely related to velocity). Hence they do not argue that an increase in the quantity of money is mechanically reflected in a proportionate rise in prices.

Instead, they contend that the demands for money for transaction purposes and liquidity purposes are *calculable functions,* just as consumption is a calculable function of income. The variables on which the demand for money depend are very complex —too complex to warrant explanation here. What is important is the idea that the relation between an increase in money supply and in transactions and financial demand can be estimated, much as the propensity to consume is estimated.

The Art of Money Management

We finally have all the pieces of the puzzle. We understand the curiously complex way in which changes in the supply of money affect changes in the expenditures of the public. It remains only to consider one aspect of the problem: the art of managing the supply of money so that the *right* increases in the supply of money will be forthcoming at the right time.

Why "art"? Is not the task of the monetary authority very clear? By increasing the supply of money, it pushes down interest rates and encourages expenditure. Hence all it has to do is to regulate the quantity of money to maintain a level of spending that will keep us at a high, but not too high, level of employment.

We have already seen some of the reasons why things are not that simple. The effect of interest rates on investment expenditure, as we previously learned, is obscure. So is the effect of liquidity on expenditure. We know that unwanted liquidity will encourage spending, but there is a time lag involved, and this lag may vary considerably at different phases of the business cycle. To add to the problem, the Federal Reserve Board can control the money supply with an eye on interest rates, or it can control it with an eye on liquidity effects, but it cannot do both at the same time. As a result, sometimes the board seems to focus entirely on the "price effect" of interest rates, and at other times on the liquidity effect of money supply. When two policies clash and there is no scientific means of judging between them, we trust to good sense, or to a "feel" of the economy. Hence the need for an "art" of money management.

SHIFTING LIQUIDITY PREFERENCES

Still another difficulty enforces the need for artful control. Suppose, for example, that the Federal Reserve creates excess reserves, in the expectation that interest rates will go down and that new loans will be pumped into investment. But suppose that at the same time, the public's "liquidity preferences" are rising because investors feel nervous and want to be more liquid. Then the shift in the quantity of money, as shown in Fig. 14·8, will be offset by a shift in liquidity preferences, and the rate of interest will not change

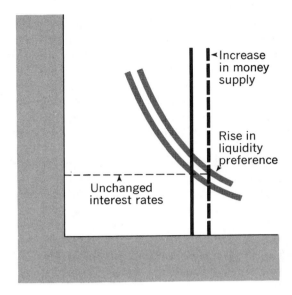

FIGURE 14 · 8
A shift in liquidity preference

at all! The new money will simply wind up in larger financial cash holdings, and none will be available for more transactions.

In other words, an attempt by the monetary authorities to drive down the rate of interest in order to encourage expenditure may be frustrated if the public uses all the additional funds for liquidity. At the bottom of the Great Depression, for example, banks had huge excess reserves because businessmen would not risk expenditure for new capital projects. People had an insatiable desire for liquidity, and no attempted reductions of the rate of interest could persuade them to spend the money they held for security.

In the same way, an attempt to raise interest rates and to halt price inflation by making credit tight may come to naught if the public reacts to higher interest rates by giving up its liquidity, thereby making funds available to others to finance increased transactions expenditure. Or take another instance: if the Fed tries to lower interest rates by increasing M, the effort may result in a general expectation of inflation and a movement out of bonds into stocks. In that case, interest rates, instead of falling, will go up! This actually happened in 1968.

CREDIT CRUNCHES

Still another difficulty of monetary management lies in *credit crunches*. These are sharp curtailments in the growth of credit. The reason for the designation "crunch" is that these curtailments do not impose their effects evenly across the economy. Tight money is not a serious deterrent to most large corporations with high credit ratings and large cash reserves of their own, but it may seriously impair the ability of states and municipalities to borrow, and it is apt to exact a real toll on residential building, where interest is a major item of cost. Even within the relatively unaffected corporate sector, a credit squeeze can hurt some companies very badly. The crunch in 1969–1970 almost caused the collapse of the Chrysler Corporation, one of the largest industrial enterprises in the nation.

Since that time, in an effort to prevent future crunches, special government lending intermediaries have been making loans to residential builders and to states and municipalities, if these borrowers are in trouble. We will have to wait and see how well they work, for the problem is that to some extent these intermediaries must take actions against the direction set by the Fed. When the Fed is trying to cut back credit, the intermediaries will be trying to extend credit.

MONETARY AND FISCAL POLICY

All these problems of monetary management help us understand why economists are generally reluctant to entrust the overall regulation of the economy to monetary policy alone. There is too much slippage between changes in the money supply and changes in expenditure; too little reliability as to the effects of changes in M on desired changes in MV.

Thus we look for our overall controls to both monetary policies and fiscal policies. Few economists today would rely solely on the money mechanism to move the general economy. Instead, they seek a combination of monetary and fiscal policies—easy money and more government spending (or tax cuts), or tight money and a public budgetary surplus.

KEY WORDS

Quantity equation

Velocity of circulation

Full employment vs. under- employment

CENTRAL CONCEPTS

1. The quantity equation $MV \equiv PT$ is an *identity saying that expenditures* (MV) *equal receipts* (PT). It was originally intended as a functional relation between M and P.
2. This statement would be true if V and T were fixed. In fact, *the velocity of circulation* (or GNP/M) *changes during the cycle*.
3. Even more important, short-run changes in output can be very marked. This is contrary to *the expectation of the early quantity theorists that the economy would always operate at full employment*.
4. When a competitive economy is operating at substantially less than full employment, an increase in M, or in MV, leads to a rise in output rather than prices. *This distinction between the effects of additional expenditure, public or private, is one of the central conceptions of modern macroeconomics*.

5. How does an increase in *M* become a larger *MV*? One critical link is the *interest rate*, or the price of money. As the price of money falls, ceteris paribus, the demand for it increases.

6. There are two kinds of demand: demand for money for *transactions purposes* and for *financial* (speculative or precautionary) *purposes*. Demand for the former rises when we need money to finance larger purchases. Demand for the latter rises when we want to be more liquid.

7. *Changes in the supply of money leave the public with larger or smaller amounts of cash than it wants at going interest rates.* It will try to get out of, or into, cash by buying or selling bonds. As bonds are sold or bought, their yield changes; and as yields change, the public changes its willingness to hold cash. At the same time, changes in interest rates are brought about by banks trying to get rid of, or to conserve, their increased or decreased reserves. Thus, *changes in interest rates will lead to changes in transactions balances and financial balances.*

8. *The rate of interest is determined by the supply of, and the demand for, money.* Monetary authorities determine the supply; transactions and financial desires determine demand.

9. Changes in *M* will affect changes in expenditure (*MV*) in ways that depend on the shapes and positions of the transactions and liquidity preference schedules. *Note that an increase or decrease in M will usually be only partly reflected in a changed MV, since liquidity balances will also expand or contract.*

10. Monetarist theorists also believe that changes in *M* directly affect expenditure by altering our *portfolios*. This *liquidity effect* leads us to convert unwanted "excess liquidity" into real assets by spending our extra cash.

11. Modern monetary theory no longer ties increases in *M* directly to *P*. It asserts that there are *calculable functions for transactions and financial purposes* that enable us to relate changes in *M* to changes in *MV*.

12. Monetary management is an art, for many reasons. The effects of interest rate changes on expenditure are unclear. So are the effects of *M* on *MV*. Shifting liquidity preference schedules make the results of monetary action hard to predict.

13. As a result, most economists advocate a close coordination of fiscal and monetary policies, rather than reliance on either one alone.

QUESTIONS

1. Why is the quantity equation a truism? Why is the interpretation of the quantity equation that M affects P not a truism?

2. Suppose you are paid $140 a week and you put it in the bank. On each of the seven days of the week, you spend one-seventh of this sum. What is your average balance during the week? Now suppose that you spend the whole sum on the first day of the week. Will your average balance be the same? What is the relation between velocity of circulation and size of average balances?

3. What considerations might lead you, as a businessman, to carry higher cash balances? Could these considerations change rapidly?

4. The basic reason why the original quantity theorists thought that M affected P was their belief that V and T were fixed. Discuss the validity of this belief.

5. Why is the level of employment a critical determinant of fiscal policy?

6. If employment is "full," what will be the effects of an increase in private investment on prices and output, supposing that everything else stays the same?

7. In what way can an increase in excess reserves affect V or T? Is there any certainty that an increase in reserves will lead to an increase in V or T?

8. Suppose that you had $1,000 in the bank. Would you be more willing to invest it if you could earn 2 percent or 5 percent? What factors could make you change your mind about investing all or any part at, say, 5 percent? Could you imagine conditions that would make you unwilling to invest even at 10 percent? Other conditions that would lead you to invest your whole cash balance at, say, 3 percent?

9. Suppose that the going rate of interest is 7 percent and that the monetary authorities want to curb expenditures and act to lower the quantity of money. What will the effect be in terms of the public's feeling of liquidity? What will the public do if it feels short of cash? Will it buy or sell securities? What would this do to their price? What would thereupon happen to the rate of interest? To investment expenditures?

10. Suppose that the monetary and fiscal authorities want to encourage economic expansion. What are the general measures that each should take? What problems might changing liquidity preference interpose?

11. Do you unconsciously keep a "liquidity balance" among your assets? Suppose that your cash balance rose. Would you be tempted to spend more?

12. Show in a diagram how a decrease in the supply of money will be reflected in lower transactions balances and in lower financial balances. What is the mechanism that changes these balances?

13. Do you understand (a) how the rate of interest is determined; (b) how it affects our willingness to hold cash? Is this in any way different from the mechanism by which the price of shoes is determined or the way in which the price of shoes affects our willingness to buy them?

The Problem
of Inflation

HOW COULD WE SPEND TWO CHAPTERS ON money and not talk about inflation? The explanation is not that we have downgraded the problem. On the contrary, we consider it so important that we are devoting this entire chapter to it. Moreover, there was another reason to defer a discussion of inflation until now. By and large, our macroeconomic chapters up to this point have covered problems about which economic knowledge is fairly secure. Now and again we have pointed out unresolved or ill-understood issues, but in the main we were on firm ground.

Beginning with inflation, that is no longer the case. We are moving now into areas where economists are very tentative and unsure. As we shall see, we know something about each of the problems of the subsequent chapters, but not nearly enough.

INFLATION IN RETROSPECT

Inflation is both a very old problem and a very new one. If we look back over history, we discover many inflationary periods. Dio-cletian tried (in vain) to curb a Roman inflation in the fourth century A.D., between 1150 and 1325 the cost of living in medieval Europe rose fourfold; between 1520 and 1650 prices again rose between 200 and 400 percent, largely as a result of gold pouring into Europe from the newly opened mines of the New World. In the years following the Civil War, the South experienced a ferocious inflation, and prices in the North doubled; during World War I, prices in the United States doubled again.

Let us focus closer on the U.S. experience up to 1950 (Fig. 15·1). Two things should be noted about this chart. *First, wars are regularly accompanied by inflation.* The reasons are obvious enough. War greatly increases the volume of public expenditure, but governments do not curb private spending by an equal amount through taxation. Invariably, wars are largely financed by borrowing, and the supply of money and the total amount of spending, public and private, rises rapidly.

Second, inflations have always been rela-

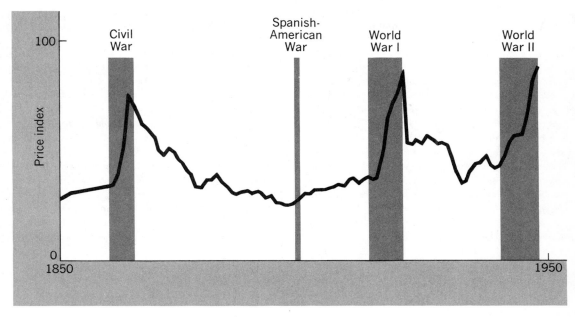

FIGURE 15 · 1
Inflation in perspective

tively short-lived in the past. Notice that prices fell during the periods 1866 to 1900 and 1925 to 1933, and that the long secular trend, although generally tilted upward, is marked with long valleys as well as sharp peaks.

RECENT INFLATIONARY EXPERIENCE

Now examine Fig. 15·2, which shows the record of U.S. price changes since 1950. Once again we notice that the outbreak of war has brought price rises, albeit relatively small ones. This is because the financing of the Korean and Vietnam wars, exactly as the preceding larger wars, did not sufficiently curtail private spending. But in a second vital regard, contemporary experience is different from that of the past. The peaks of inflationary rises have not been followed by long gradual declines. Instead, inflation seems to have become a chronic element in the economic situation, a lingering fever that has defied economic ice packs and economic antibiotics.

FIGURE 15 · 2
Wholesale prices since 1950

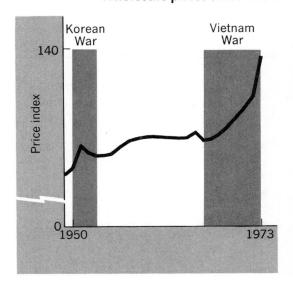

HYPERINFLATIONS

Hyperinflations are among the most destructive economic experiences that a modern economic society can undergo. In the German hyperinflation of the 1920s, for example, prices rose so rapidly that hotels and restaurants with foreign guests would not reveal the price of a meal until the diner had finished; then they would determine the "going" value of marks at that moment. Inflation mounted until a common postage stamp cost 9 billion marks, and a worker's weekly wage came to 120 trillion marks. Newspapers and magazines of the period showed people bringing home their weekly pay in wheelbarrows—billions and billions of marks literally worth less than the paper they were printed on.

Hyperinflations have also occurred in Hungary in 1923 and in China after World War II.

They are really psychological—even pathological—phenomena, rather than strictly economic ones. That is, they signal a collapse of faith in the vitality and viability of the economy. Farmers typically hoard foodstuffs, rather than accept payment in currencies that they fear will be only so much wallpaper in a matters of weeks. Merchants and manufacturers are unable to make contracts, since suppliers ask for enormous prices in anticipation of price rises to follow. Shopkeepers are reluctant to sell to customers because this means giving up the true wealth of goods for the spurious wealth of paper money that no one trusts. Thus there is flight from all paper currency and a scramble to get into goods or into commodities such as gold, in which people retain faith. The scramble means that the demand curve for goods or gold shoots out to the right, and the supply curve moves to the left as those who own goods or

WORLDWIDE INFLATION

Before we attempt to explain this perplexing phenomenon, one further fact of great significance should be noted. *It is that inflation has been a worldwide experience.* It has

TABLE 15 · 1
Worldwide Inflation

PRICE RISES IN INDUSTRIALIZED COUNTRIES

| | Average annual percentage | | |
	1959–69	1968–69	1969–72
U.S.	2.2	5.1	4.5
Australia	2.4	2.8	5.3
Canada	2.4	4.3	3.7
France	3.7	5.7	5.8
Italy	3.6	2.5	5.1
Japan	5.0	4.9	6.1
Sweden	3.7	2.6	6.9
Switzerland	3.0	2.5	5.6
U.K.	3.4	5.1	7.6
W. Germany	2.4	2.6	4.9

ravaged underdeveloped countries, where prices have often risen by 20 to 50 percent per year. And it has appeared in every industrialized nation, *even though those nations did not participate in the Korean or Indochinese wars.* As Table 15·1 shows, the United States inflationary problem has been much *less* severe than the European or Japanese experience, except for a brief period from 1968–1969. In other words, contemporary inflation seems to be a new kind of economic problem that has appeared—and resisted attempts to remedy—in all industrialized nations.

The ABC of the Inflationary Process

SUPPLY AND DEMAND ONCE AGAIN

What do we know about inflations? A good place to start is by refreshing our memories of how an individual price rises. As we have seen, prices go up when demand curves shift

gold are reluctant to sell them for paper money. Meanwhile, governments find their expenses skyrocketing and are forced to turn to the printing presses as the only way to collect the revenues they require. Finally, people find that they must *barter* goods, as in primitive economic societies.

The only cure for a hyperinflation is the abandonment of the currency in which everyone has lost faith, and the institution of a new currency that people can be once again induced to believe will serve as a reasonably stable "store of value." For example, in 1958 General de Gaulle stopped an incipient runaway French inflation when he simply announced that there would be a new franc worth one hundred of the old, deteriorating francs. Because of de Gaulle's extraordinary prestige, Frenchmen willingly changed their old 100-franc notes for new one-franc coins and then stopped trying to get "out" of money and into

goods. The same magic feat was performed in the 1920s in Germany when the government announced that there would be a new mark "backed" by land. People believed that, and hyperinflation stopped.

There is a curious aspect of hyperinflation that we might stop to notice. Why do workers trundle their wages home in wheelbarrows? Why doesn't the government simply print trillion-mark notes, so that a man's wage would fit into his pocketbook? The answer is purely bureaucratic. The printing presses are busy turning out notes in denominations that would have been suitable for the price level of, say, six months earlier. No one dares give orders for denominations that might meet needs when the notes will actually be issued. Why? Because an order to print, say, trillion-mark notes instead of billion-mark notes would be construed as *inflationary!*

to the right or when supply curves shift to the left. This happens all the time in innumerable markets. Are these price rises "inflationary"?

The question begins to sharpen our understanding of what we mean by inflation. In a price rise that takes place in the way we have described, a new stable equilibrium price is established. In an inflationary situation there is no stable outcome, since prices continue to rise. This generally means that demand curves must be continuously moving outward and that supply curves must be upward sloping. Moreover, this unstable process is not taking place in a single market (such as a continuing rise in the price of a desired commodity like gold), but in *all* or nearly all markets at the same time.

CHANGES IN TOTAL DEMAND

What could bring about such a multimarket shift? Part of the problem we already understand. The continuing rightward shift in demand curves is the result of *a continuous rise in the volume of expenditure.* More and

more dollars are earned and spent. This in turn means that the supply of money must be increasing, or that the velocity of circulation must be constantly increasing, or both. MV must be rising if the national price level is rising. You cannot have inflation unless demand curves in most markets are shifting to the right; and this in turn cannot occur unless money incomes and expenditures are rising in the economy.

THE SUPPLY CONSTRAINT: BOTTLENECKS

But this is only half the picture. There is also the question of supply. A rightward shift of a demand curve will not cause prices to rise in a market if the supply curve shifts outward to meet it, or if the industry is producing under conditions of constant or decreasing cost. Thus, corresponding to the rightward shift in total demand must come a gradual upward tilt in supply curves, as Fig. 15·3 shows.

As demand moves from D_1 to D_2, prices hardly rise at all. But the shift from D_2 to D_3 brings a sharp increase because we run into

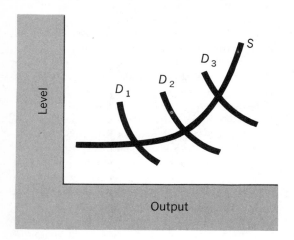

FIGURE 15 · 3
The bottleneck supply curve

bottlenecks, where output cannot be further increased, except at much higher cost. These bottlenecks, moreover, may begin to exert their constricting influence before the economy as a whole can be considered in a condition of overall full employment. Thus as demand curves for various goods and services move outward, we will experience price rises in some industries even though there is unused capacity in others, or even though considerable unemployment exists. If these industries bulk large in the pattern of production or in consumer budgets—for example, if we hit bottlenecks in steel or food output—the general price level will begin to rise.

DEMAND PULL VS. COST PUSH

Economists sometimes talk about the two processes that enter into inflation as *demand pull* or *cost push*. Demand pull focuses attention on forces that are causing thousands of demand curves to move to the right—for example, policies of easy money or expansionary fiscal policy. Cost push emphasizes the supply side, with cost curves moving to the left or sloping sharply upward.

Cost-push analyses often concentrate on the wage level as a prime causative agency for inflation. Of course, rising wages can be a source of higher costs. But it is important to distinguish between increases in *wage costs per hour* and increases in *wage costs per unit.* Wages may rise; but if *labor productivity keeps pace, cost per unit will not rise.*

Corresponding to cost push from rising wage costs per unit, there is cost push from higher profits, an argument frequently put forward by labor. Again we must distinguish between higher profits for the company and higher profits per unit. The latter may occur if the increase in demand outruns the increase in productive capacity, strengthening the market power of large companies.

THE PHILLIPS CURVE

To determine the inflationary pressure in thousands of markets, each with a different configuration of supply and demand curves, would be an impossible task. Hence, the English economist A.W. Phillips has sug-

FIGURE 15 · 4
The Phillips curve

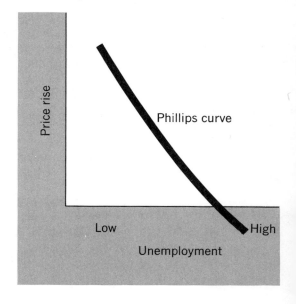

gested that we show the general relationship between higher wages and/or profits per unit and the degree of capacity utilization. As industries move toward higher rates of utilization, their costs per unit begin to mount more steeply. This is because they are operating in ever tighter markets, especially for labor. Hence Phillips has drawn a curve showing the over-all relationship between unemployment, a good indicator of capacity utilization, and the rise in prices. As Fig. 15·4 shows, the lower unemployment falls, the higher is the tendency toward inflation.

THE TRADE-OFF DILEMMA

The Phillips curve does more than point out a general relationship between employment and price rises. It also points up a fundamental dilemma. The dilemma is that we cannot choose one target for unemployment and another target for the price level *independent of each other*. We cannot, for example, "decide" to have 2 percent inflation and 2 percent unemployment, because we do not know how to reconcile low unemployment and low inflation rates. *We have to trade off unemployment against price stability.* The dilemma thus imposes a cruel choice. Governments must choose between alternatives, *both* of which are painful and costly. Before we investigate the means by which they seek to bring about whatever choice they finally make, let us inquire into the costs of these alternatives.

The Economic Costs of Unemployment

THE UNEMPLOYMENT OPTION

Suppose the government decides to lessen inflation by increasing the rate of unemployment. What does this cost?

We can begin with a fairly straightforward estimate of the losses that result from unemployment. For each percentage point of increase in the official unemployment figures, United States gross national product falls by about 3 percent, or roughly $40 billion. The reduction in GNP is much larger than the increase in officially measured unemployment because (as we have seen on pp. 53–54), the labor force and the hours worked per week both shrink as employment opportunities shrink.

Is this, then, the cost of choosing the unemployment "option"? Not quite. For the losses of output and income are by no means equally distributed. If increasing the unemployment rate from 4.5 to 5.5 percent meant that each person found himself unemployed for 14 instead of only 11 out of 250 working days, the income losses would be evenly shared among the labor force. On the other hand, if the additional one percent of unemployment meant that one percent of the working force was permanently unemployed all year, then the costs of unemployment would be entirely concentrated on this group.

If most people were asked which of the two ways of bearing the costs of unemployment were more equitable, they would probably choose the first. But in fact, the way unemployment is actually shared is closer to the second. Joblessness tends to concentrate in certain groups, especially in cyclical downswings. For instance, when the white unemployment rate rises by 1 percentage point, black unemployment rises by 2 percentage points. So, too, in 1971 when the average rate of unemployment for the labor force was more than 6 percent, the rate among married men was only 3.3 percent, whereas among young workers (16 to 19 years old) it was more than 15 percent. For white workers as a whole it was 4.5 percent; for Negro and Puerto Rican workers, 8.2 percent; among black teenagers it reached as high as 42 percent.

EASING THE COST OF UNEMPLOYMENT

To some extent, this concentrated cost of unemployment is offset by transfer payments made to some of the unemployed. Because these payments come from taxes that are mainly paid by employed persons, transfers help to some small degree to spread the burden. Unfortunately, unemployment compensation in the United States is far from generous. Although the systems differ widely among the states, in general they provide for payment of one-half of an unemployed person's income, up to some maximum weekly benefit that ranges from $105 in Washington, D.C., to $49 in Mississippi. There is also a limit on how many weeks' unemployment compensation can be claimed; usually 20 weeks. After that, there is welfare, which also varies from state to state.

OTHER COSTS

There are costs to unemployment other than those directly incurred by the unemployed. Discouraged workers who withdraw from the labor force do not count as "unemployed," as we know, but the incomes they "voluntarily" give up are also economic losses. These hidden unemployed are frequently housewives who have other means of support; but because they are not working full or part time, as they would if there were jobs available, their families will have fewer dollars to spend. Another source of loss is the decrease in overtime, often an important supplement to the earnings of blue-collar workers who are paid on an hourly basis.

Capitalists also bear some of the loss of unemployment. When the aggregate demand for goods and services falls, output declines too. As a result, profits fall; and since managers are usually reluctant to let overhead office staff go, profits may fall more rapidly

than output. As in the case of the labor force, the losses borne by firms are not evenly shared. Some industries, such as durable goods, tend to bear more than their share. Others, such as household staples, are relatively depression-proof.

The Economic Costs of Inflation

As we have seen, the costs of unemployment tend to be concentrated among certain groups or industries, rather than diffusely shared by all. Now, what of the costs of inflation? Are they also concentrated? Do they resemble the costs of unemployment?

INFLATION AND INCOME

Let us begin to answer this very important question by reviewing an important, familiar fact. It is our old identity between gross national product and gross national income. We recall that all costs of GNP must become the incomes of the factors of production. This gives us the knowledge that whenever the monetary value of GNP goes up, so must the monetary value of gross national income. This is true whether the increase in GNP results from increased output or higher prices, for in either case the factors of production must receive the monetary value of the output they have produced.

This provides a very important point of departure in comparing unemployment and inflation. *For the nation as a whole, inflation cannot decrease the total of incomes.* Here it differs sharply from unemployment. Whenever unemployment increases, there is a loss in potential GNP. But whatever the price at which GNP is sold, the real output of the nation remains the same—at least up to the point at which hyperinflation threatens to destroy the system itself.

A ZERO SUM GAME

Discussions of inflation tend to overlook this fact. They often speak of the losses that inflation brings to this or that group. Of course inflation *can* lower an individual's standard of living by raising the prices he or she must pay. *But since the total GNI is equal to GNP, one's person's loss must be transferred as a gain to another.* This in no way lessens the importance or even the dangers of inflations. But it makes clear that unlike unemployment, in which there are losers but no gainers, in inflation every loss is offset by an equal gain. We call this a zero sum game. What is important, then, is to try to weigh the benefits that inflation gives to some, against the losses it inflicts on others.

Who gains by inflation?

Speculators are one group. During an inflation everything does not rise by the same amount or at the same rate. Some items will shoot up; others lag behind, just as in a booming stock market not all stocks share alike in the rise. Speculators are those lucky or skillful individuals who have bought goods that enjoy the sharpest rises. This may be land, gold, or (in hyperinflations) food. Indeed, one of the reasons that hyperinflations result in a collapse of GNP is that more and more persons are *forced* to become speculators, seeking to sell or trade possessions for basic necessities. As individuals spend more and more time trading or scrounging, they begin to spend less and less time at their regular jobs. Thus output begins to fall, and we have the strange coexistence of an economic collapse and soaring prices.

MODERATE INFLATIONS

Hyperinflations are, fortunately, very rare. Nations have inflated as much as 200 or 300 percent a year without experiencing the breakdown and disorganization of a real runaway inflation.

In nonrunaway inflations, individuals will, of course, be gainers or losers, depending on whether their incomes go up faster or slower than prices. But we are interested in whether major *groups* can be classified as winners or losers.

FIXED-INCOME RECEIVERS

By definition, anyone who lives on a fixed income, such as an annuity, must be a loser in inflation. Therefore retirees, as a group, should be badly penalized when prices continually rise. Curiously, they are not. Undoubtedly, there exist the much advertised widows and orphans living off small pensions, but they are probably a very small group. Most retirees live on (or depend largely on) Social Security, and this is quite another story. Social Security benefits have been periodically hiked up by Congress, so that a typical recipient in 1973 was well ahead of the game in terms of the purchasing power of benefits he received. Moreover, in 1973, Congress added to Social Security a cost-of-living escalator clause that automatically adjusted Social Security payments to compensate for cost-of-living increases. Welfare recipients have also had their benefits periodically increased, and they too, have not come out behind in the race since 1950.

WHO HAS LOST?

If we look at the broadest categories of income receivers, shown in Table 15-2 on the following page, we see that the shares of income going to major groups in the economy have not changed dramatically.

The share going to wages and salaries slowly eroded during accelerated inflation, but the table does not show a considerable rise

TABLE 15·2
*Shares of total
personal income*

	Wages, salaries, and other labor income	Proprietors' income	Rental income	Dividends and interest	Gross transfers
1967	70.5	9.8	3.2	10.8	8.2
1970	71.2	8.4	3.0	8.9	9.7
1973	69.9	9.0	2.5	11.3	9.8
1974 (est.)	70.1	7.8	2.3	11.8	12.3

NOTE: Figures do not add to 100 percent, owing to rounding and other factors.

in this share during the years of slow inflation from 1950 to 1973. Proprietors' incomes (farm, business, and professional) have also slowly declined as a share of total income; and as we would expect, rental incomes lagged behind the economy (rents are fixed and normally rise more slowly than prices). Dividends and interest have increased somewhat, largely the result of soaring interest rates that have pushed up the return on bonds and savings accounts. Transfer incomes (Social Security, welfare, and unemployment compensation) have increased markedly. Not shown in the table, corporate profits plus depreciation fell sharply from about 11.4 percent of GNP in 1967 to about 9 percent in 1970, and then rose again to 11 and 12 percent in 1973 and 1974.

WHY IS INFLATION SUCH A PROBLEM?

These figures raise an important question. The great bulk of the population apparently did not suffer a major decline in its share of income—at least not until 1973–1974, as the box shows. Note that transferees—usually the lowest income group—actually increased their share. *Then why the fuss about inflation?* Why is it not a popular economic process?

There are several plausible reasons. One is that *the losing groups, such as small pro-* *prietors and landlords, are politically influential and articulate and make their losses known to a much greater extent than the winners (labor or transferees) make their gains known.*

A second reason is that inflation is worrisome just because it affects everyone to some degree. Unlike the concentrated loss of unemployment, the diffuse gains-and-losses of inflation touch us all. *They give rise to the fear that the economy is "out of control"— which indeed, to a certain extent, it is.*

Third *is the lurking fear that moderate inflation may give way to a galloping inflation.* The vision of a hyperinflation is a specter that chills everyone, and not one to be lightly dismissed. There is always the chance, albeit a small one, that a panic wave may seize the country and that prices may skyrocket while the production of goods declines.

Fourth, *the effect of inflation on incomes is not always mirrored in its effects on assets.* Some assets, such as land, typically rise markedly during inflation because they are fixed in supply and because people forgetting about the land booms and crashes of the past, want to get into something that has "solid value." But many middle-class families have their assets in savings banks or in government bonds, and they watch with dismay as the value of their savings declines. For as interest rates rise, bond prices fall, and

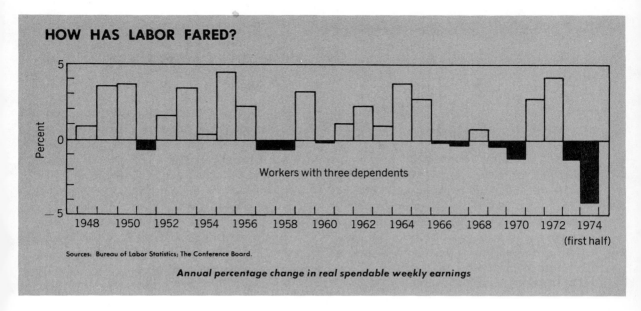

HOW HAS LABOR FARED?

Percent

Workers with three dependents

1948 1950 1952 1954 1956 1958 1960 1962 1964 1966 1968 1970 1972 1974

(first half)

Sources: Bureau of Labor Statistics; The Conference Board.

Annual percentage change in real spendable weekly earnings

stock prices do not typically stay abreast of the price level, although most people think they do. For instance, in late 1968 there was a stock market fall that brought stocks below their levels of 1966–1967; and again in early 1973, stock prices fell by a fifth, while consumer prices rose at record rates.

Last, *there is a kind of myopia that inflation produces. We blame inflation for reducing our real incomes by raising prices, but we do not give it credit for raising our incomes to pay those higher prices.* That is, for 364 days in the year we are aware of price rises as part of the inflationary process, but we do not connect the income increase we receive on the 365th day (if we get a yearly hike in pay) as being part of that selfsame process.

INFLATION VS. UNEMPLOYMENT AGAIN

Can we now compare the costs of unemployment and inflation? Three points stand out from our analysis.

1. *From the point of view of the economy as a whole, unemployment is more costly than moderate inflation.* That is because unemploy-

ment results in less production, whereas inflation does not.

2. *From the point of view of winners and losers, unemployment is also more costly than inflation.* For unlike inflation, unemployment is not a zero sum game. The losers in unemployment—the direct unemployed and the hidden unemployed—are not matched by winners who benefit from unemployment.

3. *The psychological impact of moderate inflation is probably much greater than that of moderate unemployment.* This is because we all feel affected by the inflationary process, whereas few of us worry too much about the unemployed—unless they happen to be ourselves.

Can we conclude from this that a nation should prefer inflation to unemployment—that a wise and humane policy would deliberately trade off a quite high degree of inflation in exchange for a low rate of unemployment? Some economists might recommend such a course, but it is doubtful that the nation as a whole would vote for it. Rightly or wrongly, most citizens feel that inflation is at least as great a danger as moderate unemployment, and they are not likely to support policies that reduce the joblessness of others in exchange for higher prices (or even higher prices and higher incomes!) for themselves.

The XYZ of Inflation

Until this point we have largely been concerned with conveying knowledge—what we know about inflation. Now we must change our tack. The rest of this chapter is mainly concerned with conveying ignorance. There is a great deal that we do not know about inflation, and a student should be as aware of our ignorance as of our knowledge.

THE ELUSIVE PHILLIPS CURVE

Let us begin with the Phillips curve. Consider Fig. 15·5.

The colored line shows that there is undoubtedly a *general* tendency for inflation to be inversely correlated with unemployment. When unemployment is *very* high, inflation is low, and vice versa. That much of the Phillips analysis remains. But now look at the scatter of dots within the tinted band representing the range from 3.5 to 6 percent unemployment. Compare 1964 and 1970, for instance. In 1964 an unemployment rate of just over 5 percent was associated with a rate

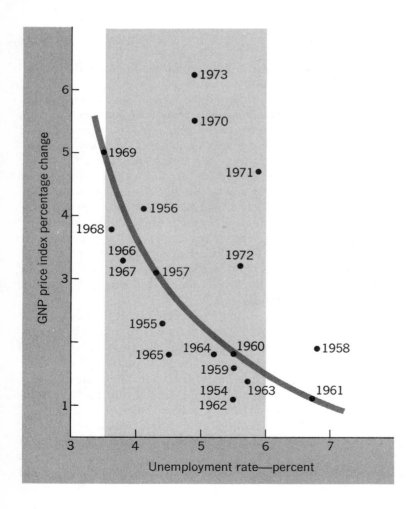

FIGURE 15 · 5
The unemployment–inflation relation

of inflation of less than 2 percent. In 1970 an unemployment rate of under 5 percent was associated with an inflation of over 5 percent.

What we have, in other words, is a relationship that is subject to such wide variations that economists have not been able to establish a function that enables them to *predict* what rate of unemployment will actually accompany a given inflation rate. This means that we cannot "target" a mix of inflation and unemployment, as our schematic diagram on p. 232 suggested, *because we do not know where the Phillips curve will be located.* Like a demand curve, it exists in our minds as a useful organizing concept, but unlike a demand curve, it is extremely difficult to locate this relationship in the real world.

A THEORY OF COINCIDENCES

Let us explore our ignorance from another angle. Consider the inflationary situation of 1973. We can easily describe many of its causes. There were poor crops and bad weather around the world. For some reason, anchovies did not appear off the coast of Peru. The Nixon administration sold a large fraction of the American grain crop to the Russians. There was a gasoline shortage because of a lack of refinery capacity and an Arab oil embargo. Lumber prices were up because foreigners were buying American lumber, made cheaper by the devaluation of the dollar. So the explanations go. Each and every price increase can be described in terms of shifts in demand and supply.

When we step back and look at the entire picture, however, this is no more than a theory of coincidences. Each price increase is caused by a particular event, not by the interrelated workings of the system. Weather, President Nixon's foreign policy, the vagaries of ocean currents, the gyrations of the foreign exchange market become the villains of the piece. These descriptions may be correct, but they provide no means of avoiding or controlling inflation. Worse, they suggest that since inflation is caused by coincidences, we should run the economy at the highest possible employment rates, since the degree of inflation this will breed is largely in the lap of the gods.

Could this be the case? Economists are reluctant to admit it. To begin with, it would mean a declaration of *total* ignorance about inflation, and we do not feel totally ignorant. We are quite sure that running the economy at 2 percent unemployment would increase the rate of inflation, even though we do not know by how much. Second, we cannot quite believe that all the incidents actually add up to inflation. Are all nations all over the world having coincidences all the time? Why didn't they have similar coincidences in the past?

AN IMPASSE FOR THEORY

The net result is that economists do not have a satisfactory *theory* of inflation. We know a lot about various aspects of inflation and something about how to dampen it (as we will see in our next section). But we do not have a clear understanding of what causes inflation or how to cure it.

At the root of our problem is the question of expectations. We are all familiar with late afternoon commentators who tell us why the stock market went up or down as a result of a Presidential speech. Often these commentators have the text of the President's speech early that morning. Why don't they go on the air and tell us what the effect of the speech *will* be? The answer is that often neither they nor anybody else can predict how a statement will affect people's outlooks. Will an announcement of stiff price controls plunge businessmen into gloomy expectations of falling profits? Or will the same speech restore confidence and send the market up?

Our ignorance about the effect of pronouncements on the market is paralleled by our ignorance about the effects of actual developments on peoples' actions in the marketplace. Will an announcement that the cost-of-living index is up over last month send people on a buying spree, in anticipation of next month's expected increase? Or will it result in a tightening of budgets for the very same reason?

Thus, our inability to predict the course of inflation stems in large part from uncertainties about expectations. Until we learn to anticipate expectations or to influence expectations, the movements of the marketplace—and of that gigantic marketplace called the economy—are likely to take us by surprise.

Controlling Inflation

Can we stop inflation? Of course—at a price. For example, wage and price controls with terrific penalties for noncompliance would surely dampen inflation. So would a decision not to increase the money supply at all. The trouble is that no one is willing to pay so great a price—the price of a police state in the first case, or of massive unemployment in the second. Therefore, we seek to control inflation with *politically acceptable* measures, and these have not been too successful.

Since World War II every major government has tried to keep the lid on inflation, but with scant results. In the United States, for example the Kennedy administration inaugurated the idea of "wage-price guidelines" that were intended to serve as an official index of productivity, to which it was hoped labor leaders would conform their demands. But the wage-price guidelines allowed for increases of only about 3.4 percent per year and were not very effective. Some unions whose productivity had gone up more rapidly than 3.4 percent claimed that they had the *right* to higher wages; other unions simply

ignored the guidelines; and most companies tried only halfheartedly to stick by them in wage bargaining sessions, because they counted on inflation itself to help them pass along any cost increases in higher prices.

Another tactic used by subsequent administrations was called "jawboning." This was simply the use of public pressure, usually through Presidential statements, to get companies (or less frequently unions) to scale down price increases. For instance in 1971, Bethlehem Steel suddenly announced that it was about to raise steel prices by 12 percent. Angry comments from the White House, coupled with stories carefully leaked to the newspapers about the possibility of relaxing steel import quotas, brought the welcome response of a much smaller (6 percent) increase from Bethlehem's main competitors. In the end, Bethlehem had to back down to the 6 percent mark.

WAGE AND PRICE CONTROLS

Still, 6 percent is a stiff price increase. Hence more and more pressure built up for the imposition of direct controls over wages and prices, which were finally instituted by the Nixon administration in 1971.

The problem with controls is that they are administratively clumsy, hard to enforce, and almost invariably evaded in one way or another. A wage and price freeze always catches someone at a disadvantage: a union that was just about to sign an advantageous but perhaps deserved contract, a store whose prices were at "sale" levels on the day that the freeze is announced, a business whose costs increase as a result of a rise in the prices of imported goods. Thus price controls lead to endless adjustment and adjudication. Moreover, unless there is a general sentiment of patriotic "pulling together" (as during World War II or the Korean war, when controls were fairly successful in repressing inflation), controls tend to lead to black or

ESCALATORS AND "INDEXING"

One way of mitigating the cost of inflation is to build escalator clauses into wage contracts, thereby guaranteeing workers that their wage rates will be automatically brought abreast of the cost-of-living index every six months or so. (This is also called "indexing" wages, since they are tied to a cost-of-living index.)

Such a policy clearly removes any loss of purchasing power for those who hold jobs, except for the brief period between adjustments. Then why not urge their widespread adoption?

Two main reasons are given by economists. One is that escalators would tend to be applied in big industries or government employments where contracts are negotiated and would not be applied in small businesses where employees are usually unorganized. Therefore it would result in a relative weakening of those whose wages were at the bottom of the scale.

The second objection is that built-in escalators would remove any incentive on the part of labor to bring the inflationary process to a halt. As long as labor's real wage was protected, what difference would it make whether inflation went faster or slower? In turn, this would remove any willingness to acquiesce in lower wage settlements or in wage guidelines or wage controls, to bring inflation to a halt.

Some economists would urge that "indexing" be applied much more broadly than in wage escalators. Professor Milton Friedman, for instance, would like to see us "index" savings accounts, bonds—indeed, all money contracts.

Such a policy would certainly mitigate the costs of inflation on fixed-money contractors, such as savings bank depositors. The worry, as with wage escalation, is that it might lower the last resistance to inflation, opening the door to accelerating price rises.

---

gray markets or to downgrading the quality of the "same" goods that are sold at fixed prices.

Not surprisingly, efforts to control wages tend to be more successful than efforts to control prices. This is because the government has an ally to help it enforce its wage regulations, namely, employers. Employers know what their employees make and have an interest in keeping wages within the legal limits. Consumers, on the other hand, usually do not know what products cost and cannot demand that stores refrain from marking up items. Renters are perhaps in the best position as consumers to enforce price controls on rents, but even they are in a weak position when they look for vacant apartments.

As a result, when controls are imposed, they tend to work fairly well for a short period of time on the wage side, while prices continue to creep upward. After a certain point, consumer resentment explodes in the form of demands from workers that their

wage restraints be loosened. In nation after nation, this process has been repeated.

INCOMES POLICY

There is, of course, an alternative. It is to curb inflation from the demand side rather than from the supply side, by imposing severe taxes that will bring the expansion of purchasing power to a halt. Once that is accomplished, the demand curve will stop its rightward movement, and a stable price level should be reached.

The problem here is obvious enough. Bringing the expansion of incomes to a halt means imposing severe taxes on the middle levels of American society where the bulk of purchasing power is concentrated. Unfortunately for anti-inflationary policy, increasing taxes on this group is political dynamite. Perhaps a truly effective tax increase could be imposed on the middle and upper middle class, if receivers of very large incomes were taxed at least as severely. This means closing the loopholes that have been stubbornly and successfully defended for many years.

It is a hard fact of political life that no government in any Western nation, including the most socially progressive such as Sweden, has succeeded in winning the political support necessary to impose a fully effective tax program. Perhaps people prefer inflation and relatively lower taxes to price stability and very high taxes. If this is the case, there is nothing the economist can do—except warn that inflation will continue.

STOP-GO

As a result of these partly economic, partly political difficulties, anti-inflationary policies here and abroad take on an aspect of "stop-go." When prices begin to rise too fast, remedial measures are put into effect. The money supply is tightened to curb spending. Governments trim their budgets. Taxes may be increased somewhat. Wage and price controls are put into effect.

For a time, these "stop" measures succeed. But then pressures mount in the opposite direction. High interest rates cut into home building. A slowdown in investment causes unemployment to rise. Tight government budgets mean that programs with important constituencies have to be cut back; Army bases are closed; social assistance programs abandoned. Businessmen chafe under controls. Hence pressures mount for a relaxation. The red light changes to green. The money supply goes up again; investment is encouraged; public spending resumes its former upward trend; controls are taken off. Before long the expected happens: prices begin to move ahead too rapidly once more, and the pendulum starts its swing in the opposite direction.

INFLATION AS A WAY OF LIFE

Does this mean that inflation has become a chronic fact of life, uncurable except at levels of unemployment that would be socially disastrous or by the imposition of severe and unpopular wage, price, and income controls?

Probably. What economists hope for is that a middle ground can be reached where the frictions generated by inflation and the real damage done by unemployment can be reduced to reasonable proportions. A price rise of 1 or 2 percent a year, for example, can be fairly easily tolerated, since a year-to-year increase in the quality of goods can be said to justify such an increase. Similarly, 3 or 4 percent unemployment (which includes voluntary unemployment and a hard core of "unemployables") is also socially acceptable, especially since both kinds of unemployment can be remedied by generous policies of unemployment compensation or by programs for retraining labor.

But it is one thing to announce such a goal and another to attain it. The simple fact remains that in no industrialized nation has anything like such an acceptable balance been achieved. In most nations, the claims of high employment quite properly take priority over those of inflation, and the rate of annual price increase has accordingly ranged from roughly 4 to 10 percent a year. As we saw at the beginning of this chapter, in this chronicle of inflationary failure, the record of the United States is by no means the worst. Unhappily, its record in combating unemployment, as we will see in our next chapter, is by no means the best.

A Problem of Affluence?

So we end our discussion of policy on much the same tentative and unsatisfying note as our discussion of theory. Yet perhaps it will help to put the unsolved problem of inflation into some perspective if we conclude with a few hypotheses of our own.

The critical fact about inflation, as we have said, is that it is a *process,* not a once-for-all jump in prices. This leads us to ask what changes might be sufficiently powerful and pervasive to bring such a process into being virtually around the world. Here are a few possibilities.

1. The shift to services

One striking fact that we notice in all industrialized nations is the movement of an ever larger fraction of their work forces into the service industries. In the U.S., as we have seen, over 60 percent of the labor force works in offices, shops, classrooms, municipal and state and federal buildings, producing the "services" that are ever more in demand in a highly urbanized, high-consumption society.

This movement has a powerful inflationary result. Productivity in the service sector tends to grow much more slowly than in the industrial or agricultural sectors. But wages in the service sectors tend to stay abreast of the wage levels set by the great industrial unions. Professor William Baumol has suggested that this major fact of life has inflationary repercussions that must be taken into account. For example, between 1962 and 1972 the consumer price index rose by 38 percent. This overall trend, however, concealed the fact that the price index of manufactured goods rose by only 27 percent, whereas the price index of services rose by 54 percent.

2. Increasing power in the marketplace

One of the most striking differences between modern inflations and those of the past is that in former days, inflationary peaks were followed by long, slow, deflationary declines, as prices and money wages both fell, particularly in times of recession. It was not uncustomary in the early years of this century

for a large company to announce an across-the-board wage cut. Indeed, that happened frequently during the Great Depression. Certainly, prices frequently declined, partly as a result of technological advance, partly through the sporadic outbreak of cutthroat competition.

All that seems a part of the past beyond recall. Since World War II, most prices and wages in every nation have shown a "ratchet" tendency. They can go up, but they rarely or never come down. This characteristic is probably due to the increasing presence of oligopolistic market structures, to stronger trade unions, and to a business climate in which wage cuts and price wars are no longer regarded as legitimate economic policies. These changes may have salutary social consequences, but they undoubtedly add to our inflationary propensities.

3. The expansionist influence of governments

A third change is equally visible throughout the Western world and Japan. It is the much larger role played by the public sector in generating demand. This does not mean that government spending is inherently inflationary. We have seen that *any* kind of spending can send prices up once we reach an area of reasonably full employment. Rather, the presence of large government sectors and the knowledge that governments are dedicated to policies of economic growth affect expectations in an inflation-producing way.

In the old days, when governments were minor contributors to GNP, and when things such as deficit spending were unknown, businesses expected bad times as well as good and planned accordingly. Investment programs tended to be short range in character; and at the first sign of a storm, sails were furled. Thus, in the typical business cycle, when an upper turning point was reached, private spending in the business sector dwindled, pulling down incomes and lessening the pressure on prices.

That has also changed. Corporations, labor leaders, and the public now expect governments to prevent recessions. Accordingly, they no longer trim their sails at the first sight of trouble on the horizon. The willingness to maintain spending serves to set a floor under the economy, adding to the ratchet-like movement of incomes and prices.

4. The effects of affluence

A last suggestion is closely related to the previous ones. It is that the staying power of labor is vastly strengthened compared with prewar days. Only a generation ago, a strike was essentially limited by the meager savings of working families or the pittance of support that unions could offer. There was no unemployment compensation, no welfare, no large union treasuries. Today, strikes are backed by very substantial staying power, and both corporations and municipalities know it. Thus there is a tendency to settle for higher wages than would be granted if the employer felt that by waiting a few weeks he could enforce a better bargain.

Add to that a change in the expectations of the public that stem directly from a more affluent society. The strikes of teachers, garbage men, transportation workers, and other groups that have added their impetus to the inflationary surge of all industrial nations are very much a modern phenomenon, in that many of these groups of workers were formerly resigned to accepting low wages. A policeman in New York City, 1920, did not think that he had a "right" to earn as much as a worker in the Ford plant in Detroit; a policeman today sees no reason why he should not. In microeconomic language, wage contours are broadening. In an affluent society, where personal aspirations are encouraged and the constraints of poverty are lessened, the established "pecking order" of an old-fashioned society gives way to a free-for-all, in which each group tries to exploit its economic strength to the hilt. While this may be good for the group concerned and may lead to a more equitable distribution of income, it also lends its momentum to the forces that push our society toward a seemingly unstoppable inflation.

A LAST WORD

It seems then that we will have to live with inflation for a very long period. In fact, only two things seem capable of arresting it. One of these is a fearful economic collapse, comparable to the worldwide depression of the 1930s. This seems unlikely and is certainly undesirable. The other is the rise of a social consensus as to what an equitable distribution of income would be, whether imposed by direct income controls or by tax measures. This would surely be the ideal way of bringing inflation to a halt, but alas, it is an objective that has so far defied our efforts.

KEY WORDS

Inflation

Hyperinflation

Inflationary
process

Demand pull/
cost push

Wage costs
per hour
and per unit

Phillips curve
trade-off

Costs of
unemployment

Inflation costs

Redistribution

Income groups

Inflationary fears

Myopia

What we do
not know

CENTRAL CONCEPTS

1. Inflation is an ancient phenomenon, often associated with wars, but usually followed by periods of declining prices. The distinguishing feature of modern inflation is that *it has been experienced in all industrialized nations*, whether or not involved in war, and that it has not shown the traditional peaks and valleys.

2. *Hyperinflations* are episodes marked by a *flight from currency into goods*. They are periods in which the intangible trust in money as a store of value disappears. Only the issuance of a new monetary unit, in which faith can be placed, will restore price stability (see box, pp. 230–31).

3. Inflation differs from an ordinary increase in prices because it is not a movement from one point of equilibrium to another, but a *continuing process*.

4. This inflationary process may derive from a continuing increase in demand—"*demand pull*"; or it may derive from increases in cost—"*cost push.*"

5. Inflation is characterized by a tendency for *wage costs to outpace productivity* increases. We must be careful to distinguish wage costs per hour (which can be compensated by increased output per hour) from wage costs *per unit*.

6. The *Phillips curve* represents the general tendency of a fully employed economy to encounter increasing costs per unit. It shows us a general "*trade-off*" between *unemployment and inflation*.

7. This trade-off presents us with a difficult dilemma: comparing the costs of unemployment with those of inflation. *The costs of unemployment* are relatively straightforward. They consist in the *loss of income and output*. This loss of income is concentrated largely on the minority who are unable to find work. It can be eased by unemployment compensation, but even then, costs remain, such as the loss of income to the hidden unemployed who withdraw from the labor force, or the losses to certain industries from underproduction.

8. The economic costs of inflation are more complex. Because GNI ≡ GNP, inflation (which raises the money value of GNP) never lowers the income of the entire nation, as unemployment does. Instead, it *redistributes the increases in the value of GNP*, so that some people's real incomes rise and others fall. *Speculators* may gain substantially in inflations, if they succeed in buying goods that will rise in money value.

9. It is difficult to single out groups, rather than individuals, who win or lose in inflation. Fixed income recipients would of course be losers, but Social Security retirees have experienced increases in benefits that more than compensate for increases in prices. Labor as a whole has probably gained. Business profits have not grown.

10. Why is inflation so critical a political issue? The reasons seem to be these: (1) the losers include *politically articulate groups*; (2) *inflation is experienced by all*, not just by a minority; (3) we worry about the possibility of a *hyperinflation*, (4) the *value of assets*, particularly middle-class assets such as savings accounts or small investments, *may fall*; and (5) a *myopia* blinds us as to the effect of inflation on our incomes as well as on the prices we pay.

11. There is much we do not know about inflation. *The Phillips curve, for example, seems to shift around, so that it gives us no predictive power within the normal range of unemployment (3 to 7 percent).* Coincidences seem to affect many prices, but we have no unified theory of why these incidents all push prices up, not down. *In fact, we lack a coherent and cogent theory of the inflationary process.* This is intimately connected with our lack of understanding about the effect of expectations on behavior.

Expectations

Controls

Incomes policy

Stop-go

Chronic inflation

12. Efforts to control inflation have included "guidelines," admonitions ("jaw-boning"), and *wage and price controls*. None have been very successful. *Incomes policy*, through tax measures, have been difficult or impossible to impose. The result has been a *stop-go* pace, in which controls are applied and inflation slowed; and then as business weakens, controls are relaxed and output (and inflation) increase.

13. Inflation seems to be a chronic condition of contemporary industrialized societies. We suggest that the root causes may be found in the following attributes of these societies: (1) a *shift to service occupations*, with lower productivity combined with wage-setting by high-productivity industries; (2) *increasing power in the marketplace* for both corporations and unions; (3) *the expanded role of government*, which buoys expectations and encourages an expansionist attitude; and (4) a change in the staying power of labor and in its aspirations in a *more affluent society*.

QUESTIONS

1. Distinguish between a change in prices in an individual market and an inflationary change. What is meant by calling inflation a "process"?

2. What is meant by "demand pull"? By "cost push"? Can you have an inflationary *process* if costs are not rising?

3. What explanations can we give for the increase in demand? For the rise in costs?

4. What kind of event might give rise to a hyper-inflation in the United States? Might a defeat in war trigger such an event? A victory? If we were to experience a runaway inflation, what measures would you counsel?

5. What is the importance of productivity in determining whether wage increases add to costs? Suppose that wages go up by 5 percent and that productivity goes up by 4 percent. Will there be an increase in costs per unit? Might this increase be absorbed by a fall in profits? Under what conditions is it likely to be passed on to consumers?

6. Is a war always inflationary? Does it depend on how it is financed? How should it be financed to minimize inflation? Does the same reasoning apply to an investment boom? (HINT: since corporations cannot tax, they must depend on savings for their expenditures.)

7. What is meant by the Phillips curve? Why is it a concept that is useful for a general understanding of the inflationary process? Why is it of little use for prediction?

8. Suppose that you could add up the costs of unemployment in terms of income lost. Suppose that you could add up the losses incurred just by those groups who are left behind in inflation (forget about the "winners"). Suppose further, that the losses imposed by inflation were greater than those imposed by unemployment. Does this mean that inflation is necessarily a worse economic disaster than unemployment? Must personal values enter into such a calculation? (If you simply compare amounts, is this also a value judgment?)

9. What measures can alleviate the costs of unemployment? The costs of inflation?

10. Why have measures to control inflation been so unsatisfactory? Why are price controls more difficult to monitor than wage controls?

11. Suppose that unemployment remains at about 5 percent and inflation rises to 10 percent a year. What measures would you propose?

12. What would you suggest as criteria for a "fair" income policy?

The Problem of Unemployment

16

AGAIN AND AGAIN IN OUR STUDY OF MACRO-economics we have come up against the problem of unemployment. And no wonder. Unemployment bulks large in our studies, because it is a problem peculiarly associated with market systems. In traditional economies we do not encounter unemployment in the same form as we do in a market system. Peasants or nomadic tribesmen or serfs may be very unproductive, extremely poor, or reduced to idleness because their institutions exclude them from land or from the ownership of animals or other wealth, but unemployment in these societies is a static condition that results from existing institutions. We do not find periods of high and low unemployment in these societies (good and bad harvests perhaps excepted), but a more or less unchanged proportion of workers to the total population. So, too, in command societies, the labor force may be poorly allocated or underutilized, but here again, unemployment appears as a fault of the planning mechanism, not as a result of the malfunction of the market machinery.

By way of contrast, the single most important social task that a market system entrusts to its "machinery" is that of finding acceptable work for the members of the society. It is also a task that the market does not perform altogether satisfactorily. From time to time, as we know, severe depressions have wracked market systems, causing unemployment to rise to heights that not only inflicted great damage on people who were unable to find work, but threatened the political and social stability of the system. In recent years, for example, one of the causes of racial unrest has been the failure of the market mechanism to provide jobs for the adolescent members of the labor force, especially among blacks, thereby contributing to the violence and unrest of the cities. Hanging over the politics of American and European societies are the memories of the trauma of the 1930s —a trauma in which mass unemployment

THE RECORD

The table (right) gives us important statistics. The terrible percentages of the Great Depression need no comment. Rather, let us pay heed to the level of unemployment in the 1960s. Here the record is mixed. During the early years of the decade we were troubled with persistent levels of unemployment much too high to be healthy. In the later years, unemployment declined sharply, but there is the discomfort of tracing much of this decline to an increase in war spending.

Part of our unemployment results from deliberate efforts made in 1970 by the Nixon administration to restrain inflation by "trading off" a limited rise in joblessness for a fall in the rate of price rise. As of the early 1970s, this trade-off was, unfortunately, more successful in producing unemployment than in slowing inflation.

Unemployment in the U.S.

Year	Unemployed (thousands)	Percent of civilian labor force
1929	1,550	3.2
1933	12,830	24.9
1940	8,120	14.6
1944	670	1.2
1960–65 av.	4,100	5.5
1966	2,875	3.8
1967	2,975	3.8
1968	2,817	3.6
1969	2,832	3.5
1970	4,085	4.9
1971	4,993	5.9
1972	4,840	5.6
1973	4,304	4.9

was a major factor in producing fascism in Europe and a crisis of faith in the United States.

Here we take one more look at the problem of unemployment—not from the viewpoint of aggregate demand, with which we are now familiar, but from another angle. We want to consider the question of *technological unemployment*—unemployment caused by the impact of machines. We want also to consider what remedies we have to combat unemployment, whatever the cause.

The Problem of Automation

For years, men have feared the effect of machinery on the demand for labor. The first-century Roman emperor Vespasian turned down a road-building machine, saying "I must have work for my poor." Shortly after Adam Smith's time, revolts of workers led by a mythical General Ludd smashed the hated and feared machines of the new textile manufacturers, which they believed to be

stealing the very bread from their mouths. To this very day, we call such antimachine attitudes "Luddite." David Ricardo, the great English economist of the early nineteenth century, shocked conventional opinion by adding a chapter "On Machinery" to the last edition of his famous *Principles of Political Economy,* in which he maintained that machines *could* displace labor, and therefore the capitalist's investment in equipment was not always in the interest of the working class.

In our own day, this lurking fear of machinery has focused on that extraordinary technology that "reads" and "hears" and "thinks" and puts human dexterity to shame. We call it automation. One of its characteristics is a feedback loop, by which the machine corrects itself, rather like a thermostat maintains a constant temperature. When such machines can make an engine block for a car almost without human supervision, it is understandable that thoughtful men should worry. There is a well-known story of Henry

Ford II showing his newly automated engine plant to the late Walter Reuther, the famed head of the United Auto Workers, and asking, "Well, Walter, how will you organize these machines?" Reuther replied, "How will you sell them cars?"

Does automation impose a wholly new and dangerous threat to employment? Let us begin to answer the question by using the tried and true method of supply and demand.

MACHINES AND SUPPLY

What has the introduction of machinery done to the supply of labor? We have already answered that question in part in Chapter 3. The effect of machinery has been vastly to increase the *productivity* of labor: a man with a tractor is incomparably more productive than a man with a shovel, not to speak of one with his bare hands.

But the effect of capital on productivity has not been evenly distributed among all parts of the labor force. On the contrary, one of the most striking characteristics of technology has been its *uneven entry* into production. In some sectors, such as agriculture, the effects of technology on output have been startling. Between 1880 and today, for instance, the time required to harvest an acre of wheat on the Great Plains has fallen from twenty hours to three. Between the late 1930s and the mid-1960s, the manhours needed to obtain a hundredweight of milk were slashed from 3.4 to 0.9; a hundredweight of chickens from 8.5 to 0.6.

Not quite so dramatic but also far-reaching in their effect have been technological improvements in other areas.

Table 16·1 shows the increase in productivity in five important branches of mining and manufacturing over the last two decades.

By way of contrast to the very great degree of technological advance in the primary and secondary sectors, we must note again the laggard advance in productivity in the tertiary sector of activity. Output per manhour in trade, for instance, or in education or in the service professions such as law or medicine or, again, in domestic or personal services such as barbering or repair work or in government has not increased nearly so much as in the primary and secondary sectors.

In the previous chapter, we noticed the inflationary consequences of this lag. Now we note the uneven entry of technology to be one main cause behind the overall migration of employment we observed in Chapter 3, (p. 40). Had we not enjoyed the enormous technical improvements in agriculture or mass production, but instead discovered vastly superior techniques of government services (in the sense of increasing the manhour output of, say, policemen or firemen or teachers), the distribution of employment might look very different.

THE INFLUENCE OF DEMAND

These strikingly different rates of increase in productivity begin to suggest a way of analyzing the effects of automation, or for that matter, any kind of labor-saving machinery. Clearly, capital equipment increases the *potential output* of a given number of workers. But will increased output be ab-

TABLE 16·1
Index of Output per Man-Hour for Production Workers

Industry	1950	1970
Coal mining	100	274
Railroad transportation	100	272
Steel	100	141
Paper and pulp	100	201
Petroleum refining	100	292

AUTOMATION AT WORK

Some years ago one of the authors of this book, visiting the New York Federal Reserve Bank, saw automation in a striking application. One of the floors of the immense Renaissance palace that is the home of the New York Fed is devoted to sorting checks that its member banks send there for deposit, so that these checks can be returned to the banks on which they were drawn.

On one entire side of this block-long floor, hundreds of women sitting at desks used a foot mechanism to operate circular files, into which,

with lightning rapidity, they sorted the checks in front of them. On the other side of the building was a single long machine, down which checks were whisked on a kind of belt mechanism. As the checks flew past, the magnetic ink numerals on each check were "read" by a machine, and the check was accordingly dropped into the appropriate slot as it traveled along the machine, much as an IBM card sorter works.

That one electronic check-reading machine performed as many "sorts" per hour as the small army of semimechanized check sorters on the other side of the aisle.

---

sorbed through expanded demand, allowing the workers to keep their jobs? Let us look at the question first in its broadest scope. We have seen that productivity has increased fastest in agriculture, next in manufacturing, least in services. What has happened to demand for the output of these sectors?

We can see this shift in demand in Table 16·2.

TABLE 16 · 2
Domestic Demand for Output

PERCENTAGE DISTRIBUTION OF DEMAND*		
	1899–1908	*1972*
Primary sector (agriculture)	16.7%	3.2%
Secondary sector (mining, construction, manufacturing)	26.0	41.0
Tertiary sector (transportation, communication, government, other • services)	57.2	55.7

*The figures actually show the *income originating in these sectors*. But we know from our macroeconomic studies that this income must have been produced by the expenditures—the demand—of society as it was distributed among the sectors.

What we see here is a shift working in a direction different from that of supply. As the productivity and potential output of the agricultural sector has risen, the demand for agricultural products has not followed suit but has lagged far behind. Demand has risen markedly for output coming from the secondary sector, but has remained roughly unchanged, in percentage terms, for the output of the tertiary service sector.

THE SQUEEZE ON EMPLOYMENT

If we now put together the forces of supply and demand, it is easy to understand what has happened to employment. The tremendous increase in productivity on the farm, faced with a shrinking proportionate demand for food, created a vast army of redundant labor in agriculture. Where did the labor go? It followed the route indicated by the growth of demand, migrating from the countryside into factory towns and cities where it found employment in manufacturing and service occupations. As Table 16·3 shows, the distribution of employment has steadily moved out of the primary and secondary, into the tertiary sector.

What we see here is the crucial role of technology in distributing employment among its various uses. As income rose,

TABLE 16 · 3
Distribution of Employment

PERCENT DISTRIBUTION OF ALL EMPLOYED WORKERS		
	1900	1972
Primary sector	38.1%	4.6%
Secondary sector	37.7	32.0
Tertiary sector	24.2	63.4

purchasing power no longer used for food was diverted to manufactured goods and homes. We would therefore expect that the proportion of the labor force employed in these pursuits would have risen rapidly. Instead, as we can see, it has fallen slightly. This is because technological improvements entered the secondary sector along with manpower, greatly increasing the productivity of workers in this area. Therefore a smaller portion of the national labor force could satisfy the larger proportional demands of the public for output from this sector.

Most important of all is the service sector. As Table 16·2 shows us, the public has not much changed the share of income that it spends for the various outputs we call services. But technological advances have not exerted their leverage as dramatically here as elsewhere, so that it takes a much larger fraction of the work force to produce the services we demand.

IMPORTANCE OF THE TERTIARY SECTOR

The conclusion, then, is that the demand for labor reflects the interplay of technology (which exerts differing leverages on different industries and occupations at different times) and of the changing demand for goods and services. Typically, the entrance of technology into industry has a twofold effect. The first is to raise the *potential* output of the industry, with its present labor force. The second is to enable the costs of the industry to decline, or its quality to improve, so that actual demand for the product will increase. But normally, the rise in demand is not great enough to enable the existing labor force to be retained along with the new techniques. Instead, some labor must now find its employment elsewhere.

There are exceptions, of course. A great new industry, such as the automobile industry in the 1920s, will keep on expanding its labor force despite improved technology, for in such cases demand *is* sufficiently strong to absorb the output of the new technology, even with a growing labor force. Then too, there is the exception of capital-saving technology, making it possible for an industry to turn out the same product with a cheaper capital equipment, thereby making it attractive to expand production and to hire more labor.

But taking all industries and all technological changes together, the net result is unambiguous. As Table 16·4 reveals, technology has steadily increased our ability to create goods, both on the farm and on the factory floor, more rapidly than we have wished to consume them, with the result that employment in these areas has lagged behind output.

TABLE 16 · 4
Output and Employment Indices

	1950	1971
Agricultural output	100	131
Agricultural employment	100	44
Manufacturing output	100	205
Manufacturing employment	100	120
1950 = 100		

THE SERVICE SECTOR

Forty percent of all consumer spending, roughly a quarter of GNP, consists of purchases of "services." A service is a utility that we purchase without buying the actual physical object from which it flows (a movie admission, not a movie film and a projector; a subway ride, not the subway).

Here it is worthwhile stressing that services are not, as we often think, just the personal ministrations of individuals, such as lawyers, fortune-tellers, accountants, and others. Many services that we buy are heavily capital-intensive; that is, use large quantities of capital per worker. To take the two examples above, movie theaters require large capital investments; subways cer-

tainly do. Wholesale and retail trade are also services, but both require large investments in land and plant; electricity and steam are services that flow from vast capital agglomerations; telephone calls are services that utilize billions of dollars worth of capital. Even travel needs aircraft, ships, hotels.

The point is that we must differentiate, when we speak of services, between those services that require large capital investments and those that do not. Strictly speaking, the division between goods and services is of less interest, from the point of view of employment, than the division between labor-intensive and nonlabor-intensive occupations, but we do not have the information we need to analyze the latter.

Note how agricultural output has increased rapidly in this period, while agricultural employment has shrunk by over 50 percent; and notice that whereas manufacturing output has more than doubled, employment in manufacturing is up by only 20 percent.

During this same period, however, our total civilian labor force increased by over 20 million. Where did these millions find employment? As we would expect, largely in the

service sector. Figures for employment in various parts of the service sector appear in Table 16·5. We might note that comparable shifts from agriculture "through" manufacturing into services are visible in all industrial nations.

THE IMPACT OF INVENTION ON COST

Our discussion of the forces of supply and demand enables us now to look more closely into the effect of introducing an individual labor-saving invention. To be sure, not all inventions by any manner of means are labor-saving. A profit-maximizing entrepreneur will not introduce a technical change into his process of production unless it lowers cost, but this cost can be capital-saving or land-saving as well as labor-saving. Fertilizer is land-saving, for example; miniaturization is often capital-saving; the oxygen process of making steel is labor-using but cost-cutting (i.e., it is relatively capital-saving).

TABLE 16 · 5
Service Employments 1950, 1972

	1950	1972	Percent increase 1950–1972
	(in millions)		
Trade	9.4	15.8	68
Services	5.4	12.3	128
Government	6.0	13.3	122
Finance and other	1.9	3.9	105
Total tertiary sector	22.7	45.3	100

LABOR-SAVING INVENTIONS

But the cost-cutting inventions that interest us here are *labor-saving* inventions or innovations, changes in technique or technology that enable an entrepreneur to turn out the same output as before, with less labor, or a larger output than before, with the same amount of labor.

Do such inventions "permanently" displace labor? Let us trace an imaginary instance and find out.

We assume in this case that an inventor has perfected a technique that makes it possible for a local shoe factory to reduce its production force from ten men to eight men, while still turning out the same number of shoes. Forgetting for the moment about the possible stimulatory effects of buying a new labor-saving machine,* let us see what happens to purchasing power and employment if the shoe manufacturer simply goes on selling the same number of shoes at the same prices as before, utilizing the new lower-cost process to increase his profits.

Suppose our manufacturer now spends his increased profits in increased consumption. Will that bring an equivalent increase in the total spending of the community? If we think twice we can see why not. For the increased spending of the manufacturer will be offset to a large extent by the decreased spending of the two displaced workers.

Exactly the same conclusion follows if the entrepreneur used his cost-cutting invention to lower the price of shoes, in the hope of snaring a larger market. Now it is *consumers* who are given an increase in purchasing power equivalent to the cut in prices. But again, their gain is exactly balanced by

---

*This is not an unfair assumption. The labor-saving technology might be no more than a more effective arrangement of labor within the existing plant, and thus require no new equipment; or the new equipment might be bought with regular capital replacement funds.

the lost purchasing power of the displaced workers.

INCOMES VS. EMPLOYMENT

Thus we can see that the introduction of labor-saving machinery does not necessarily imperil *incomes;* it merely shifts purchasing power from previously employed workers into the hands of consumers or into profits. But note also that *the unchanged volume of incomes is now associated with a smaller volume of employment. Thus the fact that there is no purchasing power "lost" when a labor-saving machine is introduced does not mean that there is no employment lost.*

Is this the end to our analysis of labor-displacing technology? It can be. It is possible that the introduction of labor-saving machinery will have no effect other than that of the example above: transferring consumer spending from previously employed labor to consumers or to entrepreneurs. But it is also possible that an employment-generating secondary effect may result. The entrepreneur may be so encouraged at the higher profits from his new process that he uses his profits to invest in additional plant and equipment and thereby sets in motion, via the multiplier, a rise in total expenditure sufficient to re-employ his displaced workers. Or in our second instance, consumers may evidence such a brisk demand for shoes at lower prices that, once again, our employer is encouraged to invest in additional plant and equipment, with the same salutary results as above. Do not fall into the trap of thinking that the new higher demand for shoes, will, *by itself,* suffice to eradicate unemployment. To be sure, shoe purchases may now increase to previous levels or even higher. But unless their incomes rise, consumer spending on other items will suffer to the exact degree that spending on shoes gains.

The moral is clear. *Labor-saving technology can offset the unemployment created by its immediate introduction only if it induces sufficient investment to increase the volume of total spending to a point where unemployment is fully absorbed.*

IMPACT OF AUTOMATION

It is in connection with our foregoing discussion that the much talked-of threat of *automation* becomes most meaningful. In the main, automation is clearly a cost-cutting and labor-saving kind of technology, although it has important applications for the creation of new products as well.

But one aspect of automation requires our special attention. It is the fact that automation represents the belated entry of technology into an area of economic activity that until now has been largely spared the impact of technical change. This is the area of service and administrative tasks that we have previously marked as an important source of growing employment. Thus the threat inherent in the new sensory, almost humanoid, equipment is not only that it may accelerate the employment-saving effects in the secondary (manufacturing) sector. *More sobering is that it may put an end to the traditional employment-absorptive effects of the tertiary service and administrative sector.*

What could be the implications of such a development? In simplest terms, it means that in the future, fewer people would be needed to produce the same quantity of services. The absorption of labor from agriculture and manufacturing into the ever-expanding service sector would now slow down or come to a halt, since the service sector could increase its output without hiring a proportionate increase in workers.

This *could,* of course, mean massive unemployment. But it need not. Just as our imaginary society limited its demand to agricultural goods and solved its labor problem by cutting the workweek, so a society that no longer needed to add labor as fast as its demands rose could easily solve the unemployment problem by more or less equitably sharing among its members the amount of labor it *did* require. To be sure, this raises many problems, not least among them the wage adjustments that must accompany such a reapportionment of hours. But it makes clear that, essentially, the challenge of automation is one of finding a new balance in our attitudes toward work, leisure, and goods, and an equitable means of sharing work (and income, the reward for work).

NEW DEMANDS

But now let us suppose that an inventor patents a new product—let us say a stove that automatically cooks things to perfection. Will such an invention create employment?

We will suppose that our inventor assembles his original models himself and peddles them in local stores, and we will ignore the small increase in spending (and perhaps in employment) due to his orders for raw materials. Instead, let us fasten our attention on the consumer who first decides to buy the new product in a store, because it has stimulated his demand.

Will the consumer's purchase result in a *net* increase in consumer spending in the economy? If this is so—and if the new product is generally liked—it is easy to see how the new product could result in sizeable additional employment.

But will it be true? Our consumer has, to be sure, bought a new item. *But unless his income has increased, there is no reason to believe that this is a net addition to his consumption expenditures.* The chances are, rather, that this unforeseen expenditure will be balanced by lessened spending for some other item. Almost surely he will not buy a regular stove. (When consumers first began buying television sets, they stopped buying as many radios and going to the movies as often.) But even where there is no direct competition, where the product is quite "new," everything that we know about the stability of the propensity to consume schedule leads us to believe that *total* consumer spending will not rise.

Thus we reach the important conclusion that new products do not automatically create *additional* spending, even though they may mobilize consumer demand for themselves. Indeed, many new products emerge onto the market every year and merely shoulder old products off. Must we then conclude that demand-creating inventions do not affect employment?

EMPLOYMENT AND INVESTMENT

We are by no means ready to jump to that conclusion. Rather, what we have seen enables us to understand that if a new product is to create employment, it must give rise to new *investment* (and to the consumption it induces in turn). If the automatic stove is successful, it may induce the inventor to borrow money from a bank and to build a plant to mass-produce the item. If consumer demand for it continues to rise, a very large factory may have to be built to accommodate demand. As a result of the investment expenditures on the new plant, GNP rises, consumers' incomes rise, and more employment will be created as they spend their incomes on various consumer items.

To be sure, investment will decline in those areas that are now selling less to consumers. At most, however, this decline can affect only their replacement expenditures, which probably averaged 5 to 10 percent of the value of their capital equipment. Meanwhile, in the new industry, an entire capital structure must be built from scratch. We can

expect the total amount of investment spending to increase substantially, with its usual repercussive effects.

When we think of a new product not in terms of a household gadget but in terms of the automobile, airplane, or perhaps the transistor, we can understand how large the employment-creating potential of certain kinds of inventions can be. Originally the automobile merely resulted in consumer spending being diverted from buggies; the airplane merely cut into railroad income; the transistor, into vacuum tubes. But each of these inventions became in time the source of enormous investment expenditures. The automobile not only gave us the huge auto plants in Detroit, but indirectly brought into being multibillion-dollar investment in highways, gasoline refineries, service stations, tourism—all industries whose impact on employment has been gigantic. On a smaller, but still very large scale, the airplane gave rise not alone to huge aircraft building plants, but to airfields, radio and beacon equipment industries, international tourism, etc., whose employment totals are substantial. In turn, the transistor offered entirely new design possibilities for miniaturization and thus gave many businesses an impetus for expansion.

INDUSTRY-BUILDING INVENTIONS

What sorts of inventions have this industry-building capacity? We can perhaps generalize by describing them as inventions that are of sufficient importance to become "indispensable" to the consumer or the manufacturer, and of sufficient mechanical or physical variance from the existing technical environment to necessitate the creation of a large amount of supporting capital equipment to integrate them into economic life.

Demand-creating inventions, then, can indeed create employment. *They do so in-*

*directly, however—not by inducing new consumer spending, but by generating new investment spending.**

Unfortunately, there is no guarantee that these highly employment-generative inventions will come along precisely when they are needed. There have been long periods when the economy has not been adequately stimulated by this type of invention and when employment has lagged as a result.

AUTOMATION AND EMPLOYMENT

Will the technology of automation be industry-building or labor-saving? *We do not know.* It is possible that the computer, the transistor, the myriad new possibilities in feed-back engineering will play the same role as the automobile and the railroad, not only giving rise to an enormous flow of investment, but opening new fields of endeavor for other new industries that will also expand. If this is the case, the demand for labor will grow fast enough to match the increase in the productivity of labor, and there will be nothing unusual to worry about.

But it is also possible that the labor-saving impact of automation will make itself felt primarily in the tertiary sector—in government, retail and wholesale trade, in banking and finance, rather than in manufacturing or agriculture. If so, as we have seen, it will introduce a hitherto unfelt pressure on employment in that sector, "freeing" labor to seek employment elsewhere.

Where? The answer must be in some fast-growing sector of industry. But which one? The employment-generating effects of

*We should mention one effect of demand-creating inventions on consumption. It is probable that without the steady emergence of new products, the long-run propensity to consume would decline instead of remaining constant, as we have seen in Chapter 7. In this way, demand-creating technology is directly responsible for the creation of employment, by helping to keep consumer spending higher than it would be without a flow of new products.

the growth of private industry have been uneven: between 1950 and 1960, for example, new jobs in the private sector accounted for only one out of every ten new jobs in the nation; from 1960 to 1972 the private sector supplied 7 out of 10 jobs. In both cases, the rest were accounted for in the public or not-for-profit sector (private schools and universities, hospitals and the like). Thus, if private industry performs in the future as poorly as in the 1950s, automation *could* present us with a very serious problem. The question is: what could we do about it?

Combating Unemployment

This question leads us to consider the whole problem of combating unemployment. Because unemployment comes from more than one source, there is more than one answer to the problem. There is also less than one answer, because, as we shall see, it is easier to prescribe the remedies for unemployment than to apply them.

1. Increasing demand

We have learned that as a general rule, anything that increases the total demand of society is apt to increase employment. This is particularly true when unemployment tends to be widespread, both in geographic location and industrial distribution. *The expansion of GNP, whether by the stimulation of private investment or consumer spending or government expenditure or net exports is generally the single most reliable means of creating more employment.*

There is, however, a problem here. Doubtless, a vast amount of employment could be created if aggregate demand were enlarged; for instance, the systematic reconstruction of our cities, a task that is becoming an increasingly pressing necessity, could by itself provide millions of jobs for decades. So could the proper care of our rapidly-growing older population, or the provision of really first-class education for large segments of the population that lack it.

The problem is that these programs require the generation of large amounts of *public demand,* and this requires the prior political approval of the electorate. If this political approval is not forthcoming, the generation of additional demand will have to be entrusted to the private sector—that is, to individual entrepreneurs in search of a profit.

Can private enterprise, without a massive public investment program, generate sufficient demand to bring about full and lasting employment? One cannot be dogmatic about such questions, but, as we have seen, there is at least some historical reason for caution in assuming that the private sector, unaided by public programs of investment, will be able to offer as much employment as the growing labor force demands. *The likelihood is that a large enough aggregate demand will require the substantial use of public expenditure, whether for urban renewal and welfare services or for other ends.*

2. Wage policy

But suppose that a very high aggregate demand is maintained, through public or private spending. Will that in itself guarantee full employment?

The answer is that it will not if the spending creates only higher incomes for workers who are already employed, rather that new incomes for workers who are unemployed. This is because much of the increase in wages is apt to be saved, in the short run, rather than spent. Thus if we want to maximize the employment-creating effect of spending, whether private or public, *we need to hold back wage raises at least until the unemployment has fallen to a socially acceptable level.* (This applies particularly to unemployment among groups such as teen-agers.)

But if raising wages can impede the process of job creation, can cutting wages encourage it? The question is not a simple one, for lower wages set into motion contrary economic stimuli. On the one hand, lower wages cut costs and thereby tempt employers to add to their labor force. On the other hand, lower wages after a time will result in less consumption spending, and will thus adversely affect business sales. The net effect of a wage cut thus becomes highly unpredictable. If businessmen feel the positive gains of a cut in costs before they feel the adverse effects of a cut in sales, employment may rise —and thereby obviate the fall in consumption spending. On the other hand, employers may *expect* that the wage cut will lead to lower sales, and their pessimistic expectations may lead them to refrain from adding to their labor forces, despite lower costs. In that case, of course, employment will not rise. On balance, most economists today fear the adverse demand effects of wage-cutting more than they welcome the possible job-creating effects.

It seems, then, that maintaining wages in the face of an economic decline and restraining wage rises in the face of an economic advance is the best way of encouraging maximum employment. It is one thing, however, to spell out such a general guideline to action and another to achieve it. *To maintain wages against an undertow of falling sales requires a strong union movement. But once times improve, this same union movement is hardly likely to exercise the self-restraint needed to forego wage raises, so that additional spending can go into the pockets of the previously unemployed.* This poses another dilemma for a market society in search of a rational high employment policy, and there is at this moment no solution in sight.

3. Remedying structural unemployment

Not all unemployment is due to insufficient demand. Some can be traced to "structural" causes—to a lack of "fit" between the existing labor force and the existing job opportunities. For instance, men may be unem-

THE GHETTO SKILL MIX

A sad example of the lack of fit between the skills demanded by employers and those possessed by the labor force is to be found in the ghetto, where typically the labor force is badly undertrained. A recent study by the First National City Bank shows this situation in New York City.

In only one category—unskilled service—was the prospective demand for labor roughly in line with the skills available. This meant a reasonable employment prospect for maids, restaurant workers, bellhops, and the like—among the lowest-paid occupations in the nation. As for the common laborer, who comprised over half the "skill pool" of the New York ghetto, his outlook was bleak indeed—less than one percent of new jobs would open in that area. Conversely, for the widest job

	Occupational distribution of ghetto unemployed, 1968	Estimated job openings, 1965–1975
White collar	13.6%	65.7%
Craftsmen	2.8	7.4
Operatives	14.7	7.7
Unskilled personal service	16.6	18.6
Laborers	52.3	0.6

market in the city—the white-collar trades that offer two-thirds of the new jobs—the ghetto could offer only one-seventh of its residents as adequately trained. If these figures have any meaning, it is that ghetto poverty is here to stay, short of a herculean effort to rescue the trapped ghetto resident.

ployed because they do not know of job opportunities in another city, or because they do not have the requisite skills to get or hold jobs that are currently being offered. Indeed, it is perfectly possible to have structural unemployment side-by-side with a lack of manpower in certain fields.

One particularly important kind of structural unemployment comes from *labor-displacing* (as compared with labor-saving) inventions. Inventions can radically alter the specific skills demanded from the labor force. The labor-saving invention of our hypothetical shoe factory, for instance, might have been a mechanical cutter operated by one man who replaced three former hand cutters. Perhaps one of the hand cutters could be retrained to operate the mechanical cutter, but it is often easier and cheaper to hire a new, young employee and to let the former employees go. In this case, their skills have become obsolete. Even if shoe sales increase, the laid-off employees will not be put back to work at their former tasks. Such workers may find themselves permanently unem-

ployed or reduced to lower incomes because they are forced to accept unskilled work.

A sharp debate has raged in the United States concerning the importance of structural reasons (as contrasted with a general deficiency of demand) in accounting for the present level of unemployment. Many observers have pointed out that the unemployed are typically grouped into certain disprivileged categories: race, sex, age, lack of training, and unfortunate geographic location. The aged and the young, the black and the unskilled, and the Massachusetts textile worker are not quickly pulled into employment by a general expansion of demand. The broad stream of purchasing power passes most of them by and does not reintegrate them into the mainstream of the economy. Hence stress is increasingly placed on measures to assist labor mobility, so that the unemployed can move from distressed to expansive areas, and on the retraining of men for those jobs offered by a technologically fast-moving society.

Retraining is, unfortunately, much easier

when it is applied to relatively few persons than when it is proposed as a general public policy affecting large numbers of unemployed. Then the question arises: for what jobs shall the unemployed be trained? *Unless we very clearly know the shape of future demand, the risk is that a retraining program will prepare workers for jobs that may no longer exist when the workers are ready for them.* And unless the *level* of future demand is high, even a foresighted program will not effectively solve the unemployment problem.

Most economists would suggest a combination of measures to combat structural unemployment. One of them is *a much more effective job-finding system* than we now have —a computerized "job bank" has been proposed. Another is *a more generous program of unemployment benefits* to give people time to look for work they want, rather than force them to settle for work they can do. *Training schools* are very valuable, especially if they are connected with a program of *public demand,* so that trainees know that jobs exist. A recent survey made by the Urban Coalition in 34 cities has estimated that over a million potential new jobs exist in the public sector—in education, welfare administration, environment control, library services, police and fire protection, hospital and sanitation improvement, etc.

4. Reducing the supply of labor

Next, the possibility exists of attacking unemployment not from the demand side, but from the supply side, by cutting the workweek, lengthening vacations, and using similar measures. Essentially, the possibility held out by shortening the workweek is that a more or less fixed quantity of work will then be shared among a larger number of workers. This is entirely feasible and possible, provided that *the decrease in hours is not offset by an increase in hourly pay rates.* In other words, once again a rational wage policy

holds the key between success and failure. Shorter hours, coupled with higher hourly wage rates, will merely raise unit costs (unless productivity rises quickly enough to compensate). This will certainly not contribute to increased employment. Shorter hours *without* increased hourly rates, on the other hand, may make it necessary for the employer to hire additional help in order to continue his established level of output.

Shortening hours of work can be a policy of despair. If people do not wish to change their working habits—the number of hours per week or the number of years in their lifetimes—then the cure for unemployment is surely to expand the demand for labor and not to diminish its supply. If private demand is inadequate to this task, then, as we have said, public demand may serve the purpose instead.

But an attack on unemployment that seeks to reduce the supply of labor, rather than to expand the demand for it, need not be a program of retreat. It can also become part of a deliberate and popularly endorsed effort to reshape the patterns and the duration of work as it now exists. Thus it may be possible to reduce the size of the labor force by measures such as subsidies that would induce younger people to remain longer in school or by raising Social Security to make it attractive for older people to retire earlier. Such policies can be useful not only in bringing down the participation rate and thus reducing "unemployment," but in affecting changes in the quality of life that would find general public approval.

5. The government as employer of last resort

Finally, we can effectively limit the problem of unemployment by formally adopting the policy of using the public sector as "employer of last resort."

This proposal, first advanced by the National Commission on Technology, Auto-

THE IMPORTANCE OF BEING THE RIGHT AGE

A special kind of structural unemployment arises because the age composition of the labor force changes, sometimes flooding the market with young untrained workers, sometimes with older workers. Take the group aged 14 to 24. This includes those who are finishing their educations, as well as those who have finished and are entering the work force. The "cohort" as a whole increased in numbers by roughly 8 to 10 percent from decade to decade in the period 1890 to 1960.

Then in the 1960s an explosion occurred. The so-called baby boom in the years immediately following World War II began to enter these age ranks. In the decade of the 1960s, the 14-to-24-year-old group increased by *52 percent*. In the 1970s it will increase by a "normal" 11 percent; in the 1980s it will *decline* by 8 percent. We can confidently predict these changes, because the members of this age group are already born.

Beginning in mid1980s, however, the rate of growth of the labor force will be very slow, except for women. Job prospects should then be very bright.

---

mation, and Economic Progress,[1] does not mean the use of the public sector as a kind of vast "work relief" program. On the contrary, the purpose is to use public employment primarily as a positive force in establishing a higher quality of life, an objective that will require a substantial expansion of much public service activity along the lines mentioned above in the proposals of the Urban Coalition. Only as a secondary objective is "the employer of last resort" to provide jobs for those who fail to find satisfactory work in the private sector or in the current career lines of public services.

THE U.S. AND EUROPEAN EXPERIENCE

As evidence of what can be done by a more vigorous attack on unemployment, using many of the above techniques, the performance of the United States in recent fairly "low unemployment" years can be compared with that of various European nations.

The lesson of Table 16·6 is clear. A tendency to generate unemployment may be an unavoidable consequence of a market sys-

[1] *Technology and the American Economy* (Washington, 1966), p. 37.

TABLE 16 · 6

Unemployment Rates, Selected Countries,* 1971

United States	5.9%
West Germany	0.7
France	2.1
Netherlands	1.4
United Kingdom	2.8
Norway	(1970) 0.8
Sweden	2.5
Denmark	1.1

*Definitions of unemployment vary slightly between the United States and European nations, but not enough to affect the basic conclusions revealed by the data.

tem, *but it is not an irremediable evil. It is possible to run a capitalist system at high levels of employment—admittedly, paying the price of a considerable degree of inflation.* The problem, then, is to bring about the political changes in the United States that may be the prerequisite for introducing the kinds of employment programs that have proved their worth in capitalism abroad. That may involve a very difficult problem of public education and persuasion, but it is a problem different from a defeatist admission that the economic system itself cannot be made to work adequately.

KEY WORDS

Technological
unemployment

Automation

Uneven entry of
technology

Supply and
demand for labor

Service sector

Labor-saving
inventions

Industry-building
inventions

Aggregate
demand

Wage policy

Wage cutting

Structural
unemployment

Retraining

Job information

Reducing the
supply of labor

Employer of
last resort

European
experience

CENTRAL CONCEPTS

1. Unemployment has been an endemic problem of market societies. We have already discussed this problem from the point of view of aggregate demand. Here we look into the important problem of *technological unemployment*.

2. *Automation* refers to a new category of machines with unusually flexible, self-correcting feedback mechanisms.

3. Machines affect both the supply of and the demand for labor. Changes on the supply side reflect the effect of machines in increasing productivity. The important point is the *uneven entry* of machines into the economy, greatly raising productivity in agriculture, raising it somewhat less (but also substantially) in manufacturing, having least effect in the services sector.

4. Employment depends on the demand for labor as well as the supply. We note that the demand for the products of the agricultural and manufacturing sectors has not risen as fast as the increase in productivity, resulting in a displacement of labor from those sectors.

5. Labor has moved, over many decades, into the services sector. The *special significance of automation is that it represents the entrance of technology into this previously labor-absorbing sector.*

6. *Labor-saving inventions* do not create a loss in income, but shift incomes previously earned by labor to other workers or to consumers (in terms of declines in price) or to profits. The inventions will create unemployment *unless these shifts give rise to investment that will create demand for additional labor.*

7. Employment-creating inventions give rise to new industries based on new demands. Automobiles are a prime example of such industry-building inventions. We do not know if automation will have such an effect on investment.

8. Unemployment can be combated in several ways. *Widespread unemployment is best attacked by increases in aggregate demand.*

9. *Wage policy* is a critical consideration in combating unemployment. If wages rise faster than productivity, employed labor will benefit; but the rise will deter the hiring of additional labor. Cutting wages is an uncertain and potentially dangerous mode of increasing employment, since the adverse effects of decreased consumption may more than offset lower costs.

10. *Structural unemployment* is an important source of joblessness. It results from a bad match between existing skills and the structure of work. *Labor-displacing inventions refer to changes in technology that make existing skills obsolete.*

11. The basic remedy for structural unemployment is retraining, but it is difficult to carry out unless one knows the skills that will be required in the future. Retraining is most successful when combined with programs of *public employment*, since their extent and skill requirements can be known in advance. Increasing *job information* is also very useful in reducing unemployment.

12. The *supply of labor can also be reduced*, thereby alleviating unemployment. This occurs when we lengthen the span of schooling or lower retirement ages.

13. The government can serve as an "*employer of last resort*," guaranteeing useful careers—not make-work jobs—if private demand is inadequate.

14. Recent European experience seems to indicate that unemployment can be held to lower levels than in the U.S.

QUESTIONS

1. What do you think accounts for the shift in demand from primary to secondary and tertiary products? In particular, what do you think is the reason for the steady growth of services as a kind of output that society seems to want?

2. Suppose that technology in the 1890s had taken the following turn: a very complex development of machines and techniques for improving public and private supervisory and administrative techniques, very clever devices that performed salesmen's and clerks' services, but almost no improvement in agricultural techniques. What would the distribution of the labor force probably look like?

3. Suppose that an inventor puts a wrist radio-telephone on the market. What would be the effects on consumer spending? What would ultimately determine whether the new invention was labor-attracting or labor-saving?

4. Suppose that another new invention halved the cost of making cars. Would this create new purchasing power? What losses in income would have to be balanced against what gains in incomes? What would be the most likely way that such an invention could increase employment? Would employment increase if the demand for cars were inelastic, like the demand for farm products—that is, if people bought very few more cars despite the fall in prices?

5. Unemployment among the black population in many cities in the late 1960s was worse than it was during the Great Depression. What steps would you propose to remedy this situation?

6. Would raising wages, and thereby creating more consumption demand, be a good way to increase employment?

7. Do you believe that there exists general support for large public employment-generating programs? Why or why not? What sorts of programs would you propose?

8. How would you encourage private enterprise to create as many *jobs* as possible?

9. Do you think that the computer, on net balance, has created unemployment? How would you go about trying to ascertain whether your hunch was accurate? Would you have to take into account the indirect effects of computers on investment?

10. What is the difference between a labor-saving and a labor-displacing invention? Which is more difficult to cope with?

11. How much inflation would *you* willingly accept, to lower unemployment to, say, 3 percent?

Problems of Economic Growth

17

FROM OUR FIRST INTRODUCTION to Adam Smith's *Wealth of Nations,* the issue of growth has been a central preoccupation of our macroeconomic investigations. Indeed, no sooner did we leave the imaginary circular flow of a static system, allowing investment to enter the picture, than growth became *the* problem of macroeconomics—too little growth bringing unemployment, too much growth pushing us toward inflation.

In this last chapter, growth once more comes into the foreground. For there are problems of growth that we have not yet met —as we shall see, problems of very great importance. In this chapter we shall deal with three of them: growth and stability; growth and the quality of life; and growth and its "limits." Perhaps these issues are more crucial and more complex than any others in the book.

The Stability of GNP

We met the issue of stability when we learned about business cycles in Chapter 4, but we have not yet explored an important aspect of the problem. Formerly, we looked into cycles as a problem involving fluctuations in demand. Now we want to investigate stability as a problem involving supply as well as demand. In particular, we want to learn more about the degree to which we utilize the *potential output* of the economy.

For even in the doldrums of recession (except for a very few severely depressed years) the economy manages to lay down a net increment of wealth in the form of investment, and this investment then adds its leverage to that of the entire stock of capital with which society works. So, too, every year, the labor force tends to grow as population increases, adding another component of potential input to the economic mechanism.

This does not mean, as we well know, that the economy will therefore automatically utilize its full resources. Unused men and unused machines are very well known to us in macroeconomic analysis. But the steady addition to the factors of production does mean that the *potential* of the economy will be steadily rising. *The possibility of growth is thus introduced into the system by the accumulation of its basic instruments of production, both human and material.* If we multiply the slowly rising hours of total labor input by a "productivity coefficient" that reflects, among other things, technology and capital, we can derive a trend line of *potential GNP.* The question we then face is to see how much of this potential volume of output we will actually produce.

ACTUAL VS. POTENTIAL GNP

As Fig. 17·1 shows, all through much of the 1950s, 1960s and early 1970s, potential output ran well ahead of the output we actually achieved. Indeed, between 1958 and 1962 the amount of lost output represented by this gap came to the staggering sum of $170 billion. Even in 1972, a prosperous year, we could have added another $55 billion to GNP— $1,000 per family—if we had brought unemployment down from the actual level of 5.6 percent to 4 percent.

DEMAND VS. CAPACITY

The problem of a potential growth rate opens an aspect of the investment process that we have not yet considered. Heretofore, we have always thought of investment primarily as an income-generating force, working through the multiplier to increase the level of expenditure. Now we begin to consider investment also as a *capacity-generating* force, working through the actual addition to our plant and equipment to increase the productive potential of the system.

No sooner do we introduce the idea of capacity, however, than a new problem arises for our consideration. If investment increases potential output as well as income, the obvious question is: will income rise fast enough to buy all this potential output? Thus at the end of our analysis of macroeconomics we revert to the question we posed at the beginning, but in a more dynamic context. At first, we asked whether an economy that saved could buy back its own output. Now we must ask whether an economy that grows can do the same.

MARGINAL CAPITAL-OUTPUT RATIO

The question brings us to consider a concept that we met earlier (p. 55) but have not yet put to much use. The *marginal capital-output ratio,* as the formidable name suggests, is not

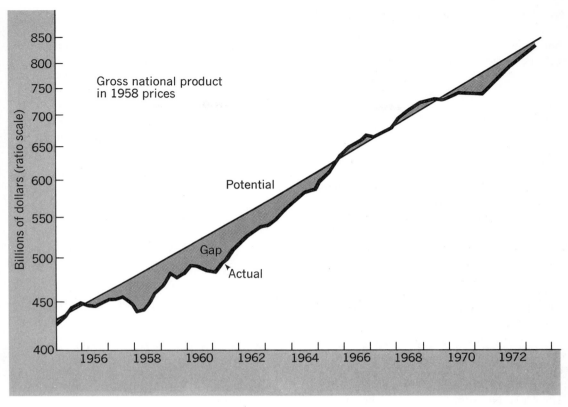

FIGURE 17 · 1
Actual and potential GNP

a relationship that describes behavior, as the multiplier does. It describes a strictly technical or engineering or organizational relationship between an *increase in the stock of capital and the increase in output that this new capital will yield.*

Note that we are not interested in the ratio between our entire existing stock of capital (most of which is old) and the flow of total output, but only in the ratio between the *new* capital added during the period and the *new* output associated with that new capital. Thus the marginal capital-output ratio directs our attention to the *net investment* of the period and to the *change in output* of the period. If net investment was $60 billion and the change in output yielded by that invest-

ment was $20 billion, then the marginal capital-output ratio was 3.

INCOME VS. OUTPUT

The marginal capital-output ratio gives us a powerful new concept to bring to bear on the problem of attaining and maintaining a high, steady rate of growth, for we can now see that the problem of steady growth requires the balancing out of two different economic processes. Investment raises productive capacity. *Increases* in investment raise income and demand. What we must now do is investigate the relationship between these two different, albeit related, economic variables.

Let us begin with a familiar formula

that shows how a change in investment affects a change in income. This is

$$\Delta Y = \frac{1}{\text{mps}} \times \Delta I,$$

which is nothing but the multiplier. For brevity, we will write it

$$\Delta Y = \frac{1}{s} \Delta I.$$

Now we need a new formula to relate I, the rate of new investment (not ΔI, the *change* in new investment), and ΔO, the change in dollar output. This will require a symbol for the marginal capital-output ratio, a symbol that expresses how many dollars' worth of capital it takes to get an additional dollar's worth of output. If we use the symbol σ (sigma), we can write this formula as $\sigma = I/\Delta O$.

For example, if we have \$10 of new investment, and output rises by \$5, then σ (the marginal capital-output ratio) must be 2 (\$10 ÷ \$5). If output rises by only \$3, σ is 3.3 (10 ÷ \$3). Note that the *lower* the marginal capital-output ratio, the *higher* the productivity of new investment.

BALANCED GROWTH IN THEORY

We now have two formulas. The first tells us by how much *income* will rise as investment grows. The second tells us the relationship between new investment and new *output*. Now, by a simple arithmetical operation, we can use our second formula to tell us the amount by which output will increase as investment increases. All we have to do is multiply both sides of the formula by ΔO and then divide both sides by σ to get $\Delta O = I/\sigma$.

This last formula tells us that if new investment is, say \$10, and the marginal capital-output ratio is, say, 2.5, then the increase in output will be \$4—that is, \$10 ÷ 2.5.

We are ready to take the last and most

important step. We can now discover *by how much investment must rise each year, to give us the additional income we will need to buy the addition to output that has been created by this selfsame investment.*

Our formulas enable us to answer that question very clearly. Increased income is ΔY. Increased output is ΔO. Since $\Delta Y = \frac{1}{s} \Delta I$, and $\Delta O = \frac{I}{\sigma}$ then ΔY will equal ΔO if $\frac{1}{s} \Delta I = \frac{I}{\sigma}$. This is the formula for balanced growth.

If we now multiply both sides of the equation by s, and then divide both sides by I, we get

$$\frac{\Delta I}{I} = \frac{s}{\sigma}$$

BALANCED GROWTH IN FACT

What does this equation mean? It tells us what *rate of growth of investment* ($\Delta I/I$) is needed to make $\Delta Y = \Delta O$. In words, it tells us by what percentage investment spending must rise to make income payments keep pace with dollar output. That rate of growth is equal to the marginal savings ratio divided by the marginal capital-output ratio. Suppose, for instance, that the marginal savings ratio (including leakages) is $\frac{1}{3}$ and that the marginal capital-output ratio (σ) is 3. Then s/σ is $\frac{1}{3} ÷ 3$ (or $\frac{1}{9}$), which means that investment would have to grow by $\frac{1}{9}$ to create just enough income to match the growing flow of output. If the rate of investment grew faster than that, income and demand would tend to grow ahead of output and we would be pushing beyond the path of balanced growth into inflation. If the rate of growth of investment were smaller than that, we would be experiencing chronic overproduction with falling prices and sagging employment.

What is the rate at which investment should rise for balanced growth in the United

States? To determine that, we would have to deal with tricky statistical problems of marginal capital-output ratios; we would have to calculate *net* investment—not easy to do; and marginal leakages would have to behave as tamely as they do in textbooks—not always the case. Moreover, to include public as well as private capital formation in the terms "investment" and "marginal capital output ratio" would also greatly complicate our computations.

Therefore we shall sidestep here the difficult empirical problems posed by the requirements for balanced growth and concentrate on the general issue that the formulation opens up. For the purpose of our discussion is to explain that there is a complex relationship between the growth in income and the growth in output. Our analysis shows that we can have a *growth gap* if our leakages are too high, so that increases in injections do not generate enough new purchasing power, or if our marginal capital-output ratio is too low, so that a given amount of investment increases our potential output (our capacity) too fast.*

POLICY FOR BALANCED GROWTH

Suppose that we are not generating income fast enough to absorb our potential output. Suppose, to go back to Fig. 17·1, that we have a persistent growth gap similar to that of the late 1950s. How can we bring the economy up to its potential?

---

*One question may have occurred to the reader. Aren't incomes and outputs *identities*? Isn't it true that GNI ≡ GNP? Then how can a growth "gap" occur? The answer lies in our familiar ex ante and ex post perspectives (see box pp. 182–83). Ex post, incomes are always the same as outputs. Ex ante they are not. The question, then, is not whether or not GNI will be equal to GNP, but *whether their identical values will be equal to potential output.* Our formula for balanced growth tells us which critical variables must be taken into account when we ask whether ex ante spending plans will bring us to a level of income and output that corresponds with *potential production.*

Our formula for balanced growth gives us the answer. The relationship between the growth of incomes and the growth of output depends above all on the rate at which investment *increases.* Thus, if expenditures fall short of the amount needed to absorb potential output, the answer is to raise the rate of investment or, perhaps more realistically, to raise the rate of growth of all expenditures, public and private. Conversely, of course, if we find ourselves pushing over the trend line of potential growth into inflation, as in the late 1960s, the indicated policy is to lower the rate of growth of investment (or of investment and government and consumption) to bring the flow of rising incomes back into balance with the rise of output.

Thus the critical element in balancing a growing economy is not the *amount* of investment needed to fill a given demand gap, but the *increase* in investment (or other injection-expenditure) needed to match a growing output capacity with a large enough demand.

PROBLEMS OF BALANCED GROWTH

But our analysis also points up an endemic problem for an expanding market system. *It is that the growth of incomes and the growth of output depend on unrelated variables.* There is nothing in the income side of the picture that ensures an appropriate magnitude for the marginal capital-output ratio. Nor is there anything on the capacity side that matches a given marginal capital-output ratio with an appropriate savings rate for the multiplier we want.

All this sets our previous discussion of fiscal and monetary policy into a more complex but more realistic framework. In trying to keep the economy on a path of balanced growth, we are trying to align two different sets of forces: one, largely technological, regulates the rate at which our capacity rises; one, largely behavioral, regulates the savings decision. This does not tell us what we want to know—exactly how fast to increase the supply of money or exactly how large our government expenditures should be—but it helps explain why a growing economy displays instability *just because it is growing*.

Growth and the Quality of Life

The second problem of growth is quite different from the first—philosophic rather than technical, imprecise and value-ridden rather than clear-cut and analytic. Yet it is no less pressing than the problem of stability. It is the question of *why growth fails to bring benefits that are proportionate to the increase in output*.

Perhaps an illustration will bring the problem home in full force. We are often fond of stating that we are twice as rich in material output as our parents, four times as rich as our grandparents, perhaps ten times richer than our Pilgrim forebears. Why then are we not twice, four, ten times as contented, satisfied, happy as they? Is it possible that growth is a process that somehow fails to offer deep and lasting satisfactions? If so, why?

THE DISBENEFITS OF GROWTH: EXTERNALITIES

We can only speculate , but speculations are better than not thinking. So let us begin by calling attention to one reason for the disappointing effects of growth. It is the possibility that *growth is the cause of many externalities* with unpleasant attributes.

In that chapter, we simply assumed the externalities were "there." Now we must recognize that many of them are the direct consequence of growth itself. The smoke, the virulent chemicals, the noise, the poisonous run-offs that make modern life disagreeable and even dangerous are all side effects of the industrial processes on which growth has depended. One reason why material growth fails to bring equal gains in well-being is that we add up the gains from growth but omit the losses it inflicts.

FAMILIARITY AND CONTEMPT

A second reason has less to do with the disutilities that flow from growth-generating processes, than with the utilities that the products of growth give us.

A new product is brought onto the market—let us say the first telephone. It is a source of excitement, wonder, joy. We are acutely conscious of the gain in well-being the flows from this miraculous instrument. We are able to talk with a sick friend; we close a business deal in a few seconds; our sense of well-being expands along with our gain in material possessions.

But now a few years pass. We are used to the telephone; we take it for granted. We call a sick friend and get a busy signal; we lose a business deal because our phone is out of order; the constant ringing of the phone is a nuisance, an interruption; we wish we could get rid of the thing, but we cannot.

This process of an initial surge, followed by a gradual decline in utilities, seems to be a common fact of life. It is probably true for total income as well as for individual goods: we are happy for a while if our income rises, then we get used to the new level and take it for granted. A cut in income that left us *above* our previous level would leave us much less happy than we formerly were.

What we encounter here is a more dynamic version of the notion of "wants" than economic theory deals with, but possibly a truer one. If our marginal utility curves are constantly moving leftward, as we become familiar with new goods or with higher levels of income, it follows that the gains in satisfaction from increasing our material wealth may be great—but will be short-lived.

MONEY AND HAPPINESS

There is still a third possible reason why growth has failed to bring a sense of increased well-being proportionate to the increase in wealth. "For most Americans," writes economist Richard Easterlin, "the pursuit of happiness and the pursuit of money come to the same thing. More money means more goods (inflation aside), and this means more of the material benefits of life." But, Easterlin asks, "What is the evidence on the relation between money and happiness? Are the wealthier members of society usually happier than the poorer? Does raising the incomes of all increase the happiness of all?"[1]

Easterlin has assembled data on the relation between wealth and happiness from some 30 surveys conducted in 19 developed and underdeveloped countries. The results are interesting—and paradoxical. In all societies, more money for the individual *is* reflected in a greater degree of happiness reported by the individual. However—and here is the paradox—raising the incomes of all does not increase the happiness of the entire society!

THE PARADOX OF WEALTH

How can we explain this paradox? Let us first examine the findings of the surveys. In every one of thirty separate surveys (eleven within the United States between 1946 and 1970; nineteen in other countries, including three communist nations), happiness was positively correlated with income. For ex-

[1]Richard Easterlin, "Does Money Buy Happiness?" *The Public Interest* (Winter, 1973).

ample, in a survey conducted among American families in December 1970, not much more than one-quarter of those in the lowest income group (under $3,000 per year) described themselves as being "very happy," whereas about half the members of the highest group (over $15,000) reported that they were "very happy." Moreover, in each intermediate income group, the proportion of "very happy" people rose steadily.

This is an impressive statistical association, although as Easterlin points out, we have to be careful that we are not dealing with "wrong-way causation" (Chap. 18, p. 302). It could be that "happier" people owe their good fortune to factors such as a better state of health or perhaps "better genes" and that their superior health or genetic endowments enable them to *make* more money. There is no doubt that some of the association between income and happiness comes from this causal relation. But another bit of evidence allows us to retain considerable confidence in the original hypothesis that money "causes" happiness. When individuals in all income groups are questioned about the reasons for their happiness or unhappiness, they typically mention three factors: family relations, health, and economic concerns. By removing one major source of worry—economic concerns—and by alleviating the problem of coping with ill-health, money can be a direct source of happiness in itself.

RELATIVE WEALTH

If this is the case, then should it not follow that the wealthier a nation becomes, the higher will be its sum total of happiness? Should we not expect to find that the overall proportion of persons calling themselves "very happy" would rise significantly as the real incomes of all groups in the nation rise?

As we have already learned, this is *not* the answer. In fact, jumping to that conclusion is another instance of the fallacy of composition—assuming that what is true for the individual must be true for society as a whole. According to the survey data, Easterlin writes, "Rich countries are not typically happier than poorer ones." Moreover, in the one nation—the United States—in which we can make comparisons over time, we find that the "profile" of happiness was not much different in 1970 from what it had been in the late 1940s, even though real income per capita, after allowance for taxes and inflation, was over 60 percent higher.

How can we explain this paradoxical outcome? The answer seems to lie in the way people estimate their degree of material well-being. They do not measure their income or possessions starting from zero. Instead, people evaluate their place on the scale of wealth by *comparing themselves with others*. Thus it is not our "absolute" level of material well-being but our relative level that determines whether or not we feel "rich" or "poor." That relative level of well-being, in turn, depends on the distribution of income; and income distribution, as we know, is slow to evidence major shifts.

WEALTH AND VALUES

This situation has two major consequences for our own society. One is that poverty, with its associated unhappiness, cannot be eradicated by simply raising the incomes of the bottom portion of the population along with those of everyone else. The families that make up the bottom groups will continue to feel "poor" and therefore unhappier than the well-to-do. *Only a change in the pattern of income distribution could be expected to eliminate the feeling of poverty and its associated unhappiness.* By the same consequence, however, a more equal distribution of income would reduce the feeling of being "rich" and its associated happiness! Whether a nation with a more equal distribution of income

would be "happier," en masse, therefore depends on our value judgments—specifically on the relative importance we would assign to an increase in the happiness of the bottom groups and a decrease in the happiness of top groups.

Second, Easterlin's conclusions suggest that we are locked in a "hedonic treadmill." We are all engaged in an effort to acquire wealth, in the expectation that it will bring happiness; but unlike the race in *Alice in Wonderland,* the race for wealth has all winners but no prizes. Does this have something to do with the chronic feeling of dissatisfaction—the complaints about the "rat race"—that are so much a part of our culture?

THE NEGLECT OF WORK

Another possibility is that growth has brought a change in the nature of the "felt work experience" that has added disutilities that largely offset the utilities of added income.

Objectively, it seems that most work experience has become easier during the last hundred years. The rigors and horrors of early industrial capitalism have largely vanished; the work day is shorter; the tasks we do are less dirty or dangerous. But with the rise in income has also come a change in aspirations and expectations. Conditions that would have been regarded as a great improvement a generation ago are as much taken for granted as the new commodities we first yearn for and then toss on the dust heap. Work becomes an experience that we no longer uncomplainingly accept, but that we regard critically. And we do not seem to like what we see.

Economics pays little heed to the felt experience of work. It concentrates on our welfare as consumers, much less on our welfare as producers. It describes as a "rising standard of living" the increasing flow of goods and services we consume, but does not pay much heed to the "standard of work experience" in the factory and office, with its machine-like pace, its clock-regulated rhythms.

This is because economics assumes that the end of economic activity is consumption. But suppose the end is production? Suppose that the main "output" of an economy were considered not the quality of its goods but the quality of its working life? Then the growth in output might be almost irrelevant to the feelings of well-being of a society.

SOCIAL BALANCE

Consider one last possibility. *It is that our well-being lags behind our growth in output because we are producing the wrong output.* We are piling up mountains of toothpaste while we ignore the possibility of providing dental care to those who cannot afford it. We are "growing" in terms of military output but not in terms of the output of public housing. Thus, we are disappointed in the effects of growth because we do not even begin to live up to the ideal of an economy in which the marginal utility of expenditures for all purposes is equal.

This state of affairs comes about for two reasons. First, the market caters to wealth, not need, obeying the demands that emanate from the existing distribution of income.

Thus growth caters to the marginal utilities of those consumers whose total utilities are already much more "saturated" than those consumers who cannot fulfill their utilities through purchasing power.

Second, our society has a very imperfect means (if indeed any at all) of judging the marginal satisfactions of collective consumption versus private consumption. John Kenneth Galbraith has described our society as one of "private affluence and public squalor." To the extent that this is true, growth fails to yield proportionate satisfactions because it lacks "social balance"; that is, a condition in which marginal utilities of expenditures for all purposes have been brought to equality.

GROWTH AND WELL-BEING

These speculations and hypotheses are difficult to test empirically (perhaps with the exception of Easterlin's findings), but they offer plausible reasons for the widely shared feeling that material growth does not yield proportionate increments in satisfaction. If true, they also suggest that growth could bring more satisfaction if means were found to eliminate some of the causes of its failure to do so.

In particular it seems reasonable to assume that the gap between output and satisfaction could be narrowed *to some extent* if we took pains to minimize the externalities associated with growth, including not least, the experience of work; if we lessened the unequal distribution of income; and if we strove for a distribution of output that tried to equalize the marginal utilities of private and public output.

Such a task is a political rather than an economic one. The estimation of marginal utilities belongs to the sphere of value judgments, where the economist bows to the political decision-making process by which societies express their preferences. But the economic considerations we have raised may help us formulate those values more thoughtfully than if we simply assume that growth, in and of itself, will bring a sense of well-being along with an increase in material wealth. Perhaps the ultimate faith of all social science is that thoughtfulness and knowledge can ultimately bring their rewards in the quality of life we experience.

The Limits to Growth

We have been considering the question of why growth yields so much less net utilities than its gross utilities—a question that asks us to reconsider the assumption that "more is always better." But we have kept until last a much more fundamental question. It is whether growth, in the form in which we have experienced it, is a process that can be maintained much longer. Good or bad, growth has been the central tendency of our society for well over two centuries. Now we must ask whether the end to that tendency lies ahead.

MATERIAL CONSTRAINTS

Growth of the kind that has characterized the history of capitalism and of industrial socialism is a process that converts the raw materials of the planet into commodities that men use for their consumption or for further production. Thus along with growth has come a steady rise in the volume of raw materials that man has extracted from the planet, and an even more rapid increase in the energy he has harnessed, both for the extraction and the processing of those raw materials.

A continuation of growth therefore depends on the continuing availability of the raw materials and energy essential for expanded industrial production. What is the outlook for these resources for the future?

Table 17·1 shows a recent estimate of the number of years that presently known and estimated future resources would supply us at present growth rates.

TABLE 17·1
Global Resource Availability

Resource	Years of global resource availability at present growth rates	
	If present resources stocks are used	If resource stocks are quintupled
Aluminum	31	55
Coal	111	150
Copper	21	48
Iron	93	173
Lead	21	64
Manganese	46	94
Natural gas	22	49
Petroleum	20	50
Silver	13	42
Tin	15	61
Tungsten	28	72

Source: Meadows, et al., *The Limits to Growth* (Washington, D.C.: Potomac Associates, 1972).

The figures are sobering, to say the least. Yet we must be careful before we take them

THE EXPONENTIAL FACTS OF LIFE

Exponential growth is a startling phenomenon. It is illustrated in the famous parable about the farmer who has a lily pond in which there is a single lily that doubles its size each day. Suppose that after a year the pond is completely covered. How long did it take for the pond to be *half* covered? The answer is—364 days. In the last day the doubling lily will completely fill the pond.

Exponential examples such as these must always be used with great care. This is because their mathematical logic does not take into effect the feedback mechanisms that inhibit the explosive behavior of exponential series. Long before the lily covered half the pond it would prob-

ably have used up the nutrient matter in the pond and ceased growing. Long before the horrendous projections of exponential population growth, in which human beings will stand on one another's shoulders in a few centuries, feedbacks would have slowed down or halted or reversed population trends. Exponential trends show the *potential* growth of variables, but this potential is rarely realized.

One last point. There is a convenient way of figuring how long it takes for any quantity to double, if we know its exponential growth rate. *It is to divide the growth rate into the number 70.* Thus if population is growing at 2 percent a year, it will double in 35 years ($70 \div 2$). If the growth rate rises to 3 percent, the doubling time drops to 23+ years ($70 \div 3$).

---

at face value. First, the *presently known reserves include only those deposits of minerals that are available with today's technology.* They do not include minerals that exist in levels of concentration that are not "economic"; that is, too costly to utilize with existing techniques. But techniques change, and with them, the volume of "economic" resources. Consider the fact that taconite, the main source of iron today, was not even considered a resource in the days when the high-grade ores of the Mesabi Range provided most of our ore.

In some cases, such as oil, economic resources may be exhausted within a relatively short time. But in general, resources probably exist in quantities sufficient to support industrial growth for centuries, especially if we consider the gigantic amounts of minerals locked into the earth's crust or present in "trace amounts" in its seas. Given the technology and the energy, we could literally "mine the seas and melt the rocks" to provide ourselves with "unlimited" resources. Moreover, the necessary technology does not seem impossible to attain. Much of it already lies within the frontier of scientific knowledge.

THE EXPONENTIAL PROBLEM

This reassuring consideration must, however, be balanced against two less assuring facts. The first is that the rate of use of resources rises with frightening rapidity because growth is an *exponential* process. Today, global industrial output is rising at about 7 percent a year, thereby doubling every 10 years. If we project this rate of growth for another fifty years, it follows that the rate of use of resources would have doubled five times (assuming that today's technology of industrial production is essentially unchanged). Thus 50 years hence we would need 32 times as large a volume of material inputs as today. A century hence, when output would have doubled ten times, we would need over a thousand times the present volume of output —and this gargantuan volume of extraction would still be relentlessly doubling.

Does this mean that we will run out of resources? We are constantly making resources, learning to use less concentrated forms of minerals and finding wholly new materials, such as plastics. Thus we may be able to expand our supply of resources exponentially, along with our use of them.

THE TECHNOLOGICAL FACTOR

All this, however, requires the appropriate technology. It is one thing to mine the seas and the rocks on paper, and another to move and refine the millions of tons of water and earth in fact. Where will we get the energy to undertake these huge labors? It is one thing to run a nuclear fusion plant on paper; another to bring it on stream. (No controllable fusion process yet exists, except in the most advanced laboratories.)

Thus we are essentially engaged in a race between technology and the exponentially rising demands for raw materials. Technology enters this race in many ways. It may enable us to recycle existing wastes, so that we do not need to extract as much new materials. It may enable us to get more usable resources from a given quantity of raw material. It may open up new modes of production that enable us to shift production techniques away from materials that are becoming scarce (and therefore expensive), to those that remain abundant and therefore cheap. It gives us new sources of energy that enable us to use materials that are now too "low grade" for economic production.

One primary question in estimating the "limits" to growth is therefore the rate at which we will develop the appropriate technology. Unfortunately, the link between research and development and economically usable technology is not clearly understood. We do not really know whether we will find an appropriate technology to permit us, for example, to run a vast private automobile fleet in the year 2000, or whether we will be able to turn out the high quality steels in the volume that would support industrialization on a global scale fifty years hence. More important, we do not know if a technology that permitted us to "mine the seas and melt the rocks" will be perfected—or whether such a technology would be compatible with other ecological and environmental considerations.

THE HEAT PROBLEM

Here we reach another problem of great importance. To extract resources on the scale required to sustain industrial growth on its present path will require the application of tremendous amounts of energy. But the production of this energy, if it uses the combustion of conventional fuels or nuclear power (including fusion power) is associated with the generation of heat. This man-made heat is the most serious environmental barrier we face.

Today the amount of heat that all our man-made energy adds to the natural heat of the sun falling on our atmosphere is trivial. But the exponential increase in this man-made heat would sooner or later pose an insurmountable problem. As two well-known economists have written:

Present emission of energy is about 1/15,000th of the absorbed solar flux. But if the present rate of growth continued for 250 years, emissions would reach 100% of the absorbed solar flux. The resulting increase in the earth's temperature would be about 50°—a condition totally unsuitable for human habitation. [1]

DOOMSDAY?

Projections such as these easily give rise to Doomsday attitudes, beliefs that we are racing hell-bent on an unalterable disaster course. This is not what economists who are concerned about the growth problem have in mind. As we have already indicated, the technology required to keep us on the present growth path may not materialize in time, thereby averting or postponing for a long period a climatic catastrophe. Sources of energy such as solar power generators or wind machines may utilize the existing heat and energy in the atmosphere to provide us with sub-

[1] Robert U. Ayres and Allen V. Kneese, *Economic and Ecological Effects of a Stationary State*, (Washington, D.C.: Resources for the Future). Reprint No. 99 (December 1972), p. 16.

stantial amounts of power that do not pour man-made heat into the air. Most important of all, a shift in the direction of economic effort away from the encouragement of wasteful industrial growth, toward the growth of services or collective consumption goods (mass transit in place of automobiles), may greatly reduce our need to increase our energy inputs.

For all these and still other reasons, a Doomsday attitude is not warranted. But that is not the same thing as saying that an attitude of extreme caution about "limitless" industrial growth is also not warranted. On the contrary, *it seems likely that industrial growth, with its heavy dependency on resources and man-made energy, cannot continue indefinitely.* If the technology of industry does not change substantially, the threshold of a dangerous degree of climatic change would be reached in less than 150 years. At that point, growth would have to cease immediately. In all likelihood, the warnings of scientists or the difficulties of sustaining growth or ecological side effects will impose a rein on industrial expansion considerably before that time, although it is impossible to specify time horizons with any degree of assurance.

ZERO GROWTH?

Thus the long-term outlook for industrial societies implies that very low or zero industrial growth lies ahead. But here it is very important to recognize that even zero industrial growth in itself is not an answer to all problems. *A zero growth society may still pollute the atmosphere.* It may still be adding unacceptable amounts of heat or other harmful wastes, even though the flow of those pollutants into the air is not increasing over time. Thus zero industrial growth is not an end in itself, any more than positive growth was an acceptable end in itself. Zero growth is useful only insofar as it leads to *zero pollution,* including heat pollution.

From this, another conclusion follows. A society may still enjoy a growth in output if that output does not contribute to pollution. A society that draws its powers from the wind and tides and sun can safely enlarge its volume of energy. A society that increases its technical efficiency, perhaps by recycling, can permit growth to occur if that growth will not be ecologically harmful. As we have many times emphasized, a society .that seeks to grow through the enrichment of the *quality* of output need not impinge on the constraints of ecological safety.

Problems of Slow Growth

Can a zero pollution society be attained? We do not know. Probably some pollution is inescapable under any system of production, certainly under an industrial system. Thus even though zero industrial growth is not a sufficient condition to bring us to (or near) a zero pollution society, *the probabilities are great that a very low pollution society would be a society in which the rate of growth of industrial output was also very low.* It might in fact be a negative rate—a decline in industrial output being compensated by a rise in service outputs.

GLOBAL INEQUALITY

Two problems must be squarely faced if we contemplate the consequences of such a very slow-growing economy. The first has to do with the unequal distribution of income (and resources) among the nations of the world. The underdeveloped nations today "enjoy" standards of living that are far below even the poorest levels in the advanced countries. Thus the prospect of an enforced slowdown in the rate of industrial output raises the specter of *an international struggle for resources,* as the poor countries attempt to build up the framework of modern industrial structures, and the developed nations continue along their present course.

The question of an impending limit to industrial growth therefore poses a major economic problem for international relations. How are the remaining easily available resources of the world to be shared? As the advanced nations continue to build up their industrial systems, will they leave the underdeveloped regions on a permanently lower level of well-being? Our analysis poses this fundamental question, but cannot answer it.

STATIONARY CAPITALISM?

Second, we must ask whether a very slow rate of industrial growth—not to mention a zero or negative rate—is compatible with capitalism. As economists from Adam Smith through Karl Marx down to the present day have pointed out, such a "stationary state" would pose very great difficulties for a capitalist system. As expansion ceased, competition among enterprises would lead to a falling rate of profit. This would directly undercut the main source of income of the capitalist class. Worse, the cessation of net investment might set into motion a downward spiral of incomes and employment that would plunge capitalism into severe depression.

Could capitalism be rescued from this fate by a much larger volume of public spending that would not add to environmental danger? Could it give up industrial expansion in exchange for programs of education, the arts, greatly improved care for the old and the very young? Could it manage the political problem of income distribution in a situation in which the growth of material output was very small, or in which material output per capita actually fell because of the demands of the underdeveloped countries?

Once again, we do not know. The impending environmental pressures surely indicate that major changes will be needed to make the economic system of the still distant future compatible with environmental constraints. Whether capitalism can make that adjustment—or whether industrial socialism can make it better—are questions that our analysis raises, but cannot answer.

A SPACESHIP ECONOMY

What is certain, however, is that *all* industrial systems, socialist as well as capitalist, will sooner or later have to change their attitudes toward growth.

For in the long run there is no alternative to viewing the earth itself as a spaceship (in Kenneth Boulding's phrase) to whose ultimately finite carrying capacity its passengers must adjust their ways. From this point of view, production itself suddenly appears as a "throughput," beginning with the raw material of the environment and ending with the converted material of the production process, which is returned to the environment by way of emissions, residuals, and so on. In managing this throughput, the task of producers is not to maximize "growth," but to do as little damage to the environment as possible during the inescapable process of transformation by which man lives. If "growth" enters man's calculations in this period of rationally controlled production, it can be only insofar as he can extract more and more "utility" from less and less material input; that is, as he learns to economize on the use of the environment by recycling his wastes and by avoiding the disturbance of delicate ecological systems.

Such a spaceship economy is probably still some distance off, although by no means so far away that our children or grandchildren may not encounter its problems. Much depends on the rate at which the Third World grows in population and productivity and on the technological means of lessening pollution in the advanced countries. Not least, a true spaceship earth would require a feeling of international amity sufficiently great so that the industrialized peoples of the world would willingly acquiesce in global production ceilings that penalized them much more severely than their poorer sister nations.

These longer perspectives begin to make us aware of the complexity of the problem of growth. Growth is desperately needed by a world that is, in most nations, still desperately poor. Yet, growth is already beginning to threaten a world that is running out of "environment." If growth inevitably brings environmental danger, we shall be faced with a cruel choice indeed. Today we have only begun to recognize the problems of pollution-generating growth, and we are engaged in devising remedies for these problems on a national basis. Ahead lies the much more formidable problem of a world in which growth may encounter ecological barriers on a worldwide scale, bringing the need for new political and economic arrangements for which we have no precedent. The true Age of Spaceship Earth is still some distance in the future, but for the first time the passengers on the craft are aware of its limitations.

KEY WORDS

CENTRAL CONCEPTS

1. This chapter is concerned with three main problems: the *stability* of the growth process; the relation between growth and the *quality of life;* and the *limits* to growth.

Potential output

Growth gap

2. We must distinguish between actual output—GNP—and *potential output*, or potential GNP. The latter is the output available from the full utilization of the growing stock of labor and capital. The difference between potential and actual output is the *growth gap.*

Marginal capital-output ratio.

3. *The problem of a high steady rate of growth is to match our increase in capacity with an equal increase in purchasing power.* Increases in capacity depend on the *marginal capital-output ratio*, σ, which describes the relationship between an increase in the stock of capital and the increased flow of output from that new stock. Increases in demand result from the multiplier, which magnifies the income effect of a *rise* in investment.

Balanced growth
$\Delta I/s$
I/σ

4. *Balanced growth* occurs when the increase in purchasing power ($\Delta I \times 1/s$) is equal to the increase in capacity (I/σ). This formulation suggests a basic problem. There is no inherent mechanism to balance the critical terms $\Delta I/s$ and I/σ.

Quality of life
Externalities

5. A second major problem relates to growth and the *quality of life.* Why do we not seem to enjoy increases in well-being proportional to those in income and output? One hypothesis is that *externalities*, which yield pervasive disutilities, are integrally connected with the process of growth.

Diminishing utilities

6. A second hypothesis is that the utilities we derive from new products—or from additional income—rapidly diminish as we become accustomed to these new goods. *The gain in utilities from growth is real but short-lived.*

Happiness and relative incomes

7. A third hypothesis is the empirical evidence that the happiness that increased incomes brings is related to *our relative position on the income scale.* As all get richer, but the hierarchy of incomes is unchanged, we do not all feel "happier."

Social balance

8. Last is the possibility that our *social balance* is very far removed from the ideal of a society in which marginal utilities of all expenditures are equal. This is partly the consequence of existing income distribution, partly of a lack of any

Criteria for well-being and growth

mechanism for estimating the marginal utilities of collective consumption vs. private consumption.

9. All this suggests the need for different criteria if growth is to bring more well-being and more material wealth. Specifically, society must take into account the disutilities it has formerly ignored, must seek a better social balance among the kinds of output in which it is realized, and should seek to minimize the hierarchies of income distribution that vitiate the gains from improving one's actual material position.

Exponential growth

10. The last and most serious problem concerns the *limits to growth*. Here the problem is to match our *exponential* rate of resource use with ample supplies of materials and energy.

Technology and resource availability

11. It is possible that *technology may make available much larger reserves of resources than now exist or may allow us to use resources much more efficiently. The principal long-run problem here is the heat pollution that combustion (including nuclear energy) adds to the atmosphere.*

Heat pollution
Doomsday predictions

12. Doomsday predictions of a catastrophic collapse due to resource exhaustion or pollution must be treated with great care. However, the facts of resource exhaustion and heat pollution warn us that *present-day industrial growth cannot continue indefinitely.*

13. Zero industrial growth, however, is not a sufficient condition for environmental safety. *Zero pollution is the necessary objective.*

Zero growth vs. zero pollution
Stationary state

14. Zero pollution would probably imply slower rates of industrial growth. This will bring *severe problems for the international distribution of wealth and may pose major problems for capitalism in a stationary state.*

QUESTIONS

1. What is meant by the marginal capital-output ratio? Is it connected with behavior? Do you think it is susceptible to social control?

2. Write the formula for changes in capacity and for changes in income. Show algebraically the conditions under which increased income matches increased output.

3. What is the difference between our original "demand gap" and a growth gap? Explain how the remedy in one case is a given amount of investment; in the other, a *change in the rate of growth* of investment.

4. Do you think it would be possible to establish empirically the change in well-being, as contrasted with income? Could we use social indicators for this purpose? Do you think that statistics on health, longevity, crime rates, etc., shed light on this matter? Surveys on "happiness"?

5. What externalities can you think of that are a direct consequence of growth?

6. Do you think the conditions of work have deteriorated? Has factory labor become more onerous or less during the last 50 years? What about commuting? What role do expectations play in the *experience* of work?

7. What value judgments are implicit in the suggestion that growth might be associated with greater well-being if the criteria suggested in the text were followed?

8. How would you go about measuring the amount of iron ore "available"? At what level of concentration would you draw the line?

9. Why does the process of combustion add heat to the atmosphere but not the utilization of wind power?

10. Is a stationary state (i.e., a state without economic growth) without environmental effects? Describe ways in which we would have growth without environmental deterioration.

11. What policies do you think should be followed to avoid a severe environmental threat to industrial society?

12. Do you think that *global* growth control is a realistic goal today? If not, what do you foresee as the long-run scenario of world economics and politics?

An Introduction to Statistics and Econometrics

18

STATISTICS ARE CENTRAL to the study of economics. Why? Because economics, more than any other social science, involves things that can be counted, concepts that can be quantified, activities that can be measured. Prices, wages, GNP itself, as we have learned, all express our ability to quantify certain aspects of social activity. This ability to quantify is often essential to our ability to analyze and control. The GNP accounts, invented in the 1930s, made it possible to develop macroeconomics. Without these accounts, only fuzzy impressionistic statements could be made about macroeconomic activity, just as only vague statements could be made about the velocity of money before we could actually measure output (see p. 217). If we could quantify "utility," we could measure welfare far better than we now do.

Hence an economist is constantly using statistics and *econometrics,* a branch of economics that combines statistical techniques with economic theory. To understand the techniques of statistics or econometrics you must learn much more than we are going to teach in this chapter. This is most emphatically not a mini-course that will substitute for a thorough study of both, but we hope that it will pave the way for further study by taking away some of the mystery surrounding the use and compilation of the numbers on which economics depends.

WHAT THIS CHAPTER IS ABOUT

You will find this longish chapter divided into eight sections, really eight sub-chapters. The first of them has to do with some over-all *cautions and warnings.* It is easy to read and does not involve any "work," unless you call learning something useful "work." Everyone should take its message to heart. Statistics are indispensable for economics, but they are also the source of much trouble for the unwary amateur.

Section II is about *Distributions and Averages.* These are concepts we use every day, as economists or in everyday life. If ever there was a word loaded with problems, it is that deceptive word *average.* This is a section that will richly repay study, and it is basically easy to master.

Section III is about *Price Indexes.* This is a more specialized subject, into which we have already looked very briefly (p. 12). It takes a little calculation to work through the construction of a price index, but the results are worth the effort, especially if you are thinking of taking further courses in economics. Then you will really have to understand "weighting" and how to convert a price index in current dollars into one in constant dollars.

Section IV is about *Sampling,* a tremendously important subject for anyone interested in empirical research. We can give you only a general idea of the often complex considerations involved in sampling, but we hope you will emerge from these few pages with a much better understanding of the general problems of sampling than you probably had before you began.

Section V brings us to econometrics and specifically to *Functions.* We have already had an introduction to functional relationships in Chapter 2, but the subject is so useful that a careful review of the field is worthwhile, particularly since functions lie at the heart of econometrics.

This brings us to *Correlations and Regression,* section VI. Here is the core of econometrics. Part of the section, about regressions, introduces you to the general notion of the techniques of one very important branch of functional analysis. It does

not try to teach you how to make an actual regression analysis, but it should make clear what you are trying to do when you sit down with a desk calculator or use a computer to work out the complex formulae of econometric analysis.

Section VII is perhaps even more important. It is a series of warnings about the meaning of *causation and correlation.* In particular, it alerts you against easy conclusions that such-and-such is the "cause" of so-and-so, just because the arithmetic "looks right." Everyone ought to look at this section, even if you have only the haziest notion of how you go about finding a "least squares" coefficient.

From here we go to section VIII, *Forecasting.* As we said in Chapter 2, prediction is one of the most important—and troublesome—aims of economic analysis. Our brief review will serve to remind you of these problems before you find yourself forecasting on the basis of flimsy data or uncertain premises.

We don't suggest that you sit down to read this chapter as a single lesson. Use it as a reference source. Perhaps you have already looked into it, when the text suggested you look ahead into certain pages. Or read it in short takes, section by section, to get a feeling for the field of statistics and econometrics. If the chapter dispels some of the fog surrounding that field and tempts you to take a course in statistics, it will have amply served its purpose.

I. Some Initial Cautions

QUALITY VS. QUANTITY

We should immediately clear up two misconceptions about statistics. The first might be called "statistics worship." It finds expression in the view that if you can't count something, it doesn't count. The second is just the opposite. It scoffs at statistics because all the important things in life are qualitative and therefore can't be measured.

Both of these *are* misconceptions, and it is important to understand why. The statistics worshipper must realize that before anyone can count anything, he must *define* it, and that definition is ultimately an act of judgment, not measurement. And the statistics scoffer must realize that before he can bring his reason to bear on social problems involving good and evil, he must have at least some notion of how *large* a good or evil he is concerned with.

Take as an illustration the problem of poverty. When Professor Galbraith wrote *The Affluent Society* in 1958, he said that one family in thirteen in America was poor. By current official statistics, one in seven is poor. Does that mean that a larger fraction of Americans are poor today? Of course not. The answer is that today the United States statistical authorities' *definition* of poverty is different from the definition used by Galbraith, so that the "growing" percentage of the poor reflects nothing more than a changing conception of what poverty means.

Thus, the extent of poverty in America is a quantitative measure founded on a qualitative definition, and the person who places a blind faith in the "facts" must remember that many of these facts change as our definition of social problems change. But isn't that just the point, asks the statistical skeptic. Since definition is everything, the problem of poverty boils down in the end to what we *think* poverty is. What is important is not what the numbers tell us, but our moral judgments from which the numbers emerge.

Of course it is true that definitions *do* come first, but they establish the unit or yardstick by which we measure the problem. Poverty may rise or fall in America if we use an unchanged yardstick. It can also rise or fall because we change its definition. But once we have made that choice of the yardstick, we use the definition to learn the magnitude of the problem *as we have defined it*. For until we know its magnitude as measured by the *same* yardstick, we cannot know how serious a problem it is, much less determine what action will be needed to remedy it.

PATTERNS OF MOVEMENT

Often, as with poverty, *the pattern of movement is as important as, or even more important than, the absolute value of the variable.* If poverty is rapidly diminishing, we may need a set of public programs very different from those needed if it seems to persist. So, too, with other measured magnitudes, such as GNP. Is GNP rising or falling, and how fast? It is no accident that most discussions of GNP in different countries tend to focus on comparative rates of growth. Changes in GNP (per capita) are probably a better measure of changes in economic welfare within a country than are efforts to measure the absolute level of GNP in one nation and to compare it with another.

Unemployment presents a similar problem. Different countries define unemployment in different ways, and the seriousness of any given level of unemployment can often be determined only by comparing the current level with its historical path. For this reason, any new statistical series should be used with caution. Its usefulness cannot be determined until we see how it moves over time and under different circumstances.

Sometimes definitions themselves are important in determining the pattern of movement of economic variables. Sometimes they are not. One of the techniques for investigating the importance of different definitions is to see if they imply that the economy is changing in different ways. If Professor Galbraith's definition of poverty yielded a pattern of movement different from the official definition (suppose poverty was growing on one definition and falling on the other) then the movement of poverty is *sensitive* to its definition. If this were true, one would want to be extremely careful when discussing poverty.

THE PROBLEM OF DEFINITIONS

The second lesson follows from the first. Words are slippery, even when no arbitrary judgment is involved. Any maker or user of statistics must be exceedingly sure of the exact meaning of the terms being used. The words *family* or *household* can be very tricky, for a household can be a single person! Another example of a treacherous definition is the one for—of all things—*motor vehicles.* If you look up the data in the *Statistical Abstract,* and read the footnotes, you will see that a "motor vehicle" includes a mobile trailer home. The result is that the motor vehicle statistics overstate the production of vehicles if you think of these as cars and trucks, and that correspondingly, the statistics for real housing investment (in which mobile trailer homes are not included) understate the value of residential construction.

UPDATING SERIES

Numbers, perhaps even more than words, have a magical authority inherent in them, but that does not mean that either are necessarily correct, even from the most impeccable sources. People make honest mistakes in gathering statistics, or mistakes creep in because of the difficulties in compiling statistics, some of which we will learn about later.

Official figures, such as those for GNP can change from one edition of the *Statistical Abstract* to the next.

The reason is that many statistical series are refined and corrected as more complete data are collected, so that virtually all figures change until the "final" returns are in. Most economic statistics are necessarily based on fragmentary data and are gradually improved as fuller information is obtained. The latest statistics are *always* subject to revision and are often marked *prelim.,* or *est.,* to warn the reader that they will be subject to change. The changes are usually not large, but occasionally large enough to alter precise calculations based on earlier data.

At regular intervals, the various government offices concerned with the collection of statistical information bring out revised—sometimes drastically revised—series of data. These revisions not only establish new "bases" and "weights" for many indices (we will come to the meaning of these terms), but involve recalculation of many past series based on new concepts, on more sophisticated data-handling techniques, and so on. (One recent controversy, for example, concerns the problem of whether or not we have accurately measured the value of the private capital stock in the United States. Economist Robert Gordon has claimed that we have "mislaid" $45 billion of this stock by failing to make allowance for various government transactions, such as the very low prices at which some companies acquired plants built by the government during World War II and subsequently sold at nominal figures to private enterprise.*)

Of course no ordinary user of official statistics can be aware of all these pitfalls or can anticipate the revisions that may alter the numbers on which he is relying. An excess of

---

*See *American Economic Review,* June 1969, and rejoinder, *ibid.,* September 1970.

wariness would only paralyze the research that we must carry on with the only data we have at hand. But a healthy pinch of caution, allowing for moderate changes in the magnitudes at hand, has saved many a researcher from trying to prove a point by relying on very *small differences in magnitudes that may later disappear.*

MOUNTAINS OUT OF MOLEHILLS

The best recent example of misusing small differences is in the handling of the monthly reports on the rate of inflation. Monthly changes are multiplied by 12 to get the annual rate of inflation published in newspaper headlines. Let's assume that in one month the rate of inflation is 0.34 percent, and in the next month it is 0.36 percent. Since the Bureau of Labor and Statistics rounds its numbers to one place to the right of the decimal, these would be reported as a 0.3 percent increase and a 0.4 percent increase. When they are multiplied by 12, they yield a 3.6 percent rate

of inflation versus a 4.8 percent rate of inflation.

In fact, the initial difference is probably well within sampling error (see below). This means that the two numbers 0.34 and 0.36 may be the same; they only appear different because of the errors inherent in any process of measurement and sampling. As a result, one should not place too much weight on month-to-month changes, but look at the pattern of movement over several months.

VISUAL DECEPTIONS

Often visual devices are used to display statistical data. These are particularly subject to misleading interpretations. Let's say we are trying to chart a crime wave over time. We have two graphs, displaying exactly the same numbers, but on different scales. In the first graph, it looks as if there were little or no change in crime; the second looks as if there were a horrendous acceleration. Can you see the reason for the difference?

FIGURE 18 · 1
Visual deceptions

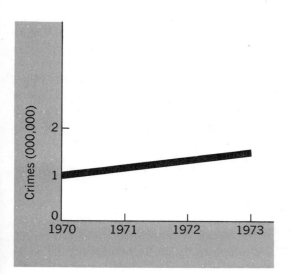

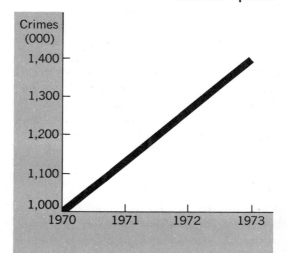

PERSPECTIVES ON DATA

Normally, the statistical "truth" about any phenomenon depends upon examining it from a number of different perspectives. Consider the much discussed question of the size of government in the U.S. economy. This is a matter we have already looked into in pp. 144ff., but it is worth reconsidering here as a general problem in statistics. The size of government will depend largely on how we define *government*. Do we mean federal government or federal plus state and local? Do we mean purchases of goods and services or all expenditures, including transfer payments? Just as a review of the difference that these definitions make, consider the following "measures" of government size:

	Percent of GNP, 1973
Federal expenditures	20
Federal state and local expenditures	31
All federal purchases	8
All government purchases	21

All these statistics accurately indicate something about the relationship of "government" and the size of the economy. The important thing, therefore, is to use the figures that are appropriate to the problem you are investigating. Are you interested in federal or total government activity? In production, purchases, or in expenditure? In the *uses* of production or expenditure? (In the last case, you will need more data, since the figures above do not show, for example, welfare vs. warfare; subsidies or public investment, etc.)

USES OF STATISTICS

These are very general warnings, but not to be taken lightly. More than one researcher has been in serious trouble because he didn't read the caption at the top of a table of figures or because he failed to check on the most recent compilations of data or because he was fooled by numbers that did not adequately reflect the changing nature of the problem he was trying to measure.

Now, at the end, a word to redress the balance. We have stressed skepticism toward statistics because the general attitude of the beginning student is generally one of blind acceptance. But too much skepticism is perhaps worse than none at all. *Carefully defined and collected data, clearly labeled and competently used, are the only way we have of measuring very important facets of our social activity.* This book would be impossible to write without statistics, and economics would be severely crippled if we could not rely on numerical magnitudes. Statistics really are an integral part of economics. The thing is to be wary of their weaknesses while appreciating their great virtues and absolute necessity.

II. Distributions and Averages

Distributions and averages are essentially statistical devices for viewing aggregate phenomena from different perspectives. For example, GNP measures total output. Sweden had an aggregate output of $39 billion in 1972; Spain had a GNP of $42 billion; the U.S. one of $1,118 billion. These numbers indicate something about the potential economic power of each country—although not very much, since Spain's ability to wage war, for example, is probably less than that of a nation such as Sweden. But even less do the numbers tell us about the amounts of goods and services that are available to typical people in each nation. To learn about this, GNP needs further examination.

MEANS

The simplest procedure is to divide total GNP by the total population to obtain the "average" GNP per person. We call this arithmetical average the *mean:* in the U.S. in 1972 it was $1,118 billion divided by 209 million individuals, or $5,353 per capita. In Sweden the per capita (mean) GNP was $4,749; in Spain, $1,221. In common usage this is what we usually have in mind when we use the word *average,* but to the statistician it is only one of several ways to give meaning to that very important word.*

MEDIANS

Means can be very misleading "averages." Suppose that one person or a very few people had virtually all the income, and the rest had very little (not so far from reality in a case like Pakistan). The mean income would then tell us very little about the income of an individual chosen at random. Hence, statisticians often use another definition of "average" called the *median.* As the word suggests, the median income is the income of the middle individual. If we lined up the population in order of income and selected the person who stood midpoint in the line, that person's income would be the median. Half the country would have smaller incomes; half larger.

ANOTHER CAUTION: CHOICE OF UNITS

Here is a good place to interject cautions about data and definitions, once more. If we were to calculate the median income of *individuals* in the United States, the answer would be zero! This is because more than half of all individuals have zero incomes. They are children, nonworking females, older retirees, and others. (You can see that it makes a difference if we choose "income" or "income plus transfers.") But it obviously

*Here is a problem in perspectives on data. If we want "average" GNP to tell us something about welfare, we probably don't want to use GNP as the measuring rod, because too much GNP becomes corporate or government end-product. Better to use an aggregate such as personal income.

makes no sense to say that the median individual in the U.S. had no income. Therefore, we focus on *family* income, on the assumption that all members of a family share equitably in the income received by the family as a whole. Actually that assumption is not true: children have much less purchasing power than adults; but it serves our general purposes to make this assumption, as long as we know that we are using the data in a special way.

MEANS AND MEDIANS

Is there a systematic difference between means and medians? There is: *medians are almost always smaller than means.* A moment's thought tells us that if the median income is $7,100, then the range of income in the poorer half of the population must be smaller than the range in the half that is richer; 50 percent of the population must receive between $1 and $7,100, and 50 percent between $7,100 and the income of the richest person in the country. *This asymmetry in the distribution of income is at the root of the difference between the two averages.*

A SIMPLE ILLUSTRATION

Perhaps the principle involved is clear to you by now. If not, an arithmetical example may help.

Assume that there are two towns, A and B, and that each consists of five families. The following table represents the distribution of income.

A	$4,000	$6,000	$7,000	$8,000	$10,000
B	$4,000	$6,000	$7,000	$8,000	$15,000

In each town, the median is $7,000, the income of the family in the middle. But notice that in town A, the distribution of income is symmetrical; that is, the median family is $1,000 away from the second and fourth families, and $3,000 away from the first and fifth families. Note, however, that this is not true of town B. The income of the top (fifth) family is much further away from the median than the income of the first family.

In town A, the median should be equal to the arithmetic mean. And, of course, it is: total income of $35,000 of town A divided by 5 equals $7,000. But in town B, because of the imbalance of income toward the wealthier side, the arithmetic mean is higher than the median: total income of $40,000 of town B divided by 5 equals $8,000. So the mean is $1,000 greater than the median in B.

In its way, town B is a highly simplified version of the country as a whole. If we lined up all the approximately 54 million families in the U.S., from poorest to richest, and picked the middle family—that is, the family with 27 million families on either side—our designated *median* household would have an income of $11,116. If instead, we added up the *incomes* of all families, in any order, and divided by 54 million, the resulting *mean* income would be $12,625.

SKEWNESS

This asymmetry in distribution is called *skewness,* a term we shall make use of subsequently. A quick way of grasping skewness is to plot data on a graph. For example, in Fig. 18·2, *A* and *B* show two hypothetical distributions, one skewed and one not. In both graphs we measure income along the horizontal axis and the number of families along the vertical axis.

The nonskewed distribution is shown in *A*, where we can see that the distribution of income is just the same on one side of the median as on the other. For example, if the median income is $8,000, we note that 5 million families have an income of $6,000 and that 5 million families have an income of $10,000, each income being the same $2,000 distance from the median figure.

This kind of unskewed frequency distribution is called a *bell-shaped curve* or a *normal* curve. Graph *B*, on the other hand, is skewed to the right. Suppose that $8,000 is the median income for this population. We

FIGURE 18 · 2
Normal and skewed distributions

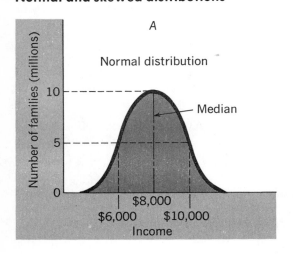

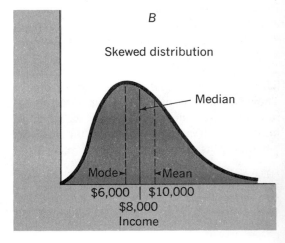

can see from the shape of the curve that there is no longer an even pairing of families on either side of this median. The incomes of the families on the right "tail" of the curve are further from the median than the incomes of those on the left "tail," and so the mean (the "old-fashioned" average) must be above the median (middle) income.

Here the mean, as we know from our definition above, is higher than the median (we suppose it to be $10,000 on the graph).

MODES

Furthermore, we can now speak of *another* kind of average, called a *mode,* which shows the particular income level on which there is the *largest number* of families. In our graph, this is represented by the figure of $6,000. Notice that in a bell-shaped distribution, the mode is the same as the median and the arithmetic mean, but this is true for only a normal, bell-shaped distribution.

WHICH AVERAGE TO USE?

If we want to express the average income in the United States, which average should we use? To know the complete truth, we would need to know the shape of the entire distribution of incomes, but we often need a summary measure. Ordinarily, we choose the median as the summary measure, because what we have in mind with the word *average* is indeed that income which is "middle-most." If we use the arithmetic mean, we distort the picture of the middle family, for we now show an amount of "average" income swollen by the presence of very large incomes at the upper end of the income register.

Sometimes, however, the mean is a better average than the median. This is the case when the distribution of income is approximately normal. Under these circumstances, the arithmetic mean has the advantage that it takes into account the *actual value* of the money incomes received by rich and poor families, whereas the median counts only the number of families on either side of the middle figure.

But bear in mind that in some kinds of distributions, the use of either average can be misleading. Say we had a country where 95 percent of the population received about $500, and the other 5 percent received more than $500, ranging up to $1 million. This is not unlike the situation in India. With such a violent skewness, we probably should use the *mode,* $500. It tells us more than either the mean or the median reveals about the distribution of income.

But suppose the upper 5 percent were all clustered around $10,000. Then we could separate the population into two main groups, one rich and one poor. Such a curve is likely to be *bimodal,* showing that a great many families cluster around one income level, and another group clusters around a wholly different level. We show such a bimodal distribution in Fig. 18·3, p. 288.

Statisticians are well aware of the difficulties of accurately representing such bimodal frequencies with "averages." Thus when you see well-conceived data that present averages—whether for IQs, academic grades, incomes, or other phenomena—you can be pretty confident that the data have only one mode and represent the kind of frequency distribution shown in Fig. 18·2.

III. Price Indexes

The problem of finding a useful way to represent "average" or typical incomes brings us to another problem when we want to reduce aggregate figures to their "real meaning." This has to do with price changes, a subject we are familiar with from our discussion in macroeconomics. In fact, in our first chapter of macroeconomics, pp. 12–13, we looked into the problem of how we change

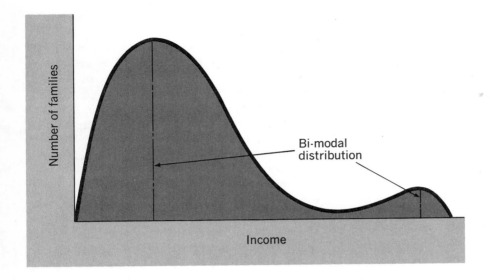

Bi-modal
distribution

FIGURE 18 · 3
Bi-modal
distribution

GNP in current dollars into GNP in constant dollars.

Here we want to investigate that problem a little more carefully. As we know, the device we use to discover changes in "real" purchasing power is a *price index*. There are many different kinds of price indexes, depending on what prices we want to measure: price indexes for wholesale commodities, for housing, for capital goods, for GNP.

Usually, when we try to discover changes in consumer well-being, we use the *Consumer Price Index,* constructed by the Department of Labor. It reflects the changing prices of a typical "market basket" of goods and services bought by an urban consumer over the period we want to investigate. By taking the prices in an initial or *base year* and the prices for the same commodities in other years, we arrive at a consumer price series, or an index of consumer purchasing power over that period.

BUILDING A PRICE INDEX

The idea of a price index is simple (although the actual statistical problems, such as collecting the data, are formidable). Let us quickly review the main steps.

Take an imaginary economy with only one consumer product, which we will call bread. Say that in the first year, which we will use as our base, bread sells for $2 per baker's dozen, and that in the second year its price is $4. What would the price index be for the second year? Elementary algebra gives us the answer:

$$\$2 \text{ is to } \$4 \text{ as } 100 \text{ is to } X$$

$$\frac{2}{4} = \frac{100}{x}$$

Solving by cross-multiplying, we get:

$$2x = 400$$
$$x = 200$$

Note that a price index is a percentage: in the above example, an index of 200 means that prices in that year are double the index (100) in the base year.

With 200 as our price index, we are now ready to compute real income in the second year in terms of base-year prices, just as we did earlier. Suppose a worker in a one-product economy was paid $5,000 the first year and $11,000 the second. What has happened to his real income? To find out, we divide this money income by the price index for that year, and then multiply the quotient by 100.

$$\frac{\$5,000}{100} \times 100 = \$5,000$$

(real income in Year 1)

$$\frac{\$11,000}{200} \times 100 = \$5,500$$

(real income in Year 2)

Thus, his real income has risen, but not by nearly so much as the sheer dollar increase indicates.

WEIGHTS

Now let's drop the assumption of a one-product economy and see what happens when there is more than one product. Assume an economy that consists of two products, bread and shoes. How would we compute a price index in this case?

Here we face a new problem. Before we can calculate *one* index for *two* products, we have to impute a proportional importance to each. For example, if more than half of consumer expenditures went for bread, then a doubling in its price would count more heavily than if the price of shoes doubled. The way we customarily deal with such a problem is *to take the amount of each product that the "typical" consumer purchased in the base year, and then compute the rise in living costs, under the assumption that the consumer will buy each product in the same proportion in succeeding years.*

Let us say that the consumer spent $100 in the base year and allotted the money in this way, between bread at $2 per unit and shoes at $10 per pair.

Product	No. units bought	×	Price	=	Total
Bread	35 dozen	×	$2	=	$70
Shoes	3 pairs	×	$10	=	$30
					$100

In the second year, the price of bread doubles to $4 and the price of shoes is cut in half to $5. If the consumer plans to buy the same number of units of each, then his new budget must look like this:

Product	No. units bought	×	Price	=	Total
Bread	35 dozen	×	$4	=	$140
Shoes	3 pairs	×	$5	=	$15
					$155

This gives us an aggregate expenditure for each year, from which we can compute the price index. Since it cost $100 to buy a typical basket of goods in the base year and $155 to buy *the same basket of goods* in the succeeding year, then the relevant index numbers are, of course, 100 and 155.

A more common way to go about this computation is *to derive "weights" from the proportional number of dollars spent on each product in the base year.* Since 70 percent of the typical consumer's money was spent on bread and 30 percent on shoes in 1967, the weights are .7 and .3, respectively.

In order to use the weights, however, we must first compute a separate price index for each product. For bread, which doubled in price, the index is 200 for the second year; for shoes, which halved in price, the index is 50. Now we multiply the index for each product by its corresponding weight and add up the results. For the base year:

Product	Index	×	Weight	=	Total
Bread	100	×	.7	=	70
Shoes	100	×	.3	=	30
					100

For the succeeding year:

Product	Index	×	Weight	=	Total
Bread	200	×	.7	=	140
Shoes	50	×	.3	=	15
					155

Again, our index numbers are 100 and 155.

Generally speaking, we assign weights by the value of purchases of the base year.* But what is more important is that the *same* weights must be used in the computation of each index number (or weights that are at least approximately the same). The consequences of doing otherwise are that an index number for one year would have little or no relation to an index number for another. If we are going to talk about fluctuations in a price level, then it must be a price level for the *same* basket of goods, as in the two products of our example, or for a basket of goods that is *relatively unchanging* in composition.

NEW GOODS

What do you do about the price of goods that do not exist in the base year? They have no base-year price. What price should they be multiplied by? There is no easy answer. Perhaps the good is a new product, such as a microwave oven, with an old function, cooking meals. In that case, government statisticians, in conjunction with an outside panel of experts, try to determine how much of the price of the new good reflects quality improvements and how much reflects price increases.

For example, suppose a conventional oven sold for $100 at the time the microwave oven was introduced at $150. Suppose further that the expert committee thought the microwave oven was 50 percent better than a conventional oven. Then the higher cost microwave oven would not show up as an increase in prices but as an increase in the quality of output. Each microwave oven produced would have the same effect on the real GNP as one and one-half conventional ovens; it would count as a $150 contribution to real GNP rather than a $100 contribution.

*For special purposes, there are also "chain indices," where weights are changed every year, as usage changes.

But suppose the committee thought that the microwave oven was *not* a quality improvement. Then each oven would show up as a $100 increase in the real GNP, just as conventional ovens. To the extent that people bought the higher price, but not higher quality microwave ovens, the prices of ovens in the GNP price indexes would go up, even though the price of conventional ovens did not change. In quality terms, you are being sold a conventional oven at a new higher price—$150.

NEW FUNCTIONS

But what can you do about products that serve completely new functions? Television sets were such an example. Since there was nothing to compare them with when they were introduced after World War II, these goods and services were evaluated at the prices for which they were first sold.

This creates a problem in measuring real growth. Most new goods are sold for very high prices when they are first introduced. Thereafter, their prices fall as they become mass produced and consumed. Let's assume that TV sets cost $500 when they were first sold in 1947. Each TV set produced would thus add $500 to the real GNP. If one million sets were produced in a year, this would add $500 million to the GNP. But let's now assume that the price of black-and-white sets fell to $100 and the government moved its base year forward to a year in which TVs cost only $100. Now the production of one million sets per year would add only $100 million to the real GNP, even though the same number had added $500 million when the government was using an earlier year as the base year.

This could be avoided by not moving the base year. But in that case the base year will rapidly become obsolete as new goods are introduced into the economy.

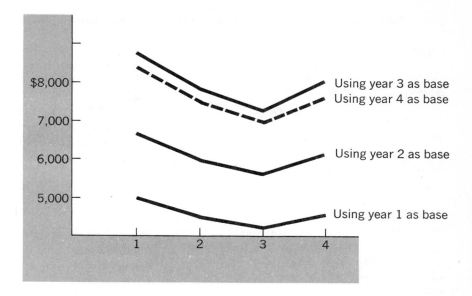

FIGURE 18·4
Shifting the base

As a result, corrections for price changes can be only an approximation of the truth. They should never be relied on "down to the last dollar" to make comparisons in real standards of living, especially if the periods being compared are widely separated in time. They are absolutely necessary to rid ourselves of the "money illusion," but they offer no more than thoughtful estimates—not precise measures—of what is happening to real standards of living over time.

APPLYING THE INDEXES

Constructing indexes is difficult; applying them is easy, and we have already given the basic rule on page 12. But let us review it for completeness.

Suppose that the results of research give us the following data:

Year	Income in current $	Price index
1	$5,000	60
2	6,000	80
3	7,000	100
4	8,000	105

It now becomes very simple to compute the changes in real income. We divide the income in current dollars in each year by the price index and multiply by 100. The answers are:

Year	Real income
1	$5,000 $\div$ 60 $\times$ 100 = $8,333
2	6,000 $\div$ 80 $\times$ 100 = 7,500
3	7,000 $\div$ 100 $\times$ 100 = 7,000
4	8,000 $\div$ 105 $\times$ 100 = 7,619

CHANGING THE BASE

Note that in this case the base year is year 3. Would it make a difference if the base year were 1 or 2? Obviously, the numbers would change. If year 1 were the base, then the "real income" in year 1 becomes $5,000 instead of $8,333. *But the relative changes over time would not be different.*

Suppose we graph the profile of real income, using each year in turn as a base. Figure 18·4 shows us that we have in fact only shifted the location of the series on the vertical scale. The *shape* of the real income series is not thereby affected.

SPLICING

Changing the base suggests that we can "splice" one time series, with a certain "base," onto another. Indeed, we can and do. As the statistical agencies "update" their bases to prevent them from becoming obsolete, they usually splice the old series onto the new, by recomputing it on the new base. The only problem here is one of interpretation. By splicing one series to another we can get charts that extend far into the past. They tend to make us forget the difficulties of making "real" corrections with which we have been concerned. Remember when you see a long time series that it has probably been spliced many times and that its apparent unbroken continuity very likely masks many difficult problems of statistical definition. Use such series with care!

IV. Sampling

Most economic data, such as family income, is collected with sampling techniques rather than complete enumeration. Few things are more disconcerting to someone who begins to work with such data than to be told that most of the "facts" which he correlates or uses are based on *samples*— that is, on figures derived from observing or counting not the entire set of objects in which he is interested, but only a fraction of that population, and often a very small fraction at that. How can the statistician presume to be telling us the exact story, the student asks, when he really knows only a part of it?

The question is a very important one. We should understand the answer, for it is true that most economic data *are* derived from samples. And yet it is also true that sampling can provide extraordinarily accurate information about "populations" that are not counted—or even *countable!* For example, during World War II, American and British statisticians estimated the totals for German war production by applying sampling methods to the serial numbers on captured equipment. After the war, many of their figures turned out to be just as accurate as the figures that the Germans compiled from the actual records of production itself. Moreover, the Allied figures were available sooner, since their method of counting took much less time.

THE LOGIC OF SAMPLING

What is the logic of sampling? It is based on a kind of reasoning that we use all the time. For example, we may complain that the streets in a city are dirty. Yet it is very unlikely that our complaint is based on an inspection of *all* the streets in the city or even a majority of them. Does this render our conclusion untrustworthy? It all depends. If we have seen a "fair" number of streets in all parts of the city, and all those we saw were dirty, we are quite justified in concluding that those we haven't seen would look much the same. But what is a "fair" number? What are the other criteria for selecting a sample that will enable us to generalize with a high degree of reliability about data that we have not observed?

SAMPLE SIZE

The first and most obvious requirement for a "fair sample" is its size. Yet, surprisingly, in making accurate statements based on samples, size turns out to be much less of a stumbling block than we might think. The U.S. Census Bureau, for example, on the basis of a sample of only about 5 percent of all families, gives a detailed and reliable description of the United States population. And if we want to study collections of data less complicated than those for the U.S. population, a sample much smaller than 5 percent will yield surprisingly good results. The Gallup and other polls forecast election results—on the whole quite accurately—on the basis of a sample of less than 100th of 1 percent of all voters.

How big a sample do we need to arrive at accurate estimates? That depends on two things: (1) how much we know about the larger "universe" of data that we are sampling, and (2) how accurate we want to be.

Suppose, for example, that we had two barrels of marbles, one filled with marbles of only two colors, white and black, and the other filled with an unknown number of colors. Obviously, the proportion of black to white marbles can be found from a much smaller sample than we would need for the second barrel, where a whole spectrum of colors and their various proportions are involved. Hence, the simpler the problem and the more clear-cut the data, the smaller the sample can be: it takes many fewer cases to establish the proportion of male to female births than to establish the pattern of average weight-to-height relation of infants at birth.

But suppose we have a "universe" that is well understood, such as our first barrel. How many marbles will we have to draw until we can make some kind of reliable statement about the *actual* proportion of black to white in the whole barrel? Here the answer depends on how accurate we want to be. Statisticians speak of "confidence intervals" to describe the fact that we can establish our own limits of reliability by increasing the size of a sample.
The "correct" sample size then turns out to depend on our need for accuracy. If we want to be 100 percent accurate, after all, we will have to check each and every marble, thereby raising the sample to the size of the population itself, assuming we make no enumeration errors—no easy task.

BIAS

Surprisingly, then, the problem of sample size is not so much of a difficulty as we might have thought, assuming that we know something about the characteristics of the population we are investigating. But suppose we do not. Suppose that we have traveled exclusively in the downtown streets of a city, not knowing there was a great slum just a few blocks away, and we based our judgments of the city as a whole on the cleanliness of the business district alone. Here we have encountered a much more serious problem. *Bias* has entered our calculations. By *bias* we mean that we have not planned our sampling technique in such a way that *each and every item in the population has an equal chance of being observed.*

Bias can enter sampling in the most unexpected ways. Suppose, for example, that the white marbles in our barrel were (unknown to us) slightly heavier than the black ones, so that when we shook up the barrel to be certain the marbles were fairly mixed, we were actually causing the white marbles to move toward the bottom. If our sample were taken from the top of the barrel, it would be biased in favor of black marbles. Or suppose that we chose our city streets absolutely by chance, but that we failed to take into account that the Sanitation Department visited different parts of the city on different days. Our sample could easily be biased in one direction or another.

Perhaps the most famous example of bias was the *Literary Digest* poll of the Roosevelt-Landon election in 1936. The magazine (long since defunct) sampled 2.3 million people, most of whom said they were going to vote for Alfred Landon. On this basis, the *Digest* predicted a landslide for the Republican candidate. In fact, as we all know, the election *was* a landslide—but for the other side.

What went wrong? Obviously, the problem was that the sample, although very large, was terribly biased. It was taken from subscription lists of magazines, telephone directories, and automobile registration lists.

In 1936, people who subscribed to magazines, had phones, and owned autos were highly concentrated in the upper brackets of income distribution. Furthermore, in that year, income had a great deal to do with party choice. The result has been used in statistics texts ever since as the perfect example of bias.

CORRECTING FOR BIASES

How do we avoid biases? The answer is to strive to choose our sample as randomly as possible—that is, in such a way that every unit in the population has an equal chance of being in our sample. A purely random sample has the best chance to duplicate, in miniature, all the characteristics of the larger "universe" it represents. Clearly, the more complex that universe, the larger the random sample will have to be to give us figures that fall within respectable confidence intervals. That is why the U.S. Bureau of the Census uses a sample *as large as* 5 percent to collect information about age, sex, race, income, place of residence and many more attributes of the population as a whole.

Getting a sample that is free of bias is by no means easy. Statisticians spend much time in devising ways to avoid the errors of bias and in detecting unsuspected errors in the work of others. Doesn't this mean, then, that sampling is a technique we should view with considerable suspicion? In fact, doesn't it more or less cast serious doubt on a good deal of what we think are "the facts"?

As we have said before, a healthy skepticism with regard to data is often very useful. But skepticism is not at all the same thing as a rejection of sampling as a statistical *technique*. Sampling is ultimately based on the laws of probability about which we know quite a bit. Hence, far from avoiding sampling, we should use our knowledge to perfect it.

Here are three reasons why sampling is both essential and reliable:

1. Samples may be the only way of obtaining information.

Suppose that you are in charge of planning the development program for a nation like India and that you need to know many facts about the birth rate, the average size of landholdings, or average incomes. *There may be no possible way of obtaining this information except by sampling.* Or suppose you are a historian interested in reconstructing the average length of life or the average family size of some period far in the past. There may be no possible method of gaining this information except by sampling (for example, using the data on gravestones), thereafter making the best adjustment you can for the inevitable biases that have crept into your sample (the poorest people didn't get gravestones). Or suppose your doctor wants to test your blood. Would you want him to test *all* of it?

2. Samples may be cheaper than counting.

Even when you can count all the items in a collection, it may not be worth your while to do so. It would take an enormous expenditure of time and effort to interview each and every householder in the U.S. about every set of facts in the decennial census. It would cost a fortune to test each and every light bulb that General Electric makes. Sampling gives us accurate enough data at a vast saving in cost and time.

3. Sampling may be more accurate than counting.

Believe it or not, sampling is often more accurate than taking a full count. For example, a census survey of every household would require the services of an army of census takers, most of whom could not be trained in all the pitfalls of interviewing. It is quite likely that the inaccuracies of their mass survey would be greater than those in the much smaller number of reports prepared by expert census takers who are careful to follow instructions to the letter. In full counts, immense amounts of data must be handled and transcribed. Clerical errors are apt to be fewer in smaller but more easily manipulated samples.

Sampling, in short, has its inescapable problems. But it is an absolutely indispensable and astonishingly reliable technique with which to deal with the overwhelming mass of data in the real world.

V. Econometrics: the Use of Functions

Now that we have an idea how sampling and other statistical techniques generate different types of economic data, we want to learn something about how data are used to test economic theories. This brings us to a relatively new use for statistics called *econometrics, a use that applies statistics to test various hypotheses about how the economy works.*

FUNCTIONAL RELATIONSHIPS

One of the central uses of econometrics is to discover functional relationships among the variables of the economic system. From Chapter 2, we are familiar with the general meaning of functional relationships, and we have again and again looked for, or applied, such relationships, as in the propensity to consume, a functional relationship between income and consumption.

Let us increase our basic knowledge by studying the consumption function further—not as a problem of empirical research, but as an exercise that will introduce us further to the vocabulary and techniques of econometrics.

For this purpose let us assume that the consumption function is this:

$$C = 2 + .8\,Y$$

This formula enables us to set up a table or schedule, relating C and Y, as follows:

If Y is equal to	*then C is equal to*			*shown on graph as point*
0	2 + .8(0)	= 2 + 0	= 2	A
10	2 + .8(10)	= 2 + 8	= 10	B
20	2 + .8(20)	= 2 + 16	= 18	C
40	2 + .8(40)	= 2 + 32	= 34	D
75	2 + .8(75)	= 2 + 60	= 62	E
100	2 + .8(100)	= 2 + 80	= 82	F

Let's now graph this relationship. Remember that each point in the two-dimensional graph represents *two* numbers; namely, C and Y.

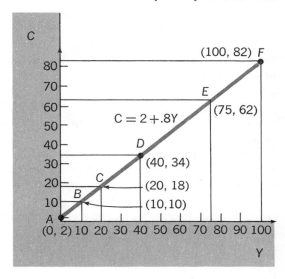

FIGURE 18·5
Propensity to consume

All this, of course, is very familiar. But now consider: *how do we know that the consumption function is a straight line?*

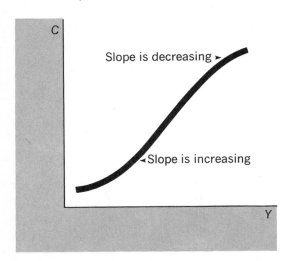

FIGURE 18 · 6
Nonlinear functions

The answer is that the word *straight* means that the line has an *unchanging slope*. If it were not a straight line, the slope would be increasing or decreasing from point to point, as Fig. 18·6 shows. By way of contrast, all lines of unchanging slope are always straight, although they need not all slope at the same angle. Figure 18·7 shows a variety of lines of *unchanging* slope, with very *different angles* of slope.

What is it about our formula that tells us that the (hypothetical) consumption function of $C = 2 + .8Y$ is a straight line? It is not the number 2, which simply tells us the value of C when $Y = 0$. This so-called *intercept* tells us where our line "begins" on the vertical axis, but it says nothing about its slope. That is determined by the second term. In this term, the number .8 is called the *coefficient* of Y, and shows the slope of the line. The "linearity" (straight line) aspect of the equation depends on the fact that Y is of the "first order"—that is, it is not squared or of a higher power. $C = 2 + .8Y^2$ would *not* be a linear function, but a curvilinear one. A

linear function is always of the form $Y = a \pm bx$.

COEFFICIENTS

The coefficient of the independent variable tells us how much the dependent variable will change for each unit of change of the independent variable. That is, .8 tells us that for each variation of $1 in income, consumption will change by 80¢. Given our unchanging coefficient, this relationship will remain the same, whether we are dealing with $1 or with $1 million. In each case, the change in C will be 80 percent the change in Y. If, in fact, the coefficient did change—if, e.g., we consumed a larger fraction of a small income than of a large one—the line would not be straight, and the equation that represented that line would not be an equation of the very simple form we have used.*

FIGURE 18 · 7
Linear functions

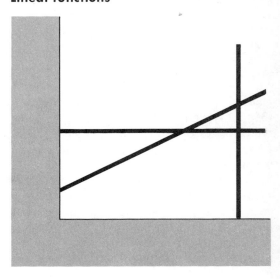

*The two numbers 2 and .8 in our formula are called *parameters*. A change in either or both parameters indicates a *shift* in the consumption line.

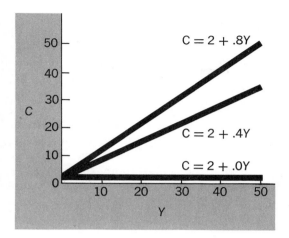

FIGURE 18 · 8
Changing coefficients

Coefficients, even of the simplest kinds, can represent all kinds of slopes. In Fig. 18·8 we show three coefficients that give rise to three slopes. The lowest line has a coefficient of zero, giving rise to a straight horizontal line parallel to the income axis. (Such a line depicts a situation in which we would not consume any more than a fixed amount, no matter how high our incomes—a highly implausible state of affairs.) The middle line shows a consumption function of approximately .4—a state of affairs in which we regularly consume 40¢ out of each additional $1 of income over the $2 intercept. The topmost line shows us our familiar coefficient of .8.

Note three final points.

1. The coefficient describes the slope of a line.

2. All lines described by unchanging coefficients are straight.

3. Econometrics commonly uses equations rather than graphs because equations can handle many more variables than we can conveniently show on a graph.

VI. Correlations and Regression

Up to this point we have spoken of functional relationships as if we knew the relationship among the variables in our equations. But one of the most difficult problems in actual economic research is to determine this relationship. In everyday language, we spend much time in econometric research trying to determine what affects what, and by how much. Once we have determined these relationships, it is relatively simple to put the results into formulas and to solve for the answers. Hence we are now going to turn to a fundamental technique of econometrics —correlation and regression—that will lead into the important problem of establishing reliable functional relationships.

THE ANALYSIS OF RELATIONSHIPS

We have come into contact with this problem in our study of the propensity to consume. There we were interested in examining the association between two variables, income and consumption. Much of econometrics is concerned with the kinds of *problems* exemplified by the income-consumption relationship, although the kinds of *activities* that econometrics investigates runs a vast gamut that includes price-quantity relations, interest rate-investment relationships, and wage-employment relationships.

What is it that we want to discover when we look into the relationship of two variables, such as income and consumption, wages and employment, or whatever? Generally, we seek to establish three things: (1) whether a change in one of these variables— say, income—or wages—is usually associated with a change in the second variable; (2) if there *is* such an association, whether a given change in one variable usually results in large or small change in the associated variable; and (3) once two variables have been shown to be linked in some way, just how precisely the relationship between the two can be described.

CORRELATION AND SCATTER DIAGRAMS

All of these problems use statistical techniques that we will not attempt to teach fully in this text. But for each of them there is also an intuitive representation that will make you familiar with the nature of these econometric questions.

The first such task, we have said, is to discover whether or not a relationship exists at all between two variables. The simplest way to test for the probable existence of such a relationship is to perform the operation we did in Chapter 7 ("A Diagram of the Propensity to Consume"), where we made a *scatter diagram* of income and consumption. In Fig. 18·9, we show two such scatter diagrams, each a visual representation of the association between two variables. On the left, we show a diagram that depicts the relationship of the heights and weights of a group of male adults; on the right we show one that portrays the heights and IQs of a group of male adults (both diagrams are fictitious).

The difference between the two diagrams is obvious. There is a clear-cut relationship between height and weight—the taller the man, the heavier he tends to be (with exceptions, of course). But there is no clear-cut relation between height and IQ: tall men are neither brighter nor more stupid than short men. In the first case, there is prima facie evidence that a correlation exists; in the second case there is none.

FIGURE 18·9
Scatter diagrams

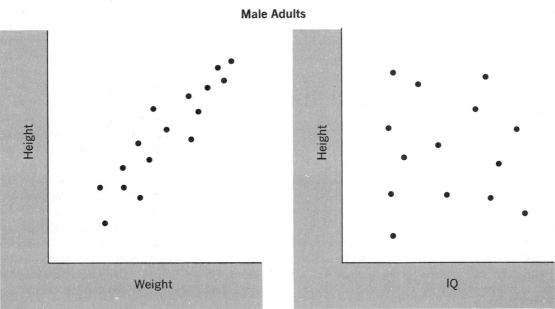

Male Adults

REGRESSION

Once we have some evidence that a correlation exists, we would like to find a way of describing it. That is, we would like to discover the value of one variable, if we know the value of the other, or the rate of change in one variable, given a change in the other. For example, we would like to know the *average change* in weight associated with an additional inch of height, or the *average change* in consumption associated with an additional dollar of income. (The last is, of course, our familiar marginal propensity to consume.)

When econometricians seek to reduce this relationship to a numerical magnitude, they speak of "running a regression" of one variable (such as height or consumption) on the other (weight or income). How do you run such a regression? The first problem, to which we shall turn in Section VII, is to establish the direction of causality—that is, whether we are regressing X on Y, or Y on X. The second problem is the procedure by which we measure the association in which we are interested. The details of computation are better reserved for a statistics course. We will just ask you to take on faith that there is a fairly simple arithmetical technique for deriving a regression line that will tell us what variable A will tend to be, given Variable B.

In Fig. 18·10, we show a very simple height-weight scatter diagram (it could be, of course an income-consumption scatter diagram) with *two* regression lines. Each line was drawn visually in an attempt to show the form of the relationship which the dots exhibit. Forget the colored lines for a moment. How do we know which is the better of the two, line A or B?

LEAST SQUARES

The answer is that we try to find the line that describes the relationship best; that is, the

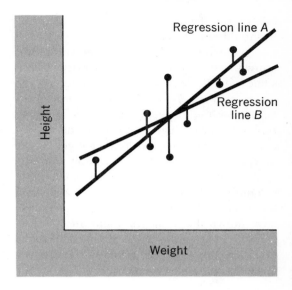

FIGURE 18 · 10
Least squares

line that lies closest to the dots. But how do we define "closest"? Here is where the colored lines enter. (1) From each dot we draw a vertical line to a given regression line (line A in our example). (2) We measure each "colored-line" distance and *square* it.* (3) We add together the squared distances.

In our diagram we have shown the distances of the dots from line A. Now we would have to do the same thing for line B, or for any other line we could draw. In the end, *we choose the line that has the smallest sum of squared distances as being the best fit.* We call this technique of finding such a line "fitting a regression by least squares." There are other ways of fitting lines, as well. We must leave these problems for a statistics

---

*Why do we square the distances? One answer is that this gives additional importance (weight) to any dots that lie considerably away from the regression line, thereby making our measure more sensitive to "exceptions" to what seems to be the rule. The mathematics of statistical theory is another, and more fundamental, reason.

course. But the basic idea of a "least squares" fit should now be plain.

What does the resulting line show? We know the answer from the propensity to consume (note the least squares line fitted on the diagram, Fig. 7·5). The regression coefficient, or the *slope* of the regression line, shows us the change in the dependent variable (*C*) associated with a change in the independent variable (*Y*). We know that this relationship can also be expressed (very roughly) in the formula on page 106, where the coefficient is .94 *Y*. Thus once again we have shown that a diagram and an equation are only two ways of depicting the same thing—in this case, the relationship between consumption and income.*

CORRELATION COEFFICIENT

There remains one last problem. We know now what we mean by correlation and by a regression analysis. We even understand, in general, the criterion by which we fit a line to a group of "dots." But we do not know how we distinguish between two correlations to determine which is better.

Once again, an example will help make the answer clear. In Fig. 18·11 we show two regression lines, *each one of which is the best fit we can get by the least squares criterion.* Yet, clearly, the line on the right shows a better correlation of *Y* on *X* than the line on the left, simply because the dots lie directly on, or just off, the regression line, whereas in

the second case they lie at some distance from it.

There is a mathematical way of describing the difference in "closeness of fit" of the two lines; it is called a *correlation coefficient.* A correlation coefficient is a number that tells us how closely our regression line fits the actual data. This coefficient always has a value between +1 and −1. If the correspondence is perfect—that is, if the dots lie exactly *on* the line, the correlation coefficient is either +1 or −1 (depending on whether the two variables move in the same direction or in directions opposite to each other). If the correlation coefficient is 0, then no correlation exists, as in the case of our example of height and IQ. Once again, we leave the calculation of the coefficient itself to a statistics course. But you can now see that the closer a correlation coefficient (for which we use the symbol *r*) is to +1 or −1, the stronger is the relationship between the two variables, and the better is the correlation.

One further piece of information. Statisticians usually use the *square* of the correlation coefficient (r^2) to describe the degree of association between two variables. In other words, a high r^2 is evidence of a "significant" relationship between two variables, and a low r^2 is evidence of the *lack* of such a relationship. This raises two questions: (1) by a "significant" correlation, do we imply that changes in one variable *cause* changes in the other? and (2) how high an r^2 is "significant"? The first of these questions we will examine in our next sections. The second is a technical matter that must be left for explanation in a course on statistics.

MULTIPLE CORRELATION

A last problem remains, to which we can only allude in passing in this introduction to correlation analysis. It is the question of how

---

*Note that we have been talking exclusively about *positive* coefficients; that is, about cases where an added inch of height is associated with an *added* amount of weight, or where an extra dollar of income is associated with *extra* consumption spending. We can also have negative regression coefficients, where the groups of "dots" would be downward sloping, and where the coefficient would have a minus sign in front of it. For example, if you graph weight on the vertical axis and life expectancy on the horizontal, you would find a downward sloping cluster of dots. Can you think of other such cases?

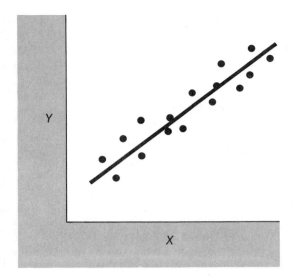
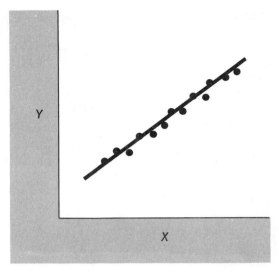

FIGURE 18 · 11
Closeness of fit

we deal with the problem of correlation when more than one variable is associated with changes in another. For instance, how do we figure out the relationship not merely between consumption and income, but between consumption and income *and* wealth *and* changes in prices *and* consumer expectations *and* still other variables that may influence consumption expenditures?

The answer is that we run what is called a *multiple regression analysis*. We do this by quantifying the relationship between the variable in which we are interested (the *dependent variable*) and the other variables (the *independent variables*), by techniques that enable us to discover the separate effect of each independent variable on the dependent variable. Once again, the techniques for doing this must be kept for a statistics course, but we should now be able to understand the meaning of the complicated formulas that emerge from multiple regression analysis.

Such a formula (purely imaginary in this case) might look like this:

$$C = .8Y + .3W - 2T$$

The purpose of such a multiple regression formula is to show us the different effects on our dependent variable, consumption (C), of various independent variables such as income (Y), wealth (W), taxes (T), and so on. What our particular formula tells us is that the net effect on consumption of $1 of added income is 80 cents, assuming that there is no change in wealth, taxes, etc.; that the net effect of an increase in wealth is 30 cents (again assuming that we have held the other variables constant); that the net effect of a rise in taxes is a *decline* in consumption (note the minus sign before the coefficient of .2), again with other variables held constant.

VII. Correlation and Causation

Regression techniques are widely used in econometric research, and we have been able only to indicate in very general terms the actual procedures that econometricians use. But the idea of correlation opens up for us a problem into which we must look very carefully.

This is the connection between *correlation and causation*. When we say that there is a high correlation between two variables—let us say cigarette smoking and heart disease—do we mean that cigarette smoking *causes* heart disease?

The question is obviously of very great importance. All sorts of disputes rage over the degree of "causation" that can be attributed to correlations. Econometrics cannot solve these disputes, because the word "cause"—as anyone knows who has ever looked into a book on philosophy—is a perplexing and elusive one. But econometrics can shed a strong light on some of the pitfalls associated with it. In particular, it makes us very cautious about declaring that such-and-such an event is the cause of another, simply because there is a high degree of correlation between them.

Here are a few examples to think about.

1. Wrong-way causation

It is a statistical fact that there is a positive correlation between the number of babies born in various cities of northwestern Europe and the number of storks' nests in those cities. Is this evidence that storks really do bring babies? The answer is that we are using a correlation to establish a causal connection in the wrong way. The true line of causation lies in the opposite direction: cities that have more children tend to have more houses, which offer storks more chimneys to build their nests in!

2. Spurious causation

It is a statistical fact that there has been a positive correlation all during the 1960s between the cost of living in Paris and the numbers of American tourists visiting there. Does that imply that American visitors are the cause of price increases in that city?

Here at least there is little danger of getting the causal links back to front; few people would argue that more Americans visit Paris *because* its prices are going up. But it would be equally difficult to argue that American tourists are the cause of rising Parisian prices, simply because the total amount of American spending is small in relation to the total amount of expenditure in Paris (with the exception of a few tourist traps).

The answer, then, is that the correlation is "spurious" in terms of causality, although it is "real" in terms of sheer statistics. The true explanation for the correlation is that the rising numbers of American visitors and the rising costs of living in Paris are both aspects of a worldwide expansion in incomes and prices. Neither is the "cause" of the other; both are the results of more fundamental, broader-ranging phenomena.

3. The problem of ceteris paribus

Finally, we must consider again the now familiar problem of *ceteris paribus*—the necessity of other things being equal. Suppose we correlate prices and sales, in order to test the hypothesis that lower prices "cause" us to increase the quantities we buy. Now suppose that the correlation turns out to be very poor. Does that disprove the hypothesis? Not necessarily. First we have to find out what happened to income during this period. We also have to find out what, if anything, happened to our tastes. We might also have to consider changes in the prices of other, competitive goods.

This problem affects all scientific tests, not just those of economics. Scientists cannot test the law of gravitation unless "other things" are equal, such as an absence of air that would cause a feather to fall much more slowly than Galileo predicted. But the trouble with the social sciences is that the "other things" are often more difficult to spot—or just to think of—than they are in the laboratory. For example, what are we to make of the fact that there is a positive correlation between shoe sizes and mathematical ability among school children? The answer, once we think about it, is that we have not held "other things" equal in one very important respect—the age of the school children. Of course older children, with bigger feet, will be able to do more arithmetic than little children. Hence the first thing to do is to see if there is a correlation between shoe sizes of children of *equal ages* and mathematical ability. Children of equal ages will also have different shoe sizes, but the correlation with problem-solving ability is hardly likely to be there.

WHAT CAN CORRELATION TELL US?

These (and still other) pitfalls make econometricians extremely cautious about using correlations to "prove" causal hypotheses. *Even the closest correlation may not show in which direction the causal influences are working;* for instance, the high correlation between the number of corporate mergers and the level of stock prices in the 1960s does not show whether mergers caused stock prices to move up, or whether booming prices encouraged companies to merge and float their new securities on a favorable market.

So, too, *the interconnectedness of the economic process often causes many series of data to move together.* In inflationary periods, for example, most prices tend to rise, or in depression many indexes tend to fall, without establishing that any of these series was directly responsible for a movement in another particular series.

And finally, econometricians are constantly on the lookout for factors that have not been held constant during a correlation, so that *ceteris paribus conditions were not in fact maintained.*

Is there an answer to these (and still other) very puzzling problems of correlation and causation? There is a partial answer. We cannot claim that a correlation is proof that a causal relationship exists. But a causal relationship is likely to exist when we can demonstrate a strong correlation, backed up by theoretical reasoning. That is, every valid economic hypothesis (or for that matter every valid hypothesis of any kind) *must* show a high and "significant" correlation coefficient between the "cause" and the "effect," provided that we are absolutely certain that our statistical test has rigorously excluded spurious correlations of various kinds and unsuspected "other things." Needless to say this is often very difficult and sometimes impossible to do with real data. A physicist can hold "other things equal" in his laboratory, but the world will not stand still just so an economist can test his theories. The net result is that correlations are a more powerful device for *disproving* hypotheses than for proving them.

All this has a very important moral. Because economists deal with quantifiable data, correlation analysis is one of the most important tools in the economist's kit. All the "laws" of economics, from supply and demand to the various relationships of macroeconomics, are constantly being subjected to highly sophisticated econometric tests, *because these are the only objective methods we have for establishing whether variable X is associated with variable Y.* Thus we constantly use correlations to buttress—but not to prove—our belief in economic relationships. Conversely, when careful correlation analysis fails to show high coefficients, there is good reason to look very skeptically at our economic hypotheses.

Hence, correlation is an indispensable part of economic science. But that is not the same thing as saying that it *is* economic science. Behind the tools of econometrics lies the process of *economic reasoning*—that is, the attempt to explain why people behave in certain ways on the marketplace, or how the hard realities of nature or technology shape and constrain the ongoing economic process. If the economic reasoning is faulty, econometrics will not set it straight: recall the puzzling inability to explain the interest rate's effect on investment (pp. 136–38). Here, in the end, we allowed the logic of theory to override the "evidence" of econometrics.

Yet, with all its problems, econometrics is the most penetrative means of empirical analysis that economics has yet developed, and our understanding of the workings of the economy would be terribly handicapped if we did not command its powerful techniques. But ultimately it is to economic theory that we look for that basic understanding itself.

VIII. Forecasting

In addition to their role in testing economic hypotheses, correlations and regressions are used to build forecasting models. Indeed, this is one of the most important functions of econometrics.

How does an econometrician attempt to forecast? We know part of the answer from our introduction to econometrics. The first step is to assemble all available statistical information concerning important economic relationships. Suppose, for example, it is known from multiple regression that the demand for automobiles can be represented by an equation in which the demand for cars is related to changes in disposable income, to changes in car prices, to credit conditions, etc. This long and complicated equation will then become one element in a model of the economy that will also contain the demand for many other final products, as well as the relationships (also econometrically derived) between or among elements such as the quantity of money and the level of prices, the level of employment and consumer disposable income, and so on.

Thus, the predictive tool of the econometrician consists of *a series of equations which depict the simultaneous interaction of those activities that the model-builder believes to be crucial in affecting the economy.* As can be imagined, this leads to extremely complex equations and systems of equations. The famous model of the Wharton School of Business of the University of Pennsylvania, for example, has some 150 equations, most of them with strings of multiple regression elements. To solve such a system of equations by pencil and paper would be impossible— or would take so long that the future would long ago have become history. Thus the computer with its lightning speeds is an integral part of the econometrician's equipment.

EXOGENOUS AND ENDOGENOUS VARIABLES

When we examine forecasting models, we find that the many variables they contain can be classified into two kinds. Many of the variables *depend* on other variables for their values; for example, automobile purchases depend on disposable income, car prices, and other variables. These are *dependent* variables in the model; that is, elements whose values will be determined by the action of the independent variables in the system.

These *exogenous* ("outside") variables must be introduced into the system to determine the values of the dependent variables. Where does the econometrician get these exogenous variables? Some of them may be known facts from which various kinds of future economic activity may be inferred by econometric analysis. For instance, the model-builder may introduce the known level of population growth as an exogenous variable on which the future level of home-building or car-buying may depend. Or exogenous variables may be based on surveys or on expected policy decisions, such as surveys of intended corporate investment or policy statements of the Federal Reserve. These and other exogenous variables are arranged along with the endogenous variables in a set of simultaneous equations that make up the econometric model and reflect the complex mechanism of the economy. The econometrician then solves the model, thus deriving values for his endogenous variables, such as consumer disposable income, automobile purchases, or GNP itself.

Here, of course, lies a central problem for econometric forecasting. We can never be certain of the accuracy of our all-important exogenous variables. We cannot predict with certainty, for instance, what the money supply will be, because we cannot know whether Federal Reserve policy will change. We cannot predict with certainty what business investment will be, because business expectations may change. To the extent that our exogenous variables are wrongly estimated, the values we derive from them for dependent elements in our model will also be wrong. In 1966, for example, the Council of Economic Advisers predicted that the rate of inflation was about to slow down. Actually, it accelerated. The mistake did not lie with the reasoning of the council or with its econometric model. It lay in the fact that the council assumed, on the basis of the data at hand, that the budget for 1967 was going to be balanced. What happened in fact was that a budgetary deficit of $9 billion was incurred to finance an expansion of the Vietnam War —a deficit that had not been included in the original budget estimates.

One way to get around such problems is to assume several sets of values for key "policy variables" and to run the model for each one. For example, a forecast put out by the Federal Reserve Bank of St. Louis has made three different predictions based on three different postulated rates of growth in the money supply. Having such a spectrum of predictions seems at first to be weaseling on

the job. But actually it serves a very useful purpose. Such alternative models show us the probable *range* of our results and can therefore tell us, for instance, if the consumption of autos will be much or little affected if the money supply grows fast or slowly.

Second, because many of the key policy variables *cannot* be accurately predicted (who can foretell with certainty what next year's federal budget will be?) a spectrum of forecasts enables individuals or corporations to make their own guesstimates about these critical variables and then to examine what the probable configuration of *other* economic variables are apt to look like, given these key assumptions.

Every person or firm bases his economic decisions on some kind of implicit or explicit estimate of future economic conditions. To try to improve these decisions, econometric forecasting is increasingly used by large industrial corporations, by financial institutions, and by governments. The results of the big models at the Brookings Institution or the Wharton School are even featured in news articles. Hence it is important to ask how well the econometric predictions have fared.

PERFORMANCE

Most econometricians would be the first to admit that their performance has been uneven. The models have worked very well— have predicted changes in the economy quite accurately—as long as things were moving along fairly steadily in one direction. But when things changed direction, *which is just when we want our models to work best,* they have not been too reliable. The influential Brookings Model, for example, did not forecast the recessions of 1957–58, or of 1960–1961. In 1968, most econometricians predicted a recession for 1969, but it did not actually take place until 1970.

What accounts for this disappointing performance? Part of the trouble lies in the problems of "specifying" the model correctly—that is, of overcoming the numerous problems of econometrics that we have touched on in past supplements. The fact that different econometric models use different multiple regression coefficients for the same variables attests in itself to the fact that there is more than one way to depict certain relationships.

Second is the problem that econometricians, as we have also made clear, ultimately rely on economics; and economists are by no means of one mind about the relative importance of certain key exogenous variables, such as the influence of fiscal or monetary policy on the price level or on GNP. Hence our models misperform because we are still in disagreement about economic theory itself.

And last, our models misperform because we cannot predict the course of certain critical exogenous variables that lie beyond the reach of economic reasoning itself. For example, no economic theory could have predicted the degree of escalation of the Vietnam War. Yet that event dominated macroeconomic behavior in the late Sixties.

THE LIMITS OF PREDICTION

Does this mean that econometric forecasting is doomed to failure? Not necessarily. The need is rather to understand better what our models can do for us and what they cannot. One thing they can certainly do is to clarify the nature of the interactions of many economic activities, so that important relationships within the economic system can be specified with much greater accuracy. A second very important purpose of models is to make clear the economic *requirements* to reach given targets, a task that is not quite the same as that of prediction, but that is no less important regarding the future.

Equally certainly, however, we cannot use our models to give us predictions about such things as the date of the next stock market crash or even the level of GNP ten years hence. When matters of volatile *behavior* are concerned, such as the psychology of the stock market, an econometric model has nothing to go by. By definition, such unforecastable psychological changes *alter* the very coefficients on which predictive equations are built.

In the same way, long-term predictions are made hazardous by events such as international crises, technological breakthroughs, or political upheavals, all of which also upset the parameters on which all prediction is ultimately based.

Here, in the realm of the exogenous, the *science* of econometric forecasting ends, and the art of forecasting begins. For it is here that the shrewd guess of the economist or the hunch of the econometrician will lead him—in the face of the established patterns of the past—to postulate that things have shifted or are about to shift and therefore to regard the results of his model with more than the usual degree of caution, or to recast the parameters on which his model is based. At this point the economist or the econometrician certainly does not claim access to the occult, but humbly confesses that scientific methods, powerful as they are, still cannot describe the shape of many things to come.

KEY WORDS

Definitions

Deceptions

Means

Medians

Skewness

Bell-shaped curve

Bi-modal

Real vs. money values

Consumer Price Index

Market basket

Weights

New goods

Base

Splicing indexes

Probability

Bias

Random selection

CENTRAL CONCEPTS

I. SOME INITIAL CAUTIONS

Statistics are always best approached with caution. *Definitions* are often key to the interpretations we place on data. Data can be out-dated, misleading if not carefully identified, deceptive if "overinterpreted" (be wary of making mountains out of molehills).

Visual tricks using data to make a point or the failure to get a rounded perspective on facts are frequent sources of statistical error—or worse—statistical *deception*.

II. DISTRIBUTIONS AND AVERAGES

Learn to distinguish between *means*—the arithmetic average—and *medians*—the middle value of a series. Mean values are usually different from medians, because data are often *skewed*.

Modes are "averages" in terms of that value which has the largest number of units. *In a normal, bell-shaped distribution, mode, mean, and median will all be the same.* This will not be the case in skewed distributions.

We must be particularly careful to guard against *bi-modal* distributions—distributions in which there are two (or more) modal clusters.

III. PRICE INDEXES

Price indexes are used to "correct" current dollar values, in order to establish "real" changes in economic magnitudes.

Price indexes can be constructed from many kinds of data. The Department of Labor's *Consumer Price Index* is an index number that measures the changing cost of a "market basket" of typical consumer goods.

It is simple to construct an index if only one good is involved. When more than one good is in the market basket, we must assign *weights* to the various items. Each is given the degree of importance proportional to its value in the "market basket."

New goods present many difficult problems for the construction of an index. To the extent that the good fulfills a *new function*, the problem is magnified because, typically, new goods fall in price.

Price indexes, once constructed, are simple to apply: current dollar values are divided by the index and then multiplied by 100. The resulting "real" series will differ in its dollar values according to which year is used as a *base*, but the relative changes from year to year will be the same. Thus indexes *can be spliced*. Be wary, however, of ignoring the statistical difficulties of long-term time series, just because they are spliced into one continuous series.

IV. SAMPLING

The logic of sampling is based on *probability*. There are well-established laws of probability that enable us to determine certain characteristics of large "universes" of data by sampling techniques.

The most important objective of good sampling is to avoid *bias*. This is accomplished by aiming for a random sample. The size of the random sample will then depend on the size of the total "universe" and on the number of its characteristics that we wish to test for.

Econometrics

Sampling, surprisingly enough, may be *more* accurate than full enumeration, as well as cheaper and easier.

*Functional
relationships*

V. ECONOMETRICS AND FUNCTIONAL RELATIONSHIPS

One main use of econometrics is the use of statistics to test economic hypotheses by statistical methods.

Another principal use is to establish the existence or nonexistence of functional relationships.

Linear graphs

Functional relationships are usually described by equations, rather than graphs, especially if the variables are numerous. *The slope of the line on all linear graphs will be determined by the coefficients* in the equation that describes the functional relationship.

Coefficients

*Associations
among variables*

VI. CORRELATIONS AND REGRESSIONS

Correlations attempt to establish *associations among variables*, and regressions are the means by which we quantify these associations.

Scatter diagrams

Scatter diagrams give us a visual clue to whether correlations exist. But we test for such correlations by a method known as *least squares..* This method gives us a *regression line* that is mathematically defined as the closest possible fit to a scatter of paired variables. The regression equation describes the nature and direction of the association between the two variables.

Least squares

Regression line

Regressions do not tell us how closely the data cluster around a given line. To establish the "tightness" of fit, we need another measure called the *correlation coefficient*.

A method known as *multiple correlation* enables us to quantify the relationship among more than two variables by holding all variables "fixed" while we test the correlation of the particular pair we wish to investigate.

*Correlation
coefficient*

VII. CORRELATION AND CAUSATION

We must be very careful about attributing causal relationships to correlated variables. There are many pitfalls: *wrong-way correlation*, *spurious correlation*, improper attention to *ceteris paribus*. All can deceive us as to the existence or nonexistence of a causal connection between variables.

*Multiple
correlation*

Causation

Correlations, when carefully interpreted, can often be useful in disproving hypotheses. They are less dependable as "proofs" of hypotheses.

VIII. FORECASTING

*Wrong-way
correlation*

Forecasting is essentially an effort to *predict the movement of dependent variables on the basis of assumptions regarding the independent variables*.

The independent variables are *exogenous*, introduced into the system from outside. They are treated as stated values that will determine or limit the values of the dependent variables.

*Spurious
correlation*

Because exogenous variables are intrinsically unpredictable, the forecasting powers of econometrics are inherently limited.

*Exogenous
variables*

Econometrics models are still invaluable as a means of examining the interrelationships among various parts of the economy and testing theories that seek to explain those relationships.

QUESTIONS

1. If someone told you that the unemployment rate was 4 percent in West Germany and 5 percent in the U.S., would you conclude that unemployment was therefore higher in the U.S.? What cautions would you advise before coming to that conclusion?

2. Draw a graph that is *calculated* to deceive someone. Example: an alarming depiction of stock price changes in the last month.

3. What is the best average to describe the "average" IQ of a population? What do you mean by "best"? What characteristics would be shown by a mean that would not be shown by a median? Would a mode be useful? Suppose instead of IQ, you wanted to show the "average" stockholdings of the same population. What answers do you now give to the questions?

4. Describe a series that is likely to be bi-modal. Try to think of one that isn't in the text. The trick is to find something that typically comes in two or more "sizes" instead of being more or less evenly spaced over the range of all sizes.

5. Write down four median incomes and four price index numbers; figure out real income for each year. Shift bases and compare your results.

6. How would you handle the problem of fitting new cars into the Consumer Price Index? How much of their price is improved quality, how much is just inflation? How would you go about making such a decision?

7. Take a market basket with two goods: bread and wine. Bread costs 50¢; wine $5.00. In year 1, you spend $10 for bread, $5 for wine. Now bread falls to 25¢, wine rises to $6.00. Can you make a weighted index from this data? Do you need to know how much you spend for bread and wine in year 2?

8. Describe some data that could be more accurately surveyed by sampling techniques than by complete enumeration. Numbers of grains of sand on a beach? Name some economic possibilities.

9. What is meant by regression? By correlation? How would you decide if a high correlation was a prima facie case for causation? Describe a highly correlated pair of variables in which causation is uncertain. Are cigarette smoking and ill-health one? How would you find out? *Could* you find out "beyond all possibility of error"?

10. Why is the forecaster's life a hard one?

Index

DATE DUE

JUN 12 '84			

30 505 JOSTEN'S